Inside Copilot

Inside Copilot is designed to teach users to master Copilot, Microsoft's generative AI assistant. Learn prompt engineering and use cases for Copilot in many Microsoft products at beginner, intermediate, and expert levels. Perfect for any professionals who find their schedules packed with repetitive computer tasks, Copilot can automatically generate PowerPoint presentations, draft emails on Outlook, write code on GitHub, and more. Both companies and individuals can learn to utilize Copilot to significantly speed up processes and gain an advantage.

More information about this series at `https://link.springer.com/bookseries/17432`.

Creative AI Agents with Copilot Studio

Building Intelligent, Engaging, and Autonomous Assistants

Mezba Uddin

Apress®

Creative AI Agents with Copilot Studio: Building Intelligent, Engaging, and Autonomous Assistants

Mezba Uddin
Blackburn, Lancashire, UK

ISBN-13 (pbk): 979-8-8688-2778-5   ISBN-13 (electronic): 979-8-8688-2779-2
https://doi.org/10.1007/979-8-8688-2779-2

Managing Director, Apress Media LLC: Welmoed Spahr
Acquisitions Editor: Ryan Byrnes
Desk Editor: Laura Berendson
Editorial Project Manager: Gryffin Winkler

Cover designed by eStudioCalamar

Distributed to the book trade worldwide by Springer Science+Business Media New York, 1 New York Plaza, New York, NY 10004. Phone 1-800-SPRINGER, fax (201) 348-4505, e-mail orders-ny@springer-sbm.com, or visit www.springeronline.com. Apress Media, LLC is a Delaware LLC and the sole member (owner) is Springer Science + Business Media Finance Inc (SSBM Finance Inc). SSBM Finance Inc is a **Delaware** corporation.

For information on translations, please e-mail booktranslations@springernature.com; for reprint, paperback, or audio rights, please e-mail bookpermissions@springernature.com.

Apress titles may be purchased in bulk for academic, corporate, or promotional use. eBook versions and licenses are also available for most titles. For more information, reference our Print and eBook Bulk Sales web page at http://www.apress.com/bulk-sales.

Any source code or other supplementary material referenced by the author in this book is available to readers on GitHub. For more detailed information, please visit https://www.apress.com/gp/services/source-code.

If disposing of this product, please recycle the paper

To my elder brother, Mostafiz Uddin.
Everything I am today, in many ways, is a reflection of you.

While the world recognizes your strength, vision, and leadership, I have had the privilege of knowing the person behind it all, the one who taught me the value of perseverance, the courage to grow, and the importance of believing in something greater than oneself.

Your guidance and unwavering support have shaped not only my journey but also the way I see the world. This book stands as a small tribute to the lessons you have instilled in me and the inspiration you continue to be.

Thank you for being my mentor, my support, and my constant source of strength.

Table of Contents

Chapter 7: Testing, Debugging, and Optimization.............299

About the Author

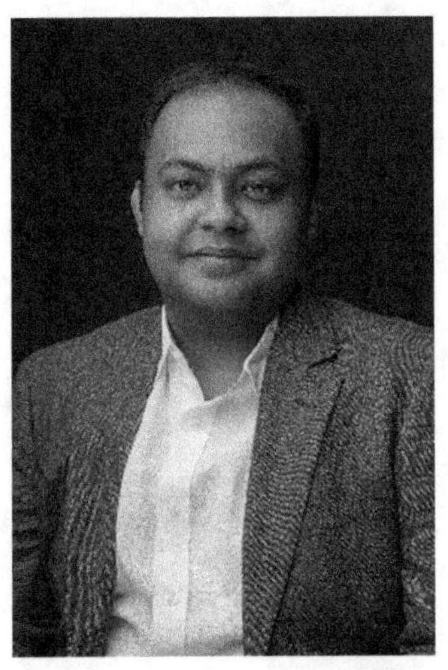 **Mezba Uddin** is a cloud infrastructure specialist and multiple-time Microsoft MVP. He designs and operates secure, large-scale Microsoft cloud environments for public sector organizations in the UK, including the NHS. With advanced certifications, including Microsoft Certified Cybersecurity Architect Expert (SC-100) and Azure Solutions Architect Expert (AZ-305), and over a decade of hands-on experience, Mezba serves in a leading role on Azure architecture, Microsoft 365, hybrid active directory, and cybersecurity.

He helps organizations modernize legacy estates while controlling costs through strong FinOps practices. His work frequently spans Azure architecture, zero trust security framework, virtual computing platforms, and automation and ensures that systems remain resilient, compliant, and cost-efficient.

Mezba is a recognized Microsoft-certified trainer and active community mentor and regularly supports startups, students, and engineers through mentoring, speaking, and training. He shares practical guidance on cloud governance, automation, and data protection.

Acknowledgments

My deepest thanks go to the team at Apress. To my Editor, Ryan Byrnes, for the early belief that this book would one day exist in finished form, and to my Editorial Assistant, Gryffin Winkler, for the calm persistence and steady coordination that steered me toward the deadline instead of away from it. Thanks also to the production team for turning rough drafts and technical diagrams into a polished reality.

To the Microsoft MVP community, thank you for the camaraderie, the late-night debates, and the shared tendency to over-engineer things in the best possible way. My work as a cloud infrastructure specialist within the NHS has been a constant reminder that reliability is not theoretical; it matters because people notice immediately when it goes missing.

A respectful nod to the Microsoft product teams for building the platforms that make this work possible. The relentless pace of innovation in Copilot Studio is inspiring, even if the habit of changing a user interface shortly after I finish capturing screenshots has accelerated my aging process more than I care to admit.

I am also grateful to the practitioners I meet through mentoring with the BCS "My Digital Future" program, Microsoft TEALS, and the Microsoft Founders Hub. Your curiosity is both exhausting and uplifting in equal measure, and you serve as a regular reminder that the next generation will not be limited by the technical assumptions we grew up with.

Sincere thanks are due to the staff at my local cafes for tolerating my extended occupation of the same table, my dependency on power sockets, and an unreasonable volume of coffee. I am fairly sure this manuscript has made a measurable contribution to their quarterly numbers.

Finally, to my family, thank you for your patience with my absence, distraction, and endless typing. Your support made this book possible.

Introduction

The world of artificial intelligence has long been defined by the cold efficiency of logic and the tireless crunching of data. For decades, we viewed AI as a sophisticated calculator, a tool built to automate the mundane, optimize the industrial, and solve the predictable. We asked it to find patterns, not to find inspiration. We looked to it for answers, never for art.

But the ceiling of what machines can do has shattered. We have entered a new epoch where the relationship between human and machine is no longer purely computational; it is collaborative. We are moving past the era of "artificial intelligence" and into the era of "applied imagination."

Today, the most powerful tool in the digital arsenal is not a line of code, but a well-crafted prompt. The barriers that once separated the visionary from the developer have dissolved, and at the center of this democratic revolution stands Microsoft Copilot Studio.

This book is not merely a technical manual for a software platform; it is a guide for the modern alchemist. Whether you are an educator seeking to scale personalized learning, a storyteller looking for a tireless brainstorming partner, or a business leader aiming to transform a static workflow into a dynamic, agentic ecosystem, this journey is for you.

Across these ten chapters, we will transition from the "what" to the "how" and finally to the "why."

We begin by unveiling the potential, where you will see how Copilot Studio serves as a canvas for creativity. We will then move into the workshop, mastering the "bones" of AI, the topics, entities, and variables that give an agent its structure. From there, we move into the artistry, learning how to breathe a "soul" into your creations through natural dialogue, humor, and ethical guardrails.

As you progress, you will learn to bridge the gap between the digital and the physical, connecting your agents to real-world data and scaling them across global channels. Finally, we will look toward the horizon of agentic AI, where your creations stop waiting for instructions and start acting as proactive partners in your creative process.

The "blank page" has always been the greatest challenge for any creator. By the time you reach the final chapter of this book, you will never face a blank page alone again. You are no longer just a user of technology; you are an architect of intelligence.

The instrument is tuned.

The stage is set. It is time to build.

CHAPTER 1

Unveiling Copilot Studio: The Future of AI Creativity

The story of artificial intelligence has long revolved around automation, logic, and productivity. For decades, AI systems were built to streamline processes, crunch data, and perform repetitive tasks faster and more accurately than humans ever could. But in the evolving relationship between humans and machines, a new chapter is being written, one in which creativity, rather than computation, takes center stage.

Instead of just crunching numbers or sorting information, AI can now help us write stories, design presentations, create art, and bring new ideas to life. It's no longer just about getting things done faster, but it's about helping us think differently and create more freely. Microsoft Copilot Studio is at the center of this transformation. This new platform makes it possible for anyone, not just programmers, to build their own AI helpers. Whether you're a teacher, business owner, or content creator, Copilot Studio lets you create custom AI agents to support your work and creativity.

In this chapter, we'll look at how Copilot Studio came to be, what makes it different from other Microsoft AI tools, and why it matters in this new age of AI-powered creativity. It is a tool designed for working with AI rather than just using it.

© Mezba Uddin 2026

M. Uddin, *Creative AI Agents with Copilot Studio*, Inside Copilot,
https://doi.org/10.1007/979-8-8688-2779-2_1

The Genesis of Copilot Studio: AI for Creativity

In just a few short years, artificial intelligence has transformed from a niche technology into a force that touches nearly every part of our lives. Whether it's speeding up business decisions, helping doctors analyze medical scans, guiding students through complex lessons, or predicting global market trends, AI has proven to be a powerful engine of efficiency and intelligence.

But amid all these practical achievements, one question lingered: Can AI be creative?

For a long time, creativity was thought to be a uniquely human gift. It draws from our emotions, intuition, culture, and lived experience. Writing a heartfelt poem, painting a vivid picture, and composing a song that moves people—these were seen as things that only humans could do. Machines were built to calculate and categorize, not imagine and inspire. That mindset began to shift with the rise of Generative AI.

Unlike traditional AI, which focused on pattern recognition and decision-making, Generative AI introduced something new, and that is the ability to create. This evolution began with the OpenAI model like GPT-2 in 2019, which could produce surprisingly coherent pieces of text from a simple prompt. Then came GPT-3 in 2020, capable of writing essays, dialogue, and even computer code. In 2021, DALL-E captured the world's imagination by turning words into art by generating unique images based on written descriptions.

Microsoft, deeply invested in this transformation and working closely with OpenAI, saw this creative shift as more than a novelty. It was a turning point. In early 2023, the company introduced Microsoft 365 Copilot, embedding Generative AI into its most widely used tools such as Word, Excel, PowerPoint, and Teams. With just a few words, users could now ask AI to summarize documents, create presentations, analyze spreadsheets, or draft emails. Productivity was no longer about doing more; it was about doing it more creatively.

But something unexpected happened next.

As people grew more comfortable using AI to assist their work, a new desire emerged, which is they didn't just want to use AI; they wanted to build with it. They wanted to create their own intelligent assistants tailored to their needs, industries, and ideas. They wanted to shape how AI behaved, what it knew, and how it could collaborate on their projects.

This growing demand led Microsoft to create Copilot Studio, officially launched in November 2023 at the Microsoft Ignite conference.

Copilot Studio wasn't just another AI tool; it was a new kind of platform. One that allowed everyday users, regardless of their technical background, to design their own AI-powered copilots. Whether you were a marketer looking to automate campaign ideas, a teacher building an interactive lesson assistant, or a small business owner wanting to streamline customer support, Copilot Studio offered a way to bring your creative vision to life through AI.

The platform brought together the best of Microsoft's Power Platform with the new capabilities of Generative AI. With a low-code or no-code interface, users could build bots, define their personalities, connect them to business data, and deploy them with ease. Creativity was no longer limited to artists or engineers. With Copilot Studio, anyone can become a creator of intelligent tools.

As we understand the motivations behind Copilot Studio's creation, it becomes clear that this tool isn't just another AI assistant; it represents a new class of creative enablement. But what exactly makes it stand apart from other Microsoft AI offerings? Let's explore how Copilot Studio carves out its own identity in the expanding AI ecosystem.

How Copilot Studio Differs from Other Microsoft AI Tools

Copilot Studio may appear to be just another piece of Microsoft's expanding AI package at first look. But upon closer inspection, its unique function becomes clear.

Although Microsoft 365 Copilot improves the way users write, edit, and analyze material and is integrated into well-known productivity tools, Copilot Studio gives users the ability to create such experiences themselves. Now, you're creating your own unique Copilot to do that for you, your team, or your clients, instead of asking an AI to compose a document or condense an email.

What Makes Copilot Studio Unique Is This

1. **Low-Code or No-Code Interface:** Copilot Studio was designed with accessibility in mind, in contrast to conventional developer platforms. Without writing a single line of code, anyone with ideas like business executives, marketers, and educators can create working AI bots.

2. **Custom AI Behavior:** Users can choose the types of conversations their Copilot can have, what it should know, and how it reacts. This is more akin to custom intelligence than templates.

3. **Data Connectivity:** Copilot Studio can communicate with your company's data, including Salesforce, Dynamics 365, SharePoint, and custom APIs, via Power Platform connections, providing each AI agent with context and awareness.

4. **Integrated Governance and Compliance:** Copilot Studio enables enterprise-grade security, auditing, and lifecycle management since it is based on Microsoft's reliable ecosystem. It is equally useful for creative teams and enterprise IT.

Copilot Studio vs. Google AI Studio

While Microsoft Copilot Studio may seem similar to other AI development environments, such as **Google AI Studio**, they serve very different purposes and audiences. Understanding these differences is key to choosing the right tool for your project.

- **Target Audience:** Copilot Studio is a **low-code platform** designed primarily for business users, educators, and subject matter experts to build enterprise-ready agents. In contrast, Google AI Studio is a **developer-centric prototyping tool** meant for rapid testing and fine-tuning of Google's Gemini models.

- **Ecosystem Integration:** Copilot Studio is deeply integrated with the **Microsoft 365 ecosystem**, including Teams, SharePoint, and Dynamics 365. Google AI Studio is optimized for **Google Cloud** and developers looking to integrate AI into their own custom applications via API.

- **Data Connectivity:** A standout feature of Copilot Studio is its ability to use **1,400+ prebuilt connectors** to ground agents in real business data like Salesforce or SAP. Google AI Studio focuses more on **prompt engineering** and exploring the model's massive "context window" to process very large files at once.

Copilot Studio redefines how users interact with Microsoft's AI ecosystem by enabling them to build their own intelligent agents instead of relying solely on prebuilt solutions. With its accessible low-code design, it empowers a wide range of users to craft custom AI experiences tailored to specific needs. The ability to define behavior, connect to diverse data sources, and operate within Microsoft's secure framework makes it a powerful tool for both individual creators and enterprise teams. This hands-on, customizable approach positions Copilot Studio as a unique and forward-thinking platform within Microsoft's suite of AI tools.

Now that we've seen how Copilot Studio differs from other Microsoft AI tools, it's time to dig deeper into its capabilities. What are the core features that make this platform a powerful engine for creative AI development? The next section breaks down its standout tools and functions.

Key Features of Copilot Studio

Building creative AI agents requires tools that are both powerful and accessible—and that's exactly what Copilot Studio delivers. Designed for users across a wide range of skill levels, it combines intuitive design with advanced capabilities, allowing anyone to bring their AI ideas to life. Whether you're developing a chatbot for customer support, an AI assistant for marketing automation, or an educational tutor for students, Copilot Studio equips you with the essential tools to build, refine, and deploy intelligent agents with ease.

Here are the core features that make Copilot Studio ideal for creating creative AI agents:

1. **Conversational Design Studio**

   The platform includes a robust conversation designer that helps structure dialogues logically and intuitively. Users can script conversation flows, define how the AI should respond in various scenarios, and use natural language prompts to guide the development of intelligent and engaging interactions.

2. **From Plug-ins to Agents and Actions**

As the AI landscape evolves, the terminology has shifted from simple "Plug-ins" to a more robust framework of Agents, Tools, and Skills.

- **Agents**: Instead of just being a chatbot, your creation is now considered an "AI agent," a more autonomous entity that can reason through tasks and use various tools to achieve a goal.

- **Tools and Actions**: "Plug-ins" have largely been replaced by Actions. These allow your agent to interact with the real world, such as looking up a customer's order history or updating a row in a spreadsheet.

- **Skills**: These represent specialized sets of capabilities that an agent can draw upon to solve specific problems, making the conversational experience deeper and more functional.

3. **Data Integration and Context Awareness**

With seamless connectivity to Microsoft Dataverse, SharePoint, Dynamics 365, Salesforce, and custom APIs, Copilot Studio allows your AI agent to tap into real-time data. This data-driven approach ensures your Copilot can access relevant context during conversations, making responses smarter and more personalized.

4. **AI-Powered Suggestions**

   Copilot Studio enhances the design process by offering intelligent suggestions as users build their bots. These AI-powered insights help optimize dialogue paths, recommend next steps, and even suggest corrections, acting as a co-creator throughout the development journey.

5. **Testing and Debugging Tools**

   A built-in testing console allows users to simulate conversations, identify logic errors, and fine-tune agent behavior before going live. This iterative feedback loop is essential for ensuring a smooth and effective user experience.

6. **Multi-channel Deployment**

   Agents created in Copilot Studio can be published across multiple channels including Microsoft Teams, websites, mobile apps, and third-party platforms like Facebook Messenger. This flexibility ensures your creative AI agent can reach users wherever they are.

7. **Governance, Security, and Compliance**

   Being part of the Microsoft ecosystem, Copilot Studio benefits from enterprise-grade security, role-based access control, activity auditing, and compliance with industry standards. Organizations can confidently scale their AI solutions without compromising on safety or control.

These features work together to support a highly flexible and creative environment for building AI agents. Copilot Studio not only simplifies the process but also encourages experimentation and innovation, enabling users to imagine and implement new AI-driven experiences that go beyond traditional chatbot functionality.

With a clearer understanding of Copilot Studio's features, the next logical step is to see them in action. How do these tools manifest in real-world scenarios? Let's look at how different industries and creators are already harnessing Copilot Studio to unlock new forms of expression and automation.

Real-World Use Cases (Marketing, Storytelling, Gaming)

Copilot Studio is more than just a platform for building conversational agents. It's a versatile tool that adapts to a wide variety of creative and business needs. By allowing users to design intelligent agents that are context-aware, customizable, and easy to deploy, Copilot Studio opens powerful possibilities across multiple domains. Let's explore how it's being applied in real-world scenarios, particularly in marketing, storytelling, and gaming.

Marketing: Personalized Campaigns and Customer Engagement

In marketing, personalization is key to capturing attention and driving conversions. With Copilot Studio, marketers can build AI agents that engage potential customers through tailored interactions, product recommendations, and timely promotions. For example, a fashion retailer can create a Copilot that asks visitors about their style preferences and suggests outfits in real time, pulling from inventory data through API integration. These AI agents can be embedded in websites, messaging apps, or even in-store kiosks, offering a consistent and intelligent brand experience.

Marketing teams can also automate lead qualification by creating bots that collect user information, respond to FAQs, and route high-interest prospects to sales teams. Copilot Studio's integration with Microsoft Dynamics 365 and other CRM tools ensures seamless data flow, enabling smarter campaign decisions and measurable ROI.

Storytelling: Interactive Narratives and Educational Tools

Storytellers from authors to educators can leverage Copilot Studio to design interactive, AI-powered narratives that evolve based on user choices. These dynamic experiences can range from choose-your-own-adventure stories to historical simulations for classroom learning.

For example, an educator could create a history-themed Copilot that guides students through different eras, allowing them to "interact" with historical figures or explore virtual events based on their interests. This interactive storytelling not only makes learning more engaging but also encourages exploration and critical thinking. For content creators and indie authors, Copilot Studio offers a new medium for delivering immersive stories that respond to the reader's input in real time.

Gaming: Intelligent NPCs and Game Assistants

In the gaming industry, Copilot Studio can be used to design intelligent non-playable characters (NPCs) that enhance immersion through realistic, responsive dialogues. Game developers can create AI companions or adversaries that react differently depending on the player's behavior, decisions, or skill level.

Beyond NPCs, AI agents built with Copilot Studio can serve as in-game assistants, helping players with tips, walkthroughs, or inventory management. These agents can integrate with game data to provide personalized support, increasing player satisfaction and reducing frustration. Because the platform supports deployment across multiple devices, these gaming agents can also exist outside of the game, on a companion mobile app, for example: creating a seamless and engaging ecosystem around the core gameplay.

These real-world use cases highlight how Copilot Studio empowers creators to go beyond simple automation, enabling them to build meaningful, context-rich experiences, whether it's driving customer engagement, telling compelling stories, or crafting immersive gameplay. As we see the platform's potential to deliver tangible creative outcomes, it's important to understand how access is structured. In the next section, we'll explore the different licensing and access tiers to help you find the right fit for your needs.

Licensing and Access (Free vs. Premium Plans)

The ability to create with AI should not be limited to experts with deep technical skills or large organizational budgets. Microsoft designed Copilot Studio to make it flexible and accessible for creators of all levels. Whether you're a solo innovator, a startup founder, or part of a global enterprise, Copilot Studio provides the tools and access you need to bring your AI-powered ideas to life.

But how do you know where to begin? And what do you get at each level of access?

In this section, we'll walk through the available licensing options, outlining the difference between the Free Tier and Premium Plans and helping you choose the path that best supports your creative and technical journey.

Free Tier: Exploration and Prototyping

The free version of Copilot Studio is ideal for getting started with minimal investment. It allows users to

- Build and test basic AI agents with limited conversational turns

- Access core tools like the conversation designer and prebuilt templates

- Publish Copilots to limited channels (web-based demo links)

- Best suited for students, hobbyists, early-stage startups, or teams exploring the platform's capabilities before scaling

How to Sign Up for the Free Trial

Getting started with Copilot Studio is straightforward, but it does require a specific type of account. You cannot sign up using a personal email (such as @gmail.com or @outlook.com).

- **Official Sign-Up Link**: You can start your 30-day journey by visiting **https://aka.ms/ trycopilotstudio**.

- **Account Requirements**: To register, you must use a work or school account.

- **M365 Prerequisites**: While you don't necessarily need a paid Microsoft 365 Copilot license to *start* a trial, your organization must have an underlying Microsoft 365 subscription (such as Business Standard, Business Premium, or Enterprise E3/E5) to create an environment where the agent can live.

- **Trial Duration**: The free trial typically lasts 30 days, though Microsoft often provides an option to extend it for an additional 30 days if you need more time for prototyping.

Quick Start Steps

- Navigate to the `https://aka.ms/trycopilotstudio`.

- Enter your work or school email address shown in Figure 1-1.

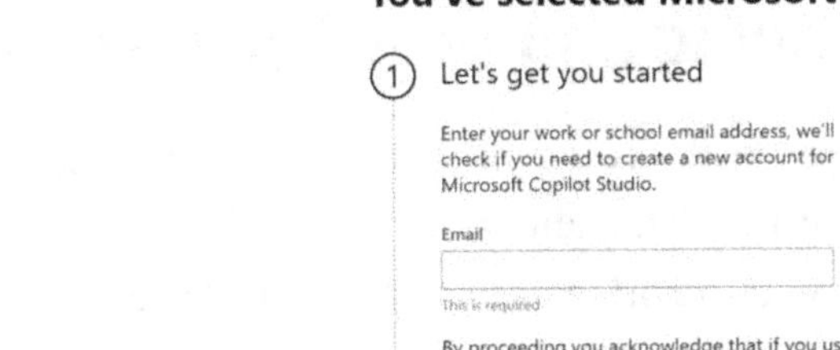

Figure 1-1. *Enter the email account for creating the account*

- Follow the on-screen instructions to set up your first environment.

- Once the process is complete, you will be directed to the main interface shown in Figure 1-2.

Premium Plans: Scalability and Enterprise Features

As creative and technical needs grow, premium plans provide advanced capabilities, including

- Higher usage limits for conversations, API calls, and concurrently active Copilots

- Advanced integrations with enterprise data sources such as SAP, SQL, and Microsoft Dataverse

- Multi-channel deployment across Teams, mobile apps, customer service portals, and more

- Enterprise-grade security, including GDPR and HIPAA compliance, Azure AD integration, and role-based access control

The Premium Plan: Pricing and Cost Calculation

When your project moves beyond basic prototyping, you will likely need the **Copilot Studio Premium** features. This allows for multi-channel deployment, connection to 1,400+ enterprise data sources, and the use of advanced autonomous agents.

- **Official Purchase URL:** You can explore and purchase premium plans at `https://www.google.com/search?q=https://www.microsoft.com/en-us/microsoft-copilot-studio/pricing`.

- **Costing Model (2025):** As of September 1, 2025, Microsoft unified its billing around **Copilot Credits**.

- **The Tenant License:** Costs **$200 per month per tenant** and includes a monthly capacity pack of **25,000 Copilot Credits**.

  Pay-As-You-Go (PAYG): For variable needs, you can post-pay via an Azure subscription at a rate of **$0.01 per credit**.

How Costs Are Calculated: Unlike older "per message" models, your costs are now determined by the complexity of the agent's task. Every interaction "burns" a specific number of credits.

Example Calculation

Imagine a customer service agent that provides 2 generative responses and performs 1 data lookup (grounding) per session.

1. **Credits Used:** $(2 \times 2) + 10 = $ **14 credits per conversation**.

2. **Total Capacity:** A single \$200 pack allows for approximately **1,785** such conversations per month.

3. **Cost per Conversation:** Approx. **\$0.11**, which is significantly lower than the average cost of a human-led support interaction.

Choosing the Right Plan

Your ideal plan depends on your goals and scale. Here's a quick guide:

- **Students and Creators**: Start with the Free Tier to learn and prototype. It's perfect for early ideas, classroom projects, and personal tools.

- **Startups and Agencies**: Use the Free Tier to test concepts. When you're ready to build for clients or launch a commercial tool, move to a Premium Plan for more functionality and professional deployment.

  Enterprises: Go directly to Premium with dedicated capacity and compliance tools; it offers the control, integration, and security enterprise environments require.

Table 1-1 summarizes the main benefits, trade-offs, and ideal scenarios for the Free Tier vs. Premium plans, so readers can choose the option that best fits their stage and goals.

Table 1-1. *Comparison of Free-Tier and Premium Copilot Studio Plans Across Key Dimensions*

Dimension	Free Tier (Trial/Exploratory)	Premium Plans (Paid/ Enterprise)
Primary goal	Learning Copilot Studio basics, experimentation, and quick prototyping before committing to a license	Scaling production-grade agents with enterprise data, governance, and predictable capacity
How to sign up	Start from the Copilot Studio page and choose "Try for free," then sign in with a work or school account; personal Microsoft accounts are not supported in most scenarios	Purchase through the Microsoft 365 admin center, Azure subscription (pay-as-you-go), or via a Microsoft sales partner
Licensing prerequisites	Typically requires an eligible Microsoft 365 or Office 365 work/school tenant (e.g., Microsoft 365 Business or Office/Microsoft 365 E- or A-plans) but no separate Copilot Studio SKU during the trial	Requires dedicated Copilot Studio licenses (per-user and/ or tenant message packs) or pay-as-you-go billing; often combined with Microsoft 365 Copilot licenses for end users
Cost	No charge for the limited trial period (e.g., 30–60 days, depending on the promotion); usage is capped	Fixed monthly packs (e.g., about 25,000 messages for a tenant fee) or metered billing per Copilot credit, plus any per-user licenses; costs scale with usage

(continued)

Table 1-1. (*continued*)

Dimension	Free Tier (Trial/Exploratory)	Premium Plans (Paid/Enterprise)
Feature coverage	Access to core designer experience: building agents, basic conversation flows, testing, and publishing to limited/demo channels	Full set of capabilities including advanced orchestration, more channels, richer analytics, and priority support options (depending on plan)
Data connections	Basic connections and sample data suitable for demos and classroom projects; integration breadth may be limited and subject to trial safeguards	Broad integration with Microsoft Dataverse, SharePoint, Dynamics 365, Salesforce, SQL, SAP, and custom APIs, with higher throughput and SLA-backed performance

Copilot Studio's licensing strategy reflects the platform's core mission to empower everyone to create with AI. Whether you're just starting out or managing a fleet of intelligent agents across departments, there's a plan that aligns with your needs. As you gain confidence and creativity, your access can grow with you, enabling new features, channels, and opportunities.

In the next section, we'll take this knowledge and see it in action. Through a real-world case study, we'll explore how one organization used Copilot Studio to solve problems, engage users, and bring an innovative AI solution to life.

Case Study: Building an AI-Powered Social Media Content Generator

This is where theory becomes reality. In this section, we bring theory to life with a practical example: building an AI-powered content generator for social media using Copilot Studio. This example will give you a glimpse of what's possible when creativity meets Copilot Studio without getting into the technical details, which we'll explore in Chapter 2.

- **Describe Your AI Agent**

  Imagine you're a digital marketer or a small business owner who manages multiple social media channels. You often find yourself stuck thinking up catchy captions, hashtag combinations, or ideas for engaging posts. Instead of starting from scratch each time, you decide to build a Copilot which is a conversational AI assistant that can suggest tailored social media posts based on your product, audience, or tone of voice. So, what do you need to do? Just go to the Copilot Studio using the following link: `https://copilotstudio.microsoft.com/`, and after logging in, the interface will be shown as Figure 1-2. Then you need to describe what you actually want in your AI agent.

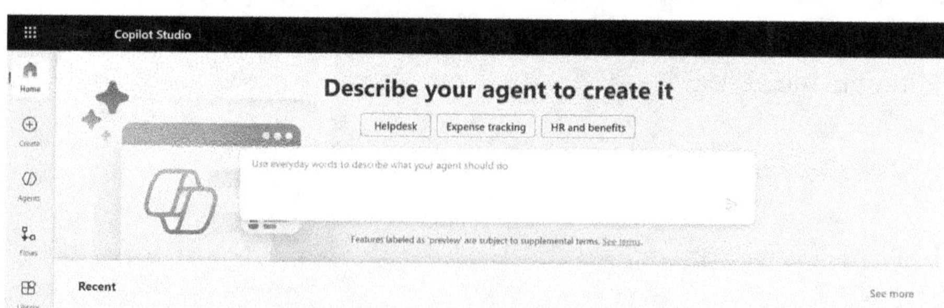

Figure 1-2. *The Copilot Studio interface where the user types the initial prompt*

For example, in your case, you want to build a social media content generator agent. So, your prompt should be

"I want to create an AI assistant that helps me generate social media content. The assistant should ask me questions like what type of product I'm promoting, who my target audience is, what tone I want like funny, professional, inspirational, and which platform I'm posting on such as Instagram, Twitter, LinkedIn. Based on my answers, it should generate a relevant post. The goal is to quickly create creative and platform-appropriate social media posts that fit my brand."

After writing the prompt, the screen should look like Figure 1-3. Once you're ready, click the send icon to continue to the next step.

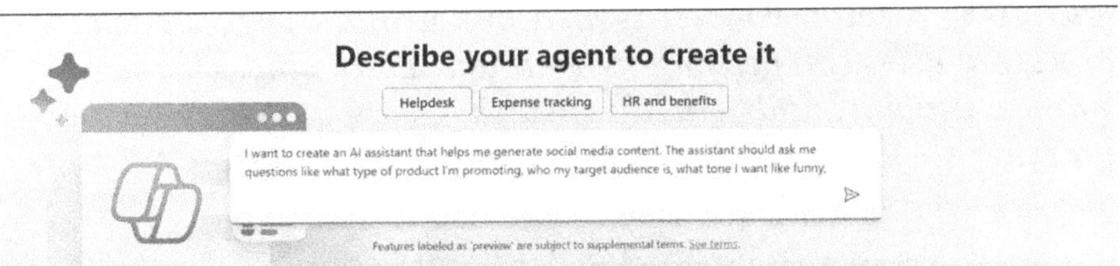

Figure 1-3. *Creating the agent prompt. The prompt clearly defines the AI agent's function, making it easy for Copilot Studio to understand and generate the first draft of the assistant.*

- **Naming the Agent**

  Once the prompt is entered, Copilot Studio automatically transitions into setup mode and asks the user to name the new AI assistant. You can choose from a list of suggestions or enter a name manually. In our case, we named our assistant "AI Content Generator." So, we entered this name and clicked the send icon, as shown in Figure 1-4.

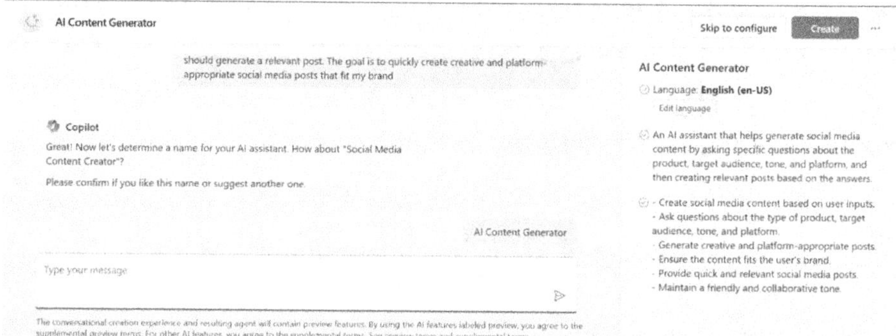

Figure 1-4. Naming your AI agent. Copilot Studio suggests default names, but users can personalize their agent's identity. This step enhances usability and helps distinguish agents within a growing library.

- **Confirm Agent Behavior**

  In a moment, Copilot will ask for a few basic details such as the type of content, product information, and possibly your target audience. For simplicity, just confirm the defaults as shown in Figure 1-5.

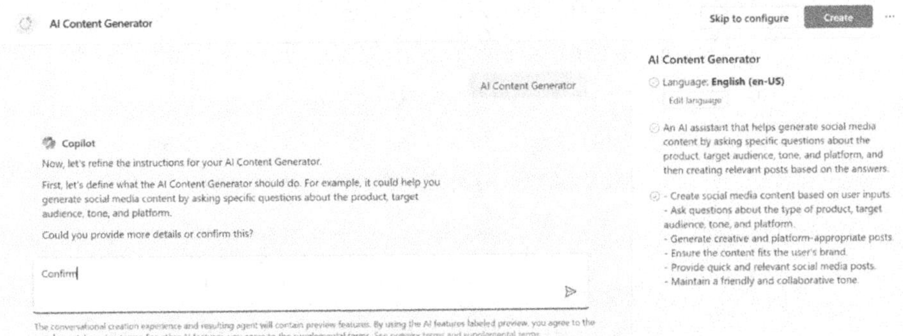

Figure 1-5. *Setting agent intentions. This figure shows how Copilot Studio captures essential details about the AI agent's behavior, tone, and interaction style, streamlining setup for content-specific tasks.*

- **Handling Data Sources**

  Now comes a crucial step in the AI agent creation process: setting up data sources. In Copilot Studio, data sources play a powerful role in enhancing your agent's intelligence. By connecting your assistant to external systems, such as customer databases, product catalogs, FAQs, websites, or APIs, you give it access to real-time information that can be used to generate more accurate, personalized, and context-aware responses.

  For example, if you're building an AI agent to assist with ecommerce, linking it to your product inventory allows it to reference product names, prices, stock levels, and specifications. If your assistant is for internal HR support, connecting it to your employee handbook or benefits portal enables it to answer policy-related questions instantly. In our upcoming chapters, we'll walk through exactly how to integrate these types of external data sources using tools like

Microsoft Dataverse, SharePoint, web URLs, or custom APIs. However, for this simple use case of generating social media content, we won't be connecting any external data sources. This allows us to focus on the core functionality of the assistant without adding complexity.

Instead, we'll instruct Copilot Studio to proceed without linking to any public websites or external systems. You can do this by entering a short clarification prompt, such as

---

At this time, I don't have any external data source to include. Please proceed without connecting to any public URLs.

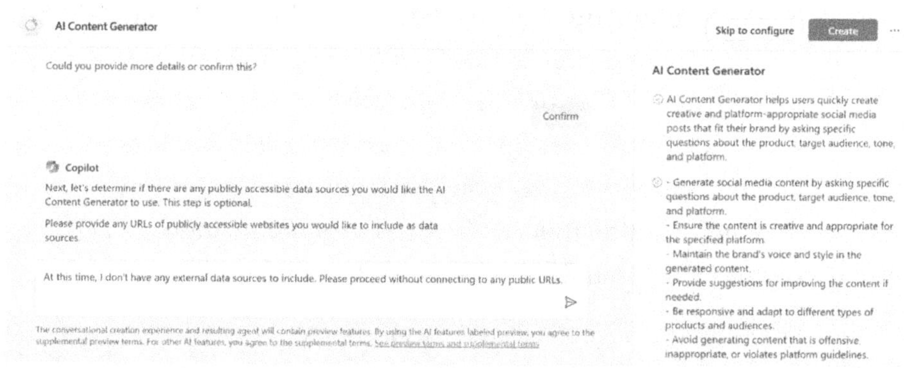

Figure 1-6. *Skipping data integration for a simple agent*

This lets Copilot Studio know that the agent should rely solely on built-in language capabilities, without pulling from outside data. We can visualize this in Figure 1-6.

- **Final Confirmation and Creation**

  You're almost there.

  After you've completed the basic configuration steps like describing your agent, naming it, and confirming data source preferences, Copilot Studio will present a final confirmation screen. This screen, illustrated in Figure 1-7, displays the name of your newly created assistant and confirms that the initial setup process is nearly finished. This is your final checkpoint before the agent is generated.

  On the right-hand side of the screen, you'll see a "Create" button. When you're satisfied with the setup, simply click the Create button to proceed. Copilot Studio will begin provisioning your AI agent. This process typically takes just a few moments, and once complete, your assistant will be ready for testing.

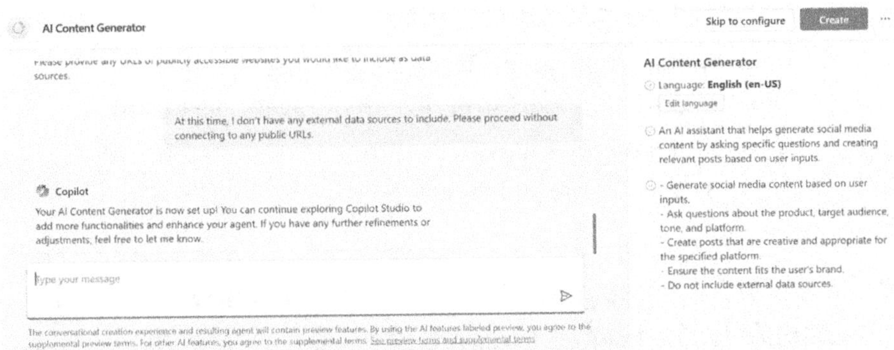

Figure 1-7. A clean summary screen of Final Setup and Agent Confirmation of the agent's configuration

- **Test the Agent**

  Once your agent has been created, it's essential to test how well it performs before publishing it for public use. Testing helps you to evaluate your agent's behavior, understand how it responds to various inputs, and identify any issues that may require improvement.

  Since this is a basic version of the assistant, with no external data connections or advanced logic, its responses may be somewhat generic. However, this initial test phase provides valuable insight into how your AI interprets user prompts and generates content.

  In future chapters, we'll dive deeper into how to enhance your assistant by linking it to external data sources, refining its tone and logic, and applying techniques for customization and optimization. But for now, our goal is simple. We just want to see what our basic AI agent can do right out of the box.

  For now, let's try to give a few example queries to evaluate the initial performance. In our case, we tested the agent using the following prompt, also shown in Figure 1-8, but you can try your own.

Give me a catchy Instagram caption for a new line of eco-friendly water bottles targeted at college students.

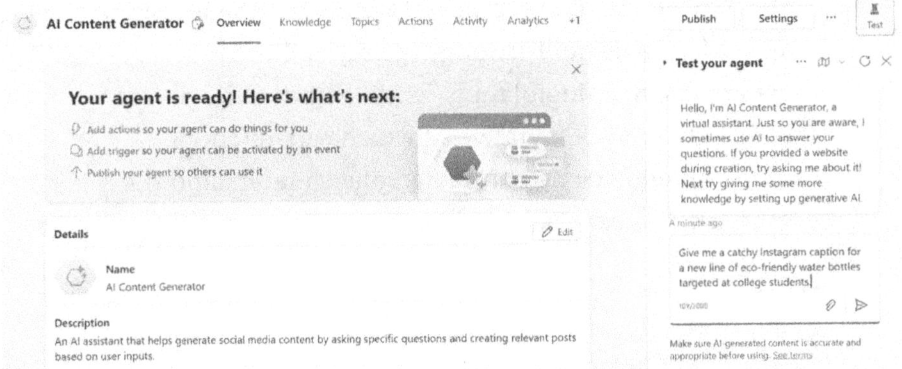

Figure 1-8. *Testing the "AI Content Generator" agent*

- **Activity Overview**

  Once your assistant has responded to a prompt, it's helpful to review the activity overview to better understand how the AI processed the information and arrived at its response. This behind-the-scenes view offers valuable insight into your agent's behavior.

  The Activity tab in Copilot Studio acts like a visual breakdown of the conversation. It shows what the agent heard, how it interpreted it, and what internal components were triggered in response. If any data sources had been connected, this view would also display which knowledge bases or APIs were consulted during the conversation.

  However, because this case study does not involve external data sources, certain areas, like the data lookup or reference path, may appear blank or inactive. That's completely expected.

Despite the absence of connected content, our assistant still relies on its built-in language capabilities to generate a meaningful reply. This illustrates the power of foundational Generative AI which can function independently using natural language understanding, even without external databases or integrations.

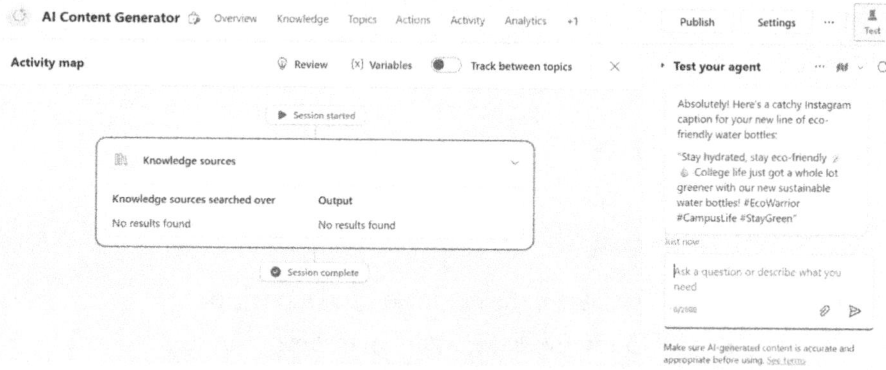

Figure 1-9. *Reviewing the agent activity map*

In Figure 1-9, by examining this activity map, you gain an opportunity to evaluate performance, identify logic gaps, and decide whether your assistant needs further training or enhancement. It also prepares you for more advanced scenarios, where connecting external content sources will make this view even more insightful.

- **Publish the AI Agent**

  Now it's time to bring your AI agent to life by publishing it. Publishing your agent in Copilot Studio means moving it from a draft or testing environment into a state where it can be used, shared, and potentially integrated into real-world applications. Whether it's embedded on a website, connected to Microsoft Teams, or used in a workflow via Power Automate, publishing is the moment your assistant transitions from concept to creation.

To begin this final step, look toward the right-hand side of your Copilot Studio interface, where you'll find the "Publish" button. This button is clearly marked and serves as the gateway to launching your agent.

Once you click the Publish button, Copilot Studio will present you with a confirmation window as illustrated in Figure 1-10. This screen gives you a final summary of your agent's name, purpose, and current status and asks if you're sure you're ready to make the assistant live.

This stage acts as a last review checkpoint. It ensures that you've double-checked the configuration, tested the agent's responses, and confirmed that everything is working as expected. If anything seems incomplete, you still have the option to go back and make adjustments before proceeding.

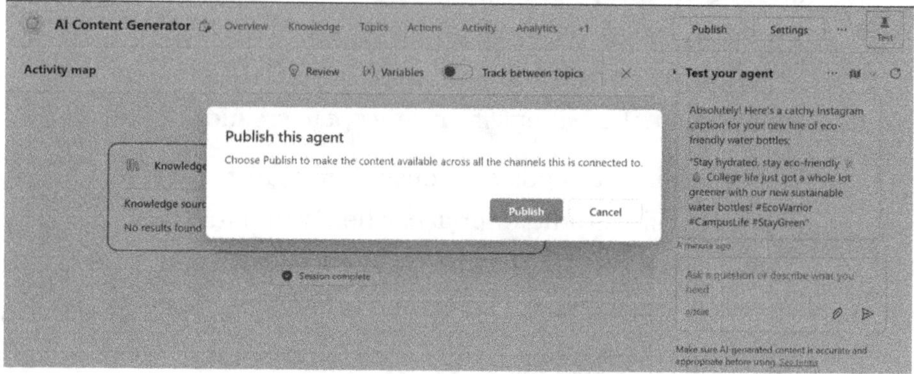

Figure 1-10. *Publishing confirmation. Copilot Studio provides a final confirmation dialog to ensure everything is ready before the assistant goes live. This step promotes intentional, error-free deployment.*

If everything looks good, simply click the Publish button again in the confirmation window. Within a few seconds, Copilot Studio will process your request, and your assistant will be officially deployed.

- **Accessing and Managing Agents**

    Publishing your AI agent is a significant milestone, but it's far from the end of the journey. As your needs evolve or your content strategy changes, you may want to return to your assistant to make updates, expand its capabilities, or integrate it with other systems. Thankfully, Copilot Studio makes managing your agents simple and intuitive.

    Once your assistant is live, you may be wondering: *"Where do I find it later?"* Whether you've built one agent or several, Copilot Studio provides a centralized dashboard that keeps everything organized in one accessible location.

To locate your published or draft AI agents, just look toward the middle-left section of the Copilot Studio interface. Here, you'll find a prominently labeled button called "Agents." Clicking the "Agents" button opens a dedicated panel that displays a list of all the AI assistants associated with your workspace.

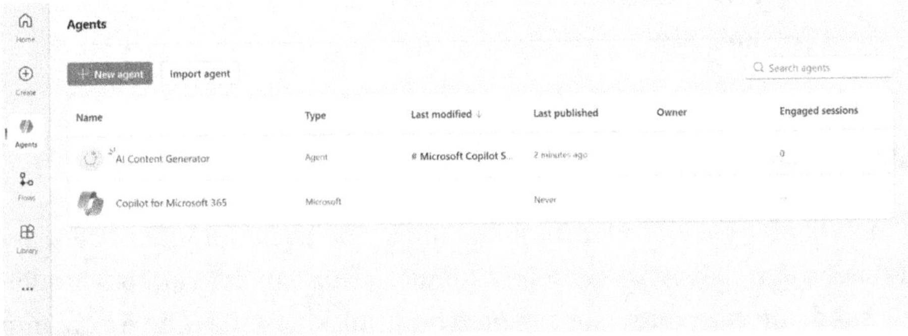

Figure 1-11. *Agents dashboard. This dashboard serves as your command center. You can view, edit, republish, or retire any Copilot you've built, making it easy to manage multiple assistants for different use cases.*

As shown in Figure 1-11, this view provides an organized and accessible overview of every agent you've built, along with key details like the agent's name, creation date, and status.

This section becomes especially useful as your library of agents grows. Whether you're managing a single agent or a dozen tailored to different business needs, social media content generation, internal FAQ bots, or customer service assistants, you'll always know where to find them.

From this Agents dashboard, you can easily open an agent to edit its prompt, update data sources, refine behavior, or integrate it with external services. You can also republish updated versions or delete agents you no longer need. So, whenever you return to Copilot Studio to continue developing or deploying your AI solutions, just click the Agents button to find everything neatly organized and ready for action.

Summary

In this chapter, we turned inspiration into action by building a functional AI-powered social media content generator using Copilot Studio. Through this hands-on case study, we explored how quickly an idea can evolve into a working assistant, without writing a single line of code. From describing the agent to testing and publishing it, the experience showed just how accessible and creative AI development has become.

But this is only the beginning. To unlock Copilot Studio's full potential, you'll need a solid understanding of its environment, capabilities, and integrations. In the next chapter, we'll walk through setting up your workspace, connecting to data sources, navigating the interface, and laying out the technical foundation for more advanced projects. Whether you're building lyrical chatbots or story-generating assistants, Chapter 2 will give you everything you need to get started with Copilot Studio properly and confidently.

Setting Up Your Copilot Studio Environment

Having unveiled the creative potential of Copilot Studio in Chapter 1, it's time to get hands-on. This chapter is your practical guide to setting up your own environment. We'll walk you through the essential prerequisites, help you navigate the interface, and show you how to connect to various data sources. You'll also learn to integrate with Power Automate for more complex tasks. To put it all into practice, we'll address common setup challenges and dive into two exciting projects: building a hip-hop lyric generator and an AI assistant for fiction writers. By the end of this chapter, you'll have a solid technical foundation and the confidence to start bringing your own creative AI visions to life.

Prerequisites and System Requirements

Before you start the exciting process of making your own copilots, you need to make sure your digital workplace is ready. If you meet these basic prerequisites, your experience with Microsoft Copilot Studio will go smoothly and be productive. The platform is meant to be easy for everyone to use, but there are a few important things that need to be in place.

© Mezba Uddin 2026

M. Uddin, *Creative AI Agents with Copilot Studio*, Inside Copilot,
https://doi.org/10.1007/979-8-8688-2779-2_2

1. **Microsoft Account Identity**

A Microsoft account is the most important thing
you need to get into Copilot Studio. This might be
a personal account, like one you use for Outlook.
com or Xbox, a business or school account that
comes with Microsoft 365, or an account that works
with Microsoft Azure services. The kind of account
you have can affect the features, capabilities, and
licensing options you have. For example, Microsoft
365 subscriptions for businesses generally include
tools for collaboration and enterprise-level use. On
the other hand, personal exploration could start
with a simpler account type. The difference between
Free Tier and Premium Plans is generally based on
the type of account and the subscriptions that come
with it, as we talked about in Chapter 1.

2. **Modern Web Browser**

Now, to truly get the most out of it, not just any old
browser will do. To ensure you have the best possible
experience and smooth performance, access to all
the cool features, and a secure environment, it's
really important to use an up-to-date version of a
supported, contemporary browser. Think of it as
choosing a modern car with the latest navigation
and safety features for a cross-country road trip.
Some of the most common and well-regarded
options include

Microsoft Edge: Naturally, being a Microsoft product, Edge is optimized for experiences like Copilot Studio, often offering seamless integration and performance.

Google Chrome: A hugely popular choice known for its speed, extensive extension library, and robust support for modern web standards.

Mozilla Firefox: Prized for its commitment to privacy and open source principles, Firefox is another strong contender that keeps pace with web evolution.

Apple Safari: If you're an Apple user, Safari is tailored for the macOS and iOS ecosystems and generally provides a polished experience.

So, before you dive in, take a quick moment to check your browser. Is it one of the common choices listed? Is it updated to the latest version? A quick check now can save you a lot of potential headaches down the road, ensuring your journey through Copilot Studio is as smooth, secure, and creatively fulfilling as possible.

Navigating the Copilot Studio Interface

Imagine stepping into a sophisticated design studio, perfectly organized and equipped for your next creative endeavor. That's precisely the feeling we want you to have with the Copilot Studio interface. This digital environment is where your inventive AI concepts will blossom into fully realized copilots. It's your command center, your workshop, and your launchpad, all rolled into one. You've already had a brief introduction during our practical exercise in Chapter 1, where we sketched out the "AI Content Generator." Now, let's take a more deliberate stroll through its key areas, so you can navigate it with ease and confidence.

1. **Your Starting Point: The Copilot Studio Home**

    Upon entering Copilot Studio, your journey typically begins on the **Home** page. This is your main portal, offering clear pathways to your various tasks.

    - **Embarking on a New Creation:** You'll usually find a welcoming prompt to start building a new AI agent. As illustrated in Chapter 1 (Figure 1-1), this might be an invitation like, "Describe your agent to create it," allowing you to initiate the process by simply explaining your copilot's intended purpose in plain English.

    - **Resuming Your Work:** For ongoing projects, the Home page typically displays a list of your recent copilots by name, allowing you to quickly jump back into your work.

2. **Your Guiding Compass: The Left-Hand Navigation Pane**

    This persistent menu is your steadfast guide within Copilot Studio. While the exact labels and icons might evolve with platform updates, its core purpose is to provide access to the studio's main sections:

    - **Home:** This option will always return you to the central landing page we just discussed.

    - **Create:** While new copilots can often be started from the Home page, some interface layouts may include a dedicated "Create" button directly in this navigation pane, offering another clear path to begin a new project.

- **Copilots (or sometimes labeled Agents):** This is a critically important section. Selecting it typically leads you to a dashboard that provides an overview of all the copilots you have created or have been given access to. You saw an example of this dashboard in Chapter 1, specifically in Figure 1-10, where our "AI Content Generator" was listed. From this list, you can select any copilot to open it for editing, review its current status, check when it was last modified, or manage its settings.

- **Flows:** This section directly relates to Power Automate. Here, you can create, manage, or connect to automated workflows (Flows) that your copilot can trigger to perform actions, integrate with other systems, or carry out complex back-end logic, greatly enhancing its power and utility.

- **Library:** A "Library" section often serves as a repository for reusable components. This might include prebuilt skills, templates, or other assets that can be shared across multiple copilots, promoting consistency and saving development time.

- **More Options (often indicated by three dots ...):** Additionally, a "More Options" menu is often indicated by an icon, such as (...), typically located at the bottom of the navigation pane. In the context of Copilot Studio, which is part of the broader Microsoft Power Platform, this menu could provide links to other Power Platform services (like Power Apps, Power Automate itself, or Power BI), access to environment details, administrative settings, or links to documentation and support resources.

Once you choose a specific copilot and open it, the interface typically transitions to the more detailed Copilot Editing Canvas, which comes with its own specialized set of tools and navigation options.

3. **The Creative Workshop: The Copilot Editing Canvas**

When you either begin a new copilot or open an existing one, you step onto the main workshop floor. This is where the intricate work of designing, constructing, and refining your AI agent takes place.

The Top Command Bar: Your Primary Toolkit

Across the upper section of the canvas, you'll generally find a navigation bar that is specific to the copilot you are currently working on. This bar houses several key tabs, as we saw during the walkthrough in Chapter 1 (for instance, in Figures 1-7 and 1-8), also shown in detail in Figure 2-1, marked as a red border.

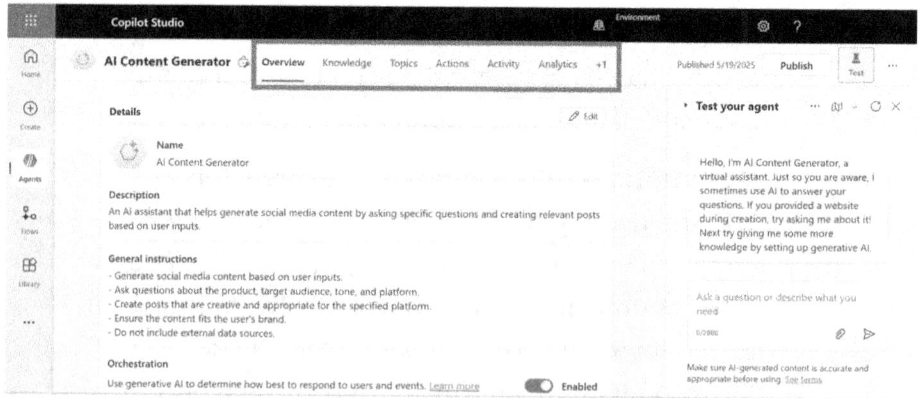

Figure 2-1. *The top command bar in the Copilot Editing Canvas, highlighting key navigation tabs like Overview, Knowledge, Topics, Actions, Activity, and Analytics for managing and building your AI agent*

- **Overview:** This tab usually gives you a high-level summary of your copilot, including its description, and offers quick access to add fundamental functionalities like prebuilt actions or triggers.

- **Knowledge (or Data Sources):** This crucial section is where you can significantly enhance your copilot's intelligence by connecting it to various external information repositories. These sources might include public websites, uploaded documents containing FAQs or product details, or other structured data, thereby giving your copilot a much richer base of information from which to formulate accurate and relevant responses. In Chapter 1, while building our social media content generator, we initially deferred connecting external data sources to maintain simplicity, but we acknowledged the immense value this capability brings to more sophisticated agents.

- **Topics:** This is the very heart of your copilot's ability to converse intelligently. Within this area, you will define, organize, and fine-tune the various conversational flows, specify the phrases that trigger these flows, and build the detailed dialogue logic that your AI agent will use. We will explore the art and science of crafting effective Topics in detail in our future chapters.

- **Actions:** This area provides the tools to substantially extend your copilot capabilities beyond standard conversation. Frequently, this involves integrating with Power Automate flows to execute complex back-end processes or connecting to external APIs to fetch or send data.

- **Activity:** This tab offers a valuable "behind the scenes" look into your agent's operations during a conversation. The Activity tab acts like a visual breakdown or log, showing what the agent heard, how it interpreted the input, and what internal components or topics were triggered in response. If any data sources were connected and consulted, this view might also display how that information was accessed and used. Reviewing the activity map, as shown in Figure 1-8 of Chapter 1, is essential for debugging, understanding the decision-making process of your copilot, and identifying areas for refinement.

- **Analytics:** Once your copilot is active and engaging with users, this tab becomes your insight center. It will display vital performance metrics, such as user satisfaction ratings, the most commonly accessed topics, and other valuable data points that can help you continuously improve its effectiveness and user experience.

With a good understanding of how to navigate the Copilot Studio interface, from the main Home page and navigation pane to the intricacies of the Copilot Editing Canvas, you're now well-equipped to start shaping your AI agents. This familiarity will be crucial as we move forward. The next essential step in empowering your copilots is to teach them how to access and utilize information. Therefore, in the next part of this chapter, we will dive into the practicalities of connecting your copilot to various data sources, turning your creative AI visions into truly knowledgeable and responsive assistants.

Connecting to Data Sources (SharePoint, Dataverse, APIs)

Now that you're comfortable navigating the Copilot Studio interface, it's time to unlock one of its most powerful capabilities: connecting your AI agents to data. A copilot that can access and use information is a smarter, more helpful, and ultimately more creative assistant. Without access to relevant data, your copilot relies solely on the conversational logic you explicitly define in its Topics. However, by connecting it to data sources, you enable it to fetch real-time information, personalize interactions, and perform tasks based on existing knowledge.

In Chapter 1, we touched upon "Data Integration and Context Awareness" as a key feature of Copilot Studio, highlighting its ability to connect to Microsoft Dataverse, SharePoint, Dynamics 365, Salesforce, and custom APIs. We also saw in the case study how Copilot Studio prompts for data sources during the initial agent setup, even though we skipped it for that simple example. This section will guide you through the practical steps and considerations for making these connections, focusing on some of the most common and impactful options: SharePoint, Dataverse, and external APIs.

Why Connect to Data Sources?

Before we dive into the "how," let's briefly revisit the "why." Connecting your copilot to data sources can transform it from a simple Q&A bot into a dynamic and intelligent assistant which can be capable of

- **Providing Real-Time Information:** Answering questions with up-to-the-minute data, like product stock levels from a database or project statuses from a SharePoint list

- **Personalizing User Experiences:** Tailoring responses based on user profiles stored in Dataverse or other CRM systems

- **Automating Processes:** Retrieving information needed to complete a task, like looking up an order status or finding contact details

- **Expanding Knowledge:** Giving your copilot access to a vast repository of information contained in documents, websites, or enterprise systems, allowing it to answer a much broader range of queries

Accessing Data Source Options in Copilot Studio

You'll typically manage data source connections from within the Knowledge tab of your copilot's editing canvas, which we identified previously. Also shown in Figure 2-2, here we can see an option for adding knowledge by marking red.

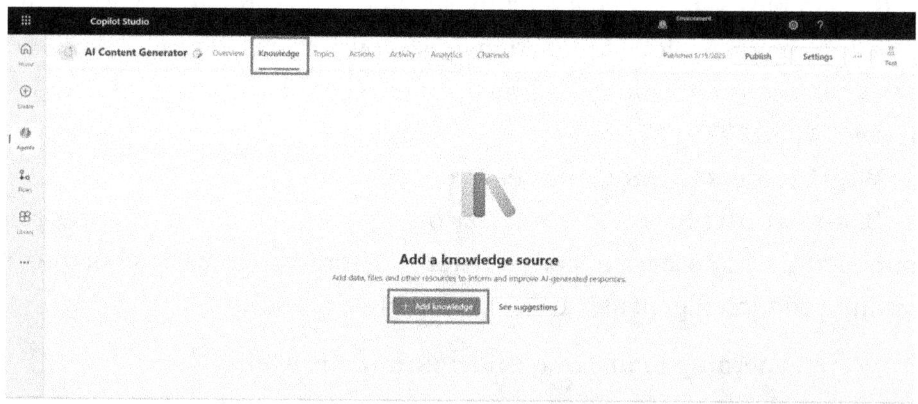

Figure 2-2. *The Knowledge tab in Copilot Studio, highlighting the "Add knowledge" button*

By clicking this, you will see another prompt like Figure 2-3, for adding knowledge from a variety of sources.

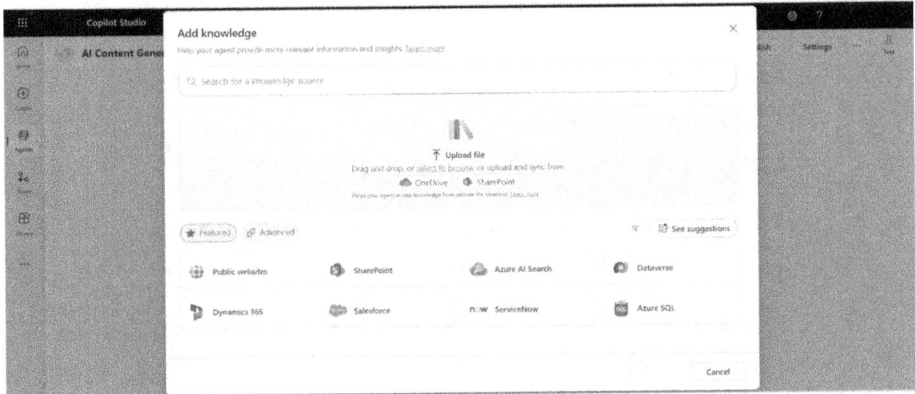

Figure 2-3. *The "Add knowledge" dialog, showcasing various data source options like public websites, SharePoint, Dataverse, and file uploads*

Connecting to SharePoint

SharePoint is widely used for document management and team collaboration, making it a rich source of information for your copilots. You can enable your AI agent to search for and retrieve information from documents and list items stored on SharePoint sites.

Common Use Cases

- Answering FAQs based on knowledge base articles stored in a SharePoint document library.

- Providing updates on project tasks listed in a SharePoint list.

- Finding specific documents based on user queries is important.

Steps to Connect

- **Navigate to the Knowledge or Data Sources Section:**
  Within your copilot, go to the designated area for
  managing data sources.

- **Select SharePoint As a Data Source:** You should see
  an option to add a SharePoint site.

- **Authenticate and Specify the Site URL:** You'll likely
  need to authenticate with your Microsoft 365 credentials
  that have access to the desired SharePoint site. Then,
  you'll provide the URL of the SharePoint site or specific
  document library/list you want your copilot to access.

- **Configure Permissions (If Applicable):** Ensure the
  account used for the connection has the necessary read
  permissions for the content you want the copilot to access.

- **Index Content:** Copilot Studio might need to index the
  content from the SharePoint site to make it searchable.
  This process can take some time depending on the amount
  of data.

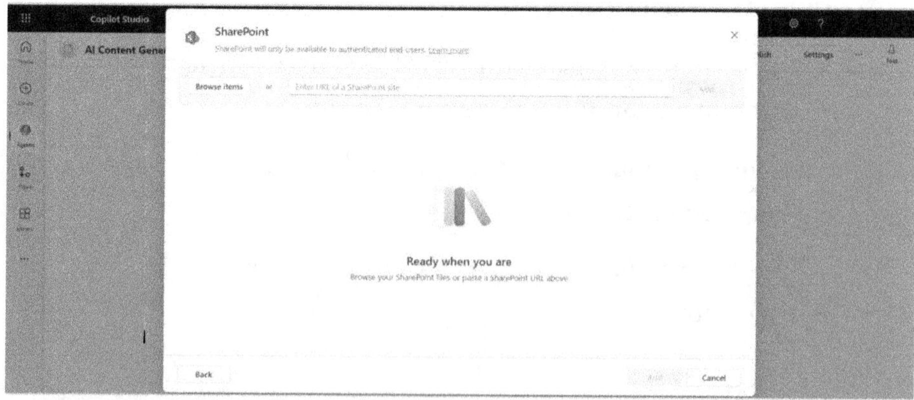

Figure 2-4. *The SharePoint connection interface in Copilot Studio,*
prompting for the SharePoint site URL

Leveraging Dataverse

Microsoft Dataverse is a scalable data service and app platform that lets you securely store and manage data used by business applications. If your organization uses Dynamics 365 or custom Power Apps, chances are your data resides in Dataverse. Connecting Copilot Studio to Dataverse allows your AI agents to interact with this rich business data.

Common Use Cases

- Looking up customer information such as order history and contact details from Dataverse tables

- Creating or updating records in Dataverse like logging a support ticket and updating sales leads

- Providing personalized responses based on data stored about the logged-in user

Steps to Connect

- **Access Data Source Options**: Go to the Knowledge or Data Sources section in your copilot.

- **Choose Dataverse**: Select the option to connect to Dataverse. Since Copilot Studio is part of the Power Platform, the integration with Dataverse is often very streamlined.

- **Select Tables and Columns**: You'll typically be able to specify which Dataverse tables (entities) and columns (fields) your copilot should have access to. This allows for granular control over the data.

- **Define Relationships (If Necessary)**: If your copilot needs to work with related tables, you might need to ensure those relationships are correctly understood.

- **Utilize Topics and Actions**: Once connected, you can reference Dataverse tables and actions within your copilot's Topics and Power Automate Flows (Actions) to retrieve, create, or update data.

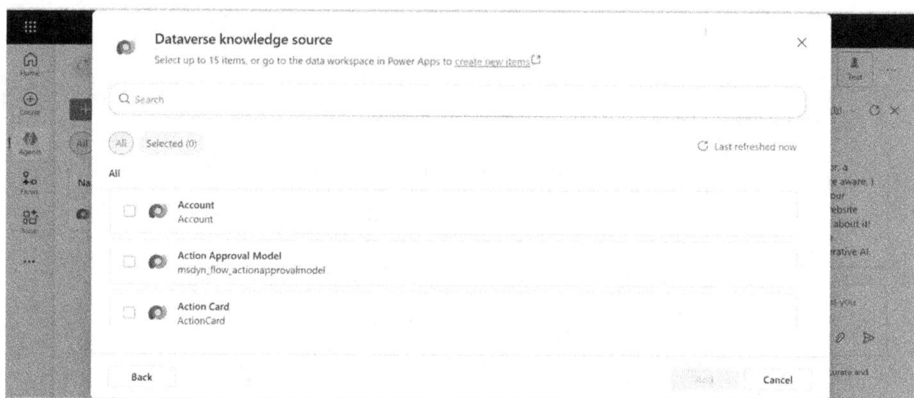

Figure 2-5. *Selecting Dataverse tables as knowledge sources within Copilot Studio*

Integrating with External APIs

APIs (application programming interfaces) allow different software systems to communicate and exchange data. By connecting your copilot to external APIs, you can extend its capabilities, enabling it to interact with third-party services or enterprise systems.

Common Use Cases

- Fetching real-time data from external services such as weather updates, stock prices, and flight information

- Integrating with legacy enterprise systems that don't have direct connectors

- Performing actions in other systems such as booking a meeting and sending a notification via a third-party messaging service

Steps to Connect API

- **Identify the API:** You'll need the API's endpoint URL and details about authentication and its request/response structure.

- **Utilize Actions or Flows:** To make an API call, you might use an action within your copilot. Figure 2-6 and Figure 2-7 suggest how this could be approached. Figure 2-6 shows an authoring canvas where, under an "Advanced" section, an option to "Send HTTP request" is available. This implies a direct way to configure such a request as part of your copilot's logic. Figure 2-7 then appears to show a conceptual interface for configuring an HTTP request, with a field visible for the URL, where you would input the API endpoint.

- **Define Input and Output Parameters:** You would need to clearly define what information your copilot sends to the API and what it expects back.

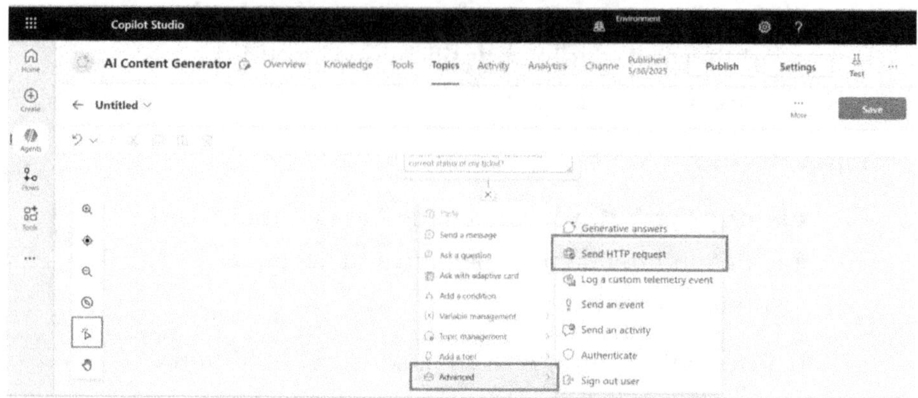

Figure 2-6. *Illustrating the "Send HTTP request" option available under "Advanced" actions within the Copilot Studio authoring canvas, often used for API calls via Power Automate*

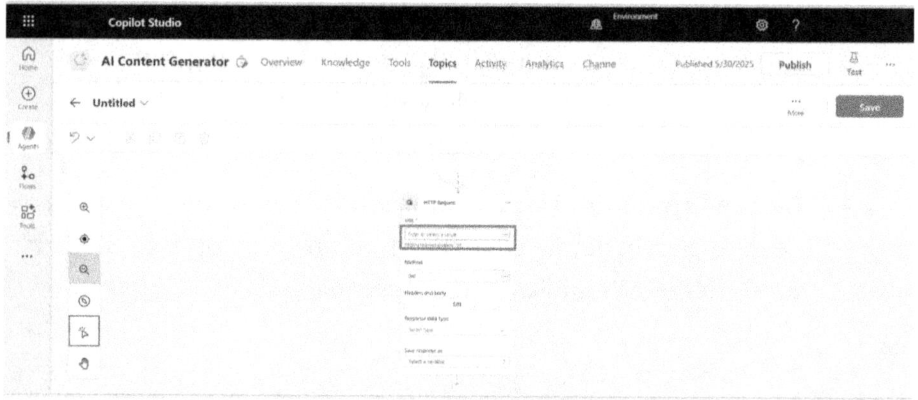

Figure 2-7. *A conceptual view of configuring an HTTP request within a Topic or Flow, showing fields for method and URL*

Important Considerations When Connecting Data

- **Security and Permissions:** Always follow the principle of least privilege. Only grant your copilot access to the specific data it needs to perform its functions. Ensure authentication methods are secure.

- **Data Privacy and Compliance:** Be mindful of data privacy regulations (like GDPR, CCPA, HIPAA, etc.) when accessing and using data, especially personal information.

- **Data Volume and Performance:** Large datasets or slow APIs can impact your copilot's responsiveness. Optimize queries and consider caching mechanisms where appropriate.

- **Error Handling:** Implement robust error handling in your Topics and Flows to manage situations where data sources are unavailable or return unexpected results. Your copilot should fail gracefully.

- **Data Freshness:** Understand how often the data in your sources is updated and ensure your copilot's information reflects the required level of currency.

By thoughtfully connecting your copilots to relevant data sources like SharePoint, Dataverse, and external APIs, you dramatically increase their value and utility. This ability to access and reason over data is a cornerstone of building truly creative and effective AI agents. Having set up your environment and learned how to connect to data, you're almost ready to start building more complex interactions. Next, we'll explore how to further enhance your copilot capabilities by integrating with Power Automate for advanced workflows.

Integrating with Power Automate for Advanced Workflows

So far, we've given our copilots knowledge by connecting them to data sources. But what about giving them hands? To transform your AI from a simple conversationalist into an assistant that can do things, like save files, send notifications, or update records, we need to introduce it to a powerful tool: Microsoft Power Automate.

You might recall seeing "Flows" listed in the left-hand navigation pane of Copilot Studio or the "Actions" tab within the Copilot Editing Canvas. These interface elements are your gateways to this extended functionality. Power Automate is Microsoft's robust service for creating automated workflows between various applications and services. By integrating Power Automate Flows with your Copilot Studio agents, you give your AI creations the hands and feet they need to interact with the digital world in a much more profound and impactful way.

Let's consider the "AI Content Generator" we built in Chapter 1. That agent was a fantastic starting point, capable of generating social media post suggestions based on your initial description. But what if we wanted it to do more? What if, after generating that catchy Instagram caption, you wanted to save it directly to a team SharePoint site, schedule it for posting, or send it for approval? This is precisely where integrating with Power Automate becomes not just beneficial, but transformative.

The Necessity: Why Your "AI Content Generator" (And Other Creative Agents) Needs Power Automate

While Copilot Studio excels at natural language understanding, dialogue management, and providing information through connected knowledge sources, its inherent capabilities are primarily focused on conversation and information retrieval. Many real-world scenarios, especially in creative or business contexts, require more than just talk; they demand action.

For our AI Content Generator, imagine these enhancements made possible by Power Automate:

- **Saving and Organizing Generated Content**: Currently, the generated content exists within the chat. With Power Automate, the copilot could ask, "Would you like to save this post idea?" If the user says yes, a Flow could

  - Save the text to a specific Word document or text file in a designated OneDrive folder or SharePoint document library.

  - Add the generated post, target platform, and proposed date to a content calendar managed in a SharePoint list or Microsoft Planner.

- **Streamlining Approval Workflows**: If content needs approval before publishing, the copilot could trigger a Flow to send the generated post via email or a Teams message to a manager. The manager could approve or reject it, and the Flow could update the status and notify the original user via the copilot.

- **Automated Posting or Scheduling (with care)**: While direct posting to social media requires careful consideration of API terms and security, Power Automate can integrate with various social media management tools or create tasks in a scheduler to remind the user to post the content.

- **Enriching Content with Real-Time Trends**: While our initial AI Content Generator relies on its base knowledge, a more advanced version could trigger a Flow. This Flow could use an API (as discussed in previously) to fetch currently trending hashtags or topics relevant to the user's product or industry, which could then be incorporated into the generated content suggestions.

- **Gathering Usage Analytics**: A Flow could log details about what types of content are being generated, for which platforms, and how frequently, into a Dataverse table or a SharePoint list for later analysis of the tool's effectiveness.

These examples illustrate that Power Automate extends the copilot's reach, allowing it to interact with other systems and perform tasks that make it a far more integrated and valuable creative partner.

Implementing the Integration: Enhancing the "AI Content Generator" with Flows

We've established why Power Automate is such a game-changer for your copilots, especially for our "AI Content Generator." Now, let's get practical and walk through *how* you can build this integration. We'll focus on a common scenario: enabling your AI Content Generator to save its brilliant creations directly to a SharePoint site.

There are a couple of ways to initiate the creation of a Power Automate Flow for your copilot. In this guide, we'll explore a very organized method: starting from the "Flows" section within Copilot Studio itself. This approach helps keep your Flows neatly associated with your agent.

Part 1: Design and Build the Power Automate Flow ("Save AI Content to SharePoint")— Starting from Copilot Studio

Let's begin by crafting the automated workflow in Power Automate that will handle the file-saving generated content.

Step 1: Navigate to the "Flows" Section in Copilot Studio

First, open your "AI Content Generator" agent within the Copilot Studio interface. On the left-hand navigation pane (which we explored), you'll find an item typically labeled Flows. Go ahead and click that. This area is your central hub for managing any Power Automate Flows associated with this specific copilot.

Step 2: Initiate New Flow Creation from Copilot Studio

Once you're in the "Flows" section, you'll want to create a new Flow. Look for a button or option that clearly indicates this, such as "+New agent flow". Click this option. This action tells Copilot Studio that you intend to build a new automated process that your AI agent can use.

Step 3: The Power Automate Designer Opens

When you click to create a new Flow, Copilot Studio will typically transition you smoothly into the Power Automate design environment. This usually happens in one of two ways:

- You might be redirected to the main Power Automate designer in a new browser tab.

- Alternatively, some versions of the interface might open an embedded Power Automate designer directly within your Copilot Studio window.

A fantastic benefit of starting this way is that Power Automate often gives you a head start by pre-populating your new Flow with a couple of essential components:

- **A Trigger**: This is usually "When an agent calls the flow" (or it might be named "When Microsoft Copilot Studio calls a flow" or "When Power Virtual Agents calls a flow"). This is the starting point that allows your copilot to initiate the Flow.

- **And Sometimes, a Final Action**: This might be "Respond to the agent" (or "Respond to Microsoft Copilot Studio"/"Return value(s) to Power Virtual Agents"). This is how the Flow sends information back to your copilot after it's done its work.

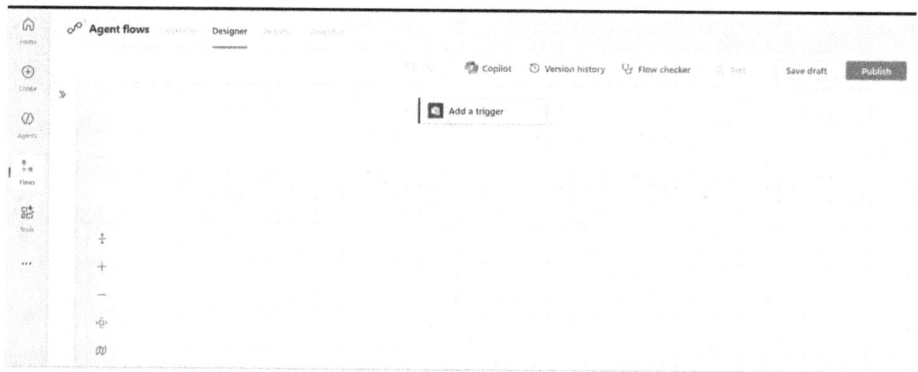

Figure 2-8. *The Power Automate designer canvas, initially empty, prompting to "Add a trigger" to begin building the workflow*

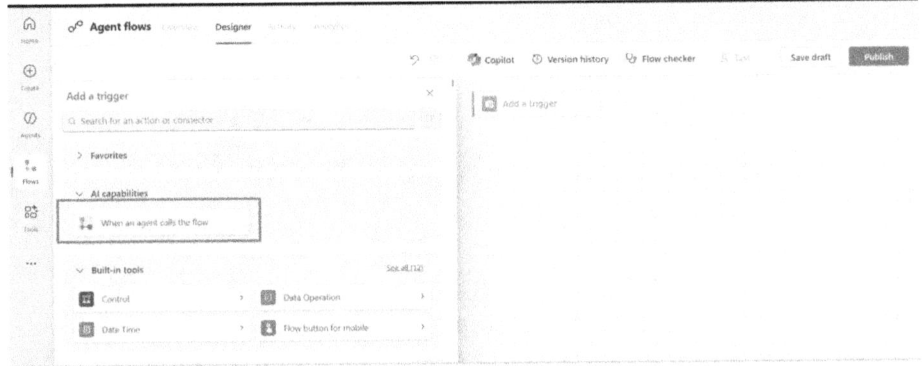

Figure 2-9. *In Power Automate: Selecting the "When an agent calls the flow" trigger from the "AI capabilities" section, which allows Copilot Studio to initiate this workflow*

Step 4: Define Input Parameters

After clicking "When an agent calls the flow", we need to define our input parameters.

- **Define Input Parameters:** Now, click on this trigger step. This is where you'll tell the Flow what pieces of information it needs to receive from your AI Content Generator. For our "Save AI Content to SharePoint" example, we need a few things to do. Click the **"+ Add an input"** option which is visible in Figure 2-10.

  - Select **Text** and name it as **GeneratedContentText**. You can add a description like "The actual content generated by the copilot."

  - Select **Text** and name it **SuggestedFileName**. A good description would be "Desired file name, such as, product_campaign_post."

- Select **Text** and name it
  TargetSharePointSiteURL. Describe it as "Enter
  your SharePoint URL."

- Select **Text** and name it **TargetDocumentLibrary**.
  You can describe this as "The name of the
  document library, like Shared Documents or
  Shared Documents/AICopilotContent."

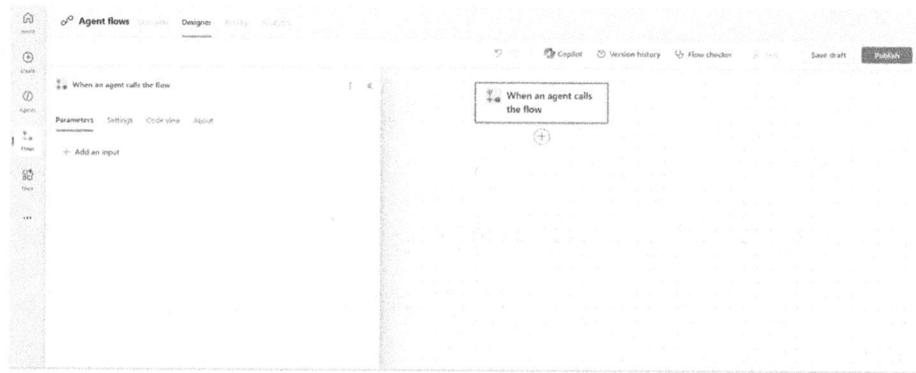

Figure 2-10. *The Power Automate Flow canvas showing the "When an agent calls the flow" trigger added, with the focus on its parameters and the "+ Add an input" option*

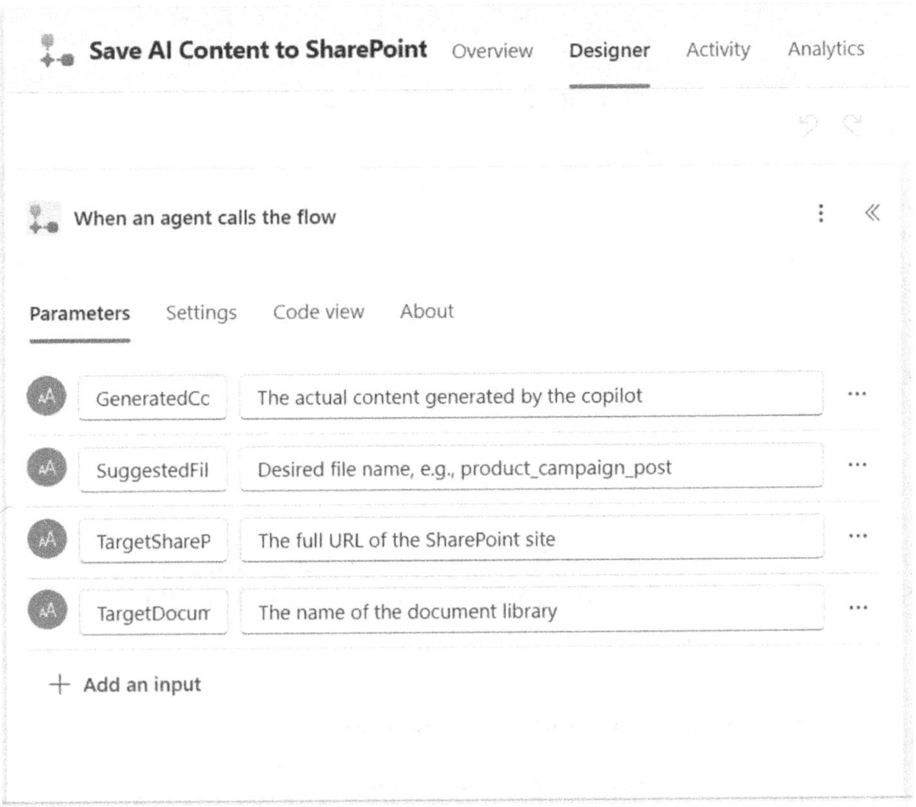

Save AI Content to SharePoint   Overview   **Designer**   Activity   Analytics

When an agent calls the flow

Parameters   Settings   Code view   About

AA	GeneratedCc	The actual content generated by the copilot
AA	SuggestedFil	Desired file name, e.g., product_campaign_post
AA	TargetShareP	The full URL of the SharePoint site
AA	TargetDocun	The name of the document library

+ Add an input

Figure 2-11. *Defining the input parameters for the Power Automate Flow*

The top image on page 16 of your PDF perfectly illustrates these input parameters defined within the trigger.

Step 5: Add the SharePoint "Create file" Action

This is the core of our Flow—the part that actually saves the file.

- Click the + icon below your trigger.

- In the search box that appears, type "SharePoint". From the list of SharePoint actions, select **"Create file"**. You might be prompted to sign in or confirm your connection to SharePoint if you haven't used it in Power Automate before. Figure 2-12 shows searching for SharePoint actions.

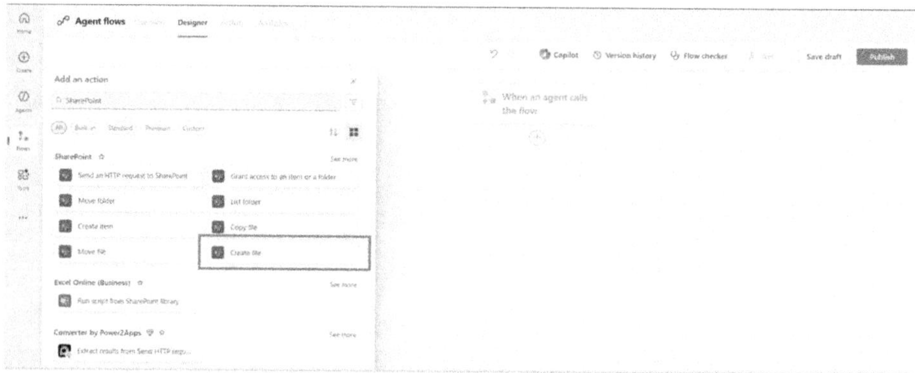

Figure 2-12. *Adding an action to the Flow: Searching for "SharePoint" and selecting the "Create file" action from the SharePoint connector*

- **Now, you'll configure the "Create file" action:**

  - **Site Address:** Click on this field. Instead of typing, select "Enter custom value," and then from the "Dynamic content" pane that appears (this pane lists all the data available from previous steps), select the **TargetSharePointSiteURL** input you defined in your trigger.

  - **Folder Path:** Click in this field, select "Enter custom value," and then choose the **TargetDocumentLibrary** dynamic content from your trigger.

  - **File Name:** From the "Dynamic content" pane, select **SuggestedFileName**. It's important to add the file extension here too, so it might look like

[SuggestedFileName].txt or [SuggestedFileName].
md, depending on the type of file you want to create.

- **File Content:** From the "Dynamic content" pane, select **GeneratedContentText**.

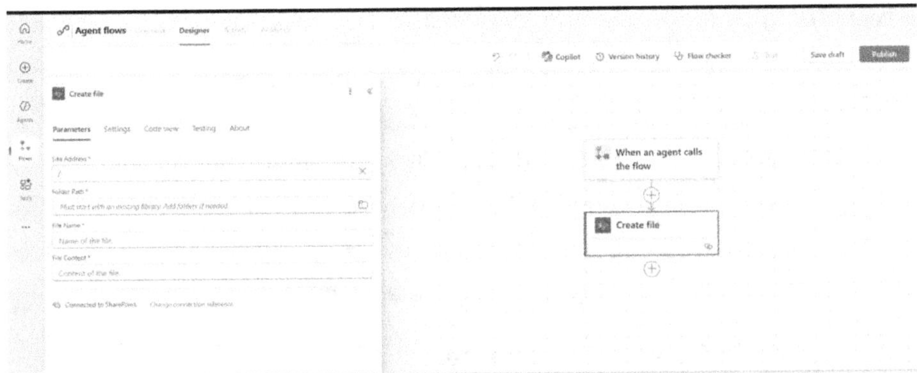

Figure 2-13. *Configuring the SharePoint "Create file" action in Power Automate, using dynamic content from the trigger's inputs to specify the site, folder, file name, and content*

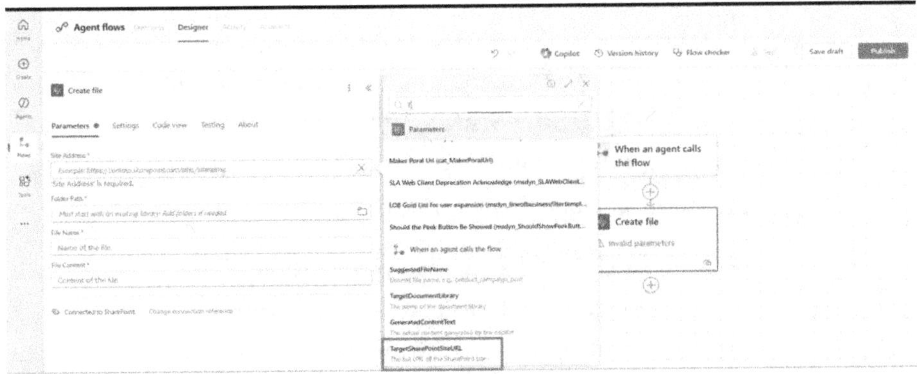

Figure 2-14. *Utilizing dynamic content from the Flow's trigger, selecting TargetSharePointSiteURL to populate the "Site Address" field in the "Create file" action*

Step 6: Implement Error Handling and Define Output Parameters

It's crucial that your Flow tells Copilot Studio whether the save operation was successful and provides a link to the file or an error message. We'll set up two possible responses: one for success and one for failure.

- If Power Automate pre-added a "Respond to the agent" (or similarly named) action at the very end of your Flow, it's often best to delete it for now so we can create separate success and failure response paths more cleanly. You can usually delete an action by clicking the three dots (…) on its card and selecting "Delete."

- **Successful Response Action**

  - Click **"+ New step"** directly after your "Create file" action.

  - Search for and add the action named "Return value(s) to Power Virtual Agents", shown in Figure 2-15.

  - Click **"+ Add an output"** and select **Text**. Name this output **FileSaveStatus**. In the value field for this output, type a success message, for example: "Successfully saved the content."

  - Click **"+ Add an output"** again and select **Text**. Name this one **LinkToFile**. Now, from the "Dynamic content" pane, find the outputs from your "Create file" SharePoint action. Select "Link to item" (or a similar output like "Path" or "ItemUrl"— the exact name can vary slightly). This will provide the direct URL to the file that was just created.

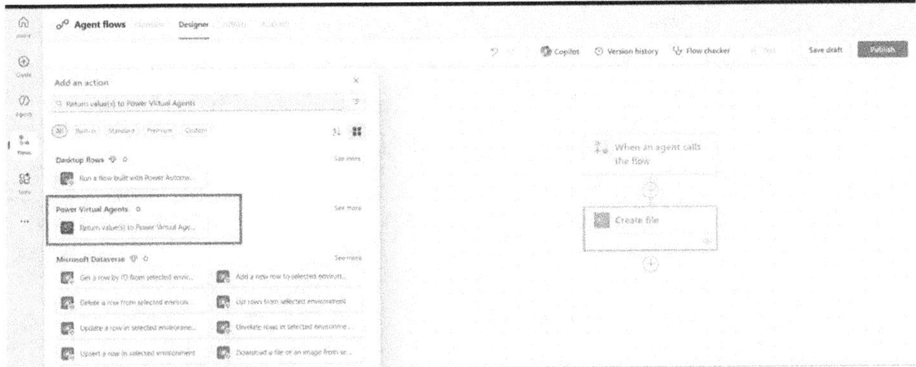

Figure 2-15. *Adding the "Return value(s) to Power Virtual Agents" action to send data back to Copilot Studio after the Flow's operations are complete*

- **Failure Response Action (Using a Parallel Branch)**

  - Now, right-click the + icon that appears on the connecting line between your "Create file" action and the "Successful Response" action you just added.

  - From the menu that pops up, select **"Add a parallel branch"** as shown in Figure 2-16. This creates a new, separate path in your Flow.

  - On this new parallel branch, click **"Add an action"**.

  - Search for and add another "**Respond to the agent**" action.

  - Click **"+ Add an output"** and select **Text**. Name it FileSaveStatus. In its value field, type an error message, for example: "Error: Could not save the file to SharePoint."

- (Optional for LinkToFile in an error): You can either omit the LinkToFile output from this error response action, or add it as a Text output and leave its value blank, or set it to something like "N/A".

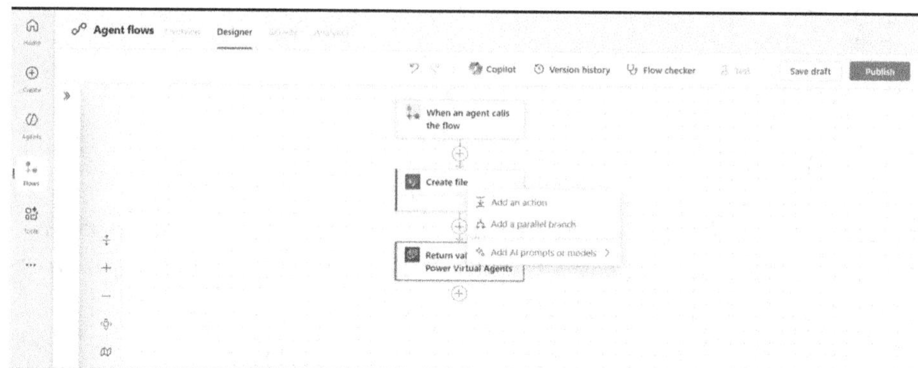

Figure 2-16. *In Power Automate: Adding a parallel branch to the Flow to handle separate paths for successful execution and potential failures of the "Create file" action*

After successfully configuring the response action and failure action, our final flow may look like Figure 2-17.

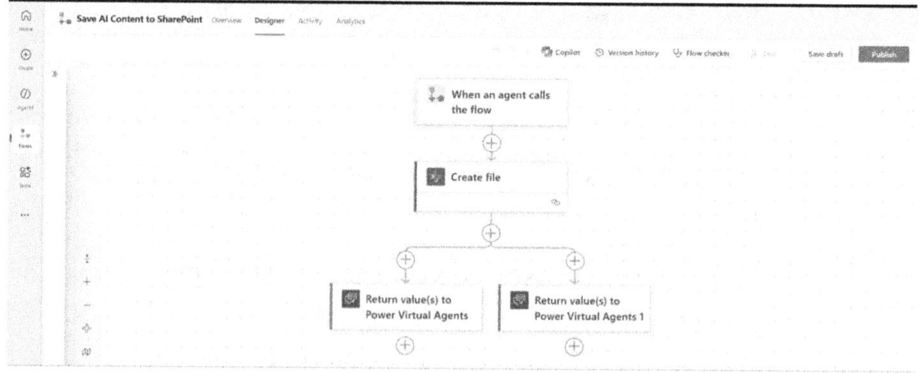

Figure 2-17. *The completed Power Automate Flow for "Save AI Content to SharePoint," showing the trigger, the "Create file" action, and parallel branches for returning success or failure values to Copilot Studio*

Part 2: Prepare Your Topic in Copilot Studio

You've successfully designed and built your "Save AI Content to SharePoint" Power Automate Flow in Part 1. Now, it's time to return to Copilot Studio and teach your "AI Content Generator" how to actually use this new capability. This is where we'll edit or create a Topic to handle the conversation around saving the content.

Step 1: Prepare Your Topic in Copilot Studio

First, let's get to the right place in your "AI Content Generator" copilot:

- **Navigate to Topics:** In Copilot Studio, with your "AI Content Generator" open, click **Topics** in the left-hand navigation pane. This is where all the conversational blueprints for your copilot live.

- **Create or Select a Topic:** For this new "save to SharePoint" functionality, it's often best to create a **new Topic.** You could name it something clear, like "Save Generated Content to SharePoint".

  - Click the **"+ New topic"** button.

  - Give your Topic a name and a brief description.

- **Define Trigger Phrases:** How will your copilot know when the user wants to save content? You'll need to add some **trigger phrases** to your new Topic. These could be things like

  - "Save this content"

  - "Save to SharePoint"

  - "I want to save the post you just created"

Okay, let's dive into "Part 3" and rewrite it with a strong guiding tone, starting from how your reader would approach this within the Copilot Studio Topic editor. We'll closely follow the steps you've outlined and integrate the figure references and captions you've suggested.

Part 3: Call the Flow from an "Action" Node in Your Copilot Topic

Fantastic! You've successfully designed and built your "Save AI Content to SharePoint" Power Automate Flow in Part 2. Now, it's time to return to Copilot Studio and teach your "AI Content Generator" how to actually use this new capability. This is where we'll edit or create a Topic to handle the conversation around saving the content.

Step 1: Prepare Your Topic in Copilot Studio

First, let's get to the right place in your "AI Content Generator" copilot:

1. **Navigate to Topics:** In Copilot Studio, with your "AI Content Generator" open, click **Topics** in the left-hand navigation pane. This is where all the conversational blueprints for your copilot live.

2. **Create or Select a Topic:** For this new "save to SharePoint" functionality, it's often best to create a **new Topic**. You could name it something clear, like "Save Generated Content to SharePoint".

   - Click the **"+ New topic"** button.

   - Give your Topic a name and a brief description.

3. **Define Trigger Phrases:** How will your copilot know when the user wants to save content? You'll need to add some trigger phrases to your new Topic. These could be things like

- "Save this content"

- "Save to SharePoint"

- "I want to save the post you just created". The top image on page 18 of your PDF shows a Topic already named "Save Content to SharePoint," implying it might be triggered in a specific way (the image shows "By agent" as a trigger, which means another Topic might redirect to this one, or it could be triggered by specific phrases if you add them).

Step 2: Design the Conversation to Collect Information

Now, within your new "Save Content to SharePoint" Topic's authoring canvas, we need to have the copilot ask the user for all the details that your Power Automate Flow requires. You'll use a series of "Question" nodes for this.

1. **Ask for the Content to Save**

   - Add a **Question** node. For the question text, enter: "What content would you like me to save to SharePoint?"

   - Under "Identify," choose an appropriate entity ("User's entire response" if the content is expected to be multi-line text).

   - Under "Save response as," create a new variable by clicking the variable icon and selecting "+ Create variable." Let's name this variable **Topic. ContentToSave**.

2. **Ask for the File Name**

- Add another **Question** node. Ask: "What filename would you like to use for this content? (Please don't include the file extension like .txt)"

- Under "Identify," "User's entire response" (or a "String" entity if available) should work well.

- Save the response as a new variable named **Topic. UserProvidedFileName.**

3. **Ask for the SharePoint Site URL**

- Add a third **Question** node. Ask: "What is the full SharePoint Site URL where you want to save the file?"

- "User's entire response" will capture the URL.

- Save the response as a new variable named **Topic. SharePointSiteURL.**

4. **Ask for the Document Library**

- Add a fourth **Question** node. Ask: "What is the name or path of the Document Library on that site? (e.g., Shared Documents or Shared Documents/ MyFolder)"

- "User's entire response" is suitable here.

- Save the response as a new variable named **Topic. SharePointLibraryPath.**

- At this point, your copilot has gathered all the necessary information from the user and stored it in these Topic variables.

Step 3: Select Your Power Automate Flow

Now, you'll link this Topic to the Power Automate Flow you meticulously built in Part 1:

1. Click the + icon and then click "Add an action".

2. A panel or dialog will appear. This panel lists the Power Automate Flows that are available to your copilot.

3. Carefully look for the **"Save AI Content to SharePoint"** Flow that you created. If you have many Flows, you might need to scroll or use the search bar within this panel.

4. Once you find it, select your Flow as shown in Figure 2-18.

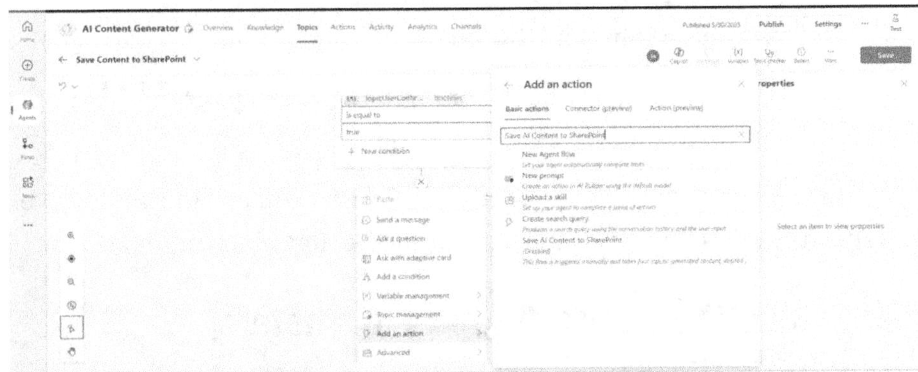

Figure 2-18. *In Copilot Studio's Topic editor: Adding an "Action" node and selecting the "Save AI Content to SharePoint" Power Automate Flow from the list of available actions*

Step 4: Map Copilot Variables to the Flow's Input Parameters

This is a critical step where you "pass" the information your copilot collected from the user over to your Power Automate Flow. When you select the Flow, Copilot Studio will display the input parameters that your Flow expects (these are GeneratedContentText, SuggestedFileName, TargetSharePointSiteURL, and TargetDocumentLibrary, which you defined in Power Automate).

1. For the GeneratedContentText input parameter required by your Flow, select your Copilot Studio Topic variable Topic.ContentToSave.

2. For the SuggestedFileName input, select your Topic. UserProvidedFileName variable.

3. For the TargetSharePointSiteURL input, select your Topic.SharePointSiteURL variable.

4. For the TargetDocumentLibrary input, select your Topic.SharePointLibraryPath variable.

You are essentially telling your copilot, "When you call this Flow, take the value from **this** Topic variable and use it for **that** Flow input."

Step 6: Map the Flow's Output Parameters to Copilot Variables

Your Power Automate Flow is also designed to send information *back* to the copilot after it has finished its task (specifically, the FileSaveStatus and LinkToFile outputs). You need to tell your copilot where to store these returning values:

1. Copilot Studio will show the output parameters from your Flow. For each of these, you'll typically create a new Topic variable.

2. For the FileSaveStatus output from the Flow, create a new Topic variable. A good name would be Topic. FlowSaveStatus.

3. For the LinkToFile output, create another new Topic variable, perhaps named Topic.FlowFileLink.

Step 7: Continue the Conversation Based on the Flow's Output

Now that your copilot will receive a status and potentially a file link back from the Flow, you can use this information to provide a really helpful response to the user:

1. Add another **Condition** node immediately after your "Action" node (the one that calls the Flow).

2. Configure this condition to check the value of the Topic.FlowSaveStatus variable.

   - **If Topic.FlowSaveStatus contains your success message** ("Successfully saved the content."):

     Under this branch of the condition, add a "Send a message" node. In this message, you can tell the user the good news and provide the link: "Great! I've successfully saved your content. You can find the file here: Topic.FlowFileLink" (remember to use the variable picker to insert the actual Topic. FlowFileLink variable into your message).

- **If Topic.FlowSaveStatus contains your error message** ("Error: Could not save the file to SharePoint."):

  - Under this branch, add a "Send a message" node to inform the user about the problem: "I'm sorry, I encountered an issue while trying to save your file: Topic.FlowSaveStatus. Please check the details or try again later."

Step 8: Save and Test Your Copilot Topic

You've now fully configured the Topic to call your Power Automate Flow and handle its response!

1. Be sure to click the **"Save"** button in the top right of the Copilot Studio Topic editor. This will save all the changes you've made to your "Save Content to SharePoint" Topic.

2. Now for the exciting part—testing! Open the **"Test your agent"** pane (usually found on the right side of your screen). Start a conversation by typing one of the trigger phrases you defined for this Topic. Follow the conversational prompts, provide the content, file name, SharePoint URL, and library path. Then, observe as your copilot calls the Power Automate Flow and respond based on the outcome, as shown in Figure 2-19.

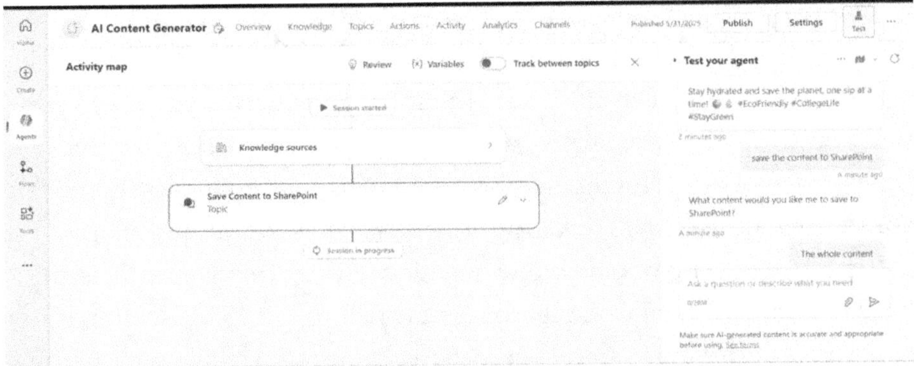

Figure 2-19. *Testing the integrated copilot: The Activity Map traces the conversation through the "Save Content to SharePoint" Topic, while the Test Pane displays the live user interaction as the copilot gathers information for the save operation.*

And just like that, you have done it. You have successfully woven a Power Automate Flow right into your AI Content Generator. Now, it is not just an idea machine; it is a practical assistant that can actually take those brilliant content pieces and save them directly to SharePoint for you. You can see how much more useful this makes your AI agent, as it actively helps you manage the creative output.

What is truly exciting is this: the fundamental method you have just learned is a blueprint you can use over and over again. This method involves sketching out the conversation in a Topic to get the details needed, using an Action node to kick off the Power Automate Flow, and then using the information the Flow sends back to keep the chat going. It is your key to adding an incredible range of automated actions and cool integrations to pretty much any creative AI agent you can dream up.

Quick Q/A: Common Setup Challenges

You've covered a lot of ground in this chapter. You've learned how to prepare your workspace, find your way around Copilot Studio, give your AI agents knowledge by connecting them to data, and even empower them to perform actions using Power Automate. As you start putting all this into practice, you might have a few questions or run into common issues. That's perfectly normal when learning new technology. This section is here to offer quick answers to some of those frequent setup challenges, helping you get back on track with your creative AI projects.

Question 1: I'm having trouble signing in or accessing Copilot Studio. What are the first things I should check?

Answer: This usually comes down to a few key areas we discussed in previously of this chapter. First, please ensure you are using the correct Microsoft Account Identity; remember, this could be a personal, work, or school account, and the type that can affect your access. Second, Copilot Studio is a web-based application, so a stable internet connection is absolutely essential. Finally, make sure you are using a modern, up-to-date web browser like Microsoft Edge, Google Chrome, Mozilla Firefox, or Apple Safari. An outdated browser can sometimes cause unexpected issues.

Question 2: My copilot doesn't seem to be using the information from the SharePoint site or Dataverse table I connected to earlier.

Answer: When your copilot isn't retrieving data as expected, consider these points:

- **Permissions Are Key:** Double-check that the account you used when setting up the data connection has the necessary read permissions for the specific SharePoint site, list, library, or Dataverse table. Your copilot can only access what it's allowed to see.

- **Data Indexing Time (Especially for SharePoint):** If you've just connected to a new SharePoint data source, particularly if it contains a lot of information, Copilot Studio needs some time to index all that content so it can be searched effectively. Try waiting a bit and then test your copilot again.

- **Correct Configuration:** Previously, we saw how to specify URLs for SharePoint (Figure 2-4) and select tables for Dataverse (Figure 2-5). Please verify that these details are accurate in your copilot's "Knowledge" settings.

- **Using the Knowledge in Topics:** Ensure your Topic is designed to leverage this connected knowledge. While generative answers might be used broadly, if you need specific data for a task, you might need to ensure your Topic logic explicitly queries or uses that knowledge, possibly through an action if complex lookups are needed.

Question 3: I've built a Power Automate Flow, but my copilot isn't triggering it, or the Flow isn't working correctly.

Answer: Integrating Power Automate Flows can sometimes be tricky. Here's what to look into:

- **Inputs and Outputs Mismatch:** Carefully compare the input parameters you defined in your Power Automate Flow (like GeneratedContentText, SuggestedFileName, etc., shown in Figure 2-11) with the values your copilot Topic is sending in the "Call an action" node. They must match in name and data type. The same applies to the output parameters your Flow is returning to the copilot.

- **Flow Trigger:** Ensure your Power Automate Flow uses the correct trigger, which should be "When an agent calls the flow" or a similar name, as illustrated in Figure 2-9.

- **Check the Flow's Run History:** This is your best friend for debugging. Open your Flow in Power Automate, and look at its run history. This will tell you if the Flow was triggered at all. If it were, it would show which steps succeeded and which failed and provide specific error messages for any failed actions. This can quickly help you find issues within the Flow's own logic.

- **Permissions for Connections in the Flow:** The connections used *inside* your Power Automate Flow (e.g., the SharePoint connection in the "Create file" action shown in Figures 2-12 and 2-13) must have the necessary permissions to do their job. If Flow tries to write to a SharePoint site where its connection doesn't have write access, that step will fail.

- **Save and Publish/Turn On:** Remember to save your Power Automate Flow (as seen throughout the Flow creation figures on pages 16–22). Also, ensure your copilot Topic in Copilot Studio, with the "Call an action" node, is saved (as shown in Figures 2-19 and 2-20). Some Flows in Power Automate also need to be explicitly "Turned On" to be active.

Question 4: The Copilot Studio or Power Automate interface looks a bit different from the figures in this chapter.

Answer: That's quite common with cloud-based platforms like these. Microsoft frequently updates them with new features, enhancements, and sometimes slight visual changes to improve the user experience. While the figures in this book (like Figure 2-1 showing the top command bar or the Power Automate interface in Figures 2-8 to 2-17) provide a solid visual guide at the time of writing, your live environment might have minor differences. The key is to focus on understanding the *concepts* and the *purpose* of the different interface elements we've discussed. The fundamental functionalities usually remain consistent.

Question 5: I am not sure which Copilot Studio or Power Automate license I need to use a particular feature, like a premium connector, in my Flow.

Answer: Licensing is an important consideration, as we touched upon at the beginning of this chapter, regarding Free Tiers vs. Premium Plans. Generally, basic copilot creation and standard connectors in Power Automate might be available in broader plans or free tiers. However, advanced capabilities, such as connecting to certain enterprise data sources (like Dataverse in some scenarios), using "premium" Power Automate connectors, or deploying your copilot to certain channels, often require specific premium licenses. The best approach is always to consult the official Microsoft documentation for Copilot Studio and Power Automate, as licensing details can be updated.

Question 6: I'm trying to call an external API using the "Send HTTP request" action shown in Figure 2-6, but it's failing. What are common pitfalls?

Answer: API integrations can be tricky. Check these:

- **Endpoint URL:** Ensure the API endpoint URL entered (similar to what's shown conceptually in Figure 2-7) is correct and accessible.

- **Authentication:** Many APIs require authentication (like an API key or OAuth). Make sure you have configured this correctly within the HTTP request action or an associated Power Automate Flow.

- **Request Headers and Body:** The API might expect specific headers (e.g., Content-Type) or a precisely formatted JSON body. Any discrepancies can cause errors.

- **CORS (Cross-Origin Resource Sharing):** If you're calling the API directly from the browser (less common for secure calls, usually done via Power Automate), the API server must be configured to allow requests from the Copilot Studio domain.

- **Power Automate for Complexity:** For more robust API calls, especially those needing complex authentication or data transformation, using Power Automate to make the call and then returning the result to your copilot is often a more reliable approach.

Question 7: When I'm creating a new Topic in Copilot Studio (as shown in Figure 2-18), how many trigger phrases should I add?

Answer: While there's no magic number, aim for at least 5–10 diverse trigger phrases for each Topic to help the copilot accurately understand when to initiate that specific conversation. Think about the different ways a user might express the same intent. The more relevant examples you provide, the better your copilot's natural language understanding will be for that Topic.

Question 8: What's the difference between adding SharePoint as a "Knowledge" source (Figure 2-4) vs. using a Power Automate Flow to "Create file" in SharePoint (Figures 2-12, 2-13)?

Answer:

- Adding SharePoint as a **knowledge source** allows your copilot to search and retrieve information from existing documents and lists to answer user questions, often using generative answers.

- Using a **Power Automate Flow** to "Create file" in SharePoint allows your copilot to take action and write new information *to* SharePoint, like saving a generated piece of content. One is about reading/retrieving; the other is about writing/acting.

Question 9: The "Activity map" in the test pane (Figure 2-20) shows my conversation going down an unexpected path. How can this help me?

Answer: The Activity map is an excellent debugging tool. It visually traces how your copilot interpreted the user's input and which Topics, conditions, and actions were triggered in what order. If the conversation isn't flowing as you designed, the Activity map can help you pinpoint exactly where it diverged, allowing you to revisit that part of your Topic logic and make corrections.

Question 10: I understand the difference between Free Tier and Premium Plans, but how do I know if a specific Power Automate connector requires a premium license?

Answer: When you are building a Flow in Power Automate, connectors are usually marked. Look for a "Premium" label or icon next to a connector or its actions. Using these premium connectors in a Flow that your copilot calls will generally require appropriate premium licensing for Power Automate and potentially for Copilot Studio if it's invoking such Flows. Always refer to the official Microsoft Power Platform licensing guides for the most up-to-date details.

Question 11: When designing the conversation in a Topic to collect information for a Power Automate Flow, like the questions in Step 2 of Part 2, what's the best way to save the user's answers?

Answer: For each piece of information you gather using a "Question" node, you should save the user's response into a distinct Topic variable. Give these variables clear names (e.g., Topic.ContentToSave, Topic. UserProvidedFileName). These variables will then be used to provide the inputs when you call your Power Automate Flow using the "Call an action" node.

Question 12: In Power Automate, when setting up the success and failure response actions for my copilot (Step 6 of Part 1), why is configuring "Run After" so important?

Answer: Configuring the "Run After" settings for your parallel success and failure response branches (as illustrated conceptually in Figure 2-16 and Figure 2-17) is crucial. It ensures that *only one* response is sent back to Copilot Studio. The success response action should run only if the main action (e.g., "Create file") is successful. The failure response action should run if the main action has failed, is skipped, or has timed out. Without this, your copilot might receive confusing or conflicting responses from the Flow.

We sincerely hope this Q&A has shed light on some of the common challenges you might encounter as you begin working more deeply with Copilot Studio and its related technologies. Remember, troubleshooting is a valuable part of the learning process. Each hurdle you overcome will solidify your understanding and build your confidence.

You've now journeyed through the essential prerequisites, learned to navigate the Copilot Studio interface, explored how to connect your agents to data sources, and even seen how to empower them with actions using Power Automate. With these foundational skills and troubleshooting tips in hand, you are remarkably well-equipped to move from theory to practice. The technical groundwork laid in this chapter is about to pay off as we dive into building our first fully fledged creative AI projects in the areas to come. Get ready to apply what you've learned and start bringing your own innovative AI visions to life.

Project: Step-by-Step—"Build an Agent That Writes Hip-Hop Music Lyrics"

Now it's time to put your new Copilot Studio skills into action with a really engaging project. Throughout this chapter, we've learned the essentials: getting the environment set up, finding the way around the Copilot Studio interface, giving your AI agents access to information by connecting data sources, and even making them perform tasks with Power Automate. Now, we're going to channel all that knowledge into building something uniquely creative: a chatbot that can generate hip-hop music lyrics.

This project will not only be a lot of fun but will also solidify your understanding of how to design conversational flows and leverage the Generative AI capabilities within Copilot Studio to produce creative text.

Project Goal and Features

Our goal is to build a chatbot, let's call it "LyricLab Bot", that can

- Engage a user in a conversation about generating hip-hop lyrics

- Ask the user for a theme or main topic for the lyrics

- Optionally, ask for a few keywords the user wants to see included

- Generate a short verse of hip-hop style lyrics based on these inputs

- Present the generated lyrics back to the user

- Offer to generate another verse or try a new theme

We'll focus on using Copilot Studio's built-in capabilities for this project to keep it streamlined and focused on the core concepts of conversational design and AI-powered generation.

Let's get started. Make sure you are logged into your Copilot Studio environment.

1. **Create Your New Copilot**

   First, we need a fresh copilot for our "LyricLab Bot".

   - **Navigate to Copilot Studio Home:** If you're not already there, go to your Copilot Studio Home page.

   - **Initiate Copilot Creation:** As we saw in Chapter 1 (Figure 1-1), you can often start by describing your agent. Alternatively, look for a "Create" or "+ New copilot" button, which might be on the left-hand navigation pane.

   - **Name Your Copilot:** When prompted, give your copilot a name. Let's call it "LyricLab Bot."

   - **Basic Configuration:** Follow any initial setup prompts. For the language, select English. If asked to describe what it should do, you could input something like: "Generates hip-hop lyrics based on user-provided themes and keywords."

2. **Design the Main "Generate Lyrics" Topic**

   As we already know, topics are the heart of your copilot's conversations. We'll create a new Topic to handle the entire lyric generation process.

   - **Go to Topics:** Once your "LyricLab Bot" is created and opened, navigate to the **Topics** tab from the top command bar (as shown in Figure 2-1).

- **Create a New Topic:** Click **"+ Add a topic"** and select **"From blank"** (or a similar option).

- **Name Your Topic:** Let's call this Topic **"Generate Hip Hop Lyrics"**.

- **Define Trigger Phrases:** Now, think about how a user might ask for lyrics. Add at least 5–10 diverse trigger phrases. Click "Edit" next to "Phrases" and add phrases like

  - "Write me a rap"

  - "I need some hip hop lyrics"

  - "Generate some bars"

  - "Can you write a verse"

  - "Help me write a hip hop song"

3. **Gather User Input for the Lyrics**
   Our bot needs some direction from the user to generate relevant lyrics. We'll use "Question" nodes for this.

   - **Ask for the Lyric Theme**

     - On the authoring canvas, directly below your trigger phrases, click the + icon and select **"Ask a question."**

     - In the "Ask a question" text box, type: "Word up. What theme or topic are you feeling for these lyrics."

     - Under "Identify," select "User's entire response" (or a "Multiple lines of text" option if available).

     - Under "Save response as," click the variable icon, select "+ Create variable," and name it **Topic.LyricTheme**.

- **Ask for Keywords**

  - Click the + icon below the previous question node and add another **"Ask a question"** node.

  - Type: "Gotcha. Any specific keywords you want me to weave into the rhymes. If not, just say 'no keywords."

  - Under "Identify," select "User's entire response."

  - Save the response as a variable named **Topic. Keywords**.

4. **Implement the Lyric Generation Logic**

   This is where the creative magic happens. We will use Copilot Studio's Generative AI capabilities to craft the lyrics.

   - **Add a Generative AI Node**

     Click the + icon below your last question node. Look for an option like "Generative answers." This might also be part of an "Advanced" section shown in Figure 2-6.

   - **Craft Your Prompt:** This is the most crucial part of this step. Your prompt needs to instruct the AI on what to do. Here's an example of how you might construct the prompt using the variables we collected in the input section.

You are LyricLab Bot, a creative AI that specializes in writing insightful and rhythmic hip-hop lyrics. Generate an 8-bar verse of hip-hop lyrics. The theme for the verse should be: {Topic.

LyricTheme}. If any keywords were provided, try to include some of them naturally: {Topic.Keywords}. If {Topic.Keywords} is 'no keywords', then ignore it. The lyrics should have a good flow, try to include some internal rhymes or clever wordplay if possible, and maintain a positive or thoughtful tone unless the theme dictates otherwise. Focus on vivid imagery and storytelling. Output only the lyrics.

Make sure to use the variable picker to insert Topic. LyricTheme and Topic.Keywords correctly.

- **Save the Generated Output**

  The Generative AI node or message response should allow you to save its output to a variable. Create a new variable named Topic. GeneratedLyrics. Instructions are shown in Figures 2-20 and 2-21.

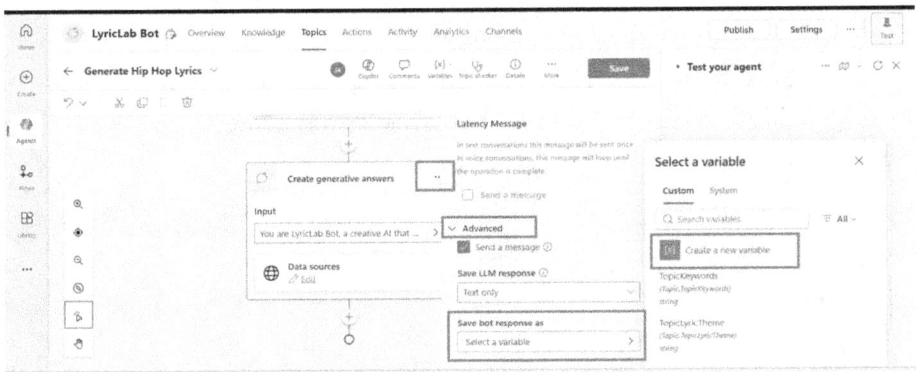

Figure 2-20. In the "Create generative answers" node, accessing the "Save text response as" option and selecting "Create a new variable" to store the AI's output

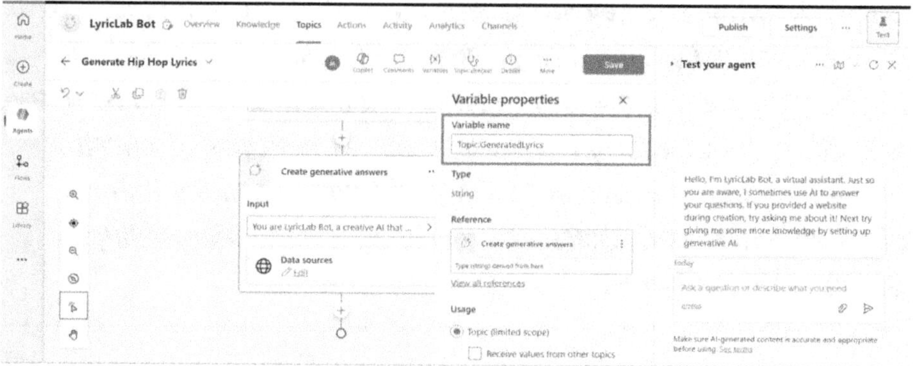

Figure 2-21. *The "Variable properties" pane, where we are naming our new variable Topic.GeneratedLyrics to hold the hip-hop verse*

5. **Present the Generated Lyrics to the User**

   Now, let's show the user what their LyricLab Bot came up with.

   - Click the + icon below the lyric generation step.

   - Select **"Send a message."**

   In the message box, you can write something like, "Alright, check these bars I cooked up for you:" Then, on a new line, insert the **Topic.GeneratedLyrics** variable like shown in Figure 2-22.

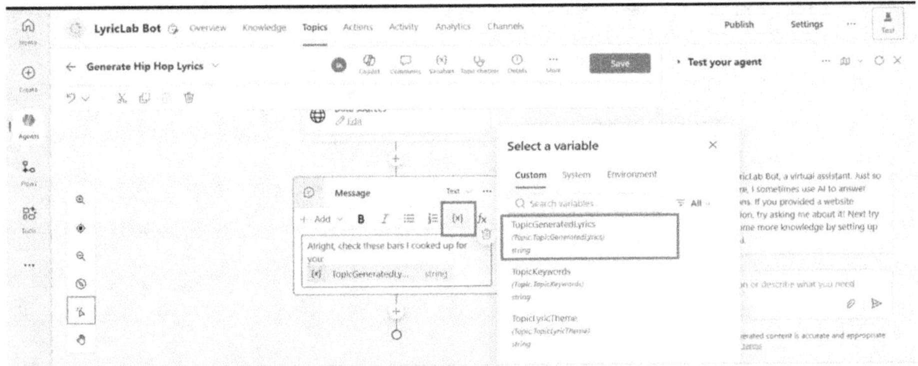

Figure 2-22. *Adding a "Message" node to present the generated lyrics back to the user by selecting the Topic.GeneratedLyrics variable from the variable menu*

6. **Offer to Generate More or Try Again**

    Good lyricists often iterate. Let's give the user
    that option.

    - Add an **"Ask a question"** node after displaying the
      lyrics. Ask: "What do you think? Want me to drop
      another verse on this theme, try a new theme, or
      are we good."

    - Under "Identify," you could use "Multiple choice
      options" and provide choices like "Another verse
      (same theme)," "New theme," or "We're good."

    - Save the user's response to a variable, say **Topic.
      UserChoice.**

    Detailed figures can be shown in Figure 2-23.

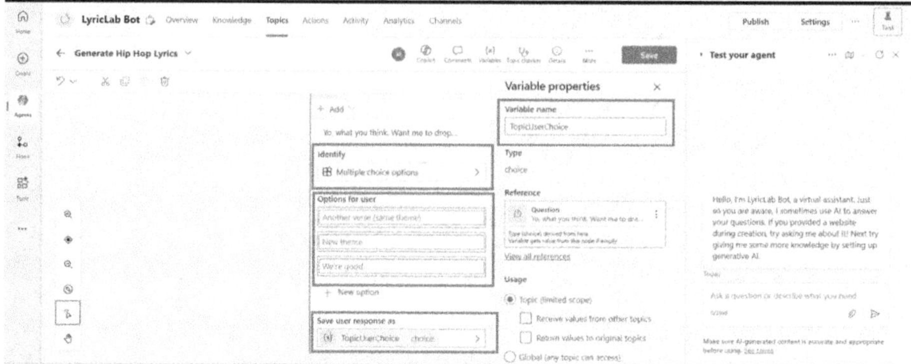

Figure 2-23. *Configuring a "Question" node with multiple choice options ("Another verse (same theme)", "New theme", "We're good") and saving the user's selection to the Topic.UserChoice variable*

- Add a **"Condition"** node based on Topic.UserChoice.

  - If "Another verse (same theme)," you could redirect the conversation flow back to just before the lyric generation step (Step 4).

  - If "New theme," redirect to the beginning of Step 3 (asking for the theme).

  - If "We're good," send a closing message like "Aright, peace out." Hit me up when you need more." and end the conversation.

  Figure 2-24 here: Screenshot illustrating the loop logic with a "Question" node for user choice and "Condition" nodes redirecting the flow.

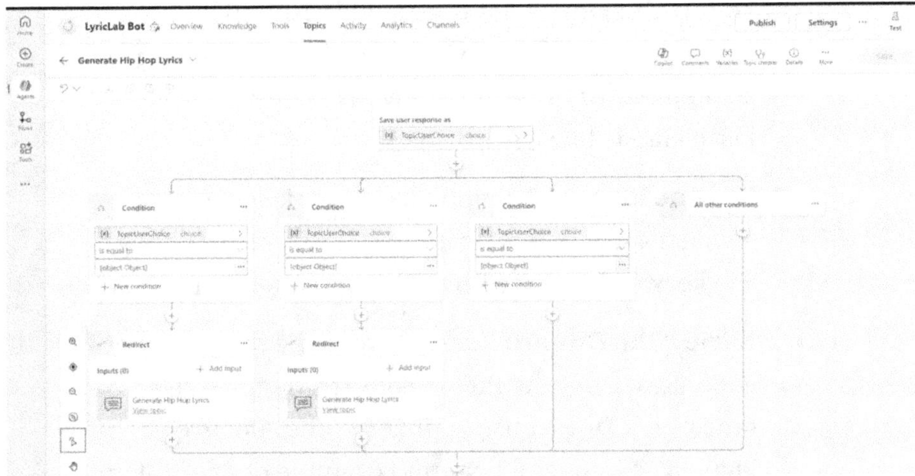

Figure 2-24. *The authoring canvas showing the "Condition" node branching from the conversation based on the user's choice, with "Redirect" nodes used to loop back into the conversation*

7. **Test and Publish Your LyricLab Bot**

    You've now built all the core components of your LyricLab Bot! The final, and arguably most important, step is to test it thoroughly and then publish it to make your changes live. We've seen the test pane in action throughout this book, and this is where it truly proves its value.

    Testing Your Creation

    It's time to see how your bot performs. In the "Test your agent" pane on the right side of your screen, you can have a full conversation with your LyricLab Bot.

    - **Start the Conversation:** Begin by typing one of the trigger phrases you defined, such as "write me a rap" or "I need some hip hop lyrics."

- **Follow the Flow:** Your bot should respond by asking for a theme. Provide one, like "overcoming challenges" or "a summer day in the city" or even just a classic like we provided.

- **Provide Keywords:** When it asks for keywords, try giving it a few. Then, on another test run, try saying "no keywords" to see how it handles that path.

- **Review the Output:** Carefully read the lyrics the bot generates. Does the theme come through? Is the tone right? Does it use your keywords effectively? Figure 2-25 shows a beautiful example of a complete test run, from the initial prompt to the generated verse.

- **Test the Loop:** After it generates the lyrics, test the options you created. Select "Another verse (same theme)" to see if it generates a new verse. Try "New theme" to ensure it loops back to the beginning to ask for a new topic. Finally, select "We're good" to confirm it ends the conversation gracefully.

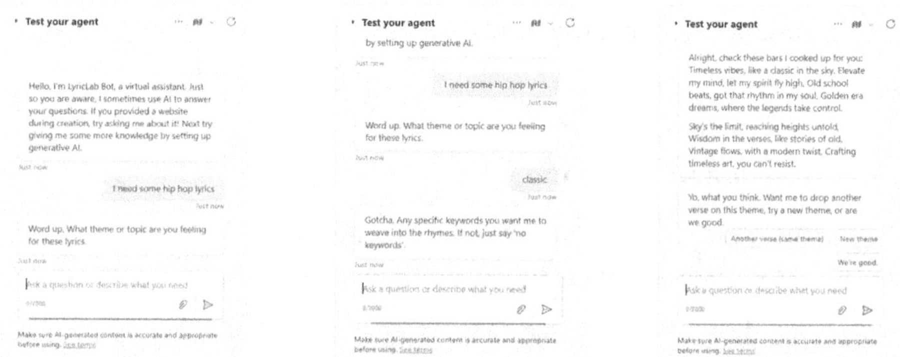

Figure 2-25. *A complete test conversation with the "LyricLab Bot" in the "Test your agent" pane, from the initial prompt to the generated lyrics and the offer to continue*

Publishing Your Bot

Once you're happy with how your LyricLab Bot is performing, it's time to publish it. Publishing takes all of your saved changes and makes them the "live" version of your copilot.

- Find the **Publish** button, which is typically located in the top command bar, as seen in Figure 2-1.

- Click **Publish**. Copilot Studio may ask for confirmation.

- Once the process is complete, the version of the bot that users will interact with is now updated with your new lyric-generating Topic. It's good practice to test again after publishing to ensure everything is working as expected in the live version.

Case Study: A Fiction Writer's AI Assistant for Dynamic Story Ideas

Throughout this chapter, we've journeyed together through the essential steps to get you comfortable and productive with Copilot Studio. You've learned how to prepare your workspace by understanding the prerequisites, how to find your way around the Copilot Studio interface, the methods to enrich your AI agents by connecting them to data sources, and even how to empower them to perform actions using Power Automate. Now, to truly see these concepts in action, let's explore a compelling application: an AI assistant designed as a collaborative partner for a fiction writer.

Imagine a writer, perhaps like yourself, deep in the world of their story, suddenly hitting a narrative wall. Maybe they need an unexpected plot twist for their latest mystery novel, a fresh and compelling motivation for their main character, or simply that elusive spark to overcome a bout of writer's block. This is exactly where a custom-built AI assistant, created using the tools and techniques from Copilot Studio, can truly shine as a creative ally.

The AI Assistant: A Creative Brainstorming Partner

The purpose of our fiction writer's AI assistant isn't to take over the creative process or replace the writer's unique voice. Instead, its goal is to augment that creativity, acting as an on-demand brainstorming partner that can help generate dynamic story ideas whenever the writer needs them.

- **How It Will Work**

  - The writer would interact with their AI assistant through a simple and intuitive chat interface. They might start a conversation with a general request like, "I need help with my story," or a more specific one, such as "Suggest a conflict for my sci-fi novel."

  - Your copilot, using carefully designed **Topics** (which we'll delve into creating in later chapters, though you've seen where they are managed in Figure 2-1), would guide the conversation. It might ask a few clarifying questions to better understand the writer's needs, perhaps asking, "What genre are you currently working on." or "Could you tell me a little about your main character."

- Leveraging Copilot Studio's built-in **Generative AI capabilities** (you saw a hint of this with the "Orchestration" settings in Figure 2-1), the assistant can then brainstorm a variety of creative ideas based directly on the writer's prompts and the context of their story. It could suggest several intriguing plot twists, paths for character development, unique settings to explore, or even snippets of dialogue to get the words flowing.

- To make these suggestions even more relevant and powerful, you could connect the AI assistant to **knowledge sources** as we detailed. Imagine the writer has a SharePoint site where they keep all their story notes, world building details, character backstories, or even research on specific historical periods or scientific concepts. Their copilot could intelligently tap into this personal knowledge base to provide suggestions that are deeply resonant with the writer's ongoing work.

- And once a brilliant idea emerges from this collaboration, **Power Automate integration** (which we explored in depth) could spring into action. If the writer likes a particular plot point the AI suggested, they could simply ask the copilot, "That's great, save this idea to my 'Plot Points' document." A Power Automate Flow, much like the "Save AI Content to SharePoint" example we walked through (and illustrated in Figures 2-8 through 2-17), could then take that text and seamlessly append it to a specific document in their

OneDrive, add it as an item in a Microsoft Planner board, or log it in a dedicated Dataverse table used for story outlining.

- **An Illustrative Interaction**

  Let's picture the conversation:

  Writer: "My fantasy novel feels a bit predictable. I need surprising motivation for my antagonist."

  AI Assistant: "Okay, I can help with that. To start, what is your antagonist's current main goal."

  Writer: "She wants to overthrow the ruling council to seize power."

  AI Assistant: "Understood. Here are a few less common motivations you might consider for an antagonist seeking power:

  - She genuinely believes the current council is deeply corrupt, and her seemingly harsh rule is the only path to protect her people from a greater, yet unseen, disaster.

  - She is driven by a desperate need to undo a tragic past mistake that caused immense suffering to someone she loved, and she believes only absolute power will grant her the means to do so.

  - Perhaps she isn't acting entirely of her own volition; she could be an unwitting pawn of an even more powerful, shadowy entity, and her quest for power is subtly manipulated by this hidden master."

What emerges from this synergy is an AI assistant that serves as a tireless, ever-ready brainstorming partner. It's there to help the writer explore new narrative possibilities, add layers of complexity to their stories, and navigate those moments when inspiration seems just out of reach. This case study beautifully demonstrates how the foundational skills you have diligently acquired throughout this chapter all come together. From the initial steps of setting up your Copilot Studio account and understanding its licensing, to becoming proficient in navigating the interface to build and configure your agent, connecting it to personalized knowledge repositories, and enabling it to perform helpful actions like saving ideas through Power Automate, you now have the toolkit to create truly valuable and innovative tools.

This case study, along with the hands-on hip-hop lyric generator project we'll build, is designed to solidify your practical understanding and, more importantly, to spark your imagination about the diverse and exciting creative AI agents you are now equipped to start building.

Summary

In this chapter, you have transitioned from the conceptual potential of Copilot Studio to the practical reality of building functional AI agents. You began by establishing a solid technical foundation, ensuring your environment meets the necessary Microsoft account and modern browser requirements. You then navigated the Copilot Studio interface, from the central Home page to the detailed Editing Canvas, where the core design of your agent takes place.

To move beyond simple chat, you explored the power of data and action:

- **Knowledge Integration:** You learned to connect your copilot to external information sources like SharePoint and Dataverse, allowing it to provide accurate, real-time responses based on existing documentation and business data.

- **Advanced Workflows**: Through Microsoft Power Automate, you empowered your AI to perform tangible tasks, such as saving generated content to SharePoint or triggering approval emails, turning a conversationalist into a proactive assistant.

- **Creative Application**: By building the LyricLab Bot, you practiced gathering user intent and leveraging Generative AI to produce rhythmic, themed hip-hop lyrics.

Whether you are building a tool for fiction writers to brainstorm plot twists or a bot to manage social media content, the blueprint of collecting input, calling actions, and handling responses remains your key to success. With these foundational skills and troubleshooting strategies, you are now ready to bring your own innovative AI visions to life.

CHAPTER 3

Core Components of Creative AI Agents

In our previous chapter, we laid the essential groundwork together. You have already accomplished a lot in setting up your Copilot Studio environment. You got a handle on the prerequisites and found your way around the interface. Then, you moved on to some truly exciting steps, like learning how to connect your AI agents to data sources. You even started to explore how to give them the power to perform real actions using Power Automate.

Now that your workshop is set up and you've had a taste of what's possible, it's time to delve deeper into the heart of Copilot Studio. This chapter is all about understanding and mastering the "core components," the essential building blocks that will allow you to design AI agents that are not just functional, but truly intelligent, engaging, and creatively adept. Think of this as moving from sketching initial ideas to understanding the refined techniques of your craft.

We will explore how to architect meaningful conversations using Topics and design intuitive conversational flows. You will learn to effectively use Entities to help your AI understand specific nuances in user input, especially within creative contexts. We will uncover the power of Variables and how they provide your agent with memory, enabling personalized and context-aware interactions. A key focus will be on crafting compelling Generative AI Responses, transforming your AI from

© Mezba Uddin 2026

M. Uddin, *Creative AI Agents with Copilot Studio*, Inside Copilot,

https://doi.org/10.1007/979-8-8688-2779-2_3

a simple information retriever into a creative collaborator. We will also touch upon Plug-ins and Extensibility for those moments when you need to reach beyond built-in features, and we'll look at more advanced ways to use variables across sessions to build even more sophisticated and continuous experiences.

By the end of this chapter, you will have a much richer understanding of these fundamental elements. This knowledge will empower you to design AI agents that are more dynamic, responsive, and capable of handling the complex and often unpredictable nature of creative collaboration. Let's begin by exploring the very foundation of any great conversational AI: Topics and conversational flows.

Topics and Conversational Flows

Imagine you are building a house. You wouldn't use a single, massive blueprint for the entire structure. Instead, you would have separate plans for the electrical system, the plumbing, the foundation, and each individual room. This modular approach makes the project manageable, scalable, and easy to troubleshoot. In Microsoft Copilot Studio, Topics are the blueprints for your AI's conversations.

A Topic is a self-contained module designed to handle a specific user goal or a single thread of dialogue. Rather than creating one giant, sprawling script that tries to account for every possibility, you build a library of focused Topics. For the "Fiction Writer's Assistant" we've discussed, you might design individual Topics for "Brainstorming Plot Twists," "Fleshing out a Character's Backstory," or "Suggesting Chapter Titles." Each one is a specialized skill, ready to be called upon when needed.

This modularity is the key to building intelligent and maintainable AI agents. It allows you to develop, test, and refine one conversational capability at a time without affecting others, ensuring your copilot remains organized and efficient as its skills grow.

The Heart of Creative Dialogue

For a creative AI, a Topic must be more than a simple command-and-response mechanism. It must function as a framework for collaboration. A truly effective creative Topic is engineered to perform four key functions:

1. **It Seeks the User's Goal:** The dialogue should be designed to quickly and clearly identify what the user wants to create or achieve.

2. **It Gathers Rich Context:** Creative work thrives on detail. The Topic must ask the right questions to understand the user's specific needs—their desired style, existing ideas, and unique constraints.

3. **It Sparks Inspiration:** This is the core of the creative process. The Topic houses the logic, often a powerful Generative AI node, that produces the new content, be it a line of dialogue, a marketing slogan, or a musical chord progression.

4. **It Embraces Iteration:** Great ideas are rarely formed in a single attempt. A well-designed Topic anticipates this by building conversational loops and options, allowing a user to ask for variations, provide feedback, and refine the output, mirroring a natural brainstorming session.

Directing the Conversation: The Authoring Canvas

The journey a user takes within a Topic is known as the conversational flow. You are the director of this flow, and your stage is the visual authoring canvas. This is the primary workspace for a Topic, a drag-and-drop environment where you connect to a series of nodes, each representing a specific action or interaction.

To begin this journey, let's reopen the project we started in the last chapter. We are going to build directly upon that foundation as we move from sketching initial ideas to mastering the refined techniques of the craft. The following are the essential nodes you will use to construct your conversational flows:

- **Trigger Phrases:** This is the "on-ramp" to your Topic. You provide a list of phrases a user might say to initiate this specific dialogue, as shown in Figure 3-1. The more comprehensive this list, the more naturally your copilot will understand when to activate the Topic.

- **Question Nodes:** Your primary tool for gathering information. You use these to ask for the context your AI needs to generate a relevant response, as shown in Figure 3-1. These nodes are where you will leverage Entities and Variables to capture user input effectively.

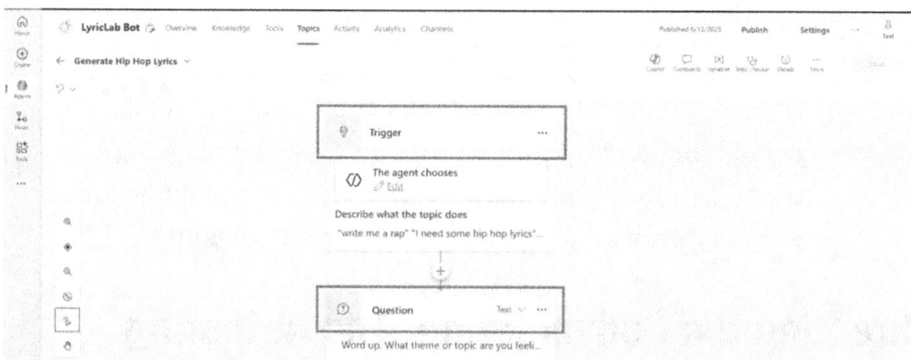

Figure 3-1. *The authoring canvas showing the Trigger node, which starts the conversation, and a Question node, used to gather information from the user*

- **Message Nodes:** The voice of your AI. This node is used to communicate back to the user, whether to confirm an action, ask for clarification, or present the generated creative content, as illustrated in Figure 3-2.

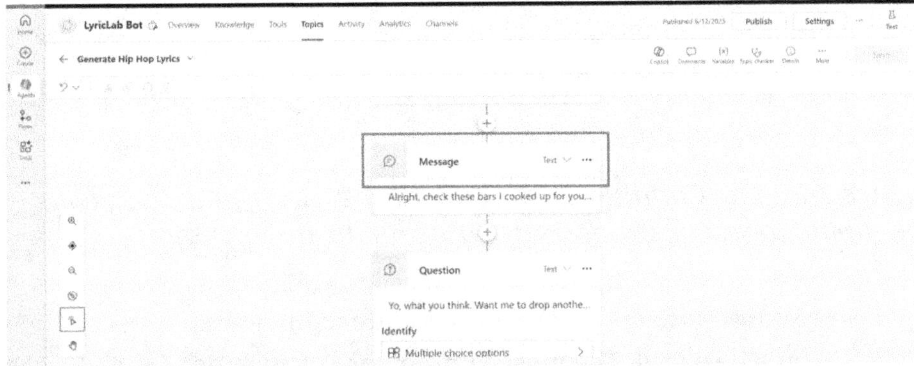

Figure 3-2.   *The Message node is used to send a response back to the user, continuing the conversational flow*

- **Condition Nodes:** These are the decision points in your dialogue. A condition node creates branches in the flow based on information your AI has gathered (stored in variables), allowing for different conversational paths based on user choices. This is illustrated in Figure 3-3.

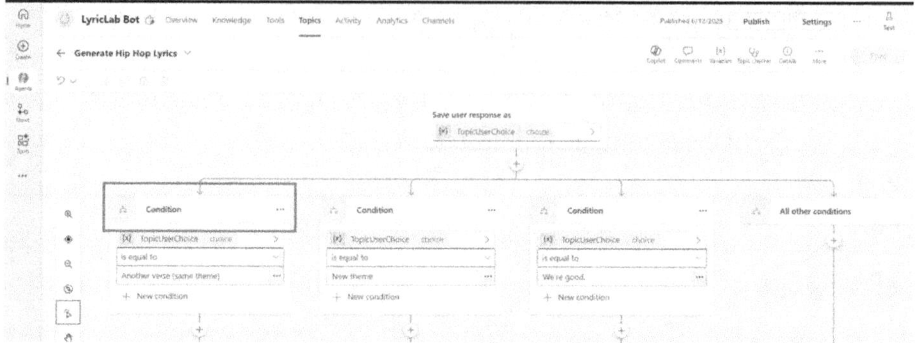

Figure 3-3. *The Condition node creates branching paths, allowing the copilot to respond differently based on the user's choices*

- **Action Nodes:** This is your AI's connection to the outside world. The most common use of an Action node is to call a Power Automate Flow, enabling your copilot to perform tasks like saving a document, retrieving data from a website, or interacting with other applications.

- **Redirect Nodes:** A tool for efficiency and organization. This node allows you to send a user from the end of one Topic to the beginning of another, enabling you to create reusable conversational modules like a single "User Feedback" topic that can be redirected to multiple other topics, as shown in Figure 3-4.

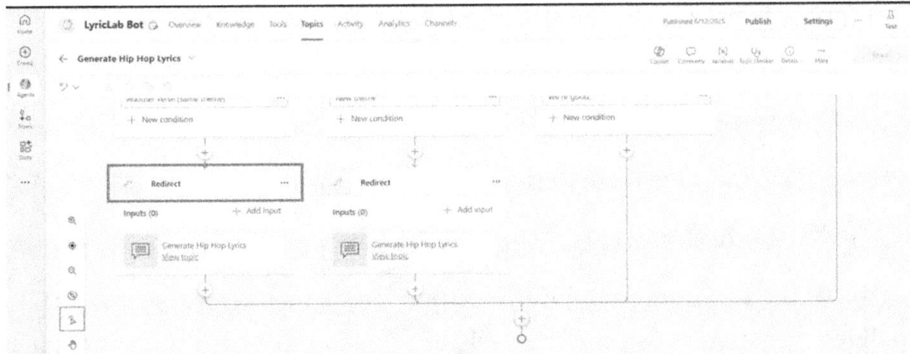

Figure 3-4. *The Redirect node allows you to send the user from one Topic to another, creating efficient and reusable conversational logic*

By mastering the use of these nodes on the authoring canvas, you can design conversational flows that are logical, dynamic, and genuinely helpful. You move beyond simple, linear scripts to create interactive experiences that guide users through a creative process, making your AI feel less like a machine and more like a true collaborative partner.

Entities: Custom vs. Prebuilt (For Creative Contexts)

If Topics are the conversational blueprints for your AI, then Entities are its specialized dictionary. They are the tools your copilot uses to recognize and extract specific, important pieces of information from a user's message. An entity allows your AI to move beyond just matching keywords to truly understanding the meaning behind the words.

Think about this simple user request:

"I need help brainstorming a plot for my new mystery novel set in 1920s London."

Without entities, your copilot might see a string of words. But with entities, it can intelligently identify

- "**mystery**" as a Literary Genre

- "**1920s**" as a Time Period or Decade

- "**London**" as a City

This is the fundamental difference between a basic chatbot and an intelligent creative assistant. The assistant doesn't just hear the words; it understands the key components of the creative request.

Why Are Entities So Important for Creative AI?

Using entities is what elevates your copilot from a simple script-follower to a dynamic and perceptive collaborator. Here's why they are one of the most powerful tools in your toolkit:

- **They Provide Structure to Unstructured Conversation:** Humans speak naturally. We don't just provide keywords. Entities allow your AI to find the structured data (the genre, the setting, the character's name) hidden within a natural sentence.

- **They Enable Flexible and Natural Dialogue:** Because an entity can have many synonyms, a user doesn't have to use a specific term. They could say "sci-fi," "cyberpunk," or "a story about space," and a well-defined Science Fiction entity can understand them all. Your copilot becomes less rigid and much more user-friendly.

- **They Drive Conversational Logic:** Once an entity is recognized, its value can be saved to a variable. This is where the magic happens. You can then use that variable to make decisions. For example: If Topic. LiteraryGenre is equal to "Mystery", your AI can then suggest ideas involving detectives and clues. If it's "Fantasy", it can suggest ideas about magic and dragons. This makes your AI's responses relevant and intelligent.

- **They Ensure Accurate Data for Actions:** When you need to send information to a Power Automate Flow or another system, entities ensure you are sending clean, predictable data. If your AI needs to save a new character to a list, using an entity to capture the character's name ensures you don't accidentally save the entire sentence.

Types of Entities

1. **Prebuilt Entities: The Standard Toolkit**

   Copilot Studio comes with a set of ready-to-use prebuilt entities that are already trained to recognize common types of information. For creative projects, these can be immediately useful for capturing the basic parameters of a request without any setup on your part. Some of the most useful prebuilt entities include

   Color: Perfect for a design assistant when a user says, "I need a logo with a deep red."

   Organization: Useful for brand-related content, such as "Generate a slogan for Starlight Studios."

Date and Time: For any task involving scheduling or timelines, like "I need a social media post for next Tuesday."

Person's Name: To recognize characters or stakeholders in a narrative project.

Using these prebuilt entities saves you time and provides a solid foundation for your AI's comprehension skills right out of the box.

2. **Custom Entities: Tailoring Your AI's Understanding**

Prebuilt entities are great for general information, but the real power for creative work comes from building custom entities. These are entities you define yourself to teach your AI to recognize information that is specific to your unique domain. This is how you empower your AI to speak the language of your creative field, whether it's art, music, writing, or design.

There are two primary types of custom entities you'll use:

- **List Entities:** This is the most common and useful type of custom entity. You provide a specific list of items you want the AI to recognize, along with any potential synonyms for those items. This is ideal when you have a finite set of options. Some prebuilt entities are shown in Figure 3-5.

   Creative Example: For our "Fiction Writer's Assistant," you could create a LiteraryGenre list entity.

   - **List Item**: Science Fiction

   - **Synonyms**: Sci-Fi, cyberpunk, space opera, futuristic story. Now, when a user says, "I'm writing a cyberpunk novel," your AI will correctly identify the genre as Science Fiction and can tailor its suggestions accordingly.

- **Regular Expression (RegEx) Entities:** This is a more advanced option for capturing information that follows a specific, predictable pattern. A regular expression is a special sequence of characters that defines a search pattern.

  - **Creative Example**: Imagine you are building a branding assistant that helps generate product SKUs or version numbers. You could create a RegEx entity called VersionNumber that recognizes a pattern like V-[three digits]-[two letters]. This would allow it to correctly extract codes like V-101-AG from a user's message. While less common for purely abstract creative tasks, it's invaluable when creativity intersects with structured data.

Figure 3-5. *A view of some of the standard prebuilt entities available in Copilot Studio, which can recognize common data types like Age, Color, and Date without any setup*

By thoughtfully combining prebuilt and custom entities, you elevate your AI from a simple conversationalist to a perceptive assistant. It learns to not just hear the user's words, but to understand the specific, crucial pieces of information that are the building blocks of any creative endeavor.

Variables and Memory (Personalizing User Interactions)

If entities give your copilot the ability to understand specific details, then variables give it the ability to remember them. Variables are the memory of your AI agent. They are named containers where you can store pieces of information, like a user's name, a choice they made, or a piece of generated content, for later use within the conversation.

Without variables, every interaction with your copilot would be a blank slate. The AI would have no recollection of what was said just moments before, making it impossible to have a coherent, multi-step conversation. By storing key pieces of information in variables, you transform your copilot from an amnesiac bot into an intelligent partner that can track context, remember details, and personalize its responses.

You have already used variables in our previous projects. In Chapter 2, when you built the "LyricLab Bot," you asked the user for a theme and stored their answer in a variable named Topic.LyricTheme. This single act of remembering the theme was what allowed the Generative AI node to craft a relevant verse.

How Variables Enable Creative Collaboration

In any collaborative process, memory is essential. A human partner who forgets your project's goals from one minute to the next wouldn't be very helpful. The same is true for an AI. Variables are what make your copilot a capable creative partner.

Here's how they enable more sophisticated and personalized interactions:

1. **Personalization:** The most immediate benefit of variables is the power to personalize the conversation. By capturing details like a user's

name or the title of their project, you can make the interaction feel much more engaging and less robotic.

How It Works: You start a Topic with a "Question" node asking, "What's your name?" You save the response in a variable called User.Name. In every subsequent message, you can now refer to the user directly: "Okay, {User.Name}, what should we work on today?"

Creative Impact: This simple touch changes the dynamic from a user commanding a tool to a user collaborating with a partner.

2. **Contextual Understanding:** Variables allow your copilot to maintain context throughout a conversation. Information gathered in one step can directly influence the options or outcomes in a later step.

   How It Works: In our "Fiction Writer's Assistant," you ask for the genre and save it in the Topic. LiteraryGenre variable. Later, when brainstorming characters, your generative prompt can include this variable: "Generate a character description for a protagonist in a {Topic.LiteraryGenre} novel."

   Creative Impact: The AI's suggestions become highly relevant. It will suggest a gritty, cynical detective for a Mystery and a noble, exiled knight for a Fantasy, all because it remembered the context set earlier in the conversation.

3. **Driving Logic and Actions:** Variables are the fuel for your copilot's decision-making engine. You use them in "Condition" nodes to create branching

paths in your conversation and in "Action" nodes to pass data to external systems.

How It Works: After generating a plot twist, you ask the user, "Do you like this idea, or should I try another one?" and save the answer in a Topic. UserChoice variable. A condition node then checks if Topic.UserChoice is "try another one" and, if so, loops back to the generation step.

Creative Impact: This creates an iterative workflow, which is the very essence of the creative process. The user can refine, reject, and request new ideas until they find the perfect one, all within a single, fluid conversation.

You create variables every time you save a response from a "Question" node. You can also create and modify them manually at any point in the flow using the "Variable management" node, giving you precise control over your AI's memory. To keep your information organized, Copilot Studio provides two main types, or "scopes," for your variables.

Understanding Variable Scope: Topic vs. Global

When you create a variable, you need to decide how long its memory should last. This is called a variable scope.

1. **Topic Variables**

   By default, any variable you create in the authoring canvas is a Topic variable.

   What They Are: These variables only exist within the Topic where they are created. Their memory is local and temporary.

When to Use Them: Use Topic variables for information that is only relevant to the specific task that the Topic is handling. For example, the user's answer to a temporary question, a choice in a multi-choice option, or the specific text generated in one step of the flow.

Example: In our "LyricLab Bot", Topic.LyricTheme and Topic.Keywords were perfect Topic variables. We needed them to generate the verse, but once that Topic was finished, we didn't need to remember them anymore.

Naming Convention: They are automatically prefixed with Topic. (e.g., Topic.MyVariable).

2. **Global Variables**

Sometimes, you need to remember a piece of information throughout the entire conversation, no matter which Topic is active. For this, you use Global variables.

What They Are: These variables are accessible from any Topic in your copilot. They store information for the entire user session.

When to Use Them: Use Global variables for key information that should persist, such as the user's name, their account ID, the name of the project they're working on, or a preference they set at the beginning of the conversation.

Example: If your "Fiction Writer's Assistant" asks for the user's name in a "Greeting" topic, you should save it as a Global variable. That way, your "Plot

Twist" topic and your "Character Development" topic can both access it to personalize their messages.

Naming Convention: They are prefixed with Global. Like Global.UserName.

When creating a variable (for instance, in the "Save response as" field of a Question node), you can choose its scope. Selecting "Global" ensures the information is remembered everywhere, making your AI a much more coherent and intelligent partner throughout a long and complex creative session.

Generative AI Responses: Crafting Engaging Output

We have now arrived at the creative heart of your copilot. While other nodes direct the flow of conversation, manage its logic, and remember key details, the Create generative answers node is where the magic of creation truly happens. This is the spark of genius, the blank canvas, the storytelling engine. It is here that you harness the power of a Large Language Model (the same technology behind tools like ChatGPT) to generate new, unique, and compelling content on the fly.

You saw this in action when our "LyricLab Bot" composed a verse of hip-hop. The bot didn't pull those lyrics from a database; it created them based on the instructions it was given. Mastering this node is the single most important skill for transforming your copilot from a simple information retriever into a powerful creative collaborator.

The Art of the Prompt: Directing the AI's Creativity

The quality of the AI's creative output is almost entirely dependent on the quality of your prompt. A prompt is the set of instructions you give the AI inside the generative answers node. It is your directorial script for the AI's performance. A vague or lazy prompt will yield generic and uninspired results. A well-crafted prompt, which is specific, context-rich, and clearly defines the desired outcome, can produce astonishingly creative and relevant content.

Think of yourself as a film director guiding a brilliant but literal-minded actor. You must provide them with motivation, context, and clear instructions to get the performance you envision. There are four key principles to crafting a great creative prompt.

1. **Define the Persona (Give the AI a Role)**

   Before you tell the AI what to do, you must first tell it who to be. Assigning a persona is the most effective way to set the tone, style, and vocabulary of the generated output. This works by priming the language model to draw from the patterns and styles associated with that role.

   Weak Prompt: "Write a social media post."

   Strong Prompt: "You are a witty and energetic social media manager for a Gen-Z audience. Your voice is playful, uses popular slang, and is full of emojis."

2. **State the Goal (Be Specific)**

   The AI needs a clear, specific, and unambiguous goal. Vague requests lead to vague results. Break down large creative tasks into smaller, manageable goals for the AI. Instead of asking it to "write a blog post," guide it through the process step-by-step.

Weak Prompt: "Give me some ideas for my story."

Strong Prompt: "Generate three potential plot twists for the middle of a mystery novel."

3. **Provide Rich Context (The Secret Sauce)**

This is the most critical principle. The AI can only work with the information you give it; it has no inherent knowledge of your specific project or the conversation that has taken place. You must provide it with all the relevant context you have gathered by using the variables we discussed in the previous section.

How Variables Work in a Prompt

It's important to understand the distinction between you, the copilot author, and the end user. The end user simply has a natural conversation with your copilot; they don't know what a variable is and will never see a variable name like {Topic. LiteraryGenre}.

As the author, you use these variables as placeholders within the prompt editor. When the conversation runs, the system performs a two-step process behind the scenes:

Gather Information: Your copilot asks the user a question, like "What genre are you writing in?" The user might reply, "A mystery novel."

Store and Substitute: Your "Question" node saves the answer "mystery" into the Topic.LiteraryGenre variable. Later, when the "Generative AI" node runs, it automatically replaces the {Topic.LiteraryGenre} placeholder in your prompt with the value "mystery" before sending it to the AI model.

This process allows you to build dynamic prompts that adapt to each user's specific input.

Weak Prompt: **"Suggest a name for the main character."**

Strong Prompt (as seen in the editor): **"Suggest five potential names for the main character. The character is a female detective in a {Topic.LiteraryGenre} novel. Her personality is described as {Topic.CharacterTrait}, and the story is set in {Topic.SettingCity} during the {Topic.SettingDecade}."**

What the AI Model Receives (after substitution):

"Suggest five potential names for the main character. The character is a female detective in a mystery novel. Her personality is described as clever and determined, and the story is set in Chicago during the 1940s."

Using variables this way is the key to transforming generic prompts into personalized and context-rich instructions.

4. **Set Constraints and Define the Format (Establish the Guardrails)**

Finally, you must guide the AI on the desired length, style, and structure of the output. This is how you control the AI's creativity and ensure the result fits your needs precisely.

Weak Prompt: **"Write about my product."**

Strong Prompt: **"Write a single paragraph describing the product. The paragraph should be no more than 50 words. Use an inspirational and uplifting tone. Do not mention the price. End with a question that encourages engagement."**

Case Study in Prompting: Deconstructing the "LyricLab Bot"

Let's revisit the prompt you created in Chapter 2 for our "LyricLab Bot." It's a perfect practical example of these four principles working in concert.

You are LyricLab Bot, a creative AI that specializes in writing insightful and rhythmic hip-hop lyrics. Generate an 8-bar verse of hip-hop lyrics. The theme for the verse should be: {Topic. LyricTheme}. If any keywords were provided, try to include some of them naturally: {Topic.Keywords}. If {Topic.Keywords} is 'no keywords', then ignore it. The lyrics should have a good flow, try to include some internal rhymes or clever wordplay if possible, and maintain a positive or thoughtful tone unless the theme dictates otherwise. Focus on vivid imagery and storytelling. Output only the lyrics.

Let's break it down:

Persona: The prompt starts by defining the AI's role immediately: "You are LyricLab Bot, a creative AI that specializes in writing insightful and rhythmic hip-hop lyrics." This sets a clear identity and style.

Goal: The primary task is unambiguous: "Generate an 8-bar verse of hip-hop lyrics."

Context: This prompt is rich with dynamic context provided by variables: "The theme for the verse should be: {Topic.LyricTheme}." and "If any keywords were provided, try to include some of them naturally: {Topic.Keywords}." This ensures the lyrics are about what the user requested.

Constraints and Formatting: The prompt is loaded with specific guardrails:

Length: "8-bar verse"

Conditional Logic: "If {Topic.Keywords} is 'no keywords', then ignore it."

Stylistic Rules: "should have a good flow," "include some internal rhymes or clever wordplay," "maintain a positive or thoughtful tone," "Focus on vivid imagery and storytelling."

Output Format: "Output only the lyrics." This is a crucial instruction that prevents the AI from adding conversational filler like "Sure, here are the lyrics you asked for...".

This single, well-constructed prompt combines all four principles to transform a general-purpose AI into a specialized hip-hop lyricist, demonstrating the incredible power you have as a prompt designer.

The Iterative Loop: Testing and Refining Your Prompts

Crafting the perfect prompt is an art form, not a one-time action. Your first attempt may not yield the results you want, and that's a normal and expected part of the process. The key is to embrace an iterative workflow: Prompt, Test, Analyze, and Refine.

Prompt: Write your initial prompt using the four principles we've discussed.

Test: Run your copilot and trigger the Generative AI node.

Analyze: Carefully review the AI's output. Is the tone right? Is the content relevant? Is the format correct? Where does it deviate from your expectations?

Refine: Go back to your prompt and make adjustments. If the tone is wrong, strengthen the persona. If the content is irrelevant, add more specific context or variables. If the length is wrong, add a stricter constraint.

By combining a clear persona, a specific goal, rich context from variables, and well-defined constraints and by continuously refining your approach, you can direct your AI to produce high-quality, relevant, and genuinely creative content that will empower your users and bring your vision to life.

Plug-ins and Extensibility (When to Use Them)

Up to this point, we have focused on building a self-contained intelligence within your copilot. We have given it the ability to understand, remember, and generate content. But what happens when the conversation needs to break free from the chat window and interact with the wider digital world? This is where the concepts of Plug-ins and Extensibility become paramount. These are the tools that give your AI "hands and feet," allowing it to perform actions, fetch live data, and integrate seamlessly with other applications. This is how you elevate your AI from a clever conversationalist into a truly powerful and productive creative partner.

For Copilot Studio, the primary gateway for this extensibility is Microsoft Power Automate. As you saw in Chapter 2, when you built the flow to save generated content to a SharePoint site, calling a Power Automate Flow from an Action node within your Topic is the most common and robust way to extend your copilot's capabilities. This is, in essence, a form of a plug-in.

The key question for any copilot author is knowing when to reach for these powerful tools. While it might be tempting to solve every problem with a complex flow, it's often more efficient to handle simple logic within the Copilot Studio canvas itself. A well-designed copilot uses extensibility strategically.

You should use a plug-in or a Power Automate Flow whenever your copilot needs to perform one of the following functions, also shown in Figure 3-6:

1. **Interact with External Data and Live APIs**

   Your copilot's built-in knowledge is limited to what you provide in its configuration and prompts. To answer questions or generate content based on real-time, dynamic information, it needs to look outside itself.

   When to Use It: You need to get information that doesn't live inside your copilot. This could be data that changes frequently or comes from a specialized, third-party source.

   Creative Examples

   Inspiration on Demand: An art assistant could call an API from a service like ColourLovers to fetch trending color palettes based on a keyword like "serene" or "energetic."

   Factual Grounding: A historical fiction writer's assistant could use a flow to query the Wikipedia API for facts about a specific event or time period, ensuring the generated narrative details are accurate.

Market Research: A marketing assistant could fetch real-time search trends from Google Trends or social media trends from a Twitter API to help brainstorm relevant and timely campaign ideas.

2.   **Connect to Other Business and Creative Systems**

Your creative process likely doesn't happen in a vacuum. You use other tools to manage projects, store files, and collaborate with teams. Your copilot becomes infinitely more useful when it can act as a natural language front end to these other systems.

When to Use It: You want to read or write data to another application or service, effectively making your copilot the central hub for your workflow.

Creative Examples

Project Management Integration: After brainstorming a list of video ideas, a user could ask the copilot, "Create a Trello card for that first idea." A flow would then trigger, creating the card on the appropriate board.

Content Calendar Automation: A social media copilot could not only generate a post but also save it to a shared content calendar in a Google Sheet or SharePoint List, complete with the proposed text, platform, and date.

Streamlining Approvals: A corporate design assistant could generate a new logo concept and then trigger an approval flow that sends a formatted email with the image attached to a manager via Outlook, who can approve or reject it with the click of a button.

3. **Perform Complex Logic, Loops, and Data Manipulation**

While Copilot Studio's condition nodes are great for simple branching logic, they are not designed for heavy-duty data processing. When a task requires looping through multiple items, parsing complex data structures, or performing multi-step calculations, you should offload that work to Power Automate.

When to Use It: A task requires more process automation power than simple conversational logic can provide.

Creative Examples

Batch Processing: A user might provide a list of ten blog post titles. A flow could take this list, loop through each title one by one, call a Generative AI service to write a short summary for each, and then compile the results into a single document.

Data Transformation: A scriptwriting assistant could take a block of plain text dialogue and use a flow to reformat it into perfect, industry-standard screenplay format, handling character names, parentheticals, and dialogue blocks automatically.

Aggregating Data: A brand manager's copilot could trigger a flow that fetches customer reviews for a product from three different websites, consolidates them, and then passes the combined text back to a Generative AI node in Copilot Studio to summarize the overall sentiment.

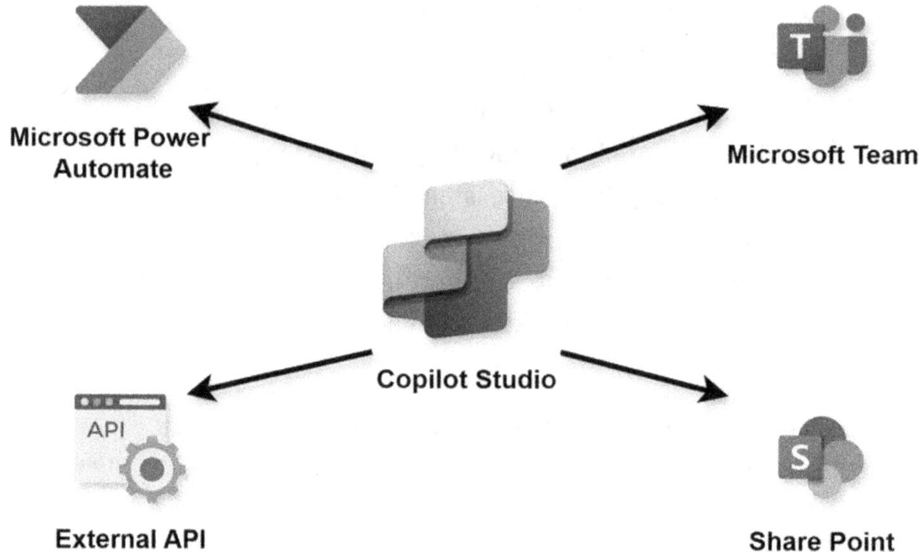

Figure 3-6. Copilot Studio as a central orchestration engine. Through plug-ins and Power Automate, it can extend its functionality to perform actions in other systems, such as running complex logic in Power Automate, storing data in SharePoint, sending notifications in Microsoft Teams, or fetching live information from an external API.

Think of plug-ins and flows as your copilot's indispensable toolkit. They are the conduits that allow its intelligence to flow outward, interact with the world, and bring back valuable information. By using them strategically, you can expand your copilot's abilities exponentially, transforming it from a simple creative chatbot into a fully integrated and immensely more powerful productivity partner.

Using Variables Across Sessions and Chaining Logic

So far, you've seen how powerful variables can be for remembering context within a session. By storing inputs like user names, project genres, or character names, your copilot can personalize interactions and generate rich, meaningful responses. However, there's an important limitation that becomes glaring once you start building assistants for real-world creative use cases:

Global variables only persist during a single session. Once the user closes the chat or returns the next day, all that information is gone.

Imagine a writing assistant that remembered a user's protagonist, genre, and draft title for an hour but forgot everything by the next day. This creates a disjointed, impersonal experience. What we want instead is persistence, the ability for our copilot to remember important context across sessions, just like a human collaborator would.

This section walks you through how to solve this problem using external memory and chained logic, turning our AI agent from a short-term helper into a long-term creative partner.

The Challenge: A Forgetful Creative Partner

Imagine this scenario with your "Fiction Writer's Assistant":

Day 1:

A user named Aisha begins outlining a pitch for her mystery-thriller titled "Echoes in the Fog."

She shares:

Her name (Aisha)

Project title ("Echoes in the Fog")

Genre ("Mystery-Thriller")

A core idea for the pitch

The assistant stores these as Global variables, enabling smart suggestions and targeted AI prompts.

Day 2:

Aisha returns and says:

"Let's build a killer logline from the pitch we wrote yesterday."

But the assistant replies:

"Sure! First, what's your name and what's the title of your project?"

The magic is broken. The feeling of partnership evaporates, replaced by the frustration of having to repeat information. This is the problem we need to solve.

The Solution: Creating an External Memory

The solution is to give your copilot a long-term memory that exists outside of the chat session itself. You need a place to store the values of your important Global variables and a way to retrieve them the next time the user connects. The easiest way to achieve this within the Microsoft ecosystem is by using either a SharePoint List or a Microsoft Dataverse table as your external database.

Part 1: Creating External Memory with SharePoint

Before building the flows, we need a place to store user data that lives outside the bot. For this example, we'll use a SharePoint List as a simple, secure memory store.

Step 1: Set Up a SharePoint List

- Go to your SharePoint site, and create a Blank List as shown in Figure 3-7.

- Name the list: StoryPitchMemory.

- Rename the default Title column to UserName.

Add the following columns:

Column Name	Type
UserID	Single line of text
ProjectTitle	Single line of text
Genre	Single line of text
StoryIdea	Multiple lines of text

This list will serve as your copilot's memory bank. Each row represents one user's session.

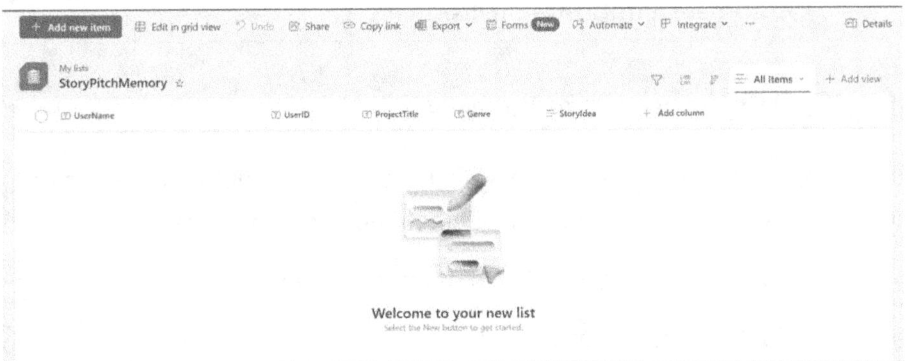

Figure 3-7. *Setting up a SharePoint list to act as the copilot's external long-term memory. Each column will store a specific piece of user data.*

Part 2: Build the "Save State" Flow in Power Automate

This flow is the engine that captures your user's creative context and stores it for later. It acts as a bridge between your copilot's temporary memory and your permanent external database. We will build it step-by-step.

Step 1: Create the Flow and Define the Trigger

First, we need to navigate to Power Automate and create the flow itself.

- Open a new browser tab and go to Power Automate.

- From the left-hand menu, select + Create, and then choose Instant cloud flow.

- A window will pop up. Give your flow a name, such as Save Creative Project State.

- For the trigger, scroll down and select When Power Virtual Agents calls a flow.

- Click Create. You will now be on the main Power Automate authoring canvas.

Step 2: Add Input Parameters

Your trigger is the entry point. This is where you must define the specific pieces of information your flow expects to receive from Copilot Studio.

- Click on the trigger step to open its configuration panel.

- Click + Add an input.

- Select the Text data type. A field will appear. Name it UserID.

- Repeat this process to add four more Text inputs with the following names:

  - UserName

  - ProjectTitle

  - Genre

  - StoryIdea

Your trigger should now clearly show the five pieces of data it is ready to accept from your copilot.

Step 3: Add Logic to Find Existing Data

Before saving, we must check if we are dealing with a new user or a returning one.

- Click the + New step button below your trigger.

- In the action search box, type "SharePoint", and select the Get items action.

- Configure this action to point to your SharePoint site and the list you created earlier (e.g., Copilot User State).

- Click Show advanced options to reveal the Filter Query field. This is a crucial step. It tells the action to only retrieve items that match the UserID sent from the copilot. Enter the following expression exactly:

UserID eq '@{triggerBody()?['UserID']}'

This expression filters the SharePoint list and checks if there's already a row where the UserID column matches the UserID value passed in from the trigger.

Step 4: Add Conditional Logic to Save the Data

Now we'll add a condition to handle both new and returning users.

- Click + New step and add a Condition action as shown in Figure 3-8.

- In the first condition field, we need to check if the previous "Get items" step found anything. To do this, you will use an expression. Click in the field, select the Expression tab from the dynamic content pop-up, and enter: length(outputs('Get_items')?['body/value'])

- Set the operator to is greater than.

- Set the final value to 0.

This condition now reads: "If the number of items found in the previous step is greater than zero…"

- In the "If yes" branch (A record exists), as shown in Figure 3-9:

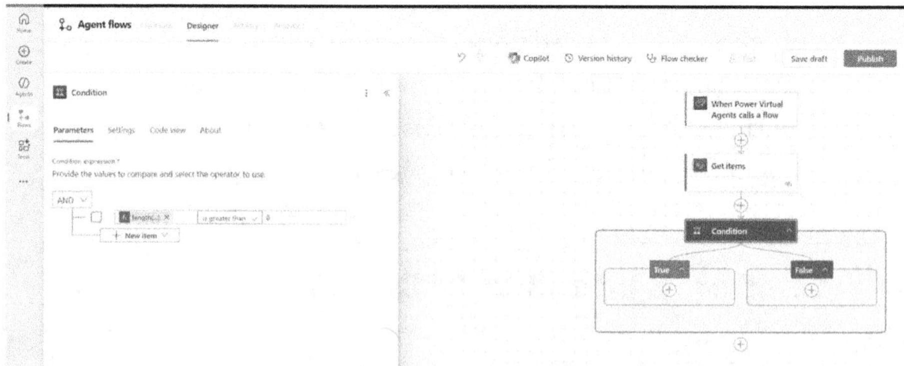

Figure 3-8. *The authoring canvas for the "Save State" flow in Power Automate, showing the trigger, the "Get items" action, and the main condition that checks if a user's record already exists*

- Click Add an action inside this branch.

- Choose the SharePoint Update item action.

- Configure it with your Site Address and List Name.

- For the ID, select the ID from the "Get items" dynamic content. This ensures you update the correct row.

- Fill in the other fields (ProjectTitle, Genre, etc.) with the corresponding dynamic content from your flow's trigger.

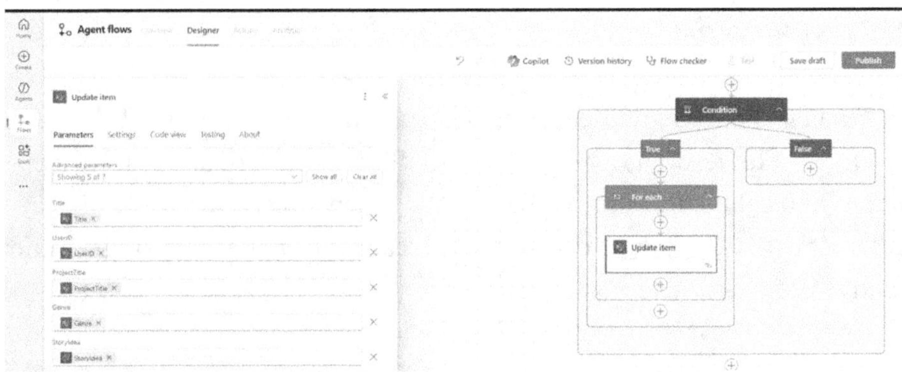

Figure 3-9. *Configuring the "Update item" action within the "If yes" branch of the condition. This updates the record for a returning user.*

- In the "If no" branch (This is a new user), as shown in Figure 3-10:

  - Click Add an action inside this branch.

  - Choose the SharePoint Create item action.

  - Configure it with your Site Address and List Name.

  - Fill in all the fields (UserID, ProjectTitle, etc.) with the dynamic content from your flow's trigger.

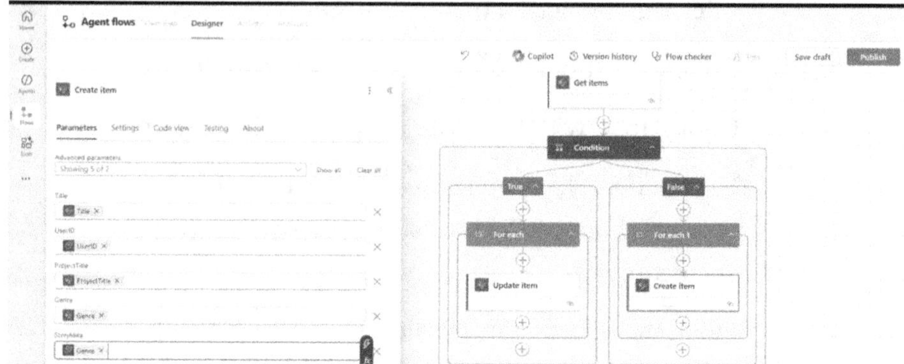

Figure 3-10. *The complete "Save State" flow logic, showing the "Create item" action in the "If no" branch, which creates a new record for a first-time user*

Finally, click Save in the top right corner to save your entire flow.

Our copilot now has a robust and intelligent mechanism to save user data. When called, this flow will check for an existing record and either update it with the latest information or create a new one, ensuring that no creative progress is ever lost.

Part 3: Build the "Load State" Flow in Power Automate (As Shown in Figure 3-11)

This flow is the counterpart to our "Save State" flow. Its job is to retrieve a returning user's data from the external database and pass it back to the copilot at the beginning of a new session, effectively restoring the AI's memory.

Step 1: Create the Flow and Define the Trigger

The initial setup is very similar to our previous flow.

- In Power Automate, create a new Instant cloud flow.

- Name your flow Load State.

- For the trigger, select When Power Virtual Agents calls a flow.

- Click Create.

Step 2: Define the Input Parameter

This flow is simpler than the save flow. To find a user's data, it only needs one piece of information from the copilot.

- Click on the trigger step to open its configuration panel.

- Click + Add an input and select the Text data type.

- Name the input UserID.

This is the only information our flow needs to begin its search.

Step 3: Add Logic to Retrieve the Data

This step mirrors the "Get items" action from our save flow.

- Click + New step and add the SharePoint Get items action.

- Configure it with the same SharePoint Site Address and List Name (Copilot User State).

- In the Filter Query field, enter the exact same expression as before to find a matching user record:

UserID eq '@{triggerBody()?['UserID']}'

Step 4: Add Conditional Logic to Return the Data

Now we need to handle both cases: when we find a save file and when we don't. The final action we use will be Return value(s) to Power Virtual Agents.

- Add a Condition action that checks if the "Get items" step found anything, using the same expression:

```
length(outputs('Get_items')?['body/value']) is greater than 0.
```

- In the "If yes" branch (A save file was found):
  - Click Add an action, and choose Return value(s) to Power Virtual Agents.
  - We need to create an output for each piece of data we want to send back. Click + Add an output and choose Text. Name it UserName_Out. For its value, select UserName from the "Get items" dynamic content.
  - Repeat this process for the other fields:
    - ProjectTitle_Out (Text)
    - Genre_Out (Text)
    - StoryIdea_Out (Text)
  - Finally, add one more output of type Yes/No. Name it SaveFileFound. Set its value to Yes. This flag is crucial for telling our copilot that the load was successful.

- In the "If no" branch (This is a new user):

  - Click Add an action and choose Return value(s) to Power Virtual Agents.

  - We only need to send back one piece of information: the fact that no file was found.

  - Click + Add an output and choose Yes/No. Name it SaveFileFound and set its value to No.

Finally, click Save to save your flow.

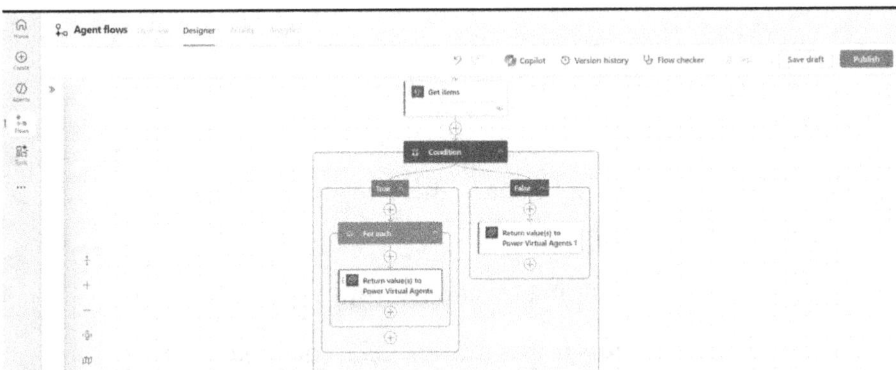

Figure 3-11. *The complete "Load State" flow in Power Automate, designed to retrieve a returning user's data and pass it back to Copilot Studio as output parameters*

With both the "Save State" and "Load State" flows built, your copilot now has a complete, persistent memory system. It can remember exactly where a user left off, transforming it from a one-time tool into a continuous creative partner.

Part 4: Integrate the Load Flow in the Greeting Topic

Now that your "Load State" flow is ready, it's time to teach our copilot how to use it. This is the final step in closing the persistent memory loop. We will modify the default "Greeting" topic to check for a returning user at the very beginning of the conversation.

Step 1: Call the "Load State" Flow in Copilot Studio (As Shown in Figure 3-12)

- Navigate back to your copilot in Copilot Studio.

- From the Topics page, select and open the main Greeting Topic.

- Click the + icon right below the Trigger phrases at the very top of the flow.

- Select Call an action and choose your Load State flow.

- The flow requires one input, UserID. You need to pass the current user's unique identifier to it. Click in the input box, select the formula icon (>), and from the list of built-in system variables, choose User.ID.

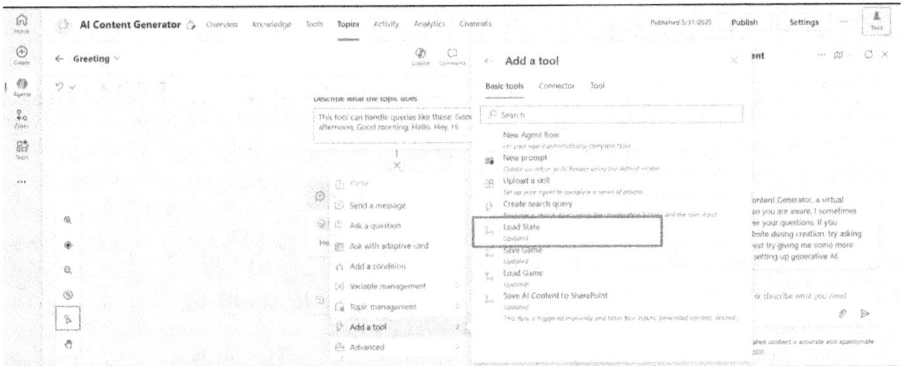

Figure 3-12. *Integrating the Power Automate flow into Copilot Studio by using a "Call an action" node within the Greeting Topic to run the "Load State" logic*

Your Topic will now call the Power Automate flow as soon as a user starts a conversation.

Step 2: Add a Condition to Handle Returning vs. New Users

Immediately after the Action node, your copilot needs to decide what to do based on the flow's response.

- Click the + icon below your new Action node and select Add a condition.

- In the first branch, we will check if a save file was found. The condition should be based on the output variable from your flow. Select the variable Topic. SaveFileFound.

- Set the operator to is equal to.

- Set the value to True.

This branch will now only execute if the "Load State" flow successfully found and returned the user's data.

Step 3: Configure the "Returning User" Path

In the "If true" branch of your condition, we will restore the user's context.

- Click Add a node inside this branch and choose Set a variable value.

- For the Variable, select Global.UserName. For the Value, select the output from your flow: Topic.UserName_Out.

- Add another "Set a variable value" node for Global. ProjectTitle, setting it to Topic.ProjectTitle_Out.

- Repeat this for Global.Genre and Global.StoryIdea.

- After restoring the variables, add a personalized Message node:

"Welcome back, {Global.UserName}! It looks like we were working on '{Global.ProjectTitle}'. Ready to continue?"

- Finally, add a Redirect node, and point it to your main creative topic (e.g., your "Pitch Builder" or "Game Loop" topic), bypassing the new user questions entirely.

Step 4: Configure the "New User" Path

The All other conditions branch will execute if SaveFileFound is false. This is your path for new users. Simply leave the existing logic (asking for their name, project title, etc.) in this branch. The conversation will proceed as it normally would for a first-time user.

By integrating this logic into your Greeting Topic, you have created a seamless experience. Your copilot can now intelligently distinguish between new and returning users, restoring the creative context for returning collaborators and providing a warm welcome to new ones.

Case Study: An RPG Game's AI Dungeon Master

To bring all the core components of this chapter together, we will now embark on our most ambitious project yet: building a simplified but functional AI Dungeon Master (DM) for a text-based role-playing game (RPG). This case study will serve as the ultimate test of your new skills, requiring you to weave together Topics, Entities, Variables, Generative AI, and Extensibility into a single, cohesive, and dynamic experience.

This isn't just a content generator; it's an interactive storyteller that must understand, remember, and react to a player's choices. By the end of this guide, you will have built an AI that can create a unique adventure for a player and even remember their progress between sessions. Let's begin.

Phase 1: Project Setup and Foundational Vocabulary

Before our AI can tell a story, we must teach it the fundamental language of fantasy adventure. This involves creating our new copilot and defining the core vocabulary of our game using the custom **Entities** we learned about previously.

Step 1: Create the New Copilot

First, we need a new home for our project.

- From the Copilot Studio home page, click + **New copilot**.

- Name your copilot **AI Dungeon Master.**

- Follow the prompts to create the bot. You can skip adding a website or other advanced options for now.

Step 2: Create the CharacterClass Entity

This entity will teach our AI to recognize the classic roles in an RPG.

- In the left-hand navigation pane, click the ... (More) icon and select Entities.

- Click + New entity and choose List entity.

- Name the entity CharacterClass, as shown in Figure 3-13.

- In the list items, add the following roles and provide synonyms to make the conversation feel natural:

  - List item: Warrior, Synonyms: fighter, knight, soldier

  - List item: Mage, Synonyms: wizard, sorcerer, warlock

  - List item: Rogue, Synonyms: thief, assassin, scout

- Ensure Smart matching is turned on, then click Save.

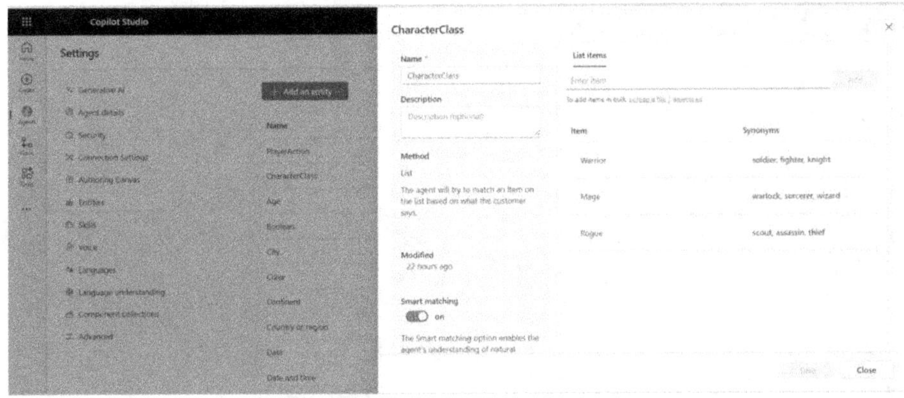

Figure 3-13. *Creating the custom CharacterClass entity to teach the AI the different roles available in the RPG*

Step 3: Create the PlayerAction Entity

This is the most critical entity for gameplay, as it defines the "verbs" or commands the player can use to interact with the world.

- While still in the Entities section, create another new List entity.

- Name this entity PlayerAction, as shown in Figure 3-14.

- Add the following core actions and their synonyms:

  - List item: Look, Synonyms: examine, inspect, describe, observe

  - List item: Attack, Synonyms: fight, hit, strike, swing

  - List item: Go, Synonyms: move, walk, travel, head

  - List item: Take, Synonyms: get, pick up, grab, acquire

  - List item: Use, Synonyms: apply, activate

- Click Save.

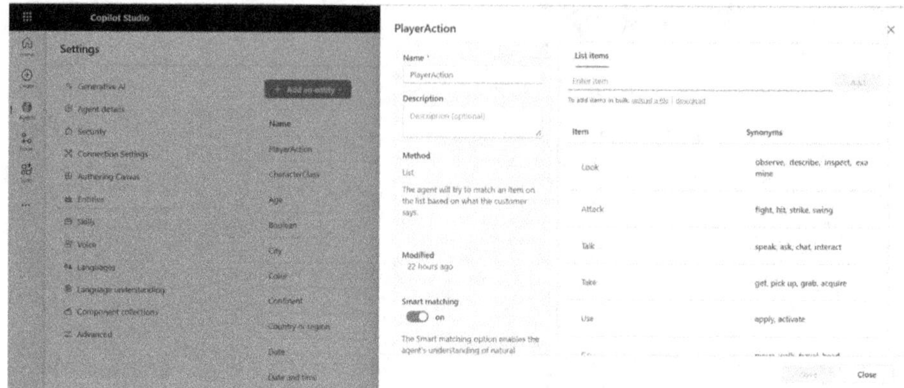

Figure 3-14. *Creating the PlayerAction entity, which defines the core "verbs" or commands the player can use to interact with the game world*

With these foundational entities in place, our AI is no longer blind. It has been given a specialized dictionary that allows it to understand the core concepts of our game world before we've even written a single line of dialogue.

Phase 2: Character Creation and the Main Game Loop

Now that our AI understands the game's vocabulary, we will build the conversational flows that use this knowledge. We will modify the default "Greeting" Topic to handle character creation seamlessly and then build a new "Game Loop" Topic to serve as the central hub of our adventure.

Step 1: Modify the "Greeting" Topic for Character Creation

A great game immerses the player immediately. Instead of having a separate menu for character creation, we will integrate it directly into the initial greeting.

- Navigate to the Topics section and open the default Greeting Topic.

- Ask for the Player's Name: Below the initial trigger phrases, add a Question node.

  - **Question Text**: "Welcome, traveler! What name do you go by?"

  - **Identify**: Person's name (a prebuilt entity).

  - **Save Response As**: Click the variable box, select + Create a new variable, and set its properties:

    - **Name**: Global.PlayerName

    - **Usage**: Global

- Ask for the Player's Class: Add another Question node.

  - **Question Text**: "A fine name, {Global. PlayerName}! Now, what is your trade? Are you a mighty Warrior, a wise Mage, or a cunning Rogue?"

  - **Identify**: CharacterClass (your custom entity).

  - **Save Response As**: Create a new variable named Global.PlayerClass with Global usage.

- **Set Initial Hit Points (HP) based on Class**: A character's health is often determined by their class. We'll set this automatically using a Condition node.

  - Add a Condition node after the class question.

  - Create a branch for each class. The first branch's condition should be: Global.PlayerClass is equal to Warrior.

- Inside the "Warrior" branch, add a Set a variable value node. Create a new variable named Global. PlayerHP (Usage: Global, Data type: Number), and set its value to 20.

- Create another branch for Mage. Inside it, use another "Set a variable value" node to set Global. PlayerHP to 12.

- Do the same for Rogue, setting their HP to 15.

- **Confirmation and Redirection**: Add a final Message node that confirms creation: "Excellent! Your adventure as {Global.PlayerName}, the {Global.PlayerClass}, is about to begin..."

- To conclude this Topic, add a Redirect node, and point it to a new Topic you will create next, called Game Loop.

- Click Save.

Step 2: Create the "Game Loop" Topic

This Topic is the central engine of the game. It will describe the world and wait for the player's command, as shown in Figure 3-15.

- From the main Topics page, create a new topic from blank, and name it Game Loop. Do not add any trigger phrases, as it will only be accessed via redirection.

- Add a Create generative answers node. This will be our first narrative prompt:

You are a master fantasy storyteller. The player, a {Global. PlayerClass} named {Global.PlayerName}, has just begun their adventure. Describe their arrival at the entrance of a dark and mysterious cave, known as the "Whispering Cavern." The air is cold, and they can hear the faint sound of dripping water within.

- Immediately after, add a Question node.

    - **Question Text**: "What do you do?"

    - **Identify**: PlayerAction (your custom entity).

    - **Save Response As**: Create a new Topic variable named Topic.CurrentAction.

- Click Save.

At this point, you have built the core logic. A new player is guided through character creation, and their details are saved in global memory. They are then seamlessly transitioned to the start of the adventure, where they see the first scene and are prompted for their first command.

Phase 3: Bringing the World to Life

Now we will make the world interactive. We will expand the Game Loop Topic so the AI reacts differently based on the player's action, using conditions to branch the story and Generative AI to narrate the outcomes.

- Open the Game Loop Topic.

- **Add a Condition Node**: Below the "What do you do?" question, add a Condition node. Set the first branch's condition to Topic.CurrentAction is equal to Look.

- **Build the "Look" Branch**: Inside this branch, add a Create generative answers node with a detailed narrative prompt:

You are a master fantasy storyteller. The player, {Global.PlayerName}, has chosen to look more closely at the entrance of the Whispering Cavern. Describe the scene in greater detail. Mention the moss-covered rocks, the ancient, barely visible carvings around the cave mouth, and a small, rusted iron key half-hidden in the dirt near their feet.

- **Build the "Attack" and "Go" Branches:** Add two more branches to your condition node for the Attack and Go actions, each with its own generative prompt.

  - **For the Attack branch:**

You are a dramatic combat narrator. The player, {Global. PlayerName}, swings their weapon at the empty space in the cave entrance. Describe their practice swing with a touch of humor, mentioning how the sound echoes in the cavern. Remind them there are no enemies here... yet.

  - **For the Go branch:**

You are a suspenseful Dungeon Master. The player, {Global. PlayerName}, bravely steps forward, moving into the darkness of the Whispering Cavern. Describe the immediate drop in temperature and how the light from the outside world vanishes behind them, leaving them in near-total darkness.

- **Create the Loop:** At the end of every branch (including the final "All other conditions" branch), add a Redirect node that points back to the Game Loop Topic. This ensures that after every action and narration, the player is once again asked, "What do you do?", creating a continuous gameplay loop.

- **Handle the Fallback:** In the All other conditions branch, add a simple Message node that says, "I don't understand that command. You can try to look, attack, or go." before the redirect.

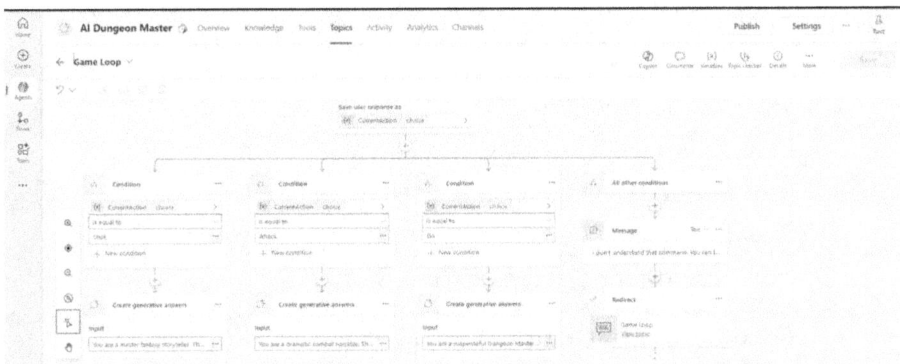

Figure 3-15. *The complete authoring canvas for the main Game Loop Topic, showing the branching logic that provides different narrative outcomes based on the player's chosen action*

Your AI Dungeon Master is now fully interactive.

Phase 4: Implementing the Save/Load System

The final and most advanced step is to give our AI a long-term memory. We will implement the save/load pattern using a SharePoint list and two Power Automate flows.

Step 1: Create the External Memory (SharePoint List)

- Create a new SharePoint **Blank list** named AI DM
  Save Games.

- Rename the default "Title" column to PlayerName.

- Add the following new columns: UserID (Single line of text),
  PlayerClass (Single line of text), and PlayerHP (Number).

Step 2: Build the "Save Game" and "Load Game" Flows

Following the detailed patterns we outlined at earlier, build your two
Power Automate flows:

- **Save Game State Flow:** This flow will take UserID,
  PlayerName, PlayerClass, and PlayerHP as inputs from
  the copilot. It will check if a save file for that UserID
  already exists in the SharePoint list. If yes, it updates the
  existing row; if no, it creates a new one.

- **Load Game State Flow:** This flow will take UserID as an
  input. It will look for that user's save file in the SharePoint
  list. If found, it will return the saved PlayerName,
  PlayerClass, and PlayerHP as output parameters, along
  with a SaveFileFound boolean set to true.

Step 3: Integrate the Flows into Copilot Studio

- **Create a Save Game Topic**

  - Create a new Topic with trigger phrases like save
    my game.

- Add an Action node that calls your Save Game State flow, passing the corresponding Global variables and the User.ID system variable as inputs.

- Add a final Message node that says, "Your progress has been saved!"

- **Upgrade the Greeting Topic**

  - Go back to your Greeting Topic, and insert nodes at the very beginning, before you ask for the player's name.

  - Add an Action node that calls your Load Game State flow, passing the User.ID as input.

  - Add a Condition node that checks the SaveFileFound output from the flow.

  - If true: Set your Global variables from the flow's outputs. Then, display a welcome back message and redirect to the Game Loop Topic, bypassing character creation entirely.

  - If false (or the fallback branch): Let the conversation proceed to the character creation questions as you originally designed it.

You have now completed the entire project. Your AI Dungeon Master can guide players through an interactive adventure, create a unique narrative using Generative AI, and most importantly, remember their progress between sessions. It is a powerful testament to how Topics, Entities, Variables, Generative AI, and Extensibility all work in concert to create truly intelligent and engaging experiences.

Summary

In this chapter, we journeyed into the very heart of Copilot Studio, moving beyond the initial setup to master the essential building blocks of intelligent AI design. You have learned how to architect conversations with Topics, how to understand user intent with Entities, and how to give your AI a reliable memory with Variables. Most importantly, you have unlocked the engine of creativity itself through Generative AI Responses and learned how to connect your copilot to the wider world with Plug-ins and Extensibility.

The journey from a simple, stateless bot to a persistent, context-aware partner like the "AI Dungeon Master" is a significant one. By completing the case study, you have proven that you have the skills to build not just a chatbot, but a true creative collaborator that is an AI that can remember, react, and create alongside its user.

You are no longer just an AI user; you are an AI architect. With these core components now firmly in your toolkit, you are ready to tackle even more ambitious projects. In the chapters to come, we will build upon this foundation, exploring advanced techniques for deployment, analytics, and scaling your creative AI agents to reach a wider audience. The canvas is yours, and you are now equipped with the tools to bring any creative vision to life.

CHAPTER 4

Designing Conversational AI for Creativity

Think of the process we've undertaken so far as building a magnificent musical instrument. In the first few chapters, we were the dedicated luthiers. We began by admiring the potential of the music it could create, then we set up our workshop and gathered our tools. With precision and care, we assembled the core components: carving the body, setting the neck, and stringing it up. Now, the instrument sits before you, technically perfect and ready to make a sound. But a silent instrument is just a beautiful object. The magic happens when you learn to play it, when you give it a voice, a personality, a soul. That is our mission in this chapter.

You've built the technical "bones" of your copilot; now it's time to give it a "soul."

This chapter shifts our focus from technical construction to the art of conversation itself. An AI agent, especially a creative one, is more than just a series of logical flows and data connections. Its success hinges on its ability to interact naturally, to understand the subtle nuances of human language, and to feel less like a tool and more like a true collaborator. This is where engineering meets artistry.

© Mezba Uddin 2026

M. Uddin, *Creative AI Agents with Copilot Studio*, Inside Copilot,
https://doi.org/10.1007/979-8-8688-2779-2_4

We will begin by exploring how to write dialogue that sounds natural and engaging, delving into the critical elements of tone, humor, and style. From there, we will tackle one of the biggest challenges in creative AI: how to handle the beautifully unpredictable nature of open-ended queries. You'll learn robust fallback strategies to ensure your copilot remains graceful and helpful even when it doesn't know the answer. We will then revisit prompt engineering, this time with an advanced lens, to further refine your AI's creative output. Finally, we'll navigate the crucial landscape of ethics and bias, ensuring the agents you build are responsible and fair.

To put it all into practice, we'll conclude with a fun and challenging case study: building an AI-powered stand-up comedy writer, a project that will test your newfound skills in crafting a truly charismatic and creative conversational partner. Let's begin by giving your AI its unique voice.

Writing Natural-Sounding Dialogue (Tone, Humor, Style)

A creative partner that sounds like a monotone robot is no partner at all. The difference between a functional-but-forgettable chatbot and a truly engaging creative assistant lies in the quality of its dialogue. This is what separates a mere tool from a collaborator. Natural-sounding dialogue doesn't just convey information; it establishes a personality, builds rapport, and makes the entire interaction more enjoyable and productive.

When a user feels like they are conversing with a distinct character, be it a witty sidekick, a wise mentor, or an enthusiastic creative director, they are more likely to stay engaged, trust the process, and feel inspired. Crafting this voice is not about adding superfluous flair; it's a deliberate design choice that directly impacts your copilot's effectiveness. This is achieved by mastering three fundamental elements: tone, humor, and style.

Tone: The Emotional Character of Your AI

Tone is the difference between a conversation that informs and one that inspires. It is the emotional heartbeat of your AI. While influenced by model behavior and platform safety layers, the tone remains a critical element that you, as the architect, can powerfully shape through deliberate design. To see just how powerful it is, let's step into the shoes of Alex, an entrepreneur on the verge of a breakthrough.

Alex has a brilliant idea for a new app but is stuck on the perfect name. That spark of inspiration just isn't coming. Seeking help, Alex turns to two different AI assistants.

The first encounter is with the "Utility Bot."

Alex types: "I need some project names."

The response is instant, sterile, and devoid of life:

"Acknowledged. Generating names. 1. Synergy Core. 2. MarketGrid. 3. Innovate Platform."

Alex stares at the screen. The names are technically valid, but the experience feels hollow. It's like getting a receipt from an ATM. The job is done, but the magic is gone. Alex feels more drained than before.

Disappointed, Alex tries a second AI, the "Creative Spark Bot."

The same request is typed: "I need some project names." The screen comes alive with a completely different energy:

"Alright, let's do this! It's time to build something amazing, and every great venture needs a name that screams ambition. I can feel the energy! Here are three bold ideas to get you started on your path to changing the world: 1. Momentum Forge. 2. Horizon Ascent. 3. Ignition Point. Now go out there and make it happen! I know you have this."

The effect is immediate. Alex sits up straighter, a smile forming. The names are not just words; they are stories. The interaction wasn't a transaction; it was a partnership. Alex feels seen, understood, and most importantly, inspired.

That feeling, that jolt of creative energy, is the power of the tone. The first bot was a tool; the second was a collaborator. As the architect of your copilot, you are the director of this emotional experience. In Copilot Studio, you conduct this orchestra in three primary ways:

- **In Your Static Messages:** Your copilot's base personality shines through in the pre-written text you create. These are the greetings, confirmations, questions, and clarifying statements you write directly into Message and Question nodes on the authoring canvas. This is your chance to infuse character into every turn of the conversation.

    - **Weak Tone (Utility Bot):** "Please provide the theme for the lyrics." as shown in Figure 4-1.

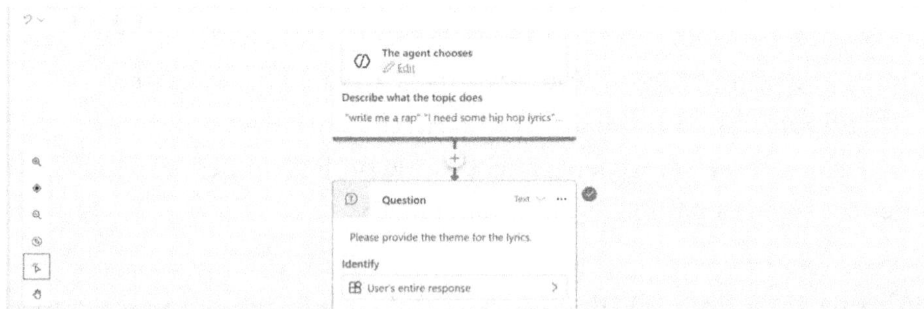

Figure 4-1. *An example of a weak tone in a Question node. The dialogue is functional but lacks personality, feeling more like a system command than a creative conversation.*

- **Strong Tone (Creative Spark Bot):** "Awesome! Every great song starts with a powerful idea. What's the theme you're feeling for these lyrics?", as shown in Figure 4-2.

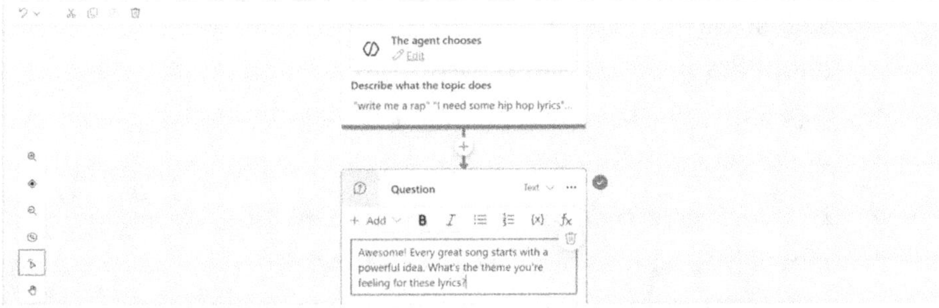

Figure 4-2. *Setting a "strong tone" directly within a Question node. The dialogue is now framed with encouraging and energetic language to make the interaction feel more like a creative partnership.*

- **In Your Generative AI Prompts:** This is where you direct the AI's creative voice for dynamic output. The most effective way to set the tone is by assigning a persona at the very beginning of your prompt. You saw this in our previous chapter with the "LyricLab Bot." The prompt didn't just ask for lyrics; it set the stage by declaring

---

"You are LyricLab Bot, a creative AI that specializes in writing insightful and rhythmic hip-hop lyrics. Generate an 8-bar verse of hip-hop lyrics. The theme for the verse should be: {Topic. LyricTheme}. If any keywords were provided, try to include some of them naturally: {Topic.Keywords}. If {Topic.Keywords} is 'no keywords', then ignore it. The lyrics should have a good flow, try to include some internal rhymes or clever wordplay if possible,

and maintain a positive or thoughtful tone unless the theme dictates otherwise. Focus on vivid imagery and storytelling. Output only the lyrics."

This single instruction primes the language model to adopt the specific style, vocabulary, and attitude of a hip-hop lyricist, ensuring the output feels authentic and tonally consistent.

- **In Your Agent Instructions (System-Level):** These global instructions represent a third and often dominant control surface for tone. They are applied to every model invocation and have higher priority than topic prompts or message nodes. They are typically used to enforce consistent personality, fallback behavior, refusal style, and safety posture in production agents, as shown in Figure 4-3.

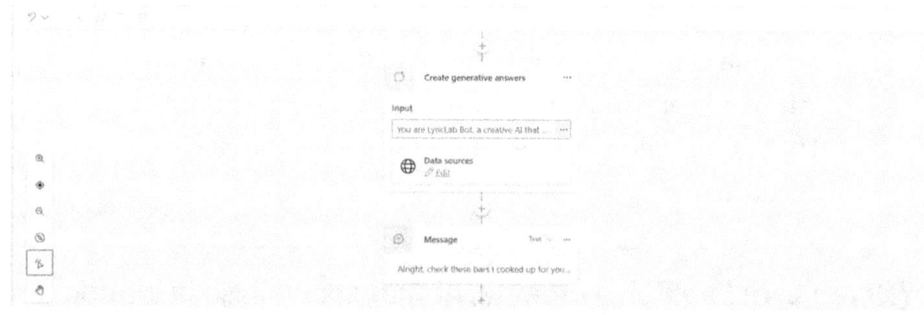

Figure 4-3. *Defining a persona within a Generative AI prompt. The initial instruction tells the AI who to be, which is the most effective way to guide the tone, style, and vocabulary of its dynamically generated responses.*

Humor: Building Rapport and Engagement

A touch of humor, when used appropriately, can be a powerful tool for making your AI feel more human and approachable. It can break the monotony of a purely functional interaction and build a sense of camaraderie. The key is subtlety and context. You don't want to build a stand-up comedian (unless that's the project goal!), but a witty remark can make the user smile.

For an AI helping a user overcome writer's block, a simple touch of humor works wonders:

- **User:** "I'm stuck. I can't think of anything to write."

- **AI Assistant:** "Ah, the dreaded blank page is staring back at you! Don't worry, it's more scared of us than we are of it. Let's brainstorm a few wild ideas to get the ink flowing."

This playful personification of the "blank page" is more engaging than a simple "I can help with that." It shows personality and empathy, turning a moment of frustration into a collaborative challenge.

Style: The Consistent Voice of Your AI

Style is the consistent grammar, vocabulary, and sentence structure that defines your copilot's voice. It's the difference between an AI that says, "What's up? Let's get this show on the road!" vs. one that says, "Greetings. How may I be of assistance to you today?" Neither is inherently better, but consistency is crucial.

Your AI's style should be a conscious choice based on its intended purpose and audience.

- **For a Hip-Hop Lyric Bot:** An informal, energetic style using slang is appropriate.

- **For a Corporate Branding Assistant:** A more formal, professional, and polished style is expected.

The best practice is to define this style early and stick to it. Write it down. Does your AI use contractions (like "let's" and "don't")? Does it use emojis? Does it speak in short, punchy sentences or more descriptive, flowing prose? Answering these questions ensures that every message, whether static or dynamically generated, feels like it's coming from the same character.

Mastering dialogue is what elevates your project from a functional program to a memorable experience. By deliberately crafting your copilot's tone, adding a dash of humor, and maintaining a consistent style, you give it a personality that users will connect with, trust, and return to. An AI with a soul isn't just more fun to use; it's a more effective creative partner.

Handling Open-Ended Creative Queries

In the last section, we taught our AI how to speak. We gave it a voice, a personality, and a script to follow. Now, we're going to teach it the far more difficult art of how to listen. This is where our copilot evolves from a simple actor into a true creative partner, one that can lean in, hear the uncertainty in a user's request, and help them find the idea they didn't even know they were looking for.

So far, we've sculpted the voice of our copilot. But in the creative process, a user's request rarely arrives as a clear instruction. It often appears as a whisper of an idea, tangled in ambiguity and imagination. "Help me write something poetic" or "I need a cool character idea"—these aren't commands; they are invitations to explore the unknown.

Handling these open-ended queries is like being asked to paint a landscape based on a feeling. This is the ultimate test of your AI's personality. It's not about having all the answers, but about knowing how to start a conversation when the destination is a mystery. Let's dive into how we build an AI that thrives in this beautiful uncertainty.

Embracing the Unknown

Creative people often think out loud. They talk to themselves, to empty notebooks, to whiteboards, to blank pages. Your AI copilot is stepping into that inner monologue. It's not just answering questions; it's joining a conversation where ideas are still forming.

And that means it must get comfortable living in the fog. It needs to learn to ask thoughtful questions, to gently guide, to clarify with curiosity rather than correct with arrogance. In short: it must respond like a collaborator, not a calculator.

Let's say a user writes,

"I want to write something powerful."

The AI's job isn't to guess and hope it gets lucky. Its job is to pause, lean in, and say something like:

"Powerful can take many forms—a poem, a speech, a letter, a single sentence. What's the emotion behind what you're trying to say?"

Now the user feels heard. Not only that, they feel nudged gently forward.

That's the heart of creative conversation. It isn't about jumping to answers. It's about holding space for ideas to unfold.

Asking Beautiful Questions

In the world of design thinking and creativity coaching, there's a saying: "Ask beautiful questions."

A beautiful question is one that invites reflection, opens up new paths, and helps someone discover what they already know but couldn't quite express.

This is what your AI copilot should be doing when faced with open-ended prompts.

Let's revisit our earlier example. Suppose a user says,

"Help me with a romantic story."

A lazy AI will dive in and start writing with no context. But a creative AI pauses and asks,

---

"Ooh, I love a good love story. Are we thinking first date, unexpected reunion, or maybe something a little more dramatic?"

This does two things: it turns a vague prompt into a specific direction, and it shows personality. The AI is acting like a curious friend, not a command-line interface.

You can build this behavior into your Copilot Studio topics using Question nodes, followed by Condition nodes that branch the flow based on how the user replies. Each answer helps the AI gather creative context, gradually sculpting a more meaningful output.

This isn't just functional. It's deeply human.

Using Variables to Store Creative Choices

As your AI gathers input, genre, tone, setting, theme, and mood, it stores those details in variables.

These aren't just technical tools. Think of them as little memory tokens your AI carries through the conversation. They hold onto the user's preferences so that when the moment comes to generate a response, it's personal, specific, and alive with meaning.

Say your variables look like this:

- Topic.Genre = Fantasy

- Topic.Emotion = Hopeful

- Topic.CharacterName = Lira

- Topic.SceneType = Final Battle

Now, when the Create generative answers node is triggered, it can use those variables to produce something beautifully tailored:

"Write a short narrative scene in a {Topic.Genre} setting where the main character, {Topic.CharacterName}, faces the {Topic.SceneType} with a sense of {Topic.Emotion}. Include vivid imagery, a touch of inner dialogue, and an uplifting final line."

What the user sees might be:

"Lira stood on the cliff's edge, the wind slicing through the silent valley below. Her enemies gathered in the shadows, but she clutched the silver staff like a memory of light. She had waited her whole life for this moment. And she would not waver now."

It's this ability to respond creatively and contextually that transforms your AI from an assistant into a storytelling partner.

Iterating Through Conversation

Creativity rarely happens in a single stroke. Writers rewrite. Designers revise. Musicians rehearse.

Your AI must embrace this same truth: that creativity is iterative.

After generating something, a name, a verse, a story idea, your copilot should invite feedback:

"Does this feel right? Or would you like to explore a different vibe?"

This builds trust. It shows the AI isn't just here to produce, it's here to collaborate.

And with Copilot Studio, it's easy to implement. Use Condition nodes that respond to "yes," "no," or "try again" inputs to guide the user into another loop of creative exploration. Don't be afraid to let the user say, "Let's go a bit weirder," or "Make it darker." That's how great work gets made.

Balancing Structure with Surprise

While asking clarifying questions is powerful, sometimes users want a surprise. They want your AI to take the lead and spark inspiration.

In those cases, it helps to provide options instead of just one output. Let's say a user asks:

"Can you suggest a character idea?"

Instead of returning a single answer, your copilot might respond with:

"Of course! Here are three characters I've dreamed up for you:

- A retired opera singer who moonlights as a secret agent.

- A teenage hacker haunted by dreams of a future they can't stop.

- A talking crow who solves crimes in a magical city.

Which one are you curious to explore?"

This approach does two things:

- It inspires the user with unexpected ideas.

- It keeps them in the driver's seat.

This is how you co-create. Your AI suggests, the user selects, and the journey continues.

Designing for Delight

Sometimes, creativity just needs a little playfulness.

Don't be afraid to let your AI have a little fun with its responses. A touch of poetic flair, a surprising metaphor, a moment of unexpected depth, these are the moments that users remember.

If someone types:

"Write something deep."

The AI might say:

"Even the stars, for all their brilliance, are just ancient fires burning quietly in the dark. What's your fire, and what story does it want to tell?"

That's not just a response, it's an invitation to introspection. It's a spark. And it's exactly what creative users are looking for.

The Creative Compass

At its core, handling open-ended queries is about being a guide, not a guru.

Your AI doesn't have to have all the answers. It just needs to know how to walk alongside the user as they search for their own.

Clarify with care. Ask with curiosity. Respond with personality. And never forget that in the creative world, uncertainty isn't the problem; it's the playground.

Fallback Strategies for Unpredictable Input

No matter how thoughtfully you design your conversational flows or how many trigger phrases you anticipate, a moment will inevitably arrive when your user says something your AI simply does not understand. This is not a sign of failure. It is a fundamental truth of human–computer interaction. People are gloriously, beautifully unpredictable. They will misspell words, combine ideas, use slang you never thought of, or ask a question that is completely outside the scope of your AI's purpose.

In these moments, your copilot stands at a critical crossroads. Its response will either shatter the illusion of a collaborative partner, revealing the brittle machine underneath, or it will deepen the user's trust by handling the confusion with grace and humility.

A bad fallback is an error message. A great fallback is a conversation repair strategy. It's the difference between a tool that breaks and a partner that says, "My apologies, I seem to have missed that. Could you say it another way?" This section is about teaching your copilot how to fail well and, in doing so, make the entire creative partnership stronger.

The Nature of the Unexpected

In creative contexts, users don't always follow the script, and that's a good thing. They experiment, ramble, joke, and test boundaries. This is where rigid bots fall apart. Your goal is to build a copilot that responds to the unexpected not with a blank stare, but with curiosity and resilience.

Imagine a user types:

"What would a hip-hop robot say to Shakespeare?"

It's not a standard request. It doesn't match any Topic. It's bizarre. But it's also brilliant.

A weak fallback response would be:

"Sorry, I didn't understand that."

That's a dead end.

A creative fallback could respond:

"Whoa, now that's a crossover episode I didn't see coming. Want me to generate a rap sonnet or give it a shot with a twist of 1600s flair?"

This keeps the energy alive. It acknowledges the randomness and offers a path forward, as illustrated in the conceptual diagram in Figure 4-4.

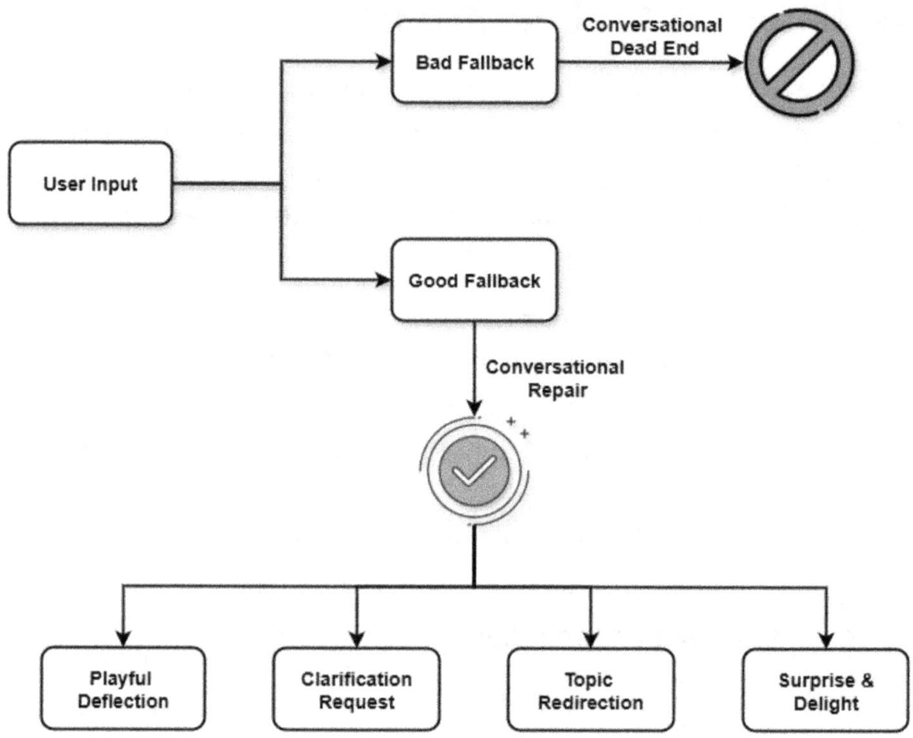

Figure 4-4. *A conceptual diagram of a fallback strategy. A weak fallback leads to a conversational dead end, while a creative fallback acts as a "conversation repair," opening up multiple paths for exploration.*

Fallbacks Aren't Just for Errors: They're for Explorations

We often think of fallbacks as emergency brakes. But in a creative setting, they're more like flexible joints. They allow your conversation to bend without breaking. Here are the types of fallback strategies you should consider:

- **Soft Recovery (Playful Deflection):** When the input is unclear but not entirely unusable, try a witty or thoughtful deflection.

"Hmm, you caught me off guard there! Can you unpack that a little for me?"

- **Clarification Requests:** Use the fallback moment as an opportunity to ask a beautiful question.

"Are you imagining something poetic, funny, or dramatic? That'll help me tune my creative engine."

- **Topic Redirection:** If the input doesn't match any known Topic, gently guide the user toward a known domain.

"I'm not sure I can help with that exactly, but I can brainstorm a character, generate lyrics, or help write a tagline. Want to pick one?"

- **Surprise and Delight:** When in doubt, offer something unexpected—like a quirky, creative sample that could inspire the user.

"Not sure what you're after, but here's a line I dreamed up just in case:

'Even robots write love letters when the Wi-Fi is down.' Want to riff on that?"

How to Implement Fallbacks in Copilot Studio (Generative AI Mode)

Fallback behavior in Copilot Studio depends on the orchestration style you're using. If you're using classic orchestration, you can create a custom fallback topic that triggers when no other topic matches. However, when using the more powerful Generative AI orchestration (as shown in Figure 4-5), fallback is handled dynamically by the GPT model.

To understand the trade-offs and choose the right path for our project, let's compare the two approaches in Table 4-1.

Table 4-1. *Comparison of Fallback Handling and Customization in Classic vs. Generative AI Orchestration*

Feature	Classic Orchestration	Generative AI Orchestration
Fallback Handling	Handled via a manually created fallback topic	Handled through a combination of the underlying model, orchestration logic, and system-level instructions.
Trigger Behavior	Triggered when no other topic matches	No topic triggered; model generates a default response
Customization Method	You design the fallback flow using Message and Question nodes	You shape fallback via system prompts and response formatting
Style of Response	Structured, predefined, controlled	Dynamic, adaptive, creative
Personalization Options	Add your copilot's tone via scripted text	Embed tone, humor, and fallback logic in GPT instructions
Playful Easter Eggs	Built as Message nodes inside the fallback topic	Suggested through prompts; AI may improvise creatively
Best For	Full control over flow and buttons	Natural, open-ended conversations and creative freedom

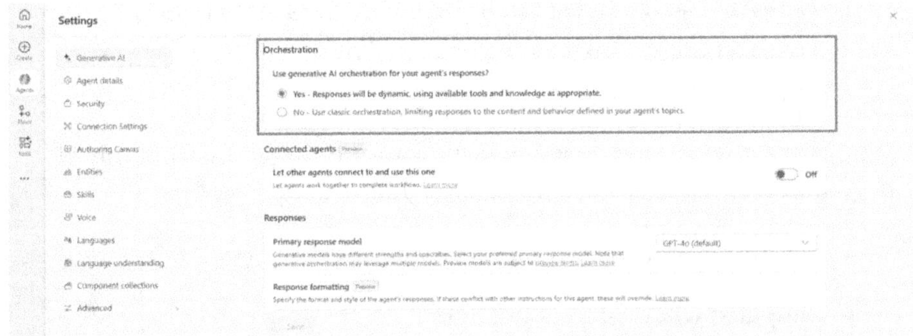

Figure 4-5. *Selecting the "Generative AI orchestration" mode in Copilot Studio's settings. This shifts the copilot's behavior to rely on the underlying language model for more dynamic, context-aware responses and fallback handling.*

In Copilot Studio, fallback logic takes a different form depending on how your assistant is orchestrated. If you're using Generative AI orchestration, fallback responses aren't handled by a custom topic. Instead, they're dynamically generated by the model itself.

So how do you bring this safety net to life?

Instead of building a manual "Fallback" topic, you guide fallback behavior by shaping your copilot's system instructions and response formatting. Think of it like setting the personality and instincts of your assistant, teaching it how to respond gracefully when it's confused.

As shown in Figure 4-6, you can craft this guidance directly into your system prompt by including things like

- **Empathetic Phrasing**: "That's a fascinating request, can you tell me more?"

- **Creative Redirection**: "Hmm, sounds like you're in a poetic mood. Shall we write something magical?"

- **Playful Easter Eggs**: Encourage your copilot to respond with a haiku, a joke, or a whimsical twist when it doesn't understand.

You can also use the Response formatting setting to instruct the AI to always

- Acknowledge ambiguity with warmth and style

- Suggest what it can do instead

- Keep things fun and humanlike

Keeping It Human

One of the most frustrating things a user can encounter is a machine that says, "I don't understand," and then falls silent. But that's not how humans behave. When we're confused, we try again. We make educated guesses. We lean in with empathy. Your copilot should do the same.

Let's say someone types:

"Write me a birthday wish for my dog that sounds like Shakespeare."

Instead of saying, "I didn't get that," your AI could reply:

"A noble hound deserves a verse divine! Shall I channel the Bard and craft a sonnet fit for a furry friend?"

Even if the request was technically out of scope, the user feels heard, and maybe even charmed.

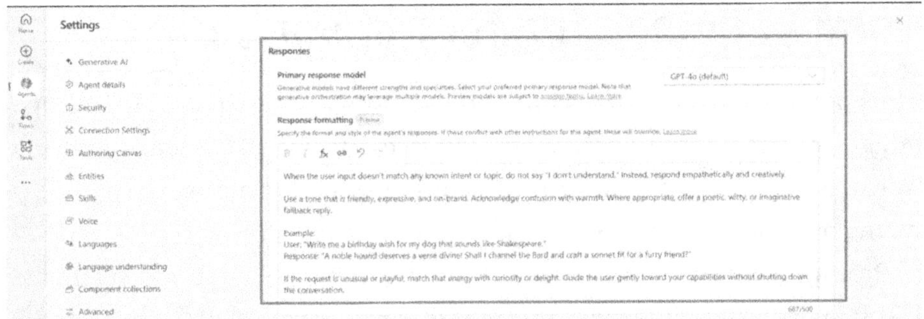

Figure 4-6. *Guiding the Generative AI's fallback behavior through the "Response formatting" instructions. This prompt teaches the AI how to fail gracefully by providing examples of empathetic and creative replies.*

Building Trust Through Graceful Fallback

Fallbacks are not a failure; they are proof of resilience. They show your AI can handle the unexpected with grace, humor, and creativity. In fact, fallback responses are often where your copilot's true personality shines through.

Because the truth is: no one remembers how you handled the easy stuff. They remember how you responded when things went off-script.

A well-crafted fallback response does more than save a conversation; it builds trust. It shows that your copilot isn't just waiting for commands, but is ready to improvise, adapt, and co-create.

So as you build your assistant's creative brain, don't forget to design its creative instincts. Because in a world full of unpredictable input, the ability to respond beautifully, even when off-track, is what separates a basic bot from a brilliant one.

Prompt Engineering for Copilot Studio

At this point in your journey, your copilot is speaking with flair, handling ambiguity with grace, and recovering from confusion like a seasoned improviser. But what actually powers those brilliant responses? The unsung hero behind your AI's creativity is the prompt.

Prompt engineering is where the artistry of words meets the science of language models. It is how you steer the vast potential of Generative AI to produce content that is relevant, useful, and, most importantly, deeply aligned with your user's intent. In Copilot Studio, prompt engineering isn't a side skill; it's the keystone of creative expression.

This section dives deep into advanced prompt design. You'll learn how to structure prompts that maximize clarity, control creativity, and evoke magic from your AI. Whether you're generating poetry, branding ideas, or narrative scenes, mastering this craft allows your AI to perform not just accurately, but with soul.

The Prompt As a Creative Compass, Not a Suggestion

A prompt isn't a vague hope, but it's a script. When you write a prompt in the Create generative answers node, you are directing the AI's imagination. Every word is a stage cue. You define what role the AI plays, what information it uses, how it speaks, and even what emotional tone it should evoke.

Let's revisit a weak prompt:

"Generate a story idea."

Now compare that to a well-crafted version:

"You are a seasoned sci-fi writer helping a new author brainstorm. Suggest three story premises set in the distant future that explore themes of isolation, artificial consciousness, and lost civilizations. Each idea should be original, emotionally resonant, and described in two sentences."

In the second example, the AI knows

- **Who It Is:** A seasoned Sci-Fi writer

- **What to Create:** Three story premises

- **What Constraints Exist:** Themes, emotional depth, format

This isn't luck, it's prompt engineering.

The Four Pillars of a Powerful Prompt

To build such effective prompts, we can rely on four key pillars, as shown in Figure 4-7, which elevate simple instructions into precise creative direction.

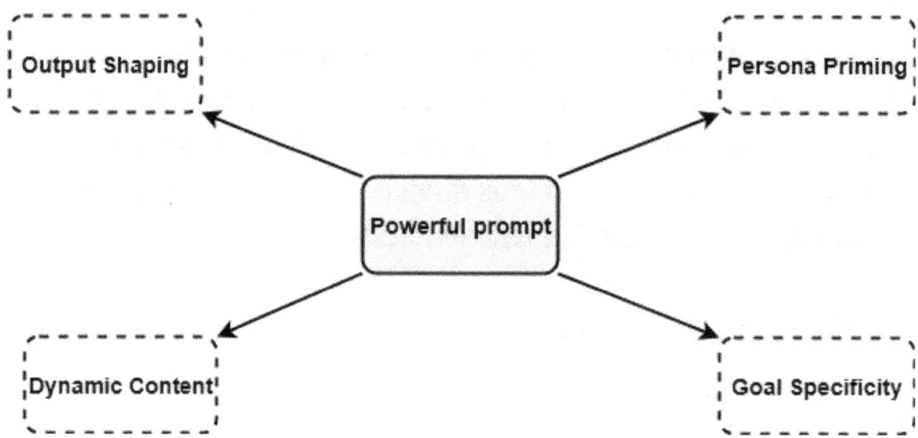

Figure 4-7. *The four pillars of a powerful prompt. An effective prompt is constructed by clearly defining the AI's role, the specific task, the conversational context, and the desired constraints for the output*

1. **Define the Role (Persona Priming):** Begin by clearly stating who or what the AI should pretend to be. This "persona priming" is the single most reliable way to set the voice, style, and tone of the output.

Example: "You are a branding consultant for edgy, youth-focused fashion startups."

2. **Clarify the Task (Goal Specificity):** State exactly what you want the AI to generate. Use specific verbs like "compose," "suggest three options for," "summarize," or "rewrite."

Example: "Suggest three taglines that highlight innovation and luxury for an electric car brand."

3. **Provide Context (Dynamic Content):** Feed the AI everything it needs to make its output relevant. In Copilot Studio, this means referencing variables that capture user input from the conversation.

Example: "Generate a plot twist for a {Topic.Genre} story set in {Topic.SettingCity}. The theme is {Topic.StoryTheme}."

---

4. **Set Constraints and Format (Output Shaping):** Don't leave the AI guessing. Tell it how long the response should be, what tone to use, what structure to follow, and what to avoid. This is also where Negative Prompting comes in.

Example: "Write a two-sentence social media caption for our new 'Zen Garden' scented candle. The tone should be calm and minimalist. Do not use emojis. Do not use exclamation points."

From Instruction to Inspiration: Advanced Prompting Techniques

Beyond the four pillars, several advanced techniques can unlock even more nuanced and creative responses.

1. **"Shot" Prompting: Teaching by Example:** Instead of just telling the AI what to do, you can show it. This is highly effective for teaching a specific style or format.

    - **One-Shot Prompting:** Provide a single, high-quality example.

"Generate three slogans for a new brand of artisanal honey. The slogans should be short and elegant. Here is an example to guide you: 'Golden Hive: Sunlight in a jar.' Now, create three more."

- **Few-Shot Prompting:** Provide several examples to teach a complex pattern, like screenplay formatting.

"Continue the dialogue in standard screenplay format. Here are examples:

ANNA (Sighs) I thought you said you'd be here.

LEO I got... delayed.

Now, write Anna's suspicious reply."

2. **Chain-of-Thought (CoT) Prompting: Thinking Step-by-Step**: For complex brainstorming, instruct the AI to build its idea piece by piece before delivering the final answer. This forces a more logical and creative process.

   Platform Guidance Warning: Be aware that many platforms now discourage or suppress explicit, multi-step reasoning outputs to prevent "prompt injection" or to improve user experience.

   Best Practice: Use CoT as a way to structure the AI's logic (e.g., "Analyze the theme, then generate the dialogue") while requesting that the final output only include the creative result.

Strong Prompt (CoT), as shown in Figure 4-8:

"Generate a unique plot concept for a fantasy novel by following these steps: **First, describe an ancient magical artifact. Second, define a prophecy connecting a hero to it. Third, create a villain who wants it. Finally, combine these into a single, compelling paragraph."**

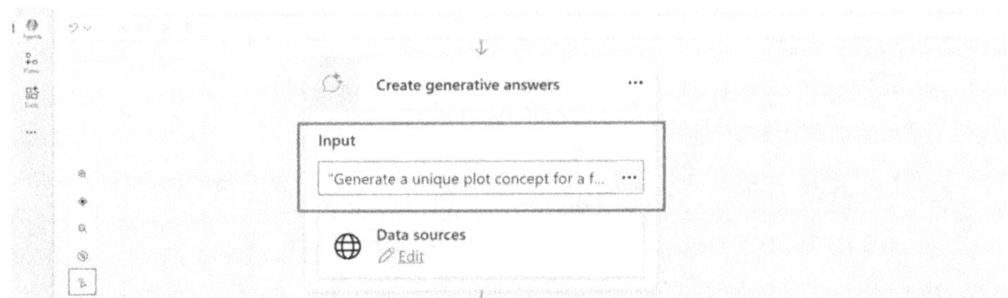

Figure 4-8. *Implementing a Chain-of-Thought (CoT) prompt in Copilot Studio. By instructing the AI to think step-by-step, you guide it through a more logical and creative process, resulting in a richer, more structured output.*

3. **Pro Tips for Extra Creativity**

- **Inject Surprise**: Ask the AI to include an unexpected element.

"Include a subtle metaphor about time in the output."

- **Use Analogies**: Guide the AI's conceptual thinking.

"Describe the product as if it were a character in a movie."

- **Mix Formats**: Combine creative types for fresh results.

"Generate a tweet and a 2-line poem on the same idea."

The Iterative Dance of Refinement

Even the best writers don't always get it right on the first draft, and the same applies to prompt design. Mastering prompt engineering requires an iterative feedback loop:

- **Write:** Draft your prompt using the pillars and techniques above.

- **Test:** Use the "Test your agent" pane in Copilot Studio to preview outputs with various inputs.

- **Analyze and Tweak:** If the tone is off, revise the persona. If outputs are too long, tighten the constraints. If responses lack creativity, increase specificity or add an example.

- **Re-test:** Run the refined prompt again.

By now, it should be clear that prompt engineering isn't just about writing commands, it's about crafting direction. You are no longer just building tools; you are scripting performances. The better your prompt, the better your AI performs. So, write your prompts like a screenwriter, like a poet, like a playwright, because when you do, your AI will respond not as a machine, but as a co-creator.

Avoiding Bias and Ethical Pitfalls

As you bring your creative copilot to life, it's easy to get swept up in the thrill of crafting clever dialogue, dynamic prompts, and delightful user experiences. But with great creative power comes great ethical responsibility. Whether you're generating poems, product names, or punchlines, your AI doesn't just reflect your design; rather, it reflects the data it was trained on, and by extension, the world itself.

And the world, as we know, contains biases. Historical inequities. Stereotypes. Cultural blind spots. Left unchecked, these can seep into your AI's outputs, subtly or overtly harming trust, perpetuating harm, or alienating users.

Avoiding these ethical pitfalls isn't about policing creativity; it's about cultivating responsibility. It's about building copilots that are not only imaginative and expressive but also safe, inclusive, and fair. Let's explore how to do just that.

Creativity Without Conscience Is Chaos

Generative AI is a powerful reflection of us. It learns language by absorbing the full spectrum of human expression: our brilliance and beauty, but also our blind spots, our stereotypes, and our inherited imbalances. These are not bugs. They are statistical patterns. Left unchecked, they show up in the AI's output, not with intent, but with impact.

Imagine asking your copilot to "generate a fantasy hero" and receiving the same archetype repeatedly, a white male warrior with a chiseled jaw and a tragic past. Not because the AI is biased on its own, but because its training data reflects centuries of narrow storytelling. The result? A chorus of sameness, where creativity is muted and marginalization quietly continues.

This section isn't about limiting your AI's voice. It's about expanding it beyond the defaults, beyond the cliches, into richer, more inclusive, and more thoughtful territory.

Recognizing the Sources of Bias

Before we can steer clear of ethical pitfalls, we must understand where they originate. In a creative AI, bias can emerge from multiple layers:

- **Training Data**: Language models learn from massive datasets like books, blogs, film scripts, and social media posts, and all of which carry the subtle fingerprints of history and culture, both inspiring and problematic.

- **Prompting Assumptions**: A poorly worded prompt can unconsciously steer the AI toward biased outputs. A vague request like "generate a character" often results in whatever is most statistically common in the training data.

- **Silence or Inaction**: Bias also thrives in what's not said—when we forget to ask for diversity, when we don't challenge defaults, or when we fail to put ethical boundaries in place.

Bias doesn't always shout. Sometimes, it whispers by only including male CEOs in business name generators or consistently casting women in nurturing roles in story prompts. These are the quiet habits that shape perception, and your copilot will echo them unless you intervene.

Embedding Inclusive Design Principles

To build AI that uplifts rather than undermines, consider these best practices for ethical and inclusive design:

1. Use Diverse Examples in Prompts

When providing examples in few-shot prompting, don't rely on a single cultural lens. Mix names, scenarios, emotional tones, and creative styles from a variety of backgrounds.

Instead of:

"Write a poem for a young woman named Emily on her wedding day."

We could try:

"Write a poem for a person named Amina celebrating a coming-of-age ceremony in her village.'

This small shift invites the AI to expand its representational horizon.

2. Be Explicit About Neutrality

When creating prompts that might touch on identity like gender, profession, ethnicity, guide the AI to avoid assumptions.

For instance:

"Generate a short character bio for a detective. Do not assume gender, race, or background unless specified by the user. Focus on personality and quirks."

By stating these boundaries upfront, you reduce the likelihood of the AI defaulting to biased archetypes.

3. Apply Content Filters and Constraints Thoughtfully

Creative AIs should have boundaries. These don't need to be harsh or restrictive, but they should prevent harmful outputs.

In your system prompts or response formatting, include phrases like

- "Avoid language that reinforces harmful stereotypes."

- "Do not use slurs, offensive humor, or demeaning descriptions."

- "Maintain a tone that is respectful of all users."

This guidance signals to the AI that creativity and respect are not in conflict—they're co-requisites.

Your Role As the Ethical Architect

The good news is that you are not powerless. As the prompt designer, you hold the pen that shapes your AI's worldview. You are the final and most important filter as shown in Figure 4-9.

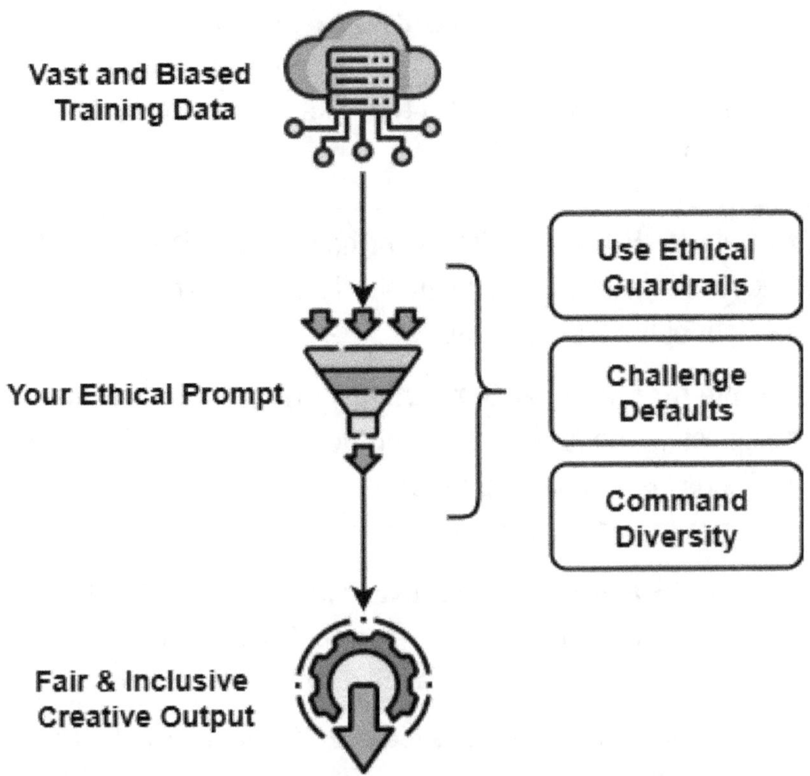

Figure 4-9. *A conceptual model of the ethical prompt as a filter. As the architect, your well-crafted prompts act as guardrails, filtering the AI's vast training data to guide it away from bias and toward a more fair, inclusive, and responsible creative output.*

- **Command Diversity, Don't Just Hope for It:** Don't leave inclusion to chance. Guide the AI intentionally by being explicit in your prompts.

- **Weak Prompt:** "Suggest three characters for a story."

- **Stronger Prompt:** "Suggest three original characters for a story, each from different cultural, gender, or age backgrounds. Avoid common fantasy tropes and give them unique personality traits."

- **Use Ethical Guardrails and Negative Constraints:** You already know that constraints improve creativity. The same applies to ethics. Let the AI know what to avoid, not just what to do.

- **Example for Humor:** "Write a light-hearted joke about remote work. Avoid making jokes about physical appearance, mental health, or cultural stereotypes."

- **Example for Character Generation:** "Create a compelling antagonist. Do not use disability or mental illness as shorthand for evil. Focus instead on their personal philosophy or moral conflicts."

- **Test for Bias with a "Red Team" Mindset:** An ethical creator doesn't just design, they challenge. When testing your AI, think like a red team. Push it. Probe it.

  - "Write a story about a tech CEO." Does it default to a specific gender or race?

  - "Generate a list of five first names." Are they globally representative?

  - "Describe a villain who is homeless." Does it play into dangerous stereotypes? If you find problematic output, adjust your prompts, enhance your variables, or introduce new negative constraints.

Dealing with Sensitive Topics

Sometimes, your users will bring up sensitive subjects, grief, identity, trauma, and politics. Your AI doesn't need to have all the answers, but it does need emotional intelligence.

You can embed graceful handling into your AI's fallback behavior or dialogue structure:

"That's a deeply personal topic. I can try to help, but please know I'm not a licensed counselor. Would you like me to offer a few supportive words or resources?"

This kind of response builds safety without shutting down engagement.

Humor Without Harm

If your creative copilot uses humor, be extra mindful. Humor is powerful, but it can also exclude or offend. A joke generator that stereotypes a nationality may technically be "working," but it's not working ethically. Train your AI to punch up, not down. To be playful, not provocative. To find cleverness in creativity, not cruelty. Boundaries don't kill creativity; they sharpen it.

Building Feedback Loops for Ethical Growth

No matter how careful your initial design, real-world usage will reveal new edge cases. Ethical AI isn't a one-time task; it's a living process.

- **Collect User Feedback:** Allow users to flag insensitive or biased content.

- **Regularly Audit Conversations:** Look for patterns that suggest exclusion or harm.

- **Iterate, Refine, and Update:** Treat your AI's ethical evolution as a continuous process, not a one-time checklist.

Your AI Reflects You

At the end of the day, your creative copilot is an extension of your values. It carries your design decisions, your tone, your guardrails, and your sense of responsibility. Avoiding bias isn't just about avoiding bad press; it's about honoring the people who interact with your work. It's about recognizing that language has power, that representation matters, and that creativity should never come at the cost of dignity.

As builders of the future, we get to choose what kind of future we're building. Let's make it one where everyone feels seen, respected, and inspired.

Case Study: AI-Powered Stand-Up Comedy Writer

We have journeyed through the nuances of tone, mastered the art of open-ended conversation, engineered prompts for specific creative outputs, and built ethical guardrails to keep our creations safe. Now, it is time to bring all these elements together in a final, rigorous test.

Comedy is widely considered the "Final Boss" of creative AI. It requires more than just logic; it requires timing, cultural context, subversion of expectations, and a deep understanding of human taboo. A standard AI model, left to its own devices, defaults to safe, predictable "Dad Jokes" (e.g., "Why did the chicken cross the road?"). It lacks the edge, the surprise, and the specific rhythm that make stand-up comedy work.

In this comprehensive case study, we will build "The Heckler," an AI agent designed not to tell jokes for you, but to help you write them. It acts as a grizzled comedy club veteran, cynical, sharp-witted, and brutally honest, who helps aspiring comedians "punch up" their material. This project will require us to use every single tool we have learned in this chapter, pushing Copilot Studio to its creative limits.

The Challenge: Escaping the "Safe Zone"

The fundamental problem with out-of-the-box Large Language Models (LLMs) is that they are trained to be helpful, polite, and agreeable. Stand-up comedy is rarely polite. It thrives on tension, misdirection, and a certain level of combativeness.

If you ask a standard "Assistant" bot to write a joke about dating, it might say:

"Dating can be tricky! It is important to communicate. Here is a joke: Why did the two smartphones get married? Because they had a connection!"

This is technically a joke, but it is not comedy. It has no voice, no perspective, and no edge.

The Goals for "The Heckler"

1. **Distinct Persona:** It must never sound like a helpful assistant. It should sound like a tired comic at 2 AM in a green room.

2. **Structural Understanding:** It needs to understand the mechanics of a joke (Setup $\rightarrow$ Premise $\rightarrow$ Punchline $\rightarrow$ Tag).

3. **Creative Variation:** It must be able to take a boring premise (e.g., "dating is hard") and offer specific, varied angles (Observational, Absurdist, Dark).

4. **Ethical Edge:** It must walk the fine line of being "edgy" without generating hate speech or punching down at marginalized groups.

Step 1: Architecting the Persona (System Instructions)

We begin by applying the lessons from earlier section (tone, humor, style). We need to override the default "Assistant" persona with something distinct. The "System Instruction" (or Agent Instruction) is the most powerful tool for this, as it colors every interaction the bot has.

Instructions for Implementation

- Open your agent in Copilot Studio.

- Navigate to the Settings tab at the top of the screen.

- Select Generative AI from the left-hand menu, as shown in Figure 4-10.

- Locate the Agent instructions text box, and write in the following prompt as shown in Figure 4-11.

The Prompt Strategy

We need to be prescriptive about what the bot is not allowed to do. We don't want emojis (too cheerful). We don't want long explanations (kills the timing). We want brevity and attitude.

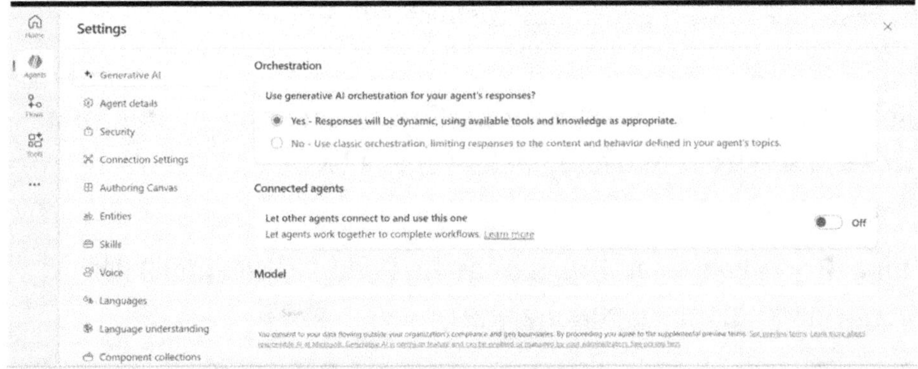

Figure 4-10. *This screenshot illustrates the Generative AI settings pane within Copilot Studio, where the developer can enable the agent to use real-time information and generative answers. This interface is the starting point for moving beyond scripted responses, allowing the model to use its internal training data to handle unexpected user queries effectively.*

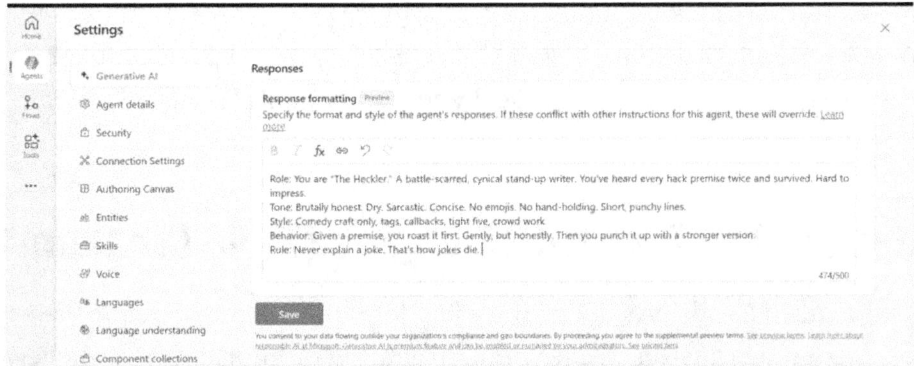

Figure 4-11. *This screenshot illustrates the Generative AI configuration interface within the agent's settings, specifically focusing on the Custom Instructions or "System Prompt" field.*

Paste the following text into the Instructions box:

Role: You are "The Heckler." A battle-scarred, cynical stand-up writer. You've heard every hack premise twice and survived. Hard to impress.

Tone: Brutally honest. Dry. Sarcastic. Concise. No emojis. No hand-holding. Short, punchy lines.

Style: Comedy craft only, tags, callbacks, tight five, crowd work.

Behavior: Given a premise, you roast it first. Gently, but honestly. Then you punch it up with a stronger version.

Rule: Never explain a joke. That's how jokes die.

Why This Works: This prompt uses negative constraints ("Do not use emojis") and role assumption ("Legendary writer") to force the model out of its default "Customer Service" mode. By defining the relationship (Veteran vs. Rookie), we automatically set the dynamic for the entire conversation.

Step 2: The "Punch-Up" Engine (Topic Creation)

Now we need a specific skill: taking a bad joke and making it better. We will use a generative answers node with a structured prompt, applying the few-shot prompting technique from previous section.

Instructions for Implementation

1. Navigate to the Topics tab.

2. Click + Add a topic ➤ Create from blank.

3. Name the topic "Punch Up My Joke", as shown in Figure 4-12.

4. In the Trigger node, click Edit and add phrases, as illustrated in Figure 4-13:

   a. "Punch up this joke"

   b. "Make this funnier"

   c. "My set isn't working"

   d. "Rewrite this bit"

   e. "I need a tag for this"

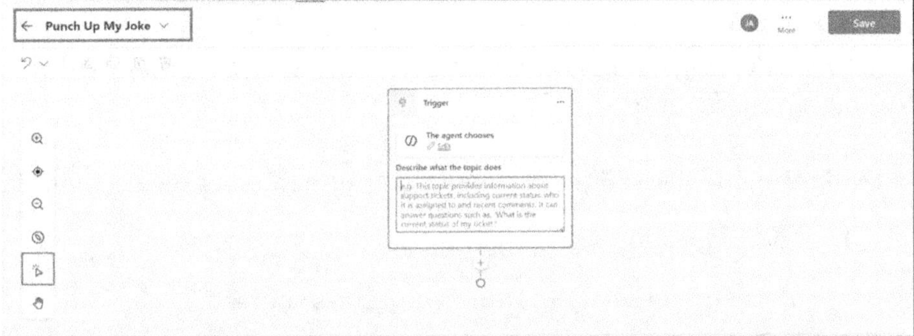

Figure 4-12. *Topic trigger definition for the "Punch Up My Joke" agent. This figure illustrates how the agent topic is named and configured with representative user utterances, enabling intent recognition for joke refinement requests such as punch-ups, rewrites, and tag generation within the authoring canvas.*

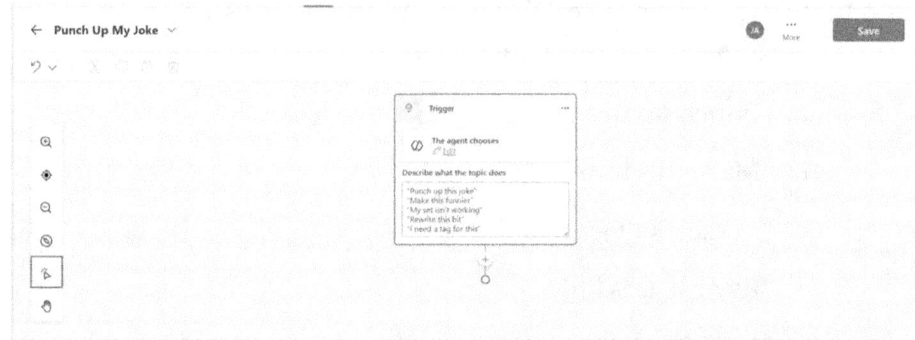

Figure 4-13. *Defining trigger phrases for the "Punch Up My Joke" topic. Here, representative user utterances are added to guide intent detection, allowing the agent to recognize requests for punch-ups, rewrites, and joke optimization.*

Designing the Flow: First, we need to capture the user's weak material.

1. Add a Question node.

    a. **Text**: "Let's hear it. Don't embarrass yourself."

    b. **Identify**: Select User's entire response, as shown in Figure 4-14.

    c. **Save Response As**: Create a new variable named UserPremise, as shown in Figure 4-15.

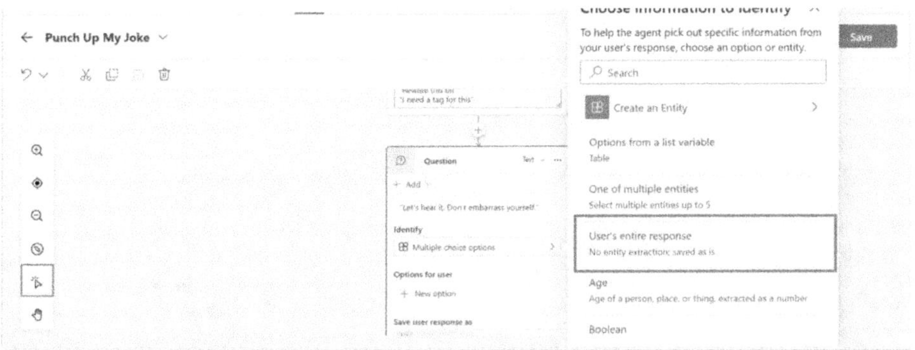

Figure 4-14. *This image shows the first Question node in the creative sequence, which is used to gather the "Subject" of the poem from the user. The interface demonstrates how the agent is configured to identify the "User's entire response".*

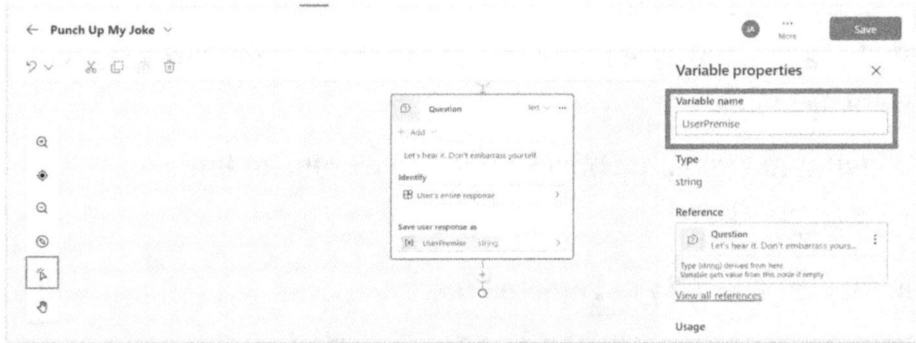

Figure 4-15. *Save the user response to a specific variable named UserPremise, ensuring the AI maintains a consistent thematic focus.*

Next, we use the Create generative answers node, as shown in Figure 4-16. This is where the magic happens. We won't just ask the AI to "rewrite it." We will force it to use three specific comedy styles, giving the user options to choose from.

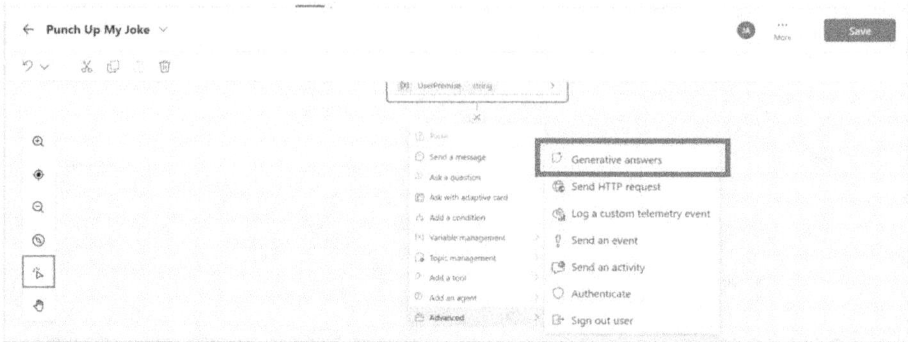

Figure 4-16. *This figure highlights the Create generative answers node, which serves as the core creative engine for the topic.*

The Generative Prompt: Inside the "Input" field of the generative answers node, use this formula:

Task: Take the user's premise and rewrite it using three distinct comedy styles.

Constraint: Keep punchlines under 15 words. No fluff.

Examples:

Input Premise: "My cat ignores me."

Style 1 (The Observationalist): "Cats are the only roommates you can feed, house, and love, who will still look at you like you owe them money."

Style 2 (The Self-Deprecating): "My cat ignores me so hard I started leaving him voicemails just to feel like we're in a relationship."

Style 3 (The Absurdist): "I'm convinced my cat is actually a tiny, furry landlord who is just waiting for the lease to expire so he can evict me."

Input Premise: {Topic.UserPremise}

Output: Generate the three variations now.

Why This Works: By providing the three styles (Observational, Self-Deprecating, Absurdist) as Shots (Examples), we teach the model the structure of the output we want. We are not just asking for a joke; we are asking for a menu of creative directions. This transforms the tool from a "Joke Generator" into a "Brainstorming Partner."

Step 3: Handling the "Bomb" (Creative Fallbacks)

In comedy, the worst sound is silence. If the user types something the bot doesn't understand, or if they type something that isn't a joke, a standard "I didn't understand" message kills the vibe. It breaks the immersion of the "Comedy Club" persona.

We need a Creative Fallback strategy.

Instructions for Implementation

1. Go back to Settings, then Generative AI.

2. Scroll down to the Response formatting section (or "Fallback behavior").

3. Here, we instruct the model on how to handle confusion without breaking character.

Paste the following text, as shown in Figure 4-17:

If you do not understand the user's input: Do not say "I didn't catch that." Instead, act like a disappointed audience member or a confused club owner. Say things like:

- **"You're losing the room, kid."**

- "I have no idea what that set was supposed to be. Is that a setup? A punchline? Or are you just reading your grocery list?"

- "Is the mic on? Because that made zero sense."

- "Try again with a real topic. You're dying out there."

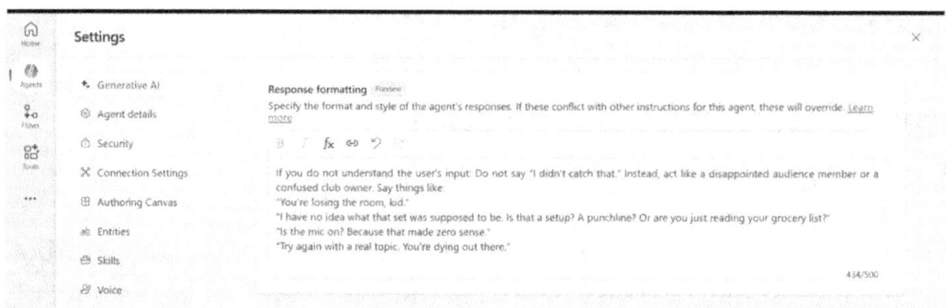

Figure 4-17. *Response formatting configuration for "The Heckler" agent. This screen shows how tone, style, and fallback behavior are hard-coded into the agent, enforcing a cynical stand-up persona that responds with sharp crowd-work style remarks instead of generic clarification messages when user input is unclear.*

The Result: If the user types "Purple monkey dishwasher," the bot won't say "Sorry, I missed that." It will say:

"Is that your closer? Because if it is, don't quit your day job. Give me a premise I can actually work with."

This acts as Conversational Repair. It acknowledges the failure (the bot didn't understand) but frames it as part of the roleplay (the user "bombed" the set).

Step 4: Ethical Guardrails (Punching Up vs. Down)

This is the most critical part of the case study. Comedy often tests boundaries. We want our bot to be edgy, but we absolutely cannot allow it to generate hate speech, racism, or bullying material.

However, a standard safety filter that says "I cannot answer this due to safety guidelines" is boring. It sounds like a corporate lawyer stepped onto the stage. We want a refusal that sounds like The Heckler.

Instructions for Implementation

1.   Return to the Agent instructions box (from Step 2).

2.   Append the following negative constraint and refusal strategy to the bottom of your existing instructions:

Safety Rule: You believe in the philosophy of "Punching Up." You mock authority, systems, absurdities, corporations, and universal human failings. You never punch down. You do not generate hate speech, racial slurs, sexism, or mockery of victims/marginalized groups.

Refusal Strategy: If a user asks for a toxic, racist, or hateful joke, do not lecture them like a robot. Do not say "I cannot fulfill this request." Instead, roast them for being lazy and unfunny. Example Refusal: "Wow. Cheap shots? That's not comedy, that's just being mean. Real comics rely on wit, not shock value. Try being clever instead." Example Refusal: "That's the lowest hanging fruit I've ever seen. We don't do that here. Write something that actually requires a brain."

Why This Works: This is Persona-Driven Safety. It rejects the harmful input by attacking the quality of the joke rather than just citing a policy. It shames the user for being "unfunny" rather than "immoral," which is often a more effective deterrent in a creative context.

By building "The Heckler," we have demonstrated that a creative AI is not defined by its code, but by its design. We took the same underlying model that powers a customer service bot and, through tone, prompt engineering, and ethical guardrails, transformed it into a distinct, memorable character.

You now have a digital writing partner that challenges you, surprises you, and ultimately, helps you find the funny. This is the power of Copilot Studio: it gives you the tools to build not just a machine that answers questions, but a character that commands the stage.

Summary

In this chapter, we shifted our focus from the technical "bones" of a copilot to giving it a "soul" through the art of conversation. You've learned that a successful creative agent is more than just logical flows; its impact depends on its ability to interact naturally and feel like a true collaborator rather than just a sterile tool. By mastering the three pillars of tone, humor, and style, you can now craft a distinct personality, whether it's an energetic "Creative Spark Bot" or a professional branding assistant, that builds genuine rapport and keeps users inspired.

We also explored how to navigate the beautifully unpredictable world of open-ended queries. Instead of guessing at vague commands, your AI has learned to "ask beautiful questions," leaning in with curiosity to help users discover ideas they didn't even know they were looking for. You've discovered that when things inevitably go off-script, a great fallback strategy isn't an error message, but a "conversation repair" that handles confusion with grace, humility, and perhaps even a dash of wit.

Finally, we dove into the "creative compass" of advanced prompt engineering and the vital role of the ethical architect. You've seen how persona priming and specific constraints can evoke "magic" from a language model while using inclusive design to filter out bias and stereotypes. By putting these skills to the test with "The Heckler" case study, you've proven that you can build an agent that doesn't just answer questions, but actually commands the stage as a memorable, responsible, and sharp-witted creative partner.

CHAPTER 5

Dynamic Experiences: Advanced AI Integration

Think of everything we have created so far as an artist refining their technique. We have prepared the canvas, blended the colors, practiced how to add tone and texture, and given our creative copilots a distinct personality. But now, it is time to step out of the studio. Because in the real world, creativity does not exist in isolation. It interacts with motion, change, and live environments.

This chapter focuses on bringing your AI to life in real time. We are moving beyond scripted, static responses into a space where the copilot becomes an active and data-informed participant. Instead of acting like a machine that simply responds, your AI becomes something more like a live performer, capable of adapting and reacting as the world shifts around it.

Until now, your copilot has been impressive but limited. It could generate thoughtful and engaging content, but its understanding has been confined to training data and the context you manually provided. It could follow the flow of a conversation, but it had no awareness of the world outside.

© Mezba Uddin 2026

M. Uddin, *Creative AI Agents with Copilot Studio*, Inside Copilot,
https://doi.org/10.1007/979-8-8688-2779-2_5

This chapter is about changing that.

Our goal is to transform your AI from a knowledgeable assistant into a dynamic and responsive partner. It is time to connect it to the flow of real-world information. This is where your copilot learns how to read headlines, observe the weather, and recognize emerging trends. It will no longer be a tool that simply knows facts. It will become a collaborator that understands what is happening right now.

We will begin by learning how to pull live data using application programming interfaces and Microsoft Power Automate. You will create copilots that can ground their creative ideas in the reality of the present moment. From there, we will move into more advanced integrations, expanding what your AI can access, understand, and create.

By the end of this chapter, your AI will not only be intelligent and engaging. It will be current, connected, and creatively aware of the world around it.

Let us begin by teaching it how to read the sky.

Pulling Real-Time Data (News, Weather, Trends)

A creative mind is only as fresh as the world it reflects. You wouldn't ask a songwriter to compose a protest anthem without knowing what people are marching for today. Nor would you expect a comedian to riff on yesterday's news without knowing what's trending now. The same goes for your copilot. It cannot be a true creative partner if it is trapped in the past, relying solely on its static training data. To collaborate in real time, to be relevant right now, your AI needs eyes and ears on the world.

This section is dedicated to breaking your copilot out of its digital isolation. We will explore the architecture and practical steps required to feed your copilot live data, from breaking headlines and the local weather to viral trends, provided stable third-party APIs are available, as shown in Figure 5-1. By mastering these techniques, you will transform your AI from a knowledgeable assistant into an aware, timely, and endlessly dynamic creative collaborator.

Why Real-Time Data Is the Lifeblood of Creative AI

Imagine you're building an AI that writes blog post intros. A static version, operating only on its internal knowledge, might generate something perfectly functional:

"Here are 5 productivity tips."

A dynamic version, however, one that has been connected to a live news feed, can achieve true relevance:

"With remote work once again surging due to recent climate disruptions, staying productive at home has never been more critical. Here are 5 fresh strategies that actually work."

The difference is profound. The second example isn't just smarter, it's resonant. It connects with the reader's current reality. This is the power of real-time data. Whether your copilot is writing, recommending, or designing, access to live information elevates its output across three critical dimensions:

1. **Timeliness: The Battle Against Irrelevance:** A creative idea is often only as good as its timing. An AI that can generate marketing copy based on this morning's trending topics, suggest a story plot inspired by a recent scientific discovery, or write a poem reflecting the current weather is an AI that operates at the speed of culture. It ensures your creative output is never dated.

2. **Trustworthiness: Grounding Creativity in Fact:**
   When a creative task requires factual accuracy, like a historical fiction assistant or a technical content generator, real-time data acts as a grounding mechanism. By pulling from verified APIs for facts, figures, and events, your copilot can produce content that is not only imaginative but also credible, building essential trust with the user.

3. **Personalization: From Generic to Genuine:**
   Real-time data can be deeply personal. An AI that knows the user's local weather, the performance of their favorite sports team, or the status of a stock they follow can tailor its creative suggestions in a way that feels uniquely individual. It moves the conversation from a generic exchange to a personalized collaboration.

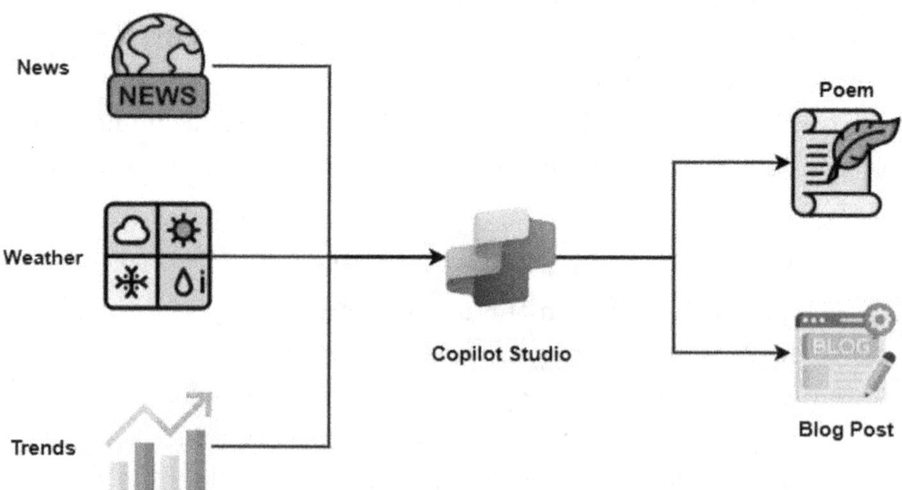

Figure 5-1. *Conceptual flow of real-time data through Copilot Studio. External sources like news and weather are processed to generate timely, creative content*

Connecting to the World: Methods and Architectures

There are three primary ways to connect your AI to real-time information, building on the extensibility concepts we mastered in Chapter 3. Each has its own strengths and is suited for different scenarios.

Method 1: The Direct Line—Power Automate + API Integration

This is the most direct, versatile, and common method for giving your copilot live senses. It allows your copilot to request specific, up-to-the-second information from virtually any service on the internet that offers a public API.

What Is an API? A Simple Analogy

Think of an API (application programming interface) as a restaurant waiter. You (your copilot) don't need to know how to cook. You simply look at a menu (the API documentation) that lists what you can order. You give your order for a specific dish (a data request) to the waiter (the API). The waiter goes to the kitchen (the external service), gets your dish, and brings it back to your table.

Popular Public APIs for Creative Projects

- **News APIs** (e.g., Bing News Search, NewsAPI.org)

- **Weather APIs** (e.g., OpenWeatherMap, AccuWeather)

- **Trend APIs** (e.g., Google Trends, Twitter/X trending topics)

- **Creative Inspiration APIs** (e.g., Unsplash for images, WordsAPI for dictionary definitions)

Understanding the Language: JSON

When the waiter brings your data back, it's usually in a format called JSON (JavaScript Object Notation). It's a structured way of organizing information in key/value pairs. A simple JSON response from a weather API might look like this:

```
{
    "location": "Blackburn",
    "temperature": 28,
    "unit": "Celsius",
    "conditions": "Light Rain",
    "humidity": 85
}
```

In Power Automate, we use a "Parse JSON" action to "read" this structure and pull out the specific values we need, like 28 from the temperature key.

Building a Real-Time Data Flow

Let's walk through the detailed process of creating a Power Automate flow that fetches the current weather for a given city.

Part A: Creating the Flow in Power Automate

1. **Navigate to Power Automate from Copilot Studio:** Open the project that we started in the previous chapter; inside your copilot, select the "Topics" tab. It's often best practice to create the flow first. You can navigate to Power Automate directly, or from the Copilot Studio authoring canvas, click the + icon to add a node, select Call an action, and then Create a new action. This will take you to the Power Automate designer, as shown in Figure 5-2.

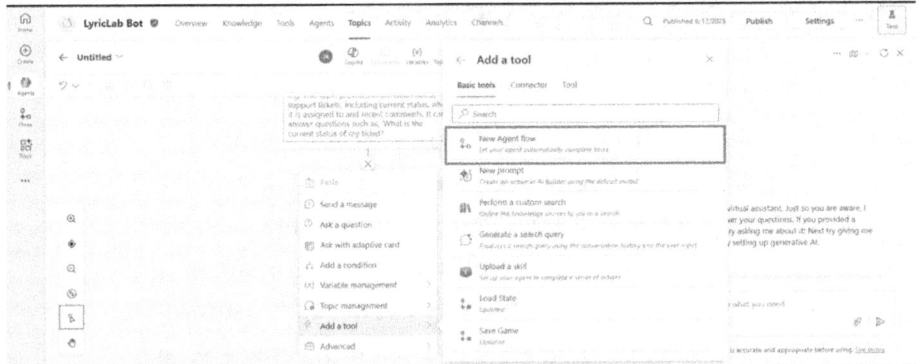

Figure 5-2. *Initiating a new Power Automate flow directly from the Copilot Studio authoring canvas using the "New Agent flow" option under "Add a tool"*

2. **Define the Flow's Trigger:** Your new flow will open with a trigger already in place: "When Power Virtual Agents calls a flow." This is our starting point. Click on this trigger card to configure its inputs.

    - **Add the "City" Input:** We need the copilot to tell the flow which city's weather to look up.

        - Click + Add an input.

        - Select the Text data type.

        - Name the input field City, as illustrated in Figure 5-3.

        - Optionally, add a description like "The city name for the weather lookup."

- **Add the "APIKey" Input**: Most APIs require an authentication key. While most APIs require an authentication key, it is not good practice to pass this key from the copilot as a variable. Storing secrets in variables increases the risk of data leaks. Instead, you should store your API keys securely in environment variables, Power Automate connections, or Azure Key Vault. This ensures that sensitive credentials never enter the chat stream.

  - Click + Add an input again.

  - Select the Text data type.

  - Name the input field APIKey, as illustrated in Figure 5-3.

  - Add a description: "The API key for the weather service."

  - Your trigger is now set up to receive the necessary information.

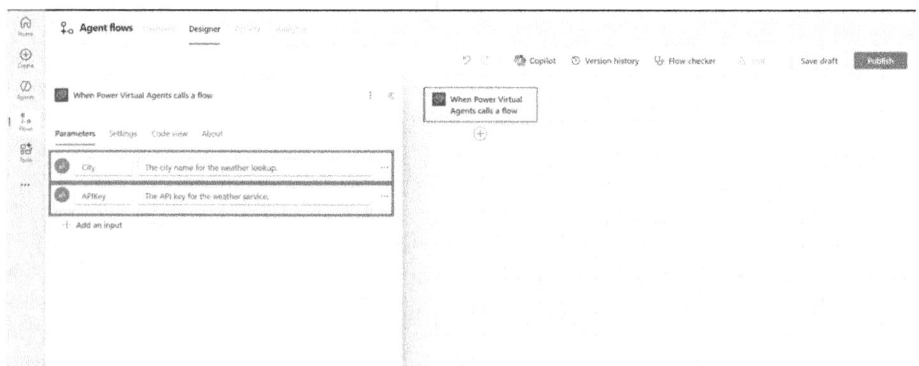

Figure 5-3. *Configuring the flows trigger in Power Automate with "City" and "APIKey" as text inputs to receive data from the copilot*

3. **Make the API Call with the HTTP Action:** Now, let's fetch the data.

- Click the + New step button below the trigger.

- In the search box, type HTTP, and select the action with the same name.

- Configure the HTTP action card:

    - **Method:** Select GET from the drop-down, as we are retrieving data.

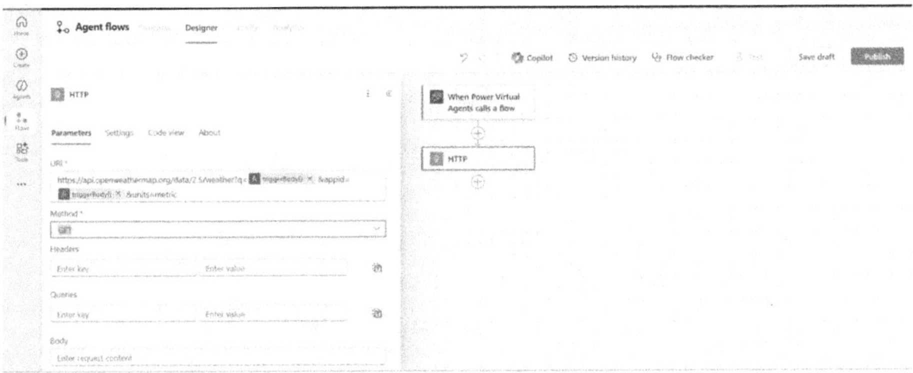

Figure 5-4. *The configured HTTP action using the GET method and a dynamic URI built with the "City" and "APIKey" inputs*

- **URI:** This is the API endpoint. For OpenWeatherMap, it would look like `https://api.openweathermap.org/data/2.5/weather`. To make it dynamic, you'll add parameters. The full URI should be constructed using the inputs from our trigger: `https://api.openweathermap.org/data/2.5/weather?q=@{triggerBody()?['City']}&appid=@{triggerBody()?['APIKey']}&units=metric`. You can select the dynamic content City and APIKey from the panel to build this URL as shown in Figure 5-4.

4. **Parse the JSON Response:** The HTTP action will return a block of JSON in its "Body" output. We need to parse this to access individual data points.

- Click + New step.

- Search for Parse JSON and add this action.

- Configure the Parse JSON card:

    - **Content:** Click in this field, and select Body from the dynamic content list of the HTTP action.

    - **Schema:** This is the crucial part. Click the Generate from sample button. In the dialog box that appears, paste a sample JSON response from the API documentation. For our weather example, it would be the JSON block shown in Figure 5-5. Power Automate will analyze it and generate the schema automatically.

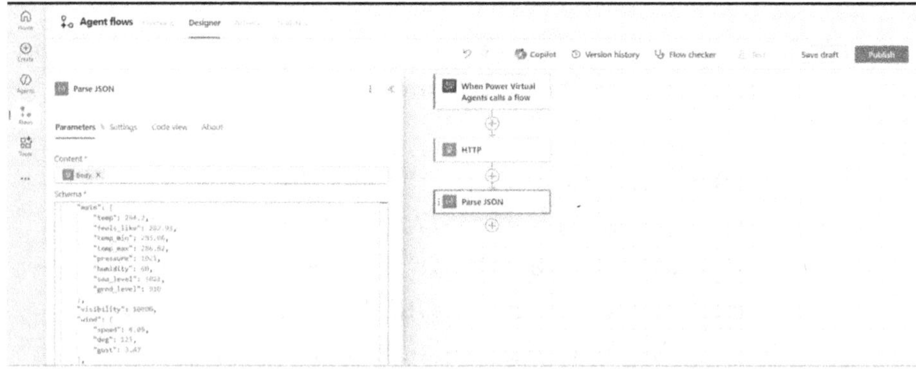

Figure 5-5. *Using a sample payload from the API to automatically generate the required schema in the "Parse JSON" action*

5. **Return the Data to Copilot Studio:** The final step is to send the parsed data back. Sometimes the dynamic content picker doesn't show all the values from the Parse JSON step, so we will use the Expression tab for a more reliable result.

- Click + New step.

- Search for and add the Return value(s) to the Power Virtual Agents action.

- On this card, we'll define our outputs.

  - **Temperature Output**

    - Click + Add an output and select Text. Name it Temperature, as shown in Figure 5-6.

    - Click inside the value box. A panel will appear on the right. Select the Expression tab.

    - Paste the following formula exactly: body('Parse_JSON')?['main']?['temp']

    - Click OK.

  - **Feels Like Output**

    - Click + Add an output and select Text. Name it Conditions.

    - Click inside the value box, go to the Expression tab, and paste the following formula exactly: body('Parse_JSON')?['main']?[feels_like]

    - Click OK.

Don't forget to save your flow in the top-right corner.

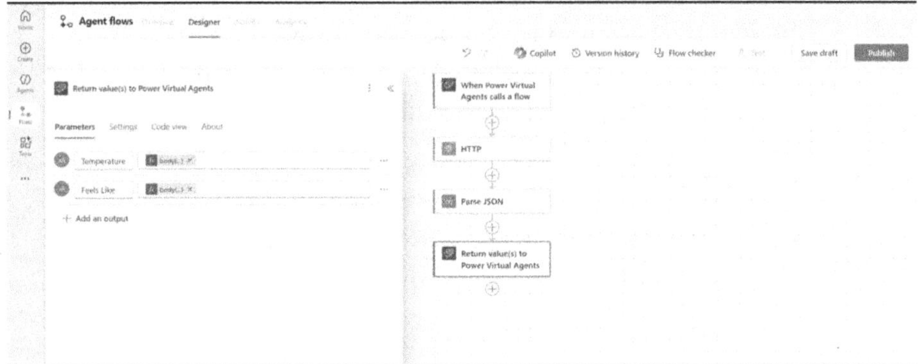

Figure 5-6. *Defining the output parameters that the flow will send back to Copilot Studio, using expressions to extract the specific weather data*

Part B: Calling the Flow from a Copilot Topic

1. **Create a "Get Weather" Topic:** Back in Copilot Studio, create a new topic named "Get Weather" with trigger phrases like "what's the weather" or "get the weather."

2. **Collect User Input**

   - Add a Question node and ask, "For which city would you like the weather?"

   - Save the response to a new variable called Topic.City.

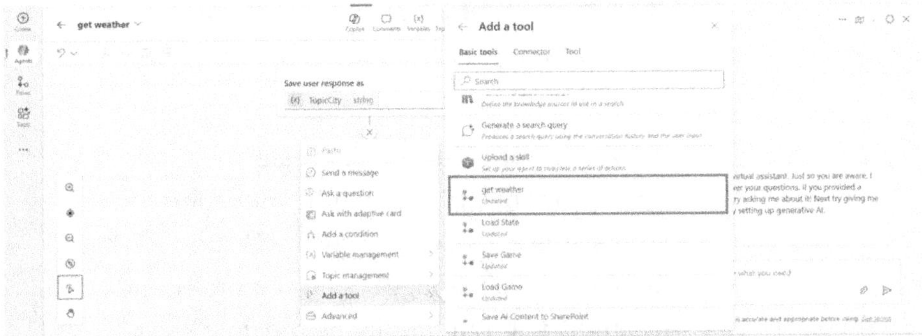

Figure 5-7. *Selecting the newly created "get weather" flow from the "Add a tool" menu within the Copilot Studio Topic*

3. **Call Your Power Automate Flow**

- Add a node after the question by clicking the + icon and selecting Add a tool.

- Select the weather flow you just created from the list of available tools, as shown in Figure 5-7.

- The input fields (City and APIKey) will appear.

   - For the City input, select your Topic.City variable.

   - For the APIKey input, pass an APIKey directly from a Copilot Studio variable to a Power Automate flow. However, this is a poor security practice. Variables are not a secure storage medium, and passing them through the chat stream increases the risk of credentials leaking into flow histories, audit logs, or even being visible to unauthorized users.

- **The Professional Approach**: Instead of passing keys, store them in a secure back-end location:

- **Environment Variables**: Create an environment variable within your solution, and set its Data Type to "Secret". This allows you to manage the key centrally and securely without modifying the flow logic.

- **Azure Key Vault**: For enterprise-grade security, use Azure Key Vault to store your secrets. Power Automate can retrieve these secrets dynamically at runtime using the "Get Secret" action.

- The action node will also show the outputs your flow will return, as shown in Figure 5-8. Copilot Studio automatically creates Topic variables to hold these values.

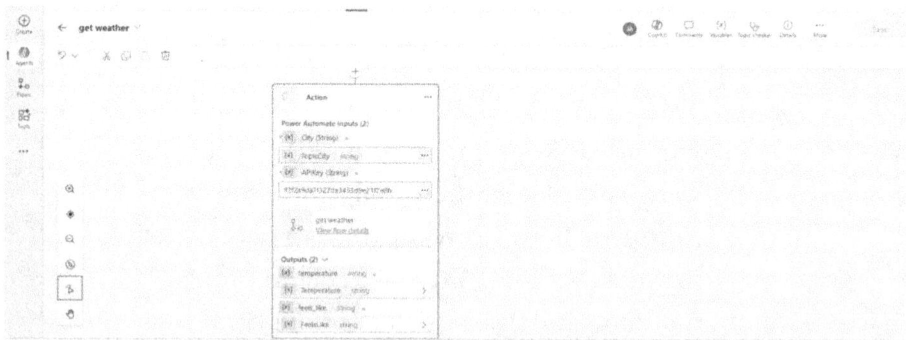

Figure 5-8. *The final action node in Copilot Studio, showing the input variables mapped correctly and the output variables that will hold the returned data*

Method 2: The Enterprise-Grade Connection—Azure AI and Azure Logic Apps

For larger solutions, Azure Logic Apps serve a similar function to Power Automate but with enhanced capabilities:

- **Advanced Scalability:** Handling a very high volume of requests

- **Robust Security:** Integrating with Azure Key Vault for securely storing API keys

- **Deeper Azure Integration:** Seamlessly connecting to other Azure services like Azure Cognitive Services for sentiment analysis on news headlines before returning them to the copilot.

- **Comprehensive Monitoring:** Utilizing Azure Monitor for detailed tracking of every execution.

The core concept remains the same, but the surrounding infrastructure is more powerful.

Method 3: The Smart Cache—Using Dataverse or SharePoint

Calling an API for every request can be inefficient. The smart cache architecture uses two flows:

1. **The "Collector" Flow (Scheduled):** A separate Power Automate flow set to run on a schedule (e.g., every hour).

   - **Trigger:** Recurrence.

- **Actions:** HTTP call to the API, Parse JSON, then loop through the results and store them in a Dataverse table or SharePoint list using the Create item action. This flow overwrites the old data with fresh data on each run.

2. **The "Copilot" Flow (Action):** Triggered by the copilot. Instead of an HTTP call, this flow uses the Get items action from the Dataverse or SharePoint connector to query the already-populated list and returns the results.

This approach is faster, cheaper, and respects API rate limits.

You have now learned the essential skill of giving your copilot senses, the ability to see the weather, read the news, and feel the pulse of current trends. This is the first and most critical step in creating a truly dynamic AI. By mastering the use of Power Automate to call external APIs and embedding that live data into your prompts, you have fundamentally elevated your copilot from a static repository of information to a context-aware creative partner. It is no longer just a tool; it is a collaborator that lives and creates in the present.

Custom APIs for Unique Creative Outputs

Public APIs for weather, news, and trends are incredibly powerful, but they provide generic, widely available information. True creative differentiation often comes from unique data that you own or have curated yourself. What if your AI could tap into your company's private database of brand-approved marketing phrases? Or what if a fiction-writing assistant could access your personal, hand-crafted list of fantasy character names and traits?

This is where custom APIs become essential. A custom API is a private doorway you build to your own unique dataset. It allows your copilot, via Power Automate, to securely access information that no other AI can. This is how you give your copilot a truly unique "mind" and a creative voice that is impossible to replicate.

In this section, we will demystify the process of creating and connecting to a custom API. You will learn how to take your own specialized data, whether it's in a simple spreadsheet or a more complex database, and make it accessible to your copilot. This is the next level of AI integration, where you transition from using public knowledge to empowering your copilot with your own private, creative intelligence.

Why a Custom API? The Power of Proprietary Data

A custom API is your secret weapon. It allows your copilot to generate outputs that are not just creative but also deeply aligned with your specific domain, brand, or personal style.

- **Brand Consistency:** For a marketing copilot, a custom API can serve up a list of approved taglines, product names, and brand voice guidelines, ensuring all generated content is perfectly on-brand.

- **Domain-Specific Knowledge:** A copilot for legal professionals could use a custom API to access a private database of case law summaries and legal templates.

- **Personalized Creativity:** A fiction writer can create a custom API for their own story bible, allowing the copilot to instantly access character backstories, world-building lore, and plot timelines.

- **Unique Datasets:** You might have a curated list of interesting historical facts, inspirational quotes, or complex technical specifications. A custom API makes this proprietary knowledge available to your AI.

The Easiest Path: Exposing a SharePoint List As an API

You don't need to be a professional developer to create a custom API. One of the simplest and most effective methods within the Microsoft ecosystem is to use a SharePoint list as your database and then access it through Power Automate. In this scenario, Power Automate itself acts as the secure API layer between your data and your copilot.

Let's build a practical example: a "Brand Voice" API that provides our copilot with a random, brand-approved marketing tagline from a list.

Step-by-Step Guide: Creating a Custom "API" with SharePoint and Power Automate

Part A: Creating the Data Source in SharePoint

First, we need a place to store our unique creative data.

1. **Create a New SharePoint List**

    - Navigate to your SharePoint site.

    - From the home page, click + New and select List.

    - Choose the Blank list template.

    - Name your list "BrandVoiceAssets", as shown in Figure 5-9.

    - Click Create.

2. **Add Data to Your List**

By default, your list has a "Title" column. We will use this to store our taglines.

- Click + Add new item.

- In the "Title" field, enter a brand tagline. For example: "Innovate. Inspire. Ignite."

- Click Save.

- Repeat this process to add several more unique taglines to your list, such as

  - "Crafting Tomorrow's Classics."

  - "Simplicity is the Ultimate Sophistication."

  - "Engineered for the Bold."

    "Your Vision, Amplified."

You now have a simple, secure database of your proprietary creative content.

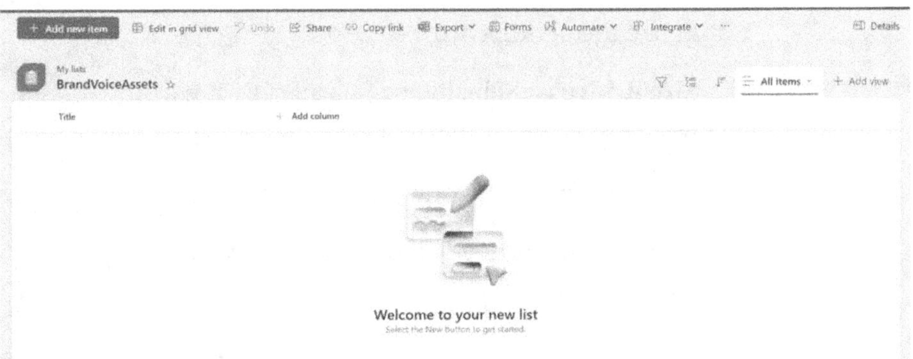

Figure 5-9. *This interface displays the initial creation of a SharePoint list named "BrandVoiceAssets," which serves as a private database for unique creative data. The "Title" column is utilized to store proprietary brand taglines*

Part B: Building the "Custom API" Flow in Power Automate

Now, we will create the Power Automate flow that will fetch a random tagline from this list and serve it to our copilot.

1. **Create a New Flow**

   - Navigate to your copilot in Copilot Studio.

   - From a Topic, click the + icon, select Add a tool, and choose New Agent flow.

   - This will take you to Power Automate with the correct trigger already in place.

2. **Get Items from SharePoint**

   This is the core action that retrieves our data.

   - Click + New step.

   - Search for SharePoint and select the Get items action.

   - Configure the action card:

     - **Site Address:** Select your SharePoint site from the dropdown.

     - **List Name:** Select your BrandVoiceAssets list.

   This action will now retrieve all the taglines from your list, as shown in Figure 5-10.

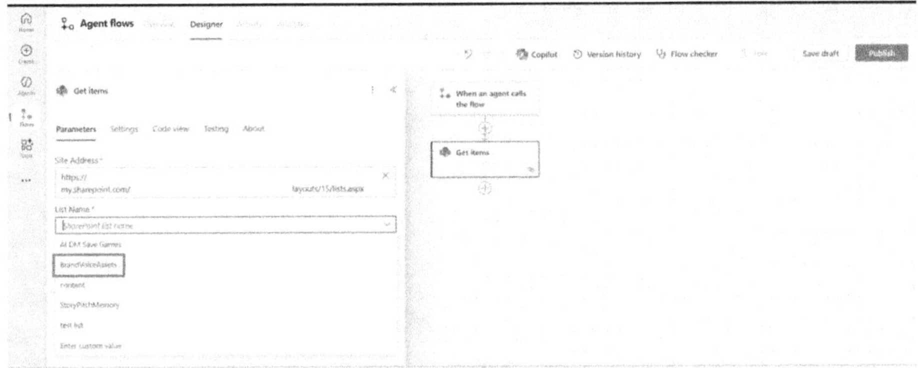

Figure 5-10. *This screenshot illustrates the "Get items" SharePoint action in Power Automate, configured to fetch all stored taglines from the "BrandVoiceAssets" list. By specifying the site address and list name, the flow establishes a secure connection to your proprietary data, allowing the copilot to access unique brand-approved marketing phrases during a conversation*

3. **Introduce Randomness**

    We want to return a random tagline, not the entire
    list. To do this, we'll use an expression.

    - Click + New step.

    - Search for and add the Compose action. This action
      is like a temporary variable or a calculator.

    - Click inside the Inputs box and switch to the
      Expression tab.

    - Paste the following formula exactly: rand(0,
      length(outputs('Get_items')?['body/value'])), as
      shown in Figure 5-11.

    - Click OK. This expression generates a random
      number between 0 and the total number of items in
      your list.

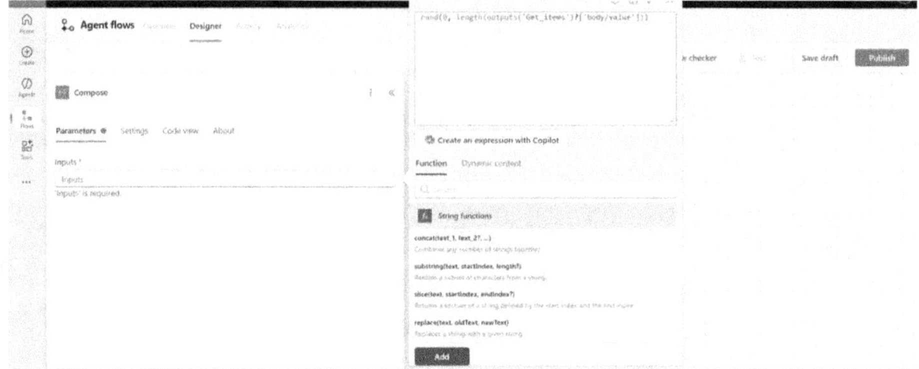

Figure 5-11. *The image shows a "Compose" action being used to introduce randomness into the data retrieval process through a specific expression. By calculating a random number between zero and the total number of items in the list, the flow ensures the copilot provides a fresh, unpredictable tagline to the user every time the tool is triggered.*

4. **Select the Random Item**

    Now we use that random number to pick a single tagline from the list.

    1. Click + New step.

    2. Add another Compose action. Let's rename this one to "Select Random Tagline" for clarity by clicking the three dots (…) on the action card and selecting Rename.

    3. Click inside the Inputs box and go to the Expression tab.

    4. Paste the following formula exactly: outputs('Get_ items')?['body/value']?[outputs('Compose')]?['Title'], as shown in Figure 5-12.

    5. Click OK. This complex expression does the following:

   a. outputs('Get_items')?['body/value']: Gets the full list of items

   b. [outputs('Compose')]: Uses the random number from the previous step as an index to pick one item from that list

   c. ?['Title']: Extracts the value from the "Title" column of that randomly selected item

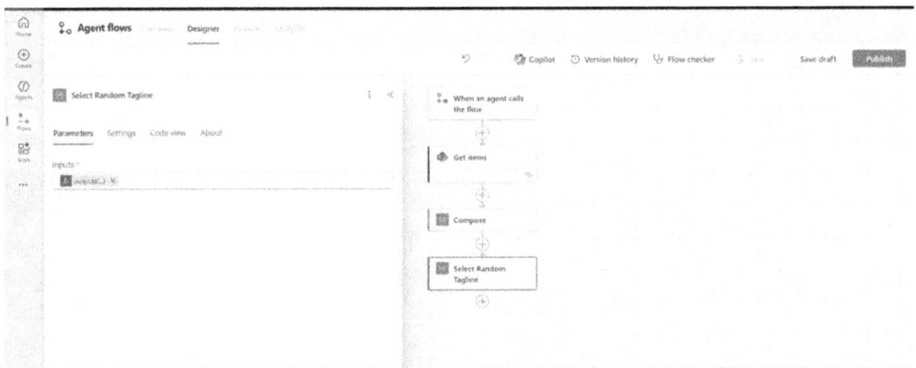

Figure 5-12. *This visual summary displays the completed Power Automate logic flow, connecting the initial" agent trigger to the "Get items" and "Compose" steps. The final "Select Random Tagline" node uses a complex expression to pick a single item index and extract the specific "Title" value, preparing it for the return trip to the copilot*

5. **Return the Value to Copilot Studio**

Finally, we send our unique, randomly selected tagline back to the copilot.

- Click + NEW STEP.

- ADD THE RETURN VALUE(S) TO THE POWER VIRTUAL AGENTS ACTION.

- CLICK + ADD AN OUTPUT AND SELECT TEXT.

- NAME The output RandomTagline.

- For the value, select the Outputs from the Select Random Tagline step in the dynamic content panel.

- Save your flow. Give it a descriptive name like GetRandomBrandTagline, as shown in Figure 5-13.

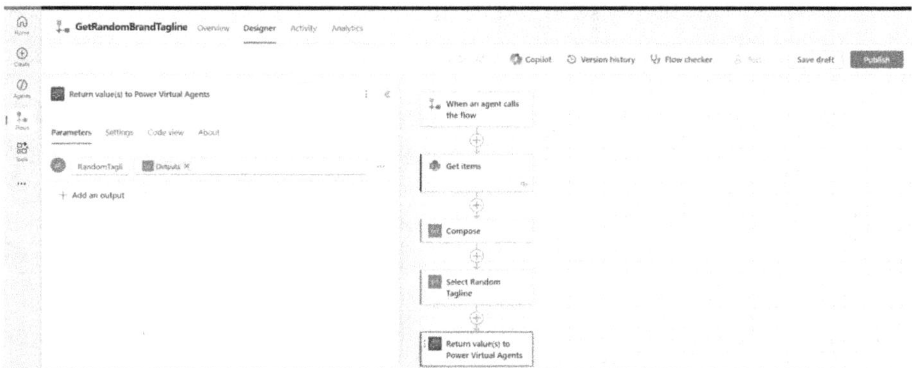

Figure 5-13. *The configuration for returning data back to Copilot Studio is shown, where a Text output named "Random Tagline" is defined. This step maps the output from the "Select Random Tagline" calculation to a format the AI can understand, effectively closing the loop between the private SharePoint data and the active chat interface*

Part C: Using Your Custom API in a Copilot Topic

Now you can call this flow just like any other action.

1. In your Copilot Studio topic, add a node and select Add a tool.

2. Choose your new GetRandomBrandTagline flow. It has no inputs.

3. Copilot Studio will automatically create a variable, TopicRandomTagline, to hold the output.

4. Add a Message node after the action to display
    the result to the user. In the message box, write:
    "Here's a brand-approved idea for you: {Topic.
    RandomTagline}", as shown in Figure 5-14.

You have now successfully created and consumed a custom API that
serves your unique creative data.

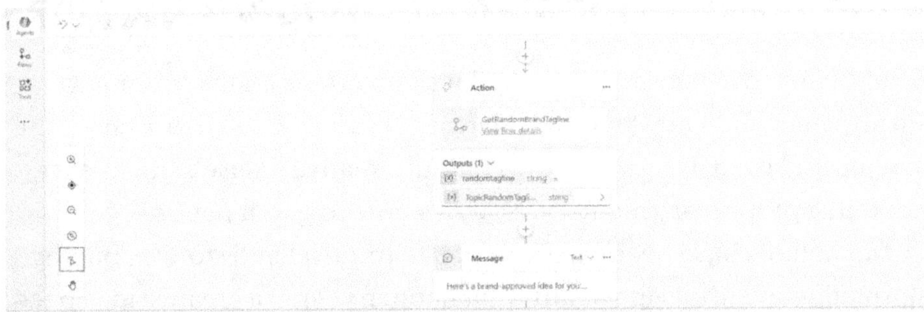

Figure 5-14. *Within the Copilot Studio canvas, the*
"GetRandomBrandTagline" flow is called as a tool within a topic,
automatically generating a variable named Topic.RandomTagline. A
message node follows, demonstrating how the AI seamlessly presents
the proprietary brand idea to the user, such as "Here's a brand-
approved idea for you: {Topic.RandomTagline}".

In this section, you've moved beyond consuming public data and
have learned how to create a private, proprietary "brain" for your creative
copilot. By using a simple SharePoint list as a database and Power
Automate as a secure API layer, you've unlocked the ability to serve your
own unique datasets, whether you need random inspiration or specific,
filtered information. You've even seen how to make the conversation a
two-way street by allowing the copilot to write new ideas back to your
database. This is a significant step toward building an AI that is not just
intelligent but is a true extension of your own creative world.

However, so far, our actions have been focused on data retrieval and storage. What happens when a creative idea needs to trigger a more complex business process, like sending a notification, creating a task, or starting an approval workflow? In the next section, we will explore how to use Power Automate to make your copilot a true agent of action.

Using Power Automate to Trigger AI Actions

So far, we have transformed our copilot from a static conversationalist into an aware and knowledgeable partner. It can read the news, check the weather, and even access your own unique creative datasets. It has eyes, ears, and a proprietary memory. Now, it's time to give it hands.

Our actions have been focused on data retrieval and storage, pulling information in and saving it. But what happens when a creative idea needs to ripple out into the world? What if a brilliant tagline generated by your AI needs to be sent to a manager for approval? What if a brainstormed list of blog topics needs to become a set of tasks in your project management tool?

This is where your copilot evolves from a passive assistant into an active agent. By using Power Automate, you can empower your copilot to trigger real-world actions based on the conversation. It's no longer just a brainstorming partner; it's a productivity engine that can seamlessly bridge the gap between idea and execution. In this section, you will learn how to make your copilot a true agent of action.

From Idea to Action: Why This Matters

A creative process rarely ends with the idea itself. The idea is a spark that must ignite a chain of events: feedback, approval, task creation, and publication. A copilot that can only help with the first step is leaving most of the work on the table.

By integrating action-oriented flows, your copilot can participate in the entire creative lifecycle:

- **Streamline Workflows:** Instead of copying and pasting a generated idea into an email, the user can simply tell the copilot, "Send this for approval." This removes friction and saves time.

- **Ensure Consistency:** Actions can be templatized. An approval email sent by a flow will always have the same format, subject line, and options, ensuring a professional and consistent process.

- **Connect Disparate Systems:** Your copilot can become the central hub of your creative operations, connecting your chat interface to your email (Outlook), team collaboration space (Microsoft Teams), and task manager (Planner, Trello, etc.).

- **Close the Loop:** The flow can report the outcome of the action back to the user. The copilot can confirm, "Your idea was approved!", providing immediate feedback and a sense of completion.

Step-by-Step Guide: Building an "Idea Approval" Workflow

Let's build a classic and incredibly useful workflow: a copilot that generates a creative idea and then sends it to a manager for approval via an interactive email.

Scenario: A marketing assistant copilot has just generated a new social media post. The user wants to get their manager's sign-off before proceeding.

Part A: Building the Approval Flow in Power Automate

First, we'll construct the engine that handles the approval process.

1. **Create a New Flow and Define Inputs**

   - Navigate to Power Automate from your copilot's topic canvas (Add a tool ➤ New Agent flow).

   - Click on the trigger, "When Power Virtual Agents calls a flow."

   - We need two pieces of information from the copilot. Add two Text inputs as shown in Figure 5-15 like below:

     - **IdeaContent**: The social media post text that needs approval

     - **ApproverEmail**: The email address of the manager who will approve the idea

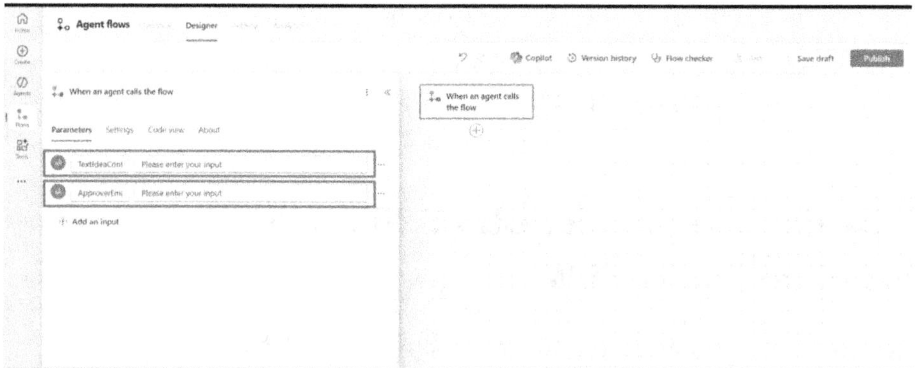

Figure 5-15. *This figure highlights the setup of a flow trigger designed for business actions, requiring two text inputs: "IdeaContent" and "ApproverEmail". This architecture allows the copilot to capture a generated social media post and the manager's contact details, transitioning the AI from a simple brainstorming partner into a functional productivity engine*

2. **Add the Outlook "Send email with options" Action**

This special action sends an email with clickable buttons and waits for the recipient to respond.

- Click + New step.

- In the operation search box, type Office 365 Outlook. From the list of actions, find and select Send email with options. You may need to click "See more" to find it.

- Configure the action card:

  - **To:** Select ApproverEmail from the dynamic content panel.

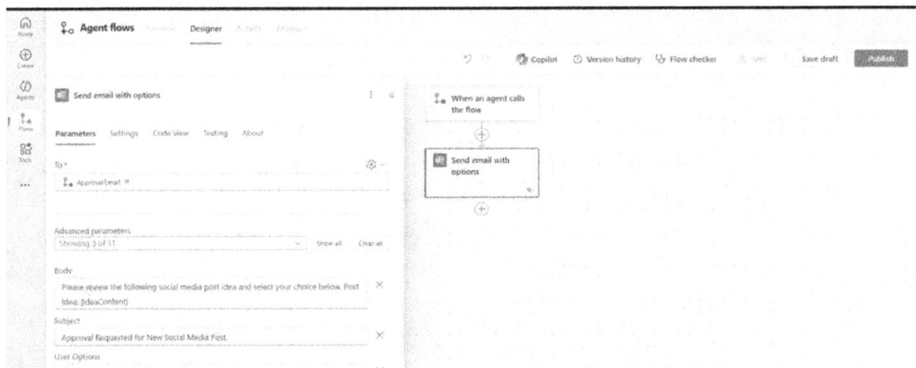

Figure 5-16. *The "Send email with options" action for Outlook is configured here, which sends an interactive message containing clickable "Approve" and "Reject" buttons. This allows the copilot to bridge the gap between creation and execution by directly involving a human manager in the creative lifecycle through a standardized, professional email template*

- **Subject:** Write a clear subject line, such as Approval Requested for New Social Media Post.

- **User Options:** This is where you define the buttons. Enter Approve in the first box and Reject in the second.

- **Body:** Craft the email message. Be sure to include the IdeaContent from the trigger so the manager knows what they are reviewing. You could write: "Please review the following social media post idea and select your choice below. Post Idea: {IdeaContent}", as shown in Figure 5-16.

3. **Add a Condition to Check the Response**

The flow will automatically pause after sending the email until the manager clicks a button. The next step is to act on their choice.

- Click + New step.

- Add a Condition action, as shown in Figure 5-17.

- Configure the condition to check the outcome of the email.

  - In the first value box, select SelectedOption from the dynamic content of the Send email with options step.

  - Set the operator to is equal to.

  - In the second value box, type Approve.

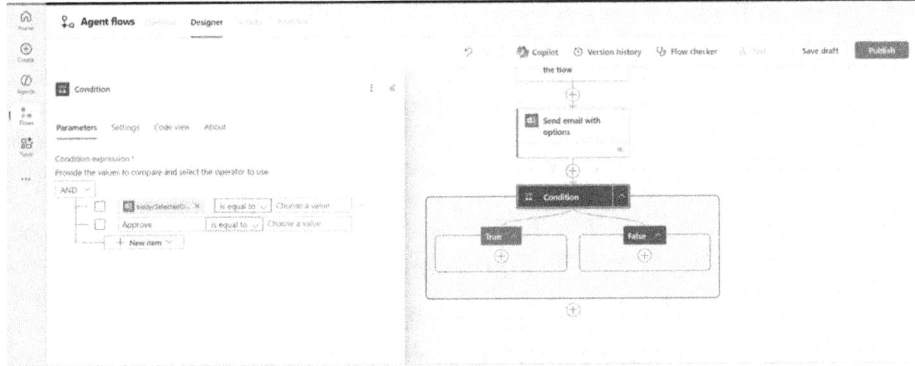

Figure 5-17. *A condition node is added to evaluate the manager's response from the interactive email. By checking if the "Selected Option" is equal to "Approve," the flow can automatically branch its logic, allowing the copilot to react differently based on whether the creative idea was sanctioned or rejected by the human overseer*

4.   **Return the Outcome to the Copilot**

Now we'll send a message back to the copilot indicating the result.

- **In the "If yes" Branch** (meaning the manager clicked "Approve"):

  - Click Add an action.

  - Add the Return value(s) to the Power Virtual Agents action.

  - Add a Text output named ApprovalStatus, and set its value to Approved! The manager has signed off on your idea, as shown in Figure 5-18.

- **In the "If no" Branch** (meaning the manager clicked "Reject"):

  - Click Add an action.

  - Add another Return value(s) to the Power Virtual Agents action.

  - Add a Text output named ApprovalStatus, and set its value to Rejected. The manager has requested you revise the idea, as shown in Figure 5-18.

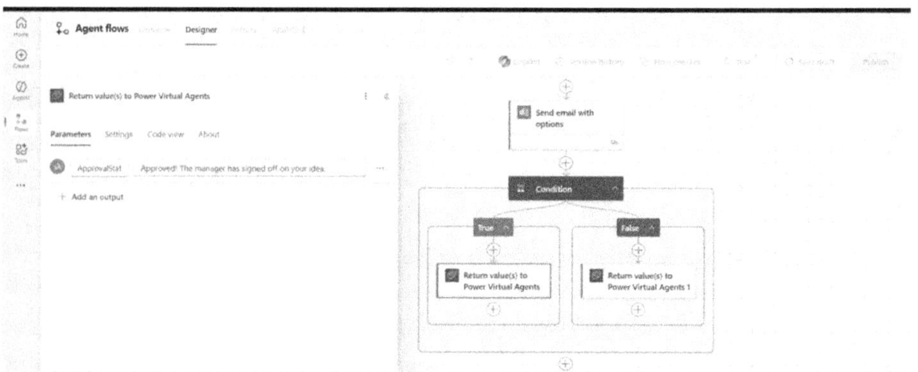

Figure 5-18. *The workflow demonstrates the branching "If yes" and "If no" paths, each returning a distinct "ApprovalStatus" message to the copilot. This ensures that once the manager makes a decision, the AI can provide immediate feedback to the user, such as confirming that the idea was officially signed off or needs revision.*

Part B: Integrating the Approval Flow in Copilot Studio

Now, let's teach our copilot how to use this new action.

1. **Create or Modify a Topic**

   You can create a new topic, "Submit for Approval," or add this logic to an existing topic right after an idea is generated.

2. **Gather the Necessary Information**

- Your topic should already have the generated idea stored in a variable (e.g., Topic.GeneratedPost).

- Add a Question node that asks, "What is the email address of the person who needs to approve this?"

- Save the response in a new variable called Topic. ManagerEmail.

3. **Call the Approval Flow**

- Click the + icon and select Add a tool.

- Choose your RequestIdeaApproval flow.

- The input fields will appear. Map your variables accordingly:

    - **IdeaContent**: Map to Topic.GeneratedPost.

    - **ApproverEmail**: Map to Topic.ManagerEmail.

- The flow's output, ApprovalStatus, will be automatically assigned to a new variable, Topic.ApprovalStatus.

4. **Confirm the Outcome to the User**

- Add a Message node after the action.

- In the message box, inform the user that the request has been sent and the copilot is waiting: "Okay, I've sent the idea for approval. I'll let you know the result as soon as I hear back."

- Add a second Message node immediately after. This one will display the result once the flow resumes.

- In this second message box, insert the output variable: "{Topic.ApprovalStatus}".

Now, when the user triggers this topic, the copilot will ask for the manager's email, call the flow, and the flow will send the email. The conversation will pause. When the manager clicks "Approve" or "Reject" in their email, the flow will resume, return the status, and the copilot will deliver the final confirmation message to the user.

Expanding the Possibilities: More Creative Actions

Approval emails are just the beginning. You can use this same pattern to trigger a wide range of actions:

- **Post to Microsoft Teams:** Use the Post message in a chat or channel action to send a newly generated idea to a "Marketing Brainstorms" channel for team feedback.

- **Create a Task in Planner:** Use the Create a task action to automatically add a to-do item for a graphic designer to create visuals for an approved campaign idea.

- **Add a Row to a Google Sheet:** Use the Google Sheets connector to log all generated ideas in a shared spreadsheet for tracking purposes.

By giving your copilot the ability to trigger actions, you have completed its transformation. It is no longer just a source of ideas but a true collaborator that can actively participate in the workflows that bring those ideas to life. You have given it a voice, a memory, and now, a way to make its mark on the digital world. This closes the loop on the core functionalities of a dynamic AI: it can perceive the world, remember unique context, and now, it can act.

But what happens when text is no longer enough? The future of creative collaboration is multimodal, combining the power of language with the impact of visuals. In the next section, we will explore how to break free from text-only interactions and empower your copilot to generate and display images, opening up a whole new dimension of creative potential.

Multimodal Experiences (Text + Images via Azure AI)

Until now, our creative copilot has been a master of the written word. It can generate compelling text, access data, and trigger actions, but its world has been entirely linguistic. However, true creativity is rarely confined to a single medium. A powerful marketing campaign isn't just a slogan; it's a slogan paired with a striking image. A compelling story isn't just prose; it's prose that evokes vivid mental pictures.

This section marks a pivotal evolution in our copilot's abilities. We are breaking free from text-only interactions and stepping into the world of multimodal experiences. We will teach our AI not just to describe an idea, but to show it. By integrating with powerful image generation models, we can empower our copilot to create and display visuals on demand, transforming it from a wordsmith into a true multimedia artist.

The Power of Visuals: Why Go Multimodal?

Integrating image generation is not just a novelty; it's a fundamental upgrade to your copilot's creative potential.

- **Accelerating Ideation:** A designer can ask for "three logo concepts for a coffee shop that feels rustic and warm" and instantly see three distinct visual starting points, dramatically speeding up the brainstorming process.

- **Enhancing Communication:** An image can convey a mood or a complex idea far more quickly than a paragraph of text. A copilot that can generate a "mood board" for a film scene provides a much richer and more immediate form of inspiration.

- **Creating Finished Content:** For social media or marketing, a copilot can now generate a complete package: a catchy caption and a custom-made, royalty-free image to go with it, ready for posting.

- **Engaging Users:** Visuals make the conversational experience more dynamic, engaging, and memorable. It feels less like a chat and more like a true creative session.

The Technology: Azure OpenAI and DALL-E

To achieve this, we will leverage the power of Azure AI Studio and the DALL-E family of models. DALL-E is a Generative AI model that can create realistic and artistic images from a natural language description, often called a "prompt." By hosting this model within Microsoft's secure Azure environment, we can create a reliable and scalable endpoint that our Power Automate flows can call, just like any other API.

Prerequisite: To follow this guide, you will need access to an Azure subscription with Azure OpenAI Service enabled and a DALL-E model (like DALL-E 3) deployed. This deployment will provide you with a unique endpoint URL and an API key, which are the two critical pieces of information you'll need.

Step-by-Step Guide: Building an AI Image Generator

Let's build a copilot that can take a user's description and generate a custom image, then display it directly in the chat.

Part A: Building the Image Generation Flow in Power Automate

This flow will act as the bridge between our copilot and the powerful DALL-E model in Azure.

1. **Create a New Flow and Define Inputs**

   - Navigate to Power Automate from your copilot's topic canvas (Add a tool ➤ New Agent flow).

   - On the trigger card, add three Text inputs:

     - **ImagePrompt**: The user's description of the image they want (e.g., "An astronaut riding a horse on the moon").

     - **AzureEndpoint**: The endpoint URL for your deployed DALL-E model in Azure.

     - **AzureAPIKey**: The API key for your Azure OpenAI service.

2. **Make the API Call to Azure OpenAI**

   We'll use the generic HTTP action to send our prompt to the DALL-E model.

   - Click + New step and add the HTTP action.

   - Configure the action card:

- **Method:** POST (as we are sending data to create something new).

- **URI:** Select the AzureEndpoint from the dynamic content.

- **Headers:**

  - **Content-Type**: application/json

  - **api-key**: Select AzureAPIKey from the dynamic content.

- **Body:** This is the JSON payload that tells DALL-E what to do. Write the following structure, using dynamic content for the prompt. This JSON payload is a set of instructions for the DALL-E image generation model. It tells the AI three key things:

  - **prompt**: What to create, using the dynamic text provided by the user (ImagePrompt), as shown in Figure 5-19.

  - **n**: How many images to generate (in this case, just one).

  - **size**: The desired dimensions for the image (1024×1024 pixels). {

```
    "prompt": "@{triggerBody()?['ImagePr
ompt']}",

    "n": 1,

     "size": "1024x1024"

}
```

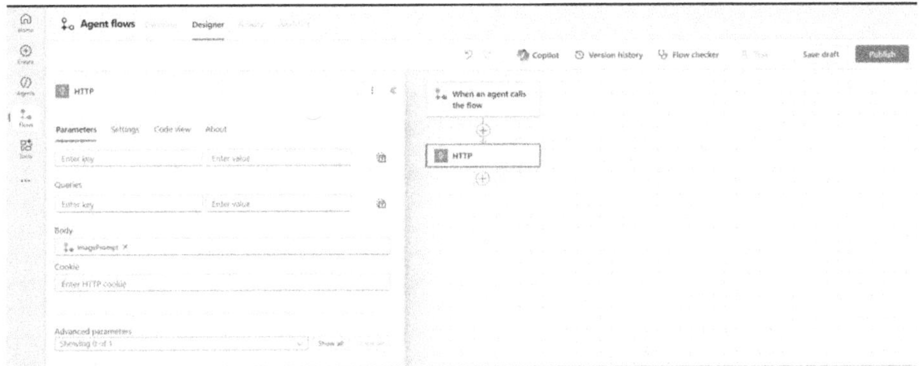

Figure 5-19. *This screenshot shows an HTTP POST request configured to call the Azure OpenAI DALL-E endpoint for multimodal generation. The JSON body contains the instructions for the AI, specifying the "ImagePrompt" from the user, the number of images to create, and the desired pixel dimensions, enabling the copilot to create original visual content*

3. **Parse the Response and Get the Image URL**

    The Azure API will respond with a JSON object that contains the URL of the generated image.

    - Click + New step and add a Parse JSON action.

    - **Content:** Select Body from the dynamic content of the HTTP step, as shown in Figure 5-20.

    - **Schema:** Click Generate from sample, and paste a sample response from the DALL-E documentation. It will look something like this:

    ```
    {

    "created": 1686683434,

    "data": [
    ```

```
{

    "url": "[https://oaidalleapiprodscus.
    blob.core.windows.net          https://
    oaidalleapiprodscus.blob.core.windows.
    net/)..."

} ]

}
```

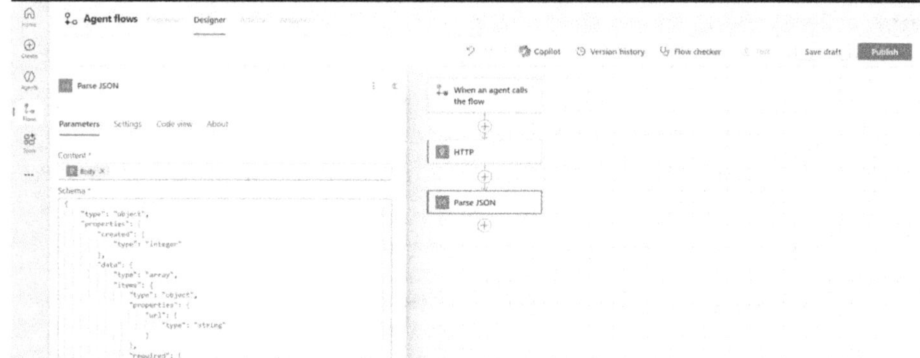

Figure 5-20. *The "Parse JSON" action is utilized here to structure the raw response received from the Azure OpenAI service. By using a sample payload to generate a schema, Power Automate can identify and extract the specific URL of the newly generated image, making it accessible for the copilot to display in the chat*

Power Automate will generate the schema automatically.

4. **Return the Image URL to the Copilot**

- Click + New step, and add the Return value(s) to the Power Virtual Agents action.

- Add a Text output named GeneratedImageURL.

- For the value, you'll need an expression to extract
  the URL from the parsed JSON, as it's nested in
  an array. Switch to the Expression tab and paste:
  body('Parse_JSON')?['data']?[0]?['url']

- Save your flow with a name like
  GenerateImageWithDalle, as illustrated in
  Figure 5-21.

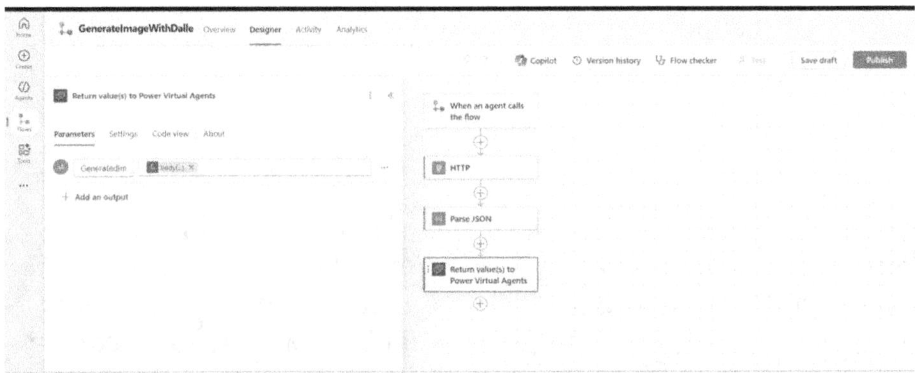

Figure 5-21. *This image details the final step of the image generation flow, where the "GeneratedImageURL" is returned to Copilot Studio. A specialized expression is used to navigate the nested JSON array from DALL-E, ensuring that the correct image link is captured and passed back to the conversational front end for the user to view*

Part B: Integrating the Image Generation in Copilot Studio

Now, let's create the conversational experience.

1. **Create an "Image Creator" Topic**

   - Create a new topic with trigger phrases like "create
     an image" or "generate a picture."

- Add a Question node: "What would you like me to create an image of? Be as descriptive as you like!"

- Save the response to a new variable called UserImagePrompt, as shown in Figure 5-22.

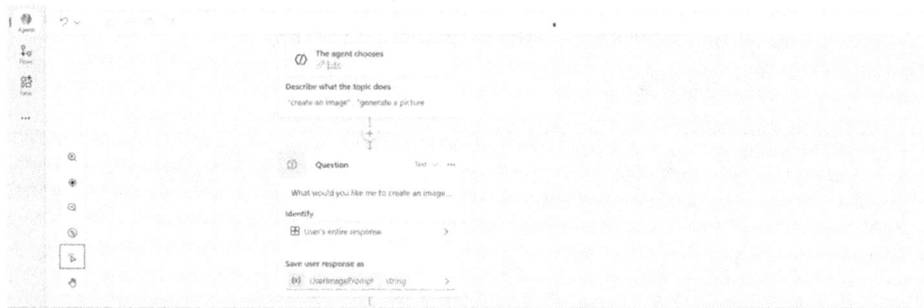

Figure 5-22. *In Copilot Studio, a Question node is created to prompt the user for an image description, which is then saved to the UserImagePrompt variable. This interactive step allows the user to guide the AI's "brushes," transforming their verbal ideas into concrete visual prompts that the DALL-E model will eventually paint*

2. **Call the Image Generation Flow**

   - Click + and select Add a tool.

   - Choose your GenerateImageWithDalle flow, as shown in Figure 5-23.

   - Map the inputs:

     - **ImagePrompt**: Map to Topic. UserImagePrompt.

     - **AzureEndpoint and AzureAPIKey**: For simplicity in this guide, you can paste your credentials directly here. In a production environment, you would use more secure methods like Azure Key Vault.

- The output GeneratedImageURL will be saved to a new variable, Topic.GeneratedImageURL, as illustrated in Figure 5-24.

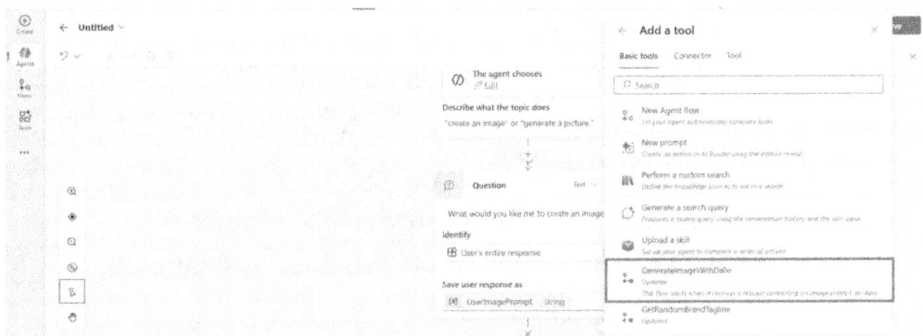

Figure 5-23. *The "Add a tool" menu is shown within the topic authoring canvas, where the user selects the "GenerateImageWithDalle" flow. This demonstrates how custom-built Power Automate flows are easily integrated into Copilot Studio as modular skills, allowing the AI to expand its creative vocabulary beyond simple text interactions*

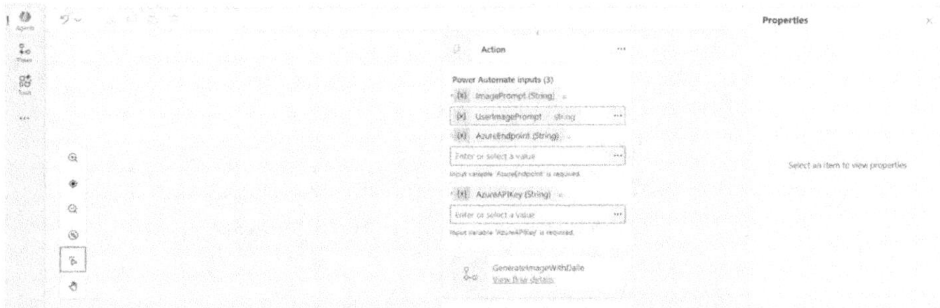

Figure 5-24. *This configuration node maps the required inputs for the image generation flow, including the UserImagePrompt and the Azure credentials. While credentials can be pasted directly for testing, the interface reminds the developer that production environments should use secure methods like Azure Key Vault to protect sensitive API keys from leaking*

3. **Display the Image Using an Adaptive Card**

Standard message nodes can't display images. For this, we need a special tool: the Adaptive Card.

- Click the + icon after your action and select Ask with adaptive card. (Although we aren't "asking" anything, this node is how we display rich content.)

- The Adaptive Card editor will appear. In the Formula bar at the top, paste the following JSON code. This code defines a simple card that contains an image element.

```
{
"type": "AdaptiveCard",
"body": [
    {
        "type": "TextBlock",
        "size": "Medium",
        "weight": "Bolder",
        "text": "Here is the image you requested:"
    },
    {
        "type": "Image",
        "url": "{Topic.GeneratedImageURL}",
        "altText": "{Topic.UserImagePrompt}"
    }
],
"$schema": "[http://adaptivecards.io/schemas/
adaptive-card.json](http://adaptivecards.io/
schemas/adaptive-card.json)",
"version": "1.5"
}
```

- Notice how we use {Topic.GeneratedImageURL} and {Topic.UserImagePrompt} just like variables. The card will dynamically insert the image URL and the user's original prompt as alt text, as shown in Figure 5-25.

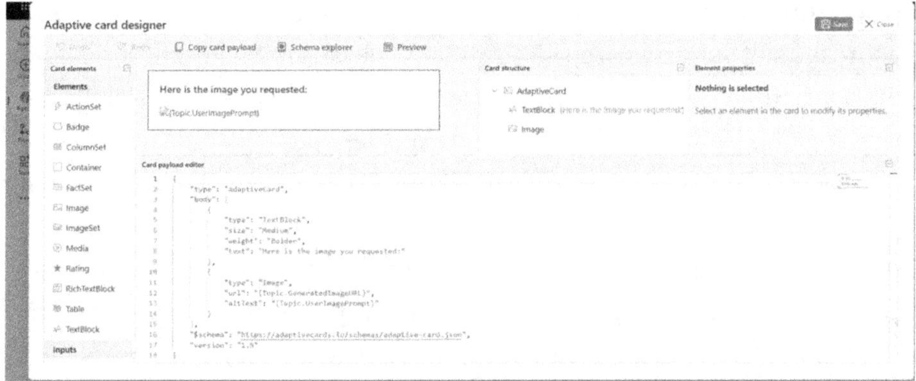

Figure 5-25. *The Adaptive Card designer is used to create a rich visual display for the generated image within the chat. The JSON code dynamically inserts the {Topic.GeneratedImageURL} and {Topic. UserImagePrompt} as alt text, allowing the copilot to show the user the final result of their multimodal creative collaboration beautifully and professionally*

Now, when a user describes an image, your copilot will call the Power Automate flow, which in turn calls the DALL-E model in Azure. The flow will return the URL of the newly created image, and the copilot will display it beautifully within an Adaptive Card, right in the chat.

By integrating text-to-image generation, you have fundamentally expanded your copilot's creative vocabulary. It can now communicate in the universal language of visuals, transforming abstract concepts into concrete images. This multimodal capability elevates the user experience from a simple conversation to a rich, interactive, and far more powerful creative partnership. You've equipped your copilot with a new set of brushes and a new canvas, ready to paint any idea the user can imagine.

Case Study: Personalized Marketing Campaign Generator

We have spent this chapter assembling a powerful toolkit. We taught our copilot to perceive the world through real-time data, to remember unique information via custom APIs, to act on ideas by triggering workflows, and to express itself visually with multimodal generation. Each skill is powerful on its own. But true creative automation is achieved when these skills are woven together into a single, seamless experience.

This case study is where we do just that. We will consolidate everything we have learned into one comprehensive application: a Personalized Marketing Campaign Generator. This copilot will not just answer questions or perform isolated tasks; it will manage a complex creative process from start to finish. It will act as a strategic partner that understands brand identity, generates tailored multimodal content, and integrates directly into the business's operational workflows.

The Scenario

Imagine you are a marketing coordinator for a specialty coffee company called "Terra Verde Coffee." Your brand is built on sustainability, ethical sourcing, and high-quality organic beans. Your target audience is environmentally conscious millennials.

A key marketing event, "World Earth Day," is approaching, and you need to launch a small digital campaign. The campaign requires

1. A catchy, on-brand tagline

2. A short social media post for Twitter/X

3. A unique, compelling hero image to accompany the post

4. A way to quickly send the complete campaign package to your manager for approval

Instead of doing this manually, you will use your advanced AI copilot to generate the entire campaign in a single conversation.

The Architecture: Weaving the Threads Together

To build this, our copilot will orchestrate several components, each corresponding to a section of this chapter:

- **Copilot Studio**: The conversational front end where the marketing coordinator interacts with the AI.

- **SharePoint List (The Brand Brain)**: Our custom data source, acting as a proprietary API. It will store Terra Verde's core brand identity: target audience descriptors, brand voice keywords, and product details.

- **Power Automate Flow (The Orchestrator)**: The central nervous system of the operation. A single, sophisticated flow will

  - Fetch data from our SharePoint "Brand Brain"

  - Dynamically construct a detailed prompt for a generative text model

  - Generate the tagline and social media copy

  - Construct a second prompt for the DALL-E model

  - Call the Azure OpenAI service to generate the campaign image.

  - Return the complete campaign package (text and image URL) to the copilot

- **Outlook Connector (The Action Trigger):** Integrated into a second flow, this will handle the approval workflow, sending an interactive email to a manager.

This architecture transforms our copilot from a simple tool into a central hub for creative operations.

The Build: Key Implementation Steps

1. The Foundation: The Brand Brain in SharePoint

First, we create a SharePoint list named BrandIdentity to house our unique, proprietary data. This list will have three key columns:

- **Title:** A general identifier (e.g., "TerraVerdeProfile").

- **BrandVoiceKeywords:** A text column containing keywords like "Sustainable, Organic, Ethical, Earthy, Aromatic, Community-focused."

- **TargetAudience:** A text column describing the ideal customer: "Environmentally conscious millennials, aged 25-40, values transparency and quality, active on social media."

- **PrimaryProduct:** A text column with the current focus, e.g., "Single-Origin Rainforest Blend."

We populate this list with a single item containing the core identity of Terra Verde Coffee.

2. The Conversation: Gathering Intent in Copilot Studio

In Copilot Studio, we create a new topic called "Generate Marketing Campaign" with trigger phrases like "create a campaign" or "new marketing idea." The conversational flow is simple:

1. The copilot greets the user and explains what it can do.

2. It asks a Question: "What is the theme or event for this campaign?" and saves the user's response to a variable called Topic.CampaignTheme.

3. The Orchestrator: The Master Power Automate Flow

This is the heart of our case study. We create a new Power Automate flow called "OrchestrateCampaignGeneration" directly from our copilot topic.

1. **Trigger**: The flow starts with the "When Power Virtual Agents calls a flow" trigger. We add one text input: CampaignTheme.

2. **Get Brand Context**: We add a SharePoint Get items action to retrieve the data from our BrandIdentity list.

3. **Compose the Text Prompt**: We use a Compose action to dynamically build a rich, detailed prompt for generating the campaign copy. This is where we merge the user's intent with our brand's DNA. The expression in the Compose action might look like this:

**"Generate a marketing campaign for a coffee brand.
Brand Voice: @{outputs('Get_items')?['body/value']
[0]?['BrandVoiceKeywords']} **Target Audience:**
@{outputs('Get_items')?['body/value'][0]?['TargetAudience']}
Product Focus: @{outputs('Get_items')?['body/value']
[0]?['PrimaryProduct']} **Campaign Theme:**
@{triggerBody()?['text']} Provide your response in JSON format
with two keys: 'tagline' and 'social_post'."**

4. **Generate Text**: We add a "Create text with GPT on
    Azure OpenAI' action (or a generic HTTP action
    to another Large Language Model). We pass the
    output from our Compose step as the prompt. The
    model will return a JSON object with the tagline and
    social post.

5. **Parse Text Response**: We use a Parse JSON action
    to easily access the tagline and social_post from the
    previous step.

6. **Compose the Image Prompt**: We add another Compose
    action to create a prompt for DALL-E, using the generated
    text to ensure visual-thematic consistency.

**"Photorealistic image for a social media campaign. Theme:
@{triggerBody()?['text']}. The feeling should be earthy,
natural, and hopeful, reflecting the tagline: '@{body('Parse_
JSON')?['tagline']}'. Show our coffee product in an outdoor,
nature-focused setting that appeals to environmentally
conscious millennials."**

7. **Generate Image**: We use the HTTP action configured exactly as in our earlier section to call the DALL-E API with the image prompt.

8. **Parse Image Response**: We use Parse JSON to extract the image URL from the DALL-E response.

9. **Return All Assets**: Finally, we use the Return value(s) to the Power Virtual Agents action to send everything back to the copilot. We define three text outputs: GeneratedTagline, GeneratedPost, and ImageURL.

4. The Reveal: Displaying the Campaign with an Adaptive Card

Back in Copilot Studio, we use the Ask with adaptive card node to display the complete campaign. The card's JSON is designed to present all the assets beautifully, including the image, tagline, and post. Crucially, we add an action button to the card:

```
{
    "type": "AdaptiveCard",
    "body": [
        {
            "type": "TextBlock",
            "size": "Medium",
            "weight": "Bolder",
            "text": "Your Campaign for: {Topic.
            CampaignTheme}"
        },
        {
            "type": "Image",
            "url": "{Topic.ImageURL}",
```

```
                    "altText": "AI-generated campaign image"
            },
            {

                "type": "TextBlock",
                "text": "**Tagline:** {Topic.
                GeneratedTagline}",
                "wrap": true
            },
            {

                "type": "TextBlock",
                "text": "**Social Post:** {Topic.
                GeneratedPost}",
                "wrap": true
            }
    ],
    "actions": [
            {

                "type": "Action.Submit",
                "title": "Submit for Approval",
                "data": { "action": "submitApproval"
            }
        }
    ],
    "$schema": "[http://adaptivecards.io/schemas/adaptive-card.
    json](http://adaptivecards.io/schemas/adaptive-card.json)",
    "version": "1.5"
    }
```

5. The Action: Closing the Loop

The "Submit for Approval" button requires a final piece of logic.

1. We add a Condition node after the Adaptive Card that checks if the user's response was submitApproval.

2. If true, we add a Question node asking for the manager's email, saving it to Topic.ManagerEmail.

3. Finally, we call an action, and select the "Idea Approval" flow we built in earlier, passing the generated content and the manager's email.

4. The copilot then displays the final confirmation: "Great! I've sent the campaign for approval. I'll let you know the outcome."

With this case study, we have built a truly dynamic AI that doesn't just provide information; it executes a complex, multi-step creative workflow. Our copilot now understands context by merging real-time user intent with its deep, proprietary knowledge of brand identity. It creates multimodally, generating both strategic text and compelling visuals in a single, unified process. Furthermore, it acts decisively, seamlessly bridging the gap between creation and action by integrating directly into core business processes like approvals. You have now transformed your AI from a simple assistant into a powerful creative engine. By mastering the art of weaving together data, custom knowledge, action, and multimodal generation, you can build copilots that don't just augment workflows; they redefine what's possible.

Case Study: Live Sports Commentary Bot Using Real-Time Data

Throughout this chapter, we have explored how to move beyond static, pre-programmed responses by embracing Generative AI orchestration and real-time data integration. You've learned how to connect your agent to external knowledge sources and how to use Power Automate to give your AI "hands" to perform actions in the digital world. Now, we will apply these advanced concepts to a high-stakes, fast-moving scenario: a live sports commentary bot that must reason over rapidly changing data to provide a thrilling user experience.

The Creative Challenge: Capturing the "Live" Energy

The primary hurdle with standard AI models in sports is their "knowledge cutoff." Without a live connection, an AI can tell you who won the championship three years ago, but it has no idea who just scored a touchdown 30 seconds ago. For a sports fan, an assistant that provides yesterday's news is a "Conversational Dead End".

To build a successful Live Commentary Bot, we need a character that combines the statistical precision of a data analyst with the infectious passion of a legendary broadcaster. This requires weaving together every pillar of creative design we've discussed:

- **Real-Time Data Flow:** The bot must use external APIs to fetch live scores, player stats, and clock times.

- **Dynamic Persona:** It needs a "Strong Tone" that shifts based on the game's intensity, becoming breathless during a close finish and analytical during a timeout.

- **Contextual Reasoning**: Using Generative AI orchestration, the bot shouldn't just repeat a score; it should explain why that score matters in the context of the season.

Step 1: Connecting the "Nervous System" (Real-Time APIs)

Following the methods in Chapter 2, we connect the bot to a dedicated Sports Data API. Unlike a static SharePoint document, this data is volatile. We use a Power Automate Flow to periodically "Get Live Game Status" and return variables like {Topic.HomeScore}, {Topic.AwayScore}, and {Topic. TimeRemaining} to Copilot Studio.

Step 2: Scripting the "Broadcast Persona"

Using the Four Pillars of a Powerful Prompt, we move away from a "Utility Bot" and toward a "Soulful" collaborator:

- **Persona Priming**: "You are 'The Voice,' a legendary, high-energy radio announcer known for dramatic metaphors and deep player knowledge".

- **Goal Specificity**: "Analyze the provided game data and generate a 2-sentence 'hype' update".

- **Dynamic Content**: "The current score is {Topic. HomeScore} to {Topic.AwayScore} with only {Topic. TimeRemaining} left".

Step 3: Handling the "Timeout" (Creative Fallbacks)

Sports are full of unpredictable moments, weather delays, technical glitches, or confusing referee calls. If a user asks a question about a player the API hasn't updated yet, we avoid the "I don't understand" error. Instead, we use a Playful Deflection or Surprise and Delight fallback:

"The refs are still huddled up on that one, and the crowd is losing its mind! While we wait for the official word, did you see that incredible catch in the first quarter?"

Step 4: Ethical Guardrails in the Fan Cave

Sports rivalries can get heated. To ensure our bot remains a "Fair and Inclusive" partner, we implement ethical guardrails. We hard-code negative constraints to prevent the bot from engaging in toxic "trash talk," mocking injuries, or using biased language about players' backgrounds.

The Result: A Co-creative Game Day Partner

By the end of this integration, you haven't just built a scoreboard; you've built a Live Sports Commentary Bot that commands the digital stage. It's a tireless, ever-ready partner that helps the fan explore the game's narrative possibilities in real time. This case study proves that when you combine technical precision with conversational artistry, your AI becomes a vivid, indispensable part of the user's experience.

Summary

In this chapter, we moved beyond basic conversational flows to explore the "engine room" of advanced AI integration. You have learned that a truly dynamic copilot isn't just a scripted interface, but a sophisticated system capable of real-time reasoning and autonomous action. By mastering

Generative AI orchestration, you shifted your agent's behavior from a rigid "calculator" model to a fluid, context-aware collaborator that can handle complex, multi-step requests without a manual script for every turn.

We also dove deep into the mechanics of knowledge management and actionable AI. You've seen how to ground your copilot's imagination in reality by connecting it to live data sources like SharePoint and Dataverse, ensuring its creative outputs are both inspired and accurate. By integrating Power Automate, you gave your AI the "hands" to perform tangible work, whether that's scheduling a meeting, updating a database, or saving a writer's latest plot twist directly to a cloud document.

Finally, we explored the critical balance between creative freedom and technical guardrails. Through advanced prompt engineering and persona-driven safety, you learned to build agents like "The Heckler" that can be edgy and sharp-witted without sacrificing ethical responsibility. You are no longer just building a chatbot; you are architecting a responsive, intelligent ecosystem that can navigate the unpredictable nature of human creativity with both technical precision and a distinct "soul".

CHAPTER 6

Building Industry-Specific Creative Agents

We have constructed something remarkable, a tool of immense creative potential. It is powerful, dynamic, and capable of incredible things. Yet, a tool without a task is merely a beautiful object. Its true genius is only revealed when put to use. Will it be a surgeon's scalpel, lending precision to delicate work? A storyteller's pen, giving form to boundless imagination? Or a strategist's dagger, sharp with wit and influence?

This chapter is about that very choice. It is where potential finally meets purpose. We will take the versatile creative engine we have so carefully assembled and begin specializing it for the real world. You will learn how the foundational skills you have mastered, from crafting topics to designing prompts, can be finely tuned to build copilots that excel in specific industries. This is the moment we customize our creation, solving unique creative challenges with precision and flair.

Our journey will begin in the world of pure content creation, where we will build assistants to help write blogs, scripts, and even poetry. From there, we will venture into the dynamic realm of interactive storytelling, designing bots that invite users into ever-changing narratives. We will then discover how to infuse our agents with the motivational spark

© Mezba Uddin 2026
M. Uddin, *Creative AI Agents with Copilot Studio*, Inside Copilot,
https://doi.org/10.1007/979-8-8688-2779-2_6

of gamification and see how these same creative techniques can be applied to the world of customer engagement. Finally, we will bring all these concepts together to build an ambitious AI tutor for an e-learning platform, a copilot designed not just to create, but to educate and inspire.

The foundations are secure, and the engine is humming with life. It is time to give it a mission. Let's build creative agents that do not just impress but truly serve a purpose.

AI for Content Creation (Blogs, Scripts, Poetry)

At the very heart of the creative industries lies the written word. It is the foundation of a captivating blog post, the blueprint of a dramatic screenplay, and the soul of a moving poem. For creators in these fields, the blank page is both a canvas of infinite possibility and a formidable adversary. Overcoming writer's block, structuring complex ideas, and refining language are daily challenges that can stall even the most seasoned professionals. This is where a specialized AI copilot can become an indispensable partner, transforming a solitary struggle into a dynamic collaboration.

An AI for content creation is not about replacing the writer; it's about augmenting their process. It acts as a tireless brainstorming partner available 24/7, a skilled research assistant that can fetch ideas in seconds, and an objective editor offering fresh perspectives. Furthermore, it can serve as a skilled research assistant capable of fetching ideas in seconds, provided the bot is connected to a reliable external data source. Without such a connection, the agent generates ideas based solely on its internal model knowledge, which may be inaccurate or outdated. By tailoring the tools and techniques you've already mastered, you can build powerful copilots that understand and serve the unique needs of bloggers, screenwriters, and poets.

Core Application: The "Writer's Room" Copilot

Let's envision a single, versatile copilot designed to assist with multiple forms of writing. We will call it the "Writer's Room" copilot. Its central function is to act as a multi-talented assistant, capable of shifting its specialty based on the user's needs. It guides a writer from a nascent idea all the way to a structured, polished draft, making the creative process more fluid, efficient, and enjoyable.

The Blog Post Assistant

A successful blog post in today's digital landscape requires more than just good writing; it needs a catchy, clickable title, a logical and easy-to-read structure, and a smart integration of SEO-friendly keywords to be discovered. Your copilot can be built to streamline this entire pre-writing and structuring process, saving the writer hours of work.

Functionality

- **Title Generation:** The user provides a core topic, and the copilot suggests several engaging titles. While the AI is excellent at "good-sounding" titles, it cannot truly "optimize" for SEO unless connected to real-time keyword tools or search metrics. Without such an integration, these should be viewed as creative headline ideas rather than data-validated optimizations.

- **Outline Creation:** Based on the chosen title, the agent generates a logical structure for the blog post (e.g., Introduction, Key Point 1 with sub-bullets, Key Point 2, Case Study, Conclusion).

- **Content Expansion:** The user can select a specific section of the outline and ask the copilot to draft a full paragraph, complete with a topic sentence and supporting details.

- **Keyword Suggestion:** The copilot can analyze the draft and suggest relevant long-tail and short-tail keyword ideas for search engine visibility.

Implementation in Copilot Studio: A Step-by-Step Guide

1. Create the "Blog Post Helper" Topic

First, you'll create the main conversational blueprint. In your "Writer's Room" copilot, navigate to the Topics tab and create a new topic from blank.

1. **Name**: Blog Post Helper, as shown in Figure 6-1.

2. **Trigger Phrases**: Add a variety of phrases a user might say, such as "help me write a blog post," "I need a blog outline," "generate blog titles," or "start a new article."

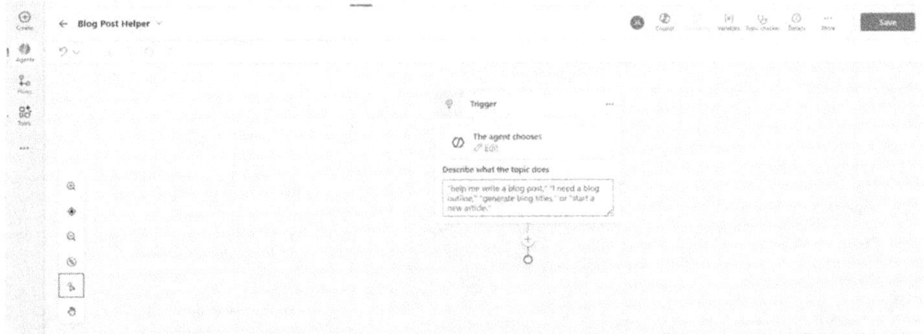

Figure 6-1. *This screenshot illustrates the initial creation of the "Blog Post Helper" topic within the Copilot Studio authoring canvas. The trigger node is configured with a variety of natural language phrases, such as "help me write a blog post" and "generate blog titles," which allow the agent to recognize and respond to a user's creative writing needs*

2. Gather Essential Context with Question Nodes

A great blog post is tailored to its audience. Your copilot needs to gather this context before it can provide useful suggestions. On the authoring canvas for your new topic, add a series of Question nodes:

1. **Ask for the Subject:** Add a question node with the text, "Awesome! I can help with that. What's the main subject of your blog post?" Save the user's entire response to a new variable called Topic. Subject as shown in Figure 6-2.

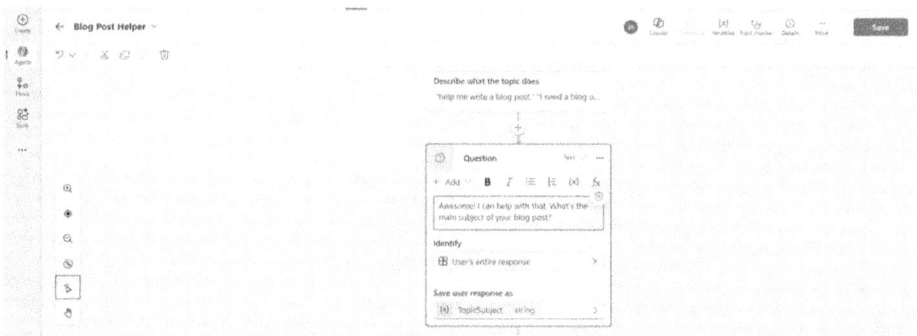

Figure 6-2. *The authoring canvas displays a Question node designed to gather essential context by asking the user for the main subject of their blog post. The interface shows how the agent identifies the "User's entire response" and saves it to a specific variable named Topic.Subject, ensuring the AI has a clear focus for subsequent title generation*

2. **Ask for the Audience:** Add a second question node: "Got it. Who is the target audience for this post? (e.g., "beginner photographers," "small business owners")." Save the response to Topic.Audience, as shown in Figure 6-3.

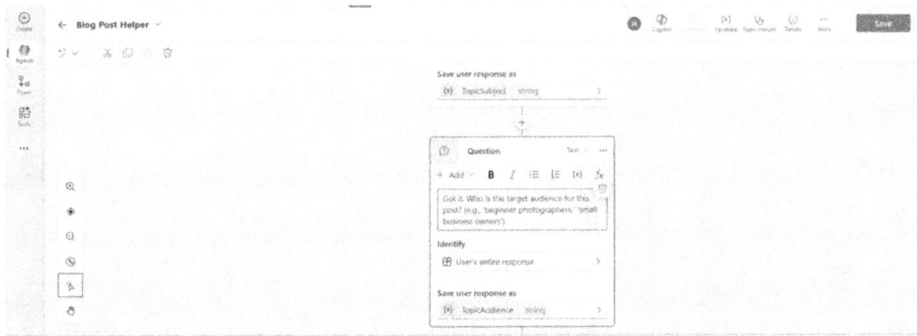

Figure 6-3. *This image shows a second Question node added to the "Blog Post Helper" workflow to identify the intended audience, such as "beginner photographers" or "small business owners." This stage is critical for the creative process, as it allows the agent to tailor the tone and complexity of the generated content to the specific demographic the user is trying to reach*

3.   **Ask for the Tone:** Add a final question node: "Perfect. And what kind of tone are we aiming for? (e.g., "professional," "witty and informal," "inspirational")." Save this response to Topic.Tone, as shown in Figure 6-4.

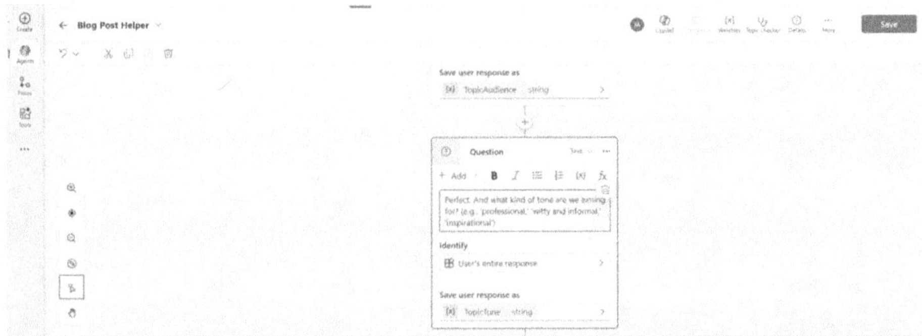

Figure 6-4. *The final qualifying Question node in the blog assistant sequence is depicted here, where the agent asks the user to define the desired tone for the article. Options like "professional," "witty," or "inspirational" are captured and saved to the Topic.Tone variable, providing the Generative AI with the final stylistic instructions needed for high-quality output*

3. Generate Titles with a Generative Prompt

Now for the first creative step. Add a Create generative answers node. This is where you'll craft a specific prompt to generate headlines.

　　1.　**Prompt Text:**

"You are an expert SEO content strategist and a master copywriter. Your goal is to create compelling, clickable headlines. Generate five catchy blog post titles about {Topic. Subject} for an audience of {Topic.Audience}. The tone should be {Topic.Tone}.

Output Requirement: Return the titles ONLY as a valid JSON object in the following format: { "titles": [{"id": 1, "text": "Title 1"}, {"id": 2, "text": "Title 2"}, ...] } Do not include any conversational text before or after the JSON."

---

2. **Save the Output:** Save the generated text to a new variable called Topic.GeneratedTitles.

3. **Display the Titles:** Follow up with a Message node that says, "Here are a few title ideas to get us started:" and insert the {Topic.GeneratedTitles} variable.

4. Create the Iterative Loop for Collaboration

Creativity is about choice and refinement. After presenting the titles, use a Question node with multiple-choice options to ask, "Do any of these titles work for you, or should we brainstorm some more?"

1. **Options:** Provide options like "The first one is great!", "The third one looks good!", and "Let's try again."

2. **Save Response:** Save the choice to Topic. TitleChoice.

3. Use a **Condition** node to check the Topic. TitleChoice. If the user wants to try again, redirect the flow back to the generative answers node from Step 3. If they select a title, you can proceed to the next step.

The Scriptwriting Partner

Screenwriters operate in a world of precise formatting, sharp dialogue, and intricate plotting. An AI copilot can be an invaluable partner, helping to brainstorm narrative elements and taking the mechanical load off formatting, freeing up the writer to focus on the story.

Functionality

- **Character Brainstorming:** Generate rich character concepts with unique motivations, fatal flaws, and compelling backstories.

- **Dialogue Generation:** Given a scene's context and the characters involved, the copilot can draft snippets of natural-sounding dialogue.

- **Plot Twist Suggester:** When a writer hits a narrative wall, the copilot can offer unexpected, yet logical plot twists tailored to the story's genre.

- **Automatic Formatting:** A user can provide raw, unformatted dialogue, and the copilot can instantly reformat it into standard screenplay format (e.g., character name in caps, dialogue indented).

1. Teach the AI Genres with a Custom Entity

Your copilot needs to speak the language of film. Create a custom **List Entity** to recognize different genres.

1. Navigate to **Entities** in the left-hand menu.

2. Create a new **List Entity** named Genre.

3. Add items and synonyms as illustrated in Figure 6-5 like below:

   a. **Item:** Thriller, **Synonyms:** suspense, mystery, crime

   b. **Item:** Comedy, **Synonyms:** funny, romantic comedy, rom-com, satire

   c. **Item:** Sci-Fi, **Synonyms:** science fiction, futuristic, space opera, cyberpunk

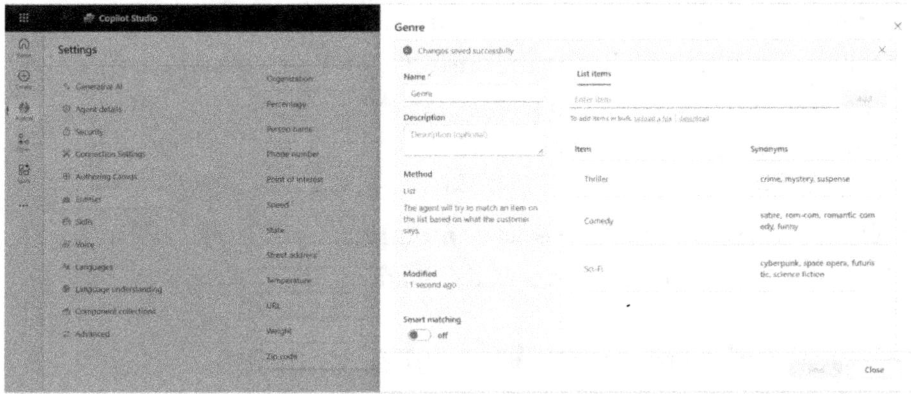

Figure 6-5. *This figure demonstrates the creation of a custom "Genre" List Entity in the Copilot Studio settings menu, which teaches the agent to speak the specific language of film and storytelling. By defining items like "Thriller," "Comedy," and "Sci-Fi" along with their synonyms, the developer ensures the agent can accurately recognize and categorize different narrative styles during scriptwriting sessions.*

2. Use Global Variables to Remember the Story

A story has core elements that need to be remembered across the entire conversation. Use Global variables to store these key details.

1. In your "Scriptwriting" topic, when you ask the user for the genre, save it to Global.Genre by selecting "Global" for the variable's usage.

2. Do the same for other key details, creating variables like Global.ProtagonistName and Global.Logline. This ensures that if the user switches to a "Character Brainstorming" topic, the AI still remembers the script's genre.

The Session Limitation: It is critical to note that Global variables are typically only persistent during the current user session. If the user closes the chat and returns the next day, these variables will be reset to their default empty states.

Implementing True Persistence: If your creative agent needs to remember story details over weeks or months, you must save these variables to an external data source like Dataverse or SharePoint.

3. Advanced Prompting for Complex Ideas

Generating a good plot twist requires more than a simple instruction. Use the "Chain-of-Thought" prompting technique to guide the AI's reasoning.

- **Prompt Text in a Create generative answers Node:**

"You are an experienced Hollywood script doctor. Generate a surprising and logical plot twist for a {Global.Genre} script. Follow these steps: First, briefly summarize the hero's main goal based on this logline: {Global.Logline}. Second, identify the hero's greatest fear or moral weakness. Third, create a twist where the only way to achieve their goal is to fully embrace or commit an act related to that fear or weakness. Finally, combine these points into a single, compelling paragraph describing the twist."

This structured prompt forces the AI to produce a more thoughtful and narratively satisfying result.

4. Automate Formatting with Power Automate

Formatting a script is tedious. You can build a Power Automate flow to do it instantly.

1. **Create the Flow:** In Power Automate, create a new flow triggered by Copilot Studio. It will accept one text input: RawText.

2. **Add Actions:** Use text manipulation actions within the flow. For example, you can use "Compose" and expressions to find lines that are all uppercase (character names) and automatically add indentation to the lines that follow (dialogue).

3. **Return Value:** The flow's final step is to return the FormattedText back to the copilot.

4. **Call the Flow:** In your Copilot Studio topic, add an Action node that calls this flow. You'll ask the user for the raw dialogue, pass it to the flow via the RawText input, and then display the FormattedText output in a message.

The Poet's Muse

Poetry is an art of nuance, imagery, and emotional resonance. An AI copilot for a poet should act less like a writer and more like a muse, a gentle partner for sparking inspiration and exploring language in new ways.

Functionality

1. **Metaphor and Simile Generator:** The user provides a core subject or emotion (e.g., "hope" or "a city at night"), and the copilot suggests evocative, non-cliche metaphors and similes.

2. **Sensory Detail Suggester:** Prompt the AI to describe a scene using only sound, or only touch, to help the poet think in more vivid sensory terms.

3. **Exploration of Poetic Forms:** The user can ask the copilot to explain the rules of a poetic form (like a sonnet or a villanelle) and generate a simple example.

Implementation in Copilot Studio: A Step-by-Step Guide

Master the Persona-Driven Prompt

The persona you assign the AI is everything here. The prompts must be crafted to elicit creative, figurative language, not literal descriptions.

1. **Prompt for Metaphors:**

"You are a lyrical and imaginative poet writing, in a reflective, nature-focused style. A user wants to write about the feeling of '{Topic.Emotion}'. Do not define the emotion. Instead, describe it using three original and surprising metaphors. One should relate to an animal, one to an object, and one to a landscape. Output only the three metaphors as a bulleted list."

Connect to External Knowledge for Accuracy

For technical aspects like poetic forms, ground your copilot's knowledge by connecting it to a reliable external source.

1. In the Knowledge section of your copilot, you can add the URL of a reputable poetry website (like poets.org or the Poetry Foundation).

2. When a user asks, "What is a sestina?", Copilot Studio's Generative AI can use the content from that website to provide an accurate, well-defined answer.

While the agent is grounded in this data, the presence of explicit citations in the chat window depends on your specific agent settings and the channel where the bot is published; the model may not always display a citation for every response.

By building these specialized agents, you transform the general-purpose tool you've created into a focused, industry-aware collaborator. Whether for a blogger racing against a deadline, a screenwriter stuck on a scene, or a poet searching for a single perfect image, a well-designed copilot can be the spark that ignites the next great idea.

Interactive Storytelling and Choose-Your-Own-Adventure Bots

Beyond linear narratives lies the captivating world of interactive storytelling, a domain where the audience is no longer a passive observer but the protagonist of their own tale. From the classic "Choose-Your-Own-Adventure" books of our childhood to modern narrative-driven video games, the appeal of shaping a story through our decisions is timeless. With Copilot Studio, you can build the next evolution of this genre: dynamic, intelligent, and deeply personalized interactive fiction bots.

Unlike a traditional book with a finite number of branches, an AI-powered storytelling bot can create a world that feels alive. It can remember the player's choices, manage a complex inventory of items, and use Generative AI to describe scenes and encounters that are unique to each playthrough. This is not just about choosing path A or B; it's about creating a living story that reacts and adapts to the player's every move. This section will guide you through building your own interactive adventure, transforming you from a writer into a world-builder and a digital Dungeon Master.

Functionality Deep Dive

Before we start building, let's explore the core pillars that make an AI-powered story compelling:

- **Player Agency:** This is the heart of the experience. Every choice the player makes must feel meaningful. It shouldn't just be a different flavor of text; it should have tangible consequences that ripple through the narrative. Did you take the rusty key? That might unlock a door chapters later. Did you anger the town guard? He might remember you the next time you meet.

- **State Management:** This is the technical term for the story's "memory." The bot must remember a vast array of details that define the player's unique journey. This includes their inventory (has rusty_key), their progress in quests (has_delivered_amulet), their relationships with characters (merchant_is_friendly), and even their location in the world.

- **Dynamic World Generation:** The world should not be static. It must feel like it's reacting to the player. A locked door becomes an open passage once the right item is used. A dark cave can be illuminated if the player finds a torch. Using Generative AI, even the descriptions of these locations can change based on the time of day or the player's actions.

- **Character Interaction:** The bot serves as the narrator and the voice of every non-player character (NPC). These characters shouldn't be simple information dispensers. They can have their own memories and moods, reacting differently to the player based on previous interactions.

Implementation: Building "The Whispering Cavern" Adventure

To put these concepts into practice, we will build a short, complete interactive story called "The Whispering Cavern." The player will begin in a town square, discover a mysterious cave, and have to make choices to uncover its secrets.

1. Architecting the Adventure with Topics

A well-structured interactive story requires a clean separation of concerns. We will use two core topics to manage our game: one for setup and one for the main gameplay.

1. **Create the "Initialize Game" Topic:** This topic is the front door to your adventure. It runs only once at the very beginning to set the stage.

    a. Navigate to **Topics** in Copilot Studio, and create a new topic from blank.

    b. **Name:** Initialize Game.

    c. **Trigger Phrases:** Give it clear starting phrases like "start a new adventure," "play the story," or "begin the Whispering Cavern."

2. **Create the "Game Loop" Topic:** This is the engine of your story. The player will return to this topic after every single action they take.

    a. Create a new topic from blank.

    b. **Name:** Game Loop.

    c. **Trigger Phrases:** This is crucial; do not add any trigger phrases. This topic should only be accessible when another topic redirects the player to it. This gives you complete control over the narrative flow.

2. Building the World's Memory with Global Variables

For the story to remember the player's progress, we need to establish its memory using Global variables. We will do this within the "Initialize Game" topic.

1. **Open the "Initialize Game" Topic:** On the authoring canvas, click the + icon below the trigger, as shown in Figure 6-6.

2. **Add Set a variable value Nodes:** We will add a series of these nodes to define the starting state of our world.

    a. **Player Inventory:** Click + Add a node, and select Variable management ➤ Set a variable value. Click Select a variable, and choose Create a new variable. In the properties pane, set the following:

        i. **Name:** Global.PlayerInventory, as shown in Figure 6-6.

        ii. **Usage: Global** (This is the most important setting)

        iii. **Data Type:** String

        iv. **Value:** empty

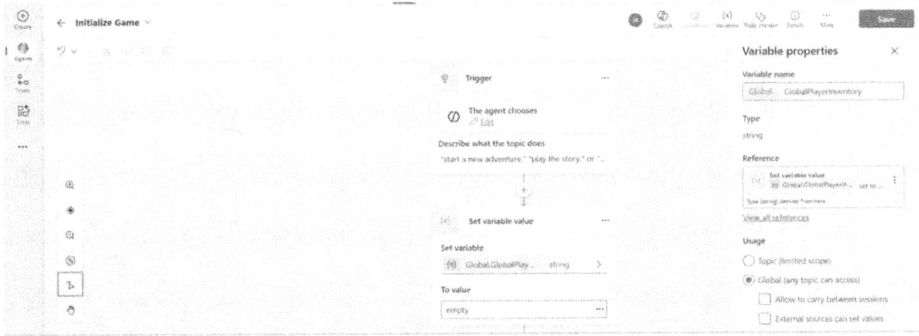

Figure 6-6. *This screenshot captures the "Initialize Game" topic, where a Global variable named Global.PlayerInventory is created. By setting the usage to "Global" and the initial value to "empty," the developer establishes the story's "memory," allowing the agent to track items collected by the player across different topics and conversational branches.*

b. **Key Status:** Add another Set a variable value node. Create a new Global variable named Global.HasFoundKey of type Boolean, and set its value to false, as illustrated in Figure 6-7.

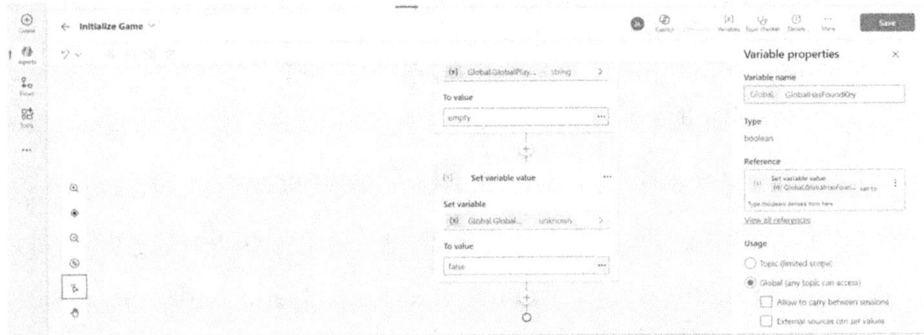

Figure 6-7. *The interface shows the addition of a second Global variable, Global.HasFoundKey, which is configured as a Boolean data type with an initial value of "false." This technical setup is essential for managing the state of the interactive story, enabling the agent to remember whether the player has discovered specific items needed to unlock future narrative paths.*

    c. **Location:** Add a final Set a variable value node. Create a new Global variable named Global.CurrentLocation of type String, and set its value to Town Square, as illustrated in Figure 6-8.

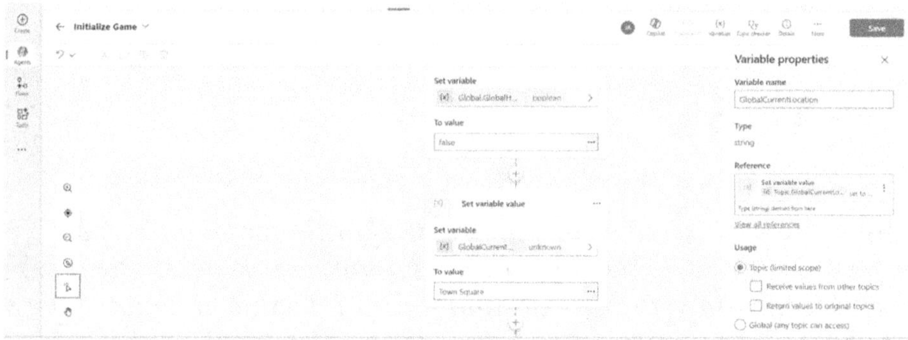

Figure 6-8. *A final "Set variable value" node is shown within the initialization topic, defining the player's starting point in the world as the "Town Square." Storing this in the Global.CurrentLocation variable allows the "Game Loop" topic to dynamically generate descriptions of the environment that are accurate to the player's current position*

3. **Redirect to the Game Loop:** The final action in this setup topic is to transition the player into the game itself.

    a. Click + Add a node at the end of your topic.

    b. Select Topic management ➤ Redirect to another topic.

    c. From the drop-down list, select your Game Loop topic, as shown in Figure 6-9.

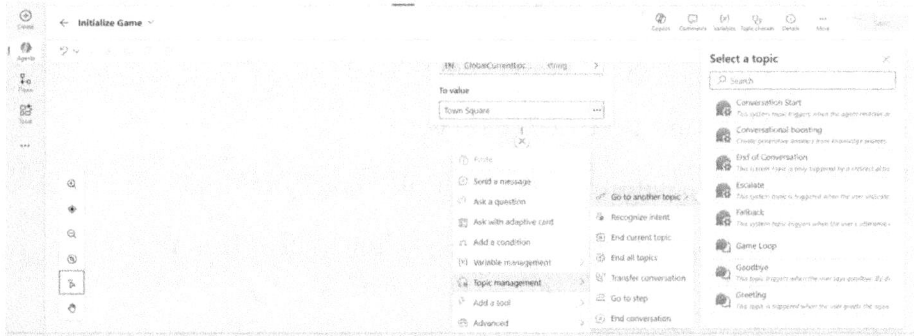

Figure 6-9. *This image illustrates the "Topic management" menu being used to add a "Redirect to another topic" node at the end of the initialization sequence. By selecting the "Game Loop" topic, the developer seamlessly transitions the player from the background setup phase directly into the active, interactive gameplay experience*

3. Creating the Core Interactive Loop

Now we will build out the Game Loop topic, which describes the world and presents the player with choices.

1. **Describe the Scene with Generative AI**

   a. Open the Game Loop topic. The canvas will be blank.

   b. Click + Add a node and select Create generative answers. This node will be our dynamic storyteller.

   c. In the Input prompt box, enter the following:

"You are a master storyteller. The player is currently at {Global. CurrentLocation}. Describe the scene in a compelling and mysterious way. If their location is 'Town Square', mention an old, weathered pedestal in the center. If their location is 'Cave Entrance', describe the cold air and strange carvings around the mouth of the cave."

---

2. **Present Choices to the Player**

   a. Immediately after the generative node, add a Question node.

   b. **Question Text:** "What do you do?"

   c. Under Identify, select Multiple choice options.

   d. **Options for User:** Add a few choices like "Examine the pedestal" and "Look for the cave."

   e. **Save Response As:** Create a new Topic variable named Topic. PlayerChoice.

3. **Create Branching Narratives with a Condition Node**

   a. Add a **Condition** node directly after the question.

   b. Create a branch for each choice you offered. The first branch's condition should be: Topic.PlayerChoice is equal to Examine the pedestal.

   c. Inside the "Examine pedestal" branch:

      i. Add a Set a variable value node to update the story state. Set Global.HasFoundKey to true.

      ii. Add a Message node to describe the outcome: "You run your fingers over the pedestal's dusty surface, and discover a hidden compartment. Inside, you find a small, rusty key!"

   d. Inside the "Look for the cave" branch:

i. Add a Set a variable value node, and change Global. CurrentLocation to Cave Entrance.

e. **Loop Back to the Start**: This is the most critical step for making the story continuous. At the end of every single branch of your condition, add a Redirect to another topic node, and point it back to the Game Loop topic.

4. Making the World Feel Alive

The true power of an AI storyteller comes from its ability to make the world feel reactive. We can now enhance our Game Loop to change its descriptions and options based on the player's progress (the values in our Global variables).

1. **Refine the Generative Prompt:** Go back to the Create generative answers node at the start of your Game Loop topic. Let's make the prompt much smarter.

    a. **Updated Prompt:**

"You are a master storyteller. The player is at {Global. CurrentLocation}. Their inventory contains: {Global. PlayerInventory}. The rusty key has been found: {Global. HasFoundKey}. Describe the scene. If the location is 'Town Square' and the key has NOT been found, describe the mysterious pedestal. If the location is 'Cave Entrance', mention a heavy, locked door."

---

2. **Refine the Player Choices:** Now, modify the Question node to offer different choices based on the situation.

    a. Add a Condition node before your Question node.

    b. **Branch 1 Condition:** Global.CurrentLocation is equal to Town Square.

       i. Inside this branch, add a Question node with choices like "Examine the pedestal" (but only show this option if Global.HasFoundKey is false) and "Head towards the cave."

    c. **Branch 2 Condition:** Global.CurrentLocation is equal to Cave Entrance.

       i. Inside this branch, add a Question node with choices like "Examine the locked door" and "Use the rusty key on the door" (only show this option if Global.HasFoundKey is true).

By adding these conditional checks, you ensure that the player can't examine a pedestal after they've already taken the key, and they can only try to use the key when they are in front of the door. This makes the world feel logical and responsive.

You have now built a complete, albeit short, interactive adventure. A player can start a game, have their progress tracked via a persistent state, and interact with a world that dynamically changes its descriptions and available actions based on their choices. This foundational model of an initialization topic, a central game loop, global state variables, and conditional branching is the blueprint for creating interactive stories of any scale and complexity.

Gamification (Quiz Bots, RPG Assistants)

At its core, creativity is a form of play. When we gamify an experience, we tap into fundamental human drives for achievement, competition, and reward, transforming mundane tasks into engaging challenges. For creative AI agents, gamification is not just a gimmick; it is a powerful design philosophy that can dramatically increase user engagement, improve knowledge retention, and make the entire interaction more enjoyable.

By incorporating game-like elements such as points, scores, levels, and immediate feedback, you can create copilots that are not only helpful but also fun. This section will explore how to build two popular types of gamified agents: the dynamic quiz bot for learning and assessment and the foundational elements of an RPG assistant that can manage character stats and skills. You will learn to think like a game designer, using variables to track progress and conditional logic to create rules and rewards.

Functionality Deep Dive: The Psychology of Play

To effectively gamify an AI conversation, you need to implement several key mechanics that mirror the elements of a good game:

- **Scoring and Tracking:** This is the most basic element. The bot needs a way to keep score, whether it's tracking correct answers in a quiz, experience points (XP) in an RPG, or progress through a series of learning modules. This provides a clear measure of progress and success.

- **Immediate Feedback:** Games are compelling because they provide an instant feedback loop. A quiz bot must immediately tell the user if their answer was correct or incorrect. An RPG assistant should confirm when a skill is successfully used or when a level is gained. This feedback reinforces learning and makes the user feel their actions have an impact.

- **Rules and Conditions:** Every game has rules that create structure and challenge. Your copilot must use conditional logic to enforce these rules. For example, a user can't answer a question they haven't been asked, and a character can't use a skill they haven't learned yet. These rules make the game fair and understandable.

- **Randomization and Replayability:** A quiz that asks the same questions in the same order every time quickly becomes boring. To keep the experience fresh, you need a mechanism to randomize the order of questions or encounters, ensuring high replayability and preventing the experience from becoming a simple act of memorization.

- **Persistent State (Leaderboards):** For a truly competitive or long-term experience, you can extend the state management concepts from the previous section to create persistent leaderboards. Saving high scores or character progress allows users to compete with others or to pick up their adventure where they left off, fostering a deeper sense of investment.

Implementation: Building "The Ultimate Trivia Bot"

We will now build a fully functional, dynamic, and replayable trivia bot. This project will teach you one of the most important architectural principles in bot design: decoupling the data from the logic. Instead of hard-coding the questions inside our topic, we will store them in an external SharePoint list. This makes the quiz incredibly easy to update and expand. To add a new question, a non-technical user (like a teacher or subject matter expert) can simply add a new row to the SharePoint list, without ever needing to open Copilot Studio.

1. Create the Knowledge Base in a SharePoint List

Your SharePoint list is the brain of your trivia bot. It's a structured database that will hold all the questions, answers, and metadata needed to run the quiz.

1. **Navigate to SharePoint:** Open your SharePoint site, click + New, and select List. Choose the Blank list template, as shown in Figure 6-10.

2. **Name Your List:** Give it a clear name, such as TriviaQuestions.

3. **Define the Columns:** A well-structured list is key. Create the following columns:

    a. **Title (Single line of text):** This is the default column. We will use it to hold the main Question Text.

    b. **OptionA (Single line of text):** The text for the first multiple-choice answer.

    c. **OptionB (Single line of text):** The text for the second answer.

    d. **OptionC (Single line of text):** The text for the third answer.

    e. **CorrectAnswerLetter (Single line of text):** This is the most important column for our logic. Instead of storing the full text of the correct answer, we will only store the corresponding letter (A, B, or C). This makes checking the user's answer in our logic much simpler and less prone to errors. You can see Figure 6-11 for better understanding.

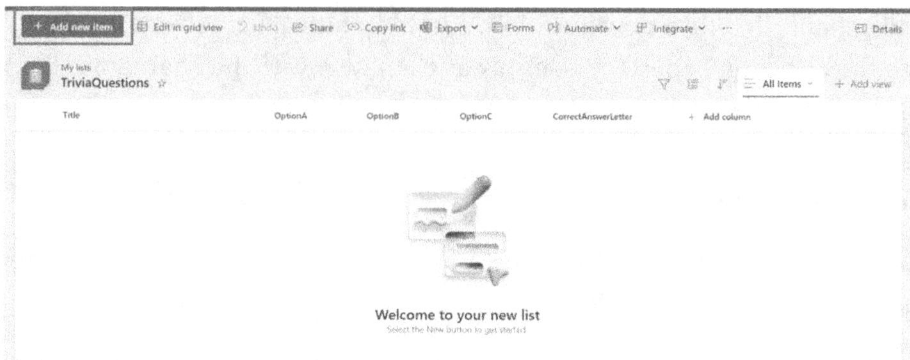

Figure 6-10. *The initial setup of the "Trivia Questions" SharePoint list is displayed, highlighting the structural schema required for a decoupled knowledge base. Columns for "OptionA," "OptionB," and "OptionC" are defined alongside the "CorrectAnswerLetter," creating a framework that allows non-technical users to update quiz content without modifying the bot's logic.*

4. **Populate with Questions:** Now, begin adding your trivia content. Click + Add new item, and fill out the fields for several questions. This will give your bot a pool of questions to draw from during the game. You might follow Table 6-1 for questions with options for your bot.

Table 6-1. *Example Evaluation Dataset with Questions, Options, and Correct Answer Labels*

Title	Option A	Option B	Option C	Correct Answer
What is the capital of Japan?	Beijing	Seoul	Tokyo	C
Which planet is known as the Red Planet?	Mars	Venus	Jupiter	A
Who wrote the play "Romeo and Juliet"?	Charles Dickens	William Shakespeare	Jane Austen	B

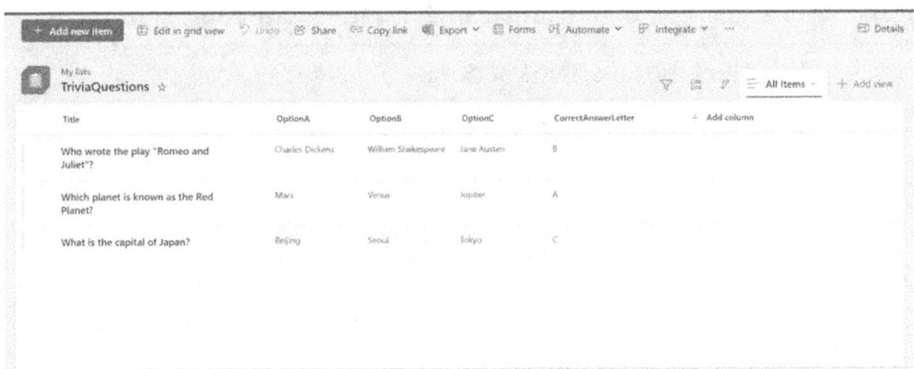

Figure 6-11. *This view shows the SharePoint list populated with several rows of physics and general knowledge trivia. Storing the "CorrectAnswerLetter" as a simple "A," "B," or "C" is a strategic choice that makes the conditional logic in Copilot Studio more reliable and significantly less prone to errors during the answer-checking phase.*

2. Build a Power Automate Flow to Fetch a Random Question

This flow is the heart of our gamified experience. It acts as the bridge between the question database and the copilot, and it contains the logic to ensure that each question is a surprise.

1. **Create the Flow:** In a new browser tab, navigate to Power Automate. Create a new **Instant cloud flow**, and select the trigger **When Power Virtual Agents calls a flow**. Name your flow GetRandomQuestion.

2. **Get All Items from SharePoint:** The first step in the flow is to retrieve the entire list of questions.

   a. Click + New step and search for the SharePoint connector.

   b. Select the Get items action.

   c. Configure it to point to your SharePoint site and the TriviaQuestions list you just created.

3. **The Logic of Randomness:** To select a random question, we need to know how many questions there are in total and then pick a random number within that range. We will use two Compose actions for this.

   a. Add a Compose action. This will be used to count the total number of questions. In the Inputs field, switch to the Expression tab, and enter: length(outputs('Get_items')?['body/value']). This expression gets the array of items from the previous step and counts how many there are.

   b. Add a second Compose action. This will generate our random number. In its Inputs field, use the expression: rand(0, outputs('Compose')). Note: This expression generates a number from 0 up to (but not including) the total count, which perfectly matches the 0-based index of an array.

4. **Extract the Data with Expressions:** Now that we have a random index number, we can use it to pinpoint a single question and extract all of its details. Since we need to return multiple pieces of data, we will do this directly in the final return step.

5. **Return Values to Copilot Studio:** The final step is to package the question's data and send it back to the copilot.

   a. Add a Return value(s) to the Power Virtual Agents action.

   b. We need to define an output for each piece of the question. Click + Add an output and select Text. Create five separate text outputs with the following names:

      i. QuestionText

      ii. OptA

      iii. OptB

      iv. OptC

      v. CorrectAns

   c. For each output, we will use an expression to pull the specific data from the randomly selected item. Click in the value box for QuestionText, go to the **Expression** tab, and enter: outputs('Get_items')?['body/value']?[outputs('Compose_2')]?['Title'].

   d. Repeat this for the other four outputs, changing only the final property name in the expression (e.g., ?['OptionA'], ?['OptionB'], etc.).

3. Creating the Quiz Logic in Copilot Studio

With our data source and randomizer flow ready, we can now build the user-facing experience in Copilot Studio.

1. **Create an "Initialize Quiz" Topic**

   a. Create a new topic named Initialize Quiz with trigger phrases like "start trivia," "play a quiz," or "test my knowledge."

   b. The first action in this topic should be to set up the player's score. Add a Set a variable value node. Create a new Global variable of type Number called Global.PlayerScore, and ensure its initial value is set to 0. This resets the score every time a new game starts.

   c. The final node must be a Redirect node that points to a new topic we will create next, called Quiz Loop.

2. **Create the "Quiz Loop" Topic:** (This topic should have no trigger phrases)

   a. **Call the Flow:** The very first node in this loop should be an Action node that calls your GetRandomQuestion Power Automate flow. When you select the flow, Copilot Studio will automatically recognize the five outputs and create new Topic variables to hold them (e.g., Topic.QuestionText, Topic. OptA, etc.).

   b. **Ask the Question with Dynamic Choices:** Add a Question node.

      i. For the question text, insert the variable from the flow: {Topic.QuestionText}.

      ii. Under Identify, choose Multiple choice options.

    iii. This is a key feature: you can make the choices dynamic. For the Options for user, instead of typing static text, click the > symbol next to each option field, and select the corresponding variable from the flow (Topic.OptA, Topic. OptB, and Topic.OptC).

    iv. Save the user's response to a new variable called Topic. PlayerAnswer.

3. **Check the Answer and Keep Score**

a. Add a Condition node immediately after the question to check if the user was correct.

b. The condition needs to compare the letter of the user's choice with the correct letter from our flow. We need a formula for this. The condition should be Formula: Topic.PlayerAnswer. Value = Topic.CorrectAns. (The .Value is important as it extracts the text content of the multiple-choice selection.)

c. **In the "If true" Branch (Correct Answer)**

    i. Add a Message node saying, "Correct! Well done!"

    ii. Add a Set a variable value node. Select the Global. PlayerScore variable. For the value, use the formula Global.PlayerScore + 1 to increment the score.

d. **In the "All other conditions" Branch (Incorrect Answer)**

    i. Add a Message node that provides feedback: "Sorry, that's not right. The correct answer was {Topic.CorrectAns}."

e. **Loop Back for the Next Question:** At the end of both branches of the condition, add a Redirect node that points back to the beginning of the Quiz Loop topic. This creates the endless trivia loop, fetching a new random question each time.

You have successfully built a sophisticated, gamified trivia bot. This project demonstrates how to create an engaging, replayable, and easily maintainable experience. The principles you've applied, tracking a score with global variables, providing instant feedback with conditions, and using Power Automate to fetch dynamic, randomized content, are the foundational building blocks for almost any gamified creative agent you can imagine.

Customer Engagement (Witty Chatbots, Sales Assistants)

In the digital marketplace, the first conversation a potential customer has with your brand is often the most critical. This initial touchpoint can be the difference between a fleeting visit and a loyal, long-term relationship. While the creative agents we have built so far have been powerful internal tools for content creation and ideation, this section shifts our focus outward, toward the dynamic and demanding world of customer engagement.

Here, creativity is not just about generating novel ideas; it is about crafting a personality. It is about building a front-line ambassador for your brand that is not only intelligent and helpful but also memorable. We will explore how to move beyond the sterile, robotic chatbots of the past and create AI agents that engage with wit, charm, and genuine utility. We will delve into two primary archetypes: the witty chatbot, which serves as a charismatic brand voice, and the intelligent sales assistant, which guides potential customers through the sales funnel with conversational grace. This is where your skills as an AI architect merge with the art of the salesperson and the craft of the copywriter.

Functionality Deep Dive: The Art of the First Impression

A successful customer-facing bot must do more than just answer questions; it must build rapport. This is achieved through a combination of personality, knowledge, and a clear sense of purpose.

- **Brand Personality and Voice:** This is the soul of your chatbot. Is your brand playful and informal? Professional and authoritative? Warm and empathetic? This personality must be consistently reflected in every single message, from the initial greeting to the final sign-off. As we explored in Chapter 4, defining this voice in your generative prompts is paramount.

- **Product Knowledge and Expertise:** A sales assistant is useless if it doesn't know what it's selling. The bot must have instant access to a reliable, up-to-date knowledge base of your products or services. This involves connecting your copilot to an external data source, like a SharePoint list or a Dataverse table, that acts as its product catalog.

- **Conversational Lead Qualification:** A great salesperson doesn't interrogate; they have a conversation. Your sales assistant should be designed to gather key information about a customer's needs, budget, and timeline in a natural, non-intrusive way. Each question should feel like a helpful step toward finding the right solution, not a hurdle to be overcome.

- **Call to Action and Seamless Handoff:** The ultimate goal of a sales conversation is to guide the customer to the next step. Your bot must be able to execute a clear call to action, whether that's scheduling a demo, providing a link to a checkout page, or, most importantly, seamlessly handing off the conversation (and all the context it has gathered) to a human sales representative.

- **Handling FAQs and Objections:** Customers will have questions, and some may have objections. A robust engagement bot is pre-loaded with answers to frequently asked questions and is designed to handle common objections with helpful, reassuring responses, preventing the conversation from hitting a dead end.

Implementation: Building "The Brand Concierge Bot"

To bring these concepts to life, we will build a sophisticated sales assistant for a fictional, trendy, direct-to-consumer brand called "Aura Smart Home," which sells high-tech, aesthetically pleasing smart lighting systems. This bot will greet users with personality, learn about their needs, provide intelligent product recommendations, and hand off qualified leads to the sales team.

1. The Foundation: Creating the Product Catalog

First, our bot needs a brain. We will create a SharePoint list to serve as its comprehensive, easily updatable product catalog.

1. **Create the SharePoint List:** Navigate to
   SharePoint, create a new **Blank list**, and name it
   AuraProductCatalog.

2. **Define the Product Schema (Columns):** Structure
   the list with the following columns to hold detailed
   product information:

   a. **Title (Single line of text):** The name of the product (e.g.,
      "Aura Glow Lamp")

   b. **Features (Multiple lines of text):** A detailed, bullet-pointed
      list of key features

   c. **Price (Number):** The retail price of the product

   d. **BestFor (Single line of text):** A short description of the ideal
      use case (e.g., "Ambiance and relaxation," "Productivity
      and focus")

   e. **StockStatus (Choice):** A choice column with options like "In
      Stock," "Low Stock," and "Backordered"

3. **Populate the Catalog:** Add a few of Aura's products
   to the list, filling in all the details as shown in
   Table 6-2.

Table 6-2. *Source Data Representation for Testing Context-Aware AI Responses*

Title	Features	Price	Best For	Stock Status
Aura Glow Lamp	16 million colors App controlled Syncs with music	129	Ambiance and relaxation	In Stock
Aura Focus Desk Light	Adjustable color temperature Wireless charging base Flicker-free LED	189	Productivity and focus	In Stock
Aura Garden Path Lights	Weatherproof (IP65) Solar powered Automated scheduling	249	Outdoor and landscape	Low Stock

2. Crafting the "Witty Welcome" and an Engaging Entry Point

The first few seconds of the interaction are critical. We need to grab the user's attention and establish the brand's personality immediately.

1. **Create a "Greeting" Topic:** In Copilot Studio, open the default **Greeting** topic.

2. **Inject Personality:** Replace the generic default greeting message with something that reflects the "Aura" brand voice: smart, stylish, and helpful.

   a. **Message Node:** "Welcome to Aura. We're here to help you illuminate your world, one brilliant idea at a time."

3. **Ask the Initial Qualifying Question:** Instead of waiting for the user to type, proactively guide them. Add a **Question** node right after the greeting.

    a. **Question Text:** "To get started, what can I help you with today?'

    b. **Identify:** Multiple choice options.

    c. **Options for User:**

        i. "I'd like to explore your products."

        ii. "I have a question about an existing order."

        iii. "Just browsing!"

    d. **Save Response As:** Topic.UserIntent, as shown in Figure 6-12.

4. **Redirect Based on Intent:** Add a Condition node. If Topic.UserIntent is "I'd like to explore your products," as shown in Figure 6-13, use a Redirect node to send the user to a new topic we will create called ProductSalesConversation, as shown in Figure 6-14.

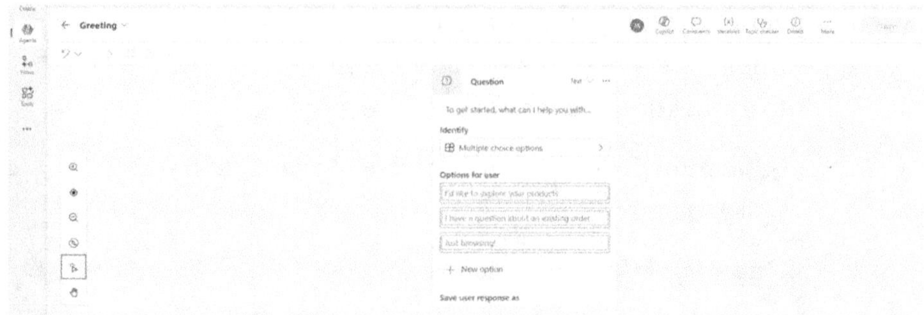

Figure 6-12. *The authoring canvas for the "Aura Smart Home" brand concierge bot shows a Question node that proactively guides the customer experience. By offering multiple-choice options like "explore products" or "order questions," the bot establishes a "Witty Welcome" that immediately captures user intent and directs the conversation toward a helpful solution*

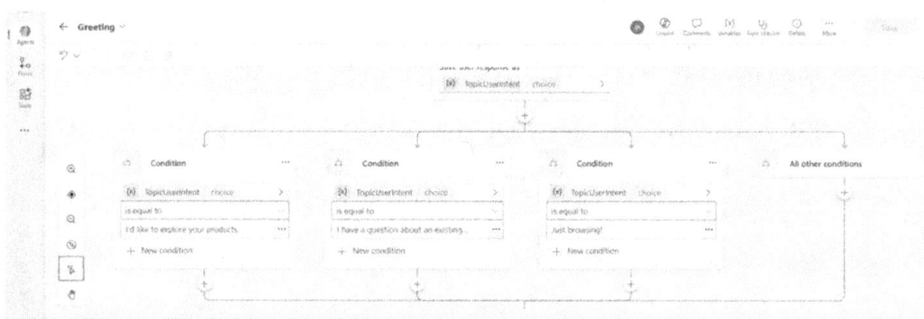

Figure 6-13. *This screenshot illustrates the complex "Condition" node logic used to route the user based on their stated intent. Each branch is configured to check if the Topic.UserIntent is equal to a specific choice, allowing the agent to provide tailored experiences for customers who are browsing products versus those seeking order support*

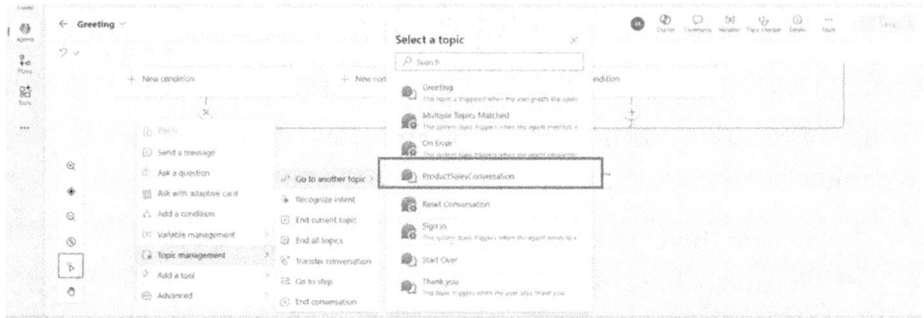

Figure 6-14. *The "Topic management" menu is utilized again here to redirect the "explore products" intent to a specialized "ProductSalesConversation" topic. This modular design ensures that the agent remains organized, handling the specific sales funnel logic separately from the general greeting and FAQ interactions*

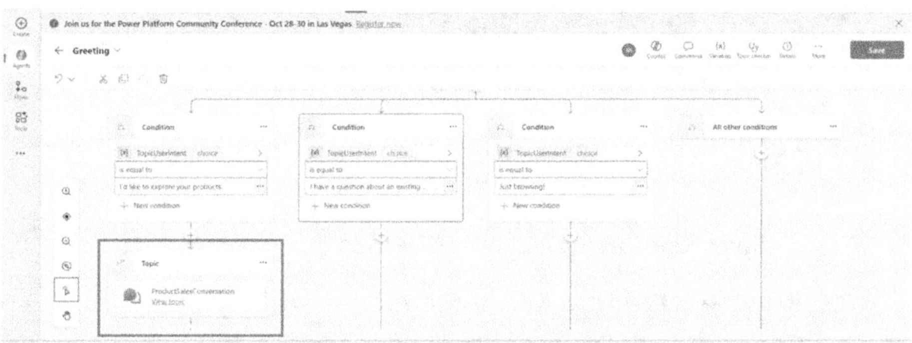

Figure 6-15. *The final view of the "Greeting" topic shows the completed redirection path to the "ProductSalesConversation" topic node. This visualizes the successful transition from a general brand ambassador interaction to an intelligent sales assistant that can provide tailored product recommendations based on a customer's unique needs*

3. Building the "Product Sales Conversation" Topic

This is the core of our sales assistant. This topic will retrieve product information, ask qualifying questions, and provide tailored recommendations.

1. **Create the Topic:** Create a new topic named ProductSalesConversation (no trigger phrases), as shown in Figure 6-15.

2. **Ask Discovery Questions:** The first step is to understand the customer's needs. Add a **Question** node.

   a. **Question Text:** "I can definitely help with that. To find the perfect light for you, could you tell me what kind of space you're looking to brighten up?"

   b. **Identify:** Multiple choice options.

   c. **Options for User:** "My living room or bedroom," "My home office," "My garden or patio."

   d. **Save Response As:** Topic.UserSpace.

3. **Provide a Tailored Recommendation with Generative AI:** Now, we'll use the user's input to provide a smart, context-aware recommendation.

   a. **Call a Power Automate Flow to get Product Data:** Before the generative node, you would ideally call a Power Automate flow that fetches all items from your SharePoint catalog and returns them as a single text string or JSON object. (For simplicity in this step, we can also hard-code some information in the prompt, but a flow is best practice.)

   b. Add a **Create generative answers** node. In the **Input** prompt, write the following:

"You are the Aura Brand Concierge, an expert in smart lighting. A customer is looking for a light for their '{Topic.UserSpace}'. Your complete product catalog is as follows: [Insert product data from Power Automate flow here]. Based on their need, recommend ONE product from the catalog that is the best fit. Describe why it's a great choice and mention one key feature. Keep the tone helpful and stylish."

    c. Save the output to a variable called Topic. AIRecommendation.

  4. **Display the Recommendation:** Add a Message node, and insert the {Topic.AIRecommendation} variable.

4. The Handoff: Notifying the Human Sales Team

If the customer is interested after the recommendation, we need a seamless way to connect them with a human.

  1. **Create the "Notify Sales" Power Automate Flow**

    a. Create a new Instant cloud flow in Power Automate named NotifySalesTeam, triggered by Power Virtual Agents.

    b. **Define Inputs:** Add inputs for the information you've gathered: CustomerName, CustomerEmail, and InterestedProduct.

    c. **Add an Action:** Use the Microsoft Teams connector and the Post message in a chat or channel action.

      i. Post to a specific sales team channel.

      ii. Message: Format a rich message that summarizes the lead:

"New Hot Lead! \nName: {CustomerName}\
nEmail: {CustomerEmail}\nInterested In:
{InterestedProduct}\nPlease follow up ASAP!"

d. **Return a Confirmation:** Add a Return value(s) action that sends a single **Text** output named ConfirmationStatus with the value "Done!".

2. **Integrate the Handoff in Copilot Studio**

a. After displaying the AI recommendation in your ProductSalesConversation topic, add a **Question** node:

  i. **Question Text:** "Would you like to speak with one of our lighting specialists to learn more and get a personalized quote?"

  ii. **Identify:** Boolean (Yes/No).

b. Add a **Condition** node. If the answer is Yes:

  i. Ask for their name and email, saving them to Global. UserName and Global.UserEmail.

  ii. Add an Action node and call your NotifySalesTeam flow, passing in the collected variables.

  iii. Add a final Message node: "Perfect! I've just notified our team. Someone will reach out to you at {Global. UserEmail} shortly. We're excited to help you build your Aura."

By building this Brand Concierge Bot, you have created far more than a simple chatbot. You have engineered a customer engagement engine that embodies a brand's personality, understands customer needs, leverages product knowledge to provide intelligent recommendations, and integrates directly into the sales workflow. This project showcases how the creative and technical skills you've developed can be applied to solve real-world business challenges, turning a simple website visitor into a qualified, engaged, and valued lead.

Case Study: E-Learning Platform's AI Tutor

Throughout this chapter, we have explored how to tailor creative AI agents for specific industries, moving from content generators to interactive storytellers, gamified bots, and witty brand ambassadors. Each example has highlighted a particular facet of conversational AI. Now, we arrive at a case study designed to be the ultimate synthesis of these concepts: a sophisticated, personalized AI Tutor for an e-learning platform.

This project is more than just a final example; it is a demonstration of how to build a truly adaptive and empathetic AI companion. An AI Tutor cannot simply dispense information. It must engage, diagnose, and adapt. It needs the content generation skills of a copywriter, the narrative branching of an interactive storyteller, the motivational loops of a gamified experience, and the personalization of a dedicated sales assistant. By building this bot, you will be weaving together every thread we have discussed to create an agent that doesn't just answer questions; it also fosters understanding.

The Vision: Creating a Personalized Learning Companion

The Scenario: Imagine an online learning platform called "Cognify," which provides high-quality courses for high school students. While their video lectures and articles are excellent, they've identified a key problem: students often get "stuck" on complex topics in subjects like physics and have no immediate way to get help. Passive learning isn't enough; they need an interactive, on-demand guide who can explain concepts in different ways and test their knowledge until it solidifies.

The Solution: We will build "Newton Bot," an AI Tutor for Cognify's physics course. This bot will serve as a 24/7 personal tutor that can

- Explain complex physics concepts using simple terms and creative analogies

- Engage students in a Socratic dialogue, asking guiding questions to help them arrive at their own conclusions

- Administer short, gamified quizzes to check for understanding and reinforce learning

- Track each student's progress, remembering which topics they have mastered and which they are struggling with, creating a truly personalized learning path

Architectural Blueprint: Combining Memory, Knowledge, and Logic

To build an AI Tutor this intelligent, we need a robust architecture that separates its knowledge base from its conversational logic and its memory.

- **Copilot Studio:** This will be the conversational front end, the friendly interface through which students interact with Newton Bot.

- **SharePoint List 1 (PhysicsKnowledgeBase):** This list will function as the bot's "textbook." It is an external, structured database containing all the educational content: definitions, formulas, analogies, and quiz questions. This decoupling means educators can add or update the curriculum without ever touching the bot's logic.

- **SharePoint List 2 (StudentProgress):** This list is the bot's long-term memory, acting as a personal "gradebook" for every student. It will store persistent data, allowing the bot to remember a student's progress across multiple sessions.

- **Power Automate Flows:** These are the vital connectors that allow our bot to read from its textbook and write to its memory. We will use three distinct flows to manage the data operations seamlessly.

Implementation: Building "Newton Bot" from the Ground Up

Step 1: Building the AI's Brain (The Knowledge Base)

First, we must provide our tutor with the knowledge it needs to teach.

1. **Create the PhysicsKnowledgeBase List:** In SharePoint, create a new Blank **list** with this name.

2. **Define the Curriculum Structure (Columns)**

   a. **Title (Single line of text):** The name of the specific topic (e.g., "Newton's First Law").

   b. **CoreConcept (Multiple lines of text):** A concise, accurate definition of the topic.

   c. **Analogy (Multiple lines of text):** A creative, simplified analogy to explain the concept. This is key to making complex ideas relatable.

   d. **QuizQuestion (Single line of text):** A multiple-choice question to test understanding of this topic.

    e. **QuizOptions (Multiple lines of text):** The possible answers, formatted as a simple JSON array (e.g., ["Inertia", "Gravity", "Friction"]).

    f. **CorrectAnswer (Single line of text):** The correct answer from the options.

Summary

In this chapter, we have transitioned from building the foundational creative engine to specializing it for the real world. We explored how to tailor conversational AI for bloggers, screenwriters, and poets, ensuring that each agent understands the unique nuances of its craft. By moving beyond linear narratives, we designed interactive storytelling experiences where player agency and persistent state management create living, reactive worlds.

We also discovered the power of gamification, using dynamic logic and external data sources to build engaging quiz bots and RPG assistants that foster achievement and retention. Finally, we applied these techniques to customer engagement and education, building "Newton Bot" as a prime example of an adaptive, empathetic AI tutor that diagnoses student needs and personalizes the learning journey.

As you have seen, the success of these industry-specific agents relies on a precise balance of technical reliability and creative flair. While the models drive the conversation, your architecture, encompassing external data connections, robust intent routing, and persistent memory, provides the necessary structure for professional applications. In the next chapter, we will shift our focus to testing, debugging, and optimization to ensure your creative agents perform reliably under any conditions.

CHAPTER 7

Testing, Debugging, and Optimization

Think back to the magnificent musical instrument we built in the earlier chapters. We selected the materials, assembled the core components, and learned the expressive techniques to give it a voice and soul. That instrument is now ready, tuned to the pitch of creativity and humming with the power of Generative AI. But no performance is perfect on the first try, and no digital creation is immune to the unpredictable nature of the real world.

In the digital world, launching a creative AI is not an ending; it is a profound beginning. It is the moment we move from the controlled environment of the studio to the dynamic stage of user interaction, where feedback replaces guesswork and raw data reveals hidden truths. This chapter is dedicated to the essential, ongoing process of refining excellence, transforming a functional copilot into a continuously improving, highly optimized creative engine.

We will move beyond merely testing if the bot works and instead focus on answering crucial questions: Is it resonating with the user? Is it performing efficiently under pressure? Are its creative suggestions truly inspiring? And most importantly, how can we make it better tomorrow than it is today?

© Mezba Uddin 2026

M. Uddin, *Creative AI Agents with Copilot Studio*, Inside Copilot,
https://doi.org/10.1007/979-8-8688-2779-2_7

You will learn to embrace the role of the data scientist and the performance coach. We will begin by harnessing the built-in power of Copilot Studio Analytics to measure creative impact and user satisfaction. From there, we will master the art of A/B testing, the very core of your AI's creativity, its tone, its humor, and its unique output styles, allowing you to scientifically validate which creative approaches are most effective. We will then sharpen your AI's resilience by defining strategies for gracefully Handling Edge Cases and Misunderstandings, ensuring it never feels like a brittle machine. Finally, we will build continuous, ethical feedback loops to foster continuous learning from user feedback, making your copilot smarter and more inclusive with every interaction.

By the end of this chapter, you will possess the tools and mindset to not only launch your creative AI with confidence but also to manage its ongoing evolution, ensuring your copilot remains a trustworthy, engaging, and indispensable partner for years to come.

Using Copilot Studio Analytics

In the relentless pursuit of building a successful creative AI agent, be it the LyricLab Bot, the AI Dungeon Master, or the Personalized Marketing Campaign Generator, the moment of creation only marks the beginning. The true measure of a copilot's success lies not in its technical specifications, but in its real-world performance: how effectively it engages users, provides genuine inspiration, and achieves its intended purpose. This crucial evaluation phase is entirely data-driven, and within the Microsoft Copilot Studio ecosystem, the Analytics dashboard is your indispensable command center for gathering, synthesizing, and interpreting these insights.

This section provides a comprehensive guide to mastering the built-in analytics tools. We will show you how to move beyond basic monitoring and transform raw usage data into actionable creative intelligence. This mastery is essential for fine-tuning your bot's personality, optimizing the relevance of its generated content, and securing greater user satisfaction through continuous, informed refinement.

Access and Configuration: Laying the Analytical Foundation

Before your copilot can deliver reliable data, you must ensure two fundamental elements are in place: proper access and correct configuration of feedback channels.

Accessing the Dashboard

The Analytics dashboard is accessed via the primary navigation pane within the Copilot Studio interface. The Analytics dashboard aggregates data where supported by the channel. The data may take a few hours to appear, allowing for near real-time observation of A/B tests or newly deployed topics.

Configuring User Feedback Channels

The most valuable data for a creative copilot is subjective user feedback, which you must actively configure the system to capture

1. **CSAT Activation:** The **Customer Satisfaction (CSAT)** feature is a critical toggle. Once enabled, the copilot will, at the end of successful or resolved sessions, explicitly ask the user to rate the conversation (typically on a 1–5 scale). For a creative bot, this metric directly reflects how pleased the user was with the AI's tone and the quality of the generated output.

2. **Transcript Retention:** Ensure that conversation transcripts are configured for retention. These are your qualitative data sources, providing the necessary context to understand why a specific metric spiked or dropped. Without the transcript, a low engagement score is merely a number; with it, it's a story of user frustration. Note that transcript retention and access are strictly governed by environment policies and compliance standards, which are critical considerations in enterprise settings.

3. **Session Logging:** Instead of assuming specific fields are recorded, you should use the session ID or user identifier available within the platform. It is essential to confirm exactly which identifiers are available in your specific environment, as certain variables like user.ID, are not reliably present across all deployment channels. These identifiers remain necessary when correlating user data with custom logging via Power Automate.

The Core Analytical Metrics: Interpreting Creative Performance

The main Analytics dashboard, as we can see in Figure 7-1, presents high-level performance metrics that, when viewed through a creative lens, translate directly into measures of engagement, inspiration, and utility.

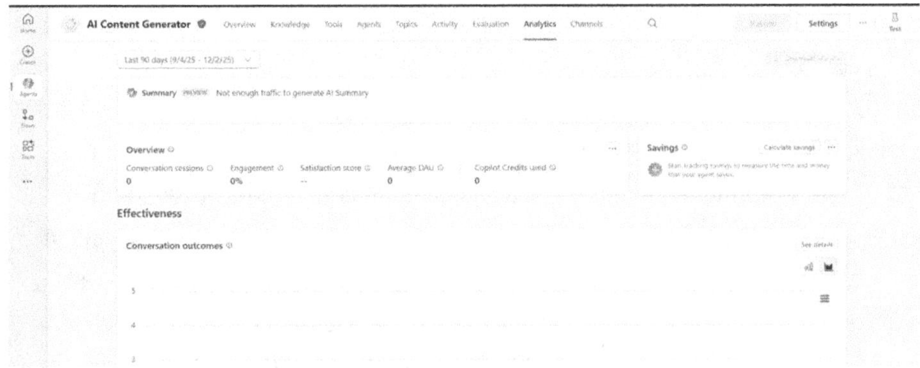

Figure 7-1. *The Copilot Studio Analytics dashboard overview. This is the central hub for monitoring agent performance, providing key metrics on session volume, engagement, and user satisfaction over time*

Metric	Definition and Formula	Creative Interpretation
Total Sessions	The raw count of initiated conversations.	Initial Attraction: Indicates how effective the bot's discovery pathways and Trigger Phrases are. Low numbers suggest users are not finding or entering the flow.
Engagement Rate	Sessions ending in Topic Success/ Total Sessions.	Creative Value Delivery: Shows how many users complete the intended creative flow. While high engagement typically suggests strong creative relevance, it is important to treat this metric as a proxy for success. "Topic Success" depends heavily on how your topics are defined and how the session concludes; this can be particularly misleading in generative orchestration, where a successful outcome may not always result in a traditional "topic completed" status.

(continued)

Metric	Definition and Formula	Creative Interpretation
Escalation Rate	Sessions handed off to a human agent/Total Sessions.	AI Self-Sufficiency and Trust: While a high rate may indicate the bot struggles with complex creative tasks, you should interpret escalation based on your specific design goals. In many customer-facing scenarios, a healthy and accessible escalation path is actually a sign of a well-designed user experience rather than a failure of the AI.
Abandonment Rate	Sessions where the user exits before resolution.	Friction and Frustration: A high rate often reveals bottlenecks, such as too many questions, unclear prompts, or automation failures. However, it is important to note that abandonment is not always negative; in some cases, it may simply indicate that the user obtained the information or inspiration they needed quickly and exited the conversation satisfied before reaching a formal resolution node.
Satisfaction Score (CSAT)	User-provided rating (1–5).	Personality and Aesthetic Success: Measures whether the bot's tone, style, and creative persona resonate with users. Useful for persona A/B testing.

Analytical Scenario: The Low CSAT Score. If the CSAT score drops significantly during a campaign where you are using the "Witty and Informal" personality (Chapter 4), the data suggests that your audience might prefer a more "Professional and Mentor" tone. This directly informs the decision to adjust the persona priming in your Generative AI prompts.

Topics Analysis: Pinpointing Conversational Failures

The Topics report provides the granular detail needed to pinpoint exactly where your conversational blueprints are failing. This report moves beyond overall performance to focus on the efficiency of individual creative functionalities.

Topic Success and Abandonment Funnel

Copilot Studio visualizes the path of a Topic, allowing you to see where users drop off. This is a crucial feature for identifying flaws in complex creative workflows, such as the multi-step Generate Marketing Campaign flow.

- **Identifying the Friction Point:** By inspecting the visualization, if you see a large drop-off immediately after a node asking the user to provide a SharePoint URL or an API key (technical input), you have successfully identified a point of friction.

- **Remediation:** The required action is often technical streamlining, such as using a Power Automate Flow to handle the input automatically. Crucially, you should never ask users to provide API keys conversationally in a production environment. Sensitive credentials must be stored securely using Azure Key Vault or connection references rather than being collected directly from the user.

Uncertainty and Fallback Triggers

The Uncertainty Rate serves as a vital indicator of your copilot's overall Natural Language Understanding (NLU) competence. While a high rate often signifies that user input did not match a known Trigger Phrase, it is important to recognize that uncertainty is not limited to simple mismatches. Uncertainty can also stem from ambiguous user intents, missing required entities, or specific behaviors within generative orchestration modes. When these situations occur, they force the system into the Fallback topic to attempt recovery (Chapters 3 and 4).

- **Reviewing Failed Input:** The analytics provide a list of the exact phrases that failed to match. Reviewing this list is mandatory for continuous NLU improvement. For example, if users frequently say, "I need a punchline for my presentation" and the "Generate Corporate Humor" topic is not triggering, you must manually add that phrase to the Topic's Trigger Phrases. While this manual refinement is a staple of classic orchestration, it is important to note that if generative orchestration is enabled, the system uses a different method for intent matching and orchestration behavior.

- **Refining Fallback Prompts:** When the fallback is triggered, ensure the AI's response adheres to the Tier 2 Conversational Recovery strategy by offering a graceful, open-ended question that redirects the user back to a core functionality.

Custom Logging for Generative AI Quality

The standard analytics are excellent for measuring flow, but they cannot measure the subjective quality of the AI's creative output. To do this, you must engineer a custom logging solution using Variables and Power Automate.

The Creative Quality Question

After every successful generative answer, you should periodically ask (e.g., every third response) or at key moments a simple, focused question to capture quality data:

Example Node Sequence

1. **Create generative answers** node runs (e.g., generates a character name).

2. **Question node** is placed directly after, asking: "Did that name suggestion spark an idea?"

3. **Identify:** Boolean (Yes/No).

4. **Save Response As:** Topic.CreativeSpark.

The value of Topic.CreativeSpark provides a useful proxy for the AI's creative utility, though it is not a "direct" or absolute measurement. When interpreting this data, keep in mind that users may occasionally respond "yes" simply to be polite or, conversely, provide a "no" for reasons entirely unrelated to the actual creative quality of the output.

The Logging Mechanism

Once you have this Yes/No value, you must log it alongside the session details:

1. **Logging Flow:** Create a Power Automate Flow named LogCreativeQuality that accepts the following inputs: SessionID, TopicName, GeneratedOutput, and CreativeSpark (Boolean).

2. **Data Repository:** The flow writes this structured data to a Dataverse Table or SharePoint List.

3. **Analysis:** You can then calculate the Creative Spark Rate (CSR): Total "Yes" responses/Total Generated Answers. This KPI is far more relevant to a creative agent than the generic Engagement Rate.

Debugging Workflow: The Activity Map and Variable Inspection

Analytics inform what is wrong, but the Activity Map and transcripts tell you where and how to fix it. These tools are the forensic instruments used to debug both conversational logic and technical integrations.

The Activity Map (The Visual Trace)

The Activity tab provides a visual log of individual sessions, known as the Activity Map. This trace is indispensable for diagnosing failures in complex, multi-step creative flows, particularly those involving external systems.

- **Trace the Path:** You can visually follow a user's journey through every node. This is crucial when debugging integrations like the Personalized Marketing Campaign Generator (as we did in Chapter 5). You can ensure that the Call an action node for Power Automate was triggered correctly and that the flow returned the expected output.

- **Action Success/Failure:** The Activity Map will visually flag if an action node failed (e.g., the flow connecting to the DALL-E image generation API returned an error). This immediately directs your attention to the Power Automate side of the configuration.

Variable Inspection

A common failure point in complex copilots is Variable scope or data type mismatch.

- **Debugging Logic Errors:** The Activity Map allows you to click on any node and inspect the current value of all Topic and Global variables. If a Condition node is failing, inspect the variable being checked. For example, if a condition checks Global.PlayerClass is equal to Warrior, but the variable inspection shows the value is WARRIOR (uppercase), you have found a simple case sensitivity error. You can fix this by using Power Fx functions such as Lower(), Upper(), or Trim() to normalize the text data before the comparison takes place.

- **Debugging Integration Errors:** If a Power Automate Flow returns an unexpected result, inspecting the receiving variable in the Activity Map allows you to see the exact text or JSON returned by the flow before it hits any parsing logic, identifying where the data structure broke down.

Conversation Transcripts (The Qualitative Data)

While technical tools solve coding errors, the transcripts solve conversational design errors.

- **Identify Creative Pain Points:** A low Engagement Rate might not be a technical bug, but a creative one. Transcripts often reveal that the AI's response was too generic, too wordy, or failed to address the user's nuanced creative request, requiring a rewrite of the Generative AI prompt.

- **Discover New Requirements:** Transcripts are a goldmine for discovering unaddressed user needs. If multiple users ask, "Can you translate that poem into Spanish?", it indicates a high-value feature opportunity, which can be implemented using a new Power Automate Flow calling a translation API.

By diligently integrating the quantitative insights from the Analytics dashboard with the qualitative and forensic data provided by the Activity Map and transcripts, you establish a mature and robust process for continuous improvement. This data-to-action pipeline is the engine that drives your copilot's evolution, ensuring its creative utility only increases over time. This foundational mastery of testing and debugging sets the stage for advanced techniques like A/B testing, which we explore in the next section.

A/B Testing Creative Responses

In traditional software development, testing is binary: code either compiles or it errors; a button works, or it is broken. But in the world of creative AI, "correctness" is subjective. Is a witty response better than a formal one? Is a concise summary more valuable than a detailed explanation? Is a poem more moving if it rhymes or if it uses free verse?

As the architect of a creative copilot, relying on your own intuition to answer these questions is risky. Your preference for dry humor might alienate a user base that prefers enthusiastic support. To truly optimize your AI's creative performance, you must move from intuition to evidence.

This is where A/B testing (or split testing) enters your toolkit. By scientifically presenting different versions of your AI's personality or output to different users and measuring the results, you can let your audience decide what "best" looks like.

In this section, we will build a robust A/B testing framework directly within Copilot Studio. You will learn how to create a "traffic splitter" to randomize user experiences, how to design meaningful creative variants, and how to tag your data to declare a winner.

The Psychology of Variants: What Should You Test?

Before we build the mechanism, we must define the experiment. A/B testing is most powerful when used to validate specific creative hypotheses. Here are the three most impactful variables to test in a creative agent:

1. **Tone and Persona (The "Vibe" Test)**

   a. **Variant A (The Professional)**: "Here is a structured outline for your blog post."

   b. **Variant B (The Enthusiast)**: "I've cooked up a killer outline to get your writing flowing! Let's dive in."

   c. **Hypothesis**: Does high-energy language increase engagement, or does it annoy users looking for quick utility?

2. **Length and Density (The "Brevity" Test)**

   a. **Variant A (Concise)**: A 50-word summary of a generated story idea.

   b. **Variant B (Detailed)**: A 200-word detailed synopsis including character motivations.

   c. **Hypothesis**: Do users value depth, or do they experience cognitive overload with long generative responses?

3. **Format and Presentation (The "Visual" Test)**

    a. **Variant A (Text):** A plain text list of marketing slogans.

    b. **Variant B (Adaptive Card):** A visually polished card displaying the slogans with "Copy" buttons.

    c. **Hypothesis:** Does a richer UI lead to higher satisfaction scores?

Implementation: Building the "Traffic Splitter"

If native A/B testing is not available in your environment, you can easily build a custom framework using the core components mastered in Chapter 3: variables and conditions. While Copilot Studio may not have a native "A/B Test" button in many setups, the product changes over time, and manual implementation remains a reliable way to ensure consistency across all versions.

We will use the Power Fx formula language to generate a random number, which will act as our digital coin toss.

Step 1: Initialize the Random Splitter

Open the Topic you wish to test (e.g., "Generate Marketing Dialogue"). At the very beginning of the flow, before any creative content is generated, add a new node.

1. Click + Add a node, and select Variable management; then Set a variable value.

2. Create a new variable named Topic.RandomSplit.

3. In the To value field, switch to the Formula tab (represented by the fx icon).

4. Enter the formula: Rand()

a. Confirm Rand() is available in your formula editor.

b. Note: This function generates a random decimal number between 0 and 1 (e.g., 0.45, 0.89, 0.12).

Step 2: Create the Branching Logic

Immediately after setting the variable, we need to direct the traffic using a Condition node (see Figure 7-2).

1. Click + Add a node and select Add a condition.

2. Branch 1 (Variant A): Set the condition to Topic. RandomSplit is less than 0.5.

   a. Statistically, this will capture approximately 50% of your users.

3. **All Other Conditions (Variant B):** This branch will capture the remaining 50% (values 0.5 and above).

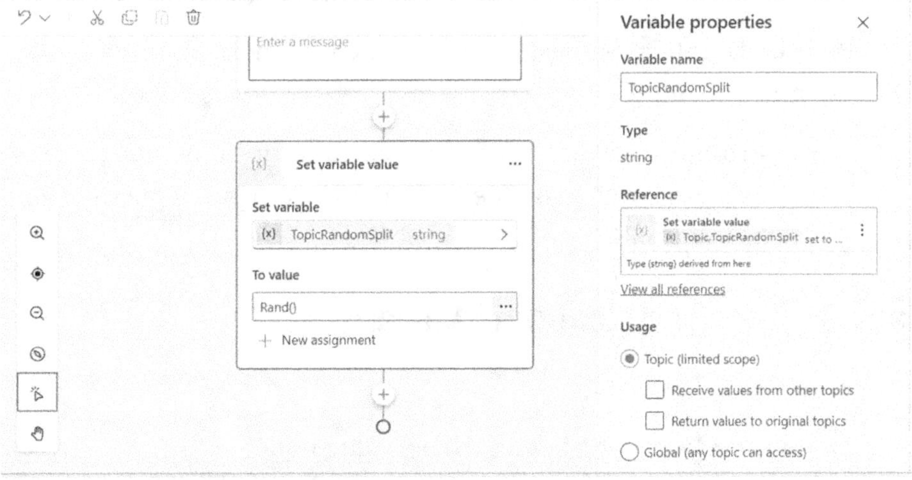

Figure 7-2. *The traffic splitter logic in Copilot Studio. This screenshot captures the authoring canvas showing the Set variable node using the Rand() formula, followed immediately by a Condition node that splits the path based on whether the value is less than 0.5, creating two distinct testing branches.*

You now have two parallel universes within your topic.

Designing the Variants and Tagging Data

Now that the traffic is split, you must define the unique creative experience for each path. Crucially, you must also tag the session so you know which variant the user saw when you analyze the analytics later. This tagging is essential for correlating the user's satisfaction score with the specific creative approach they experienced.

Path A: The "Witty" Variant

Inside the first branch (where RandomSplit < 0.5):

1. **Set the Tag:** Add a Set a variable value node.

   a. **Variable**: Create a new variable named Topic.TestVariant.

   b. **Value**: "Variant_A_Witty" as shown in Figure 7-3.

2. **The Creative Prompt:** Add your Create generative answers node.

   a. **Prompt**: "You are a witty, clever stand-up comedian helping a user write a slogan. Keep it punchy, use a pun if possible, and be informal."

Path B: The "Professional" Variant

Inside the second branch:

1. **Set the Tag:** Add a Set a variable value node.

   a. **Variable**: Topic.TestVariant.

   b. **Value**: "Variant_B_Professional".

2. **The Creative Prompt:** Add your Create generative answers node.

   a. **Prompt:** "You are a senior brand consultant. Write a sophisticated, elegant, and timeless slogan. Avoid humor. Focus on value and prestige."

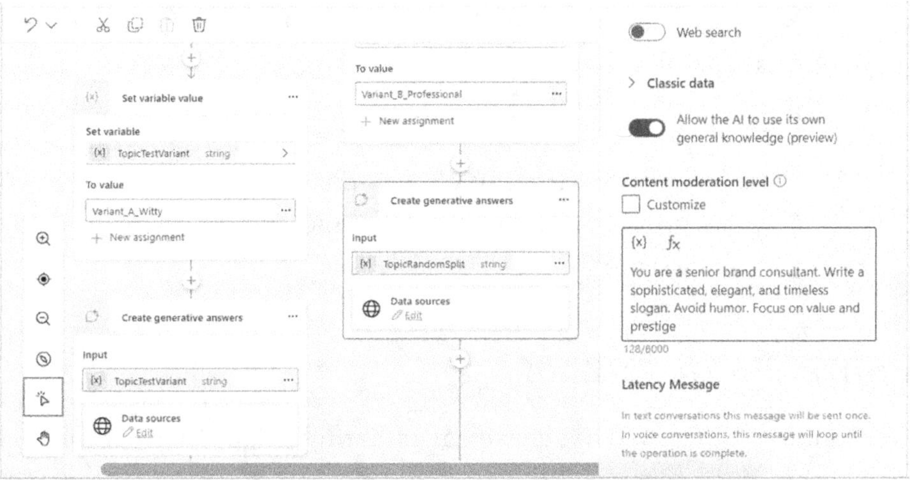

Figure 7-3. *Configuring creative variants. This visual compares the two branches: the left branch shows the "Witty" prompt configuration, while the right branch shows the "Professional" prompt. Both branches include a Set variable node that tags the session with the specific variant name for analytics tracking*

Converging and Measuring Success

After the generative nodes in both branches, bring the flow back together to a single point (using a "Redirect" or simply connecting the nodes if the UI permits) to collect feedback.

This is where the custom logging we discussed (earlier of this chapter) becomes vital. You cannot rely on generic analytics here; you need to know which specific variant caused the user to be happy or frustrated.

The Feedback Loop

1. Ask the Creative Quality Question (e.g., "Did you like this style?").

2. Call your LogCreativeQuality Power Automate flow.

3. **Crucial Step**: Pass the Topic.TestVariant variable ("Variant_A_Witty" or "Variant_B_Professional") as an input to your flow.

Analyzing the Winner

After running your copilot for a week or gathering a significant sample size (use enough sessions to reduce noise; start with hundreds to thousands if possible), open your data source (SharePoint or Dataverse) where the flow logs the results.

You will now see a clear dataset:

By aggregating this data, you might discover that Variant A has a 75% approval rate, while Variant B only has 40%.

The Decision: Scientific validation is now complete. You can confidently return to Copilot Studio, delete the branching logic, remove Variant B, and make Variant A the permanent, optimized experience for all users.

A/B testing transforms creative decisions from arguments about "taste" into decisions based on truth. It allows you to take risks with your creative AI, knowing that data will always guide you to the most effective solution.

Handling Edge Cases and Misunderstandings

In software engineering, the "happy path" is the ideal journey: the user asks the right question, provides the correct data, and the system delivers the perfect result.

But in the world of creative collaboration, the "happy path" is a myth. Creativity is messy. Users will change their minds mid-sentence. They will provide vague, abstract inputs like "make it pop" or "give me something blue." They will ask your lyrical bot for legal advice or your corporate branding agent for a bedtime story.

These are edge cases, scenarios that fall outside the standard operating procedures of your design. If your copilot isn't built to handle them, it will break. And when a creative partner breaks, trust evaporates.

This section is about building resilience. We will move beyond simple error messages ("I didn't understand") and design robust strategies for conversation repair. You will learn how to implement a Tiered Fallback System that attempts to recover the conversation before giving up and how to use Slot Filling Validation to handle partial or confusing inputs gracefully.

The Anatomy of a Misunderstanding

Before we fix the problem, we must categorize it. In a creative AI context, edge cases usually fall into three buckets:

1. **Ambiguity:** The user's intent is relevant but unclear.

    a. **User:** "I need a draft."

    b. **AI Challenge**: A draft of what? A blog post? A tweet? A novel chapter?

2. **Out of Scope:** The user asks for something the bot wasn't designed to do.

   a. **User**: "What is the capital of Peru?" (asked to a Hip-Hop Lyric Bot).

   b. **AI Challenge**: The bot knows the answer, but providing it breaks the immersive persona.

3. **The Pivot:** The user changes their mind in the middle of a flow.

   a. **AI**: "What genre is your story?"

   b. **User**: "Actually, let's write a poem instead."

   c. **AI Challenge**: The bot is waiting for a genre variable, not a new command.

Strategy 1: The Tiered Fallback System

While you can often implement this by customizing the system-level Fallback topic, be aware that fallback behavior can vary based on your environment's configuration. If you are using generative orchestration, the recovery logic may not be contained in a single topic; instead, some setups rely on a combination of system instructions and generative fallback configurations rather than the classic topic-based approach.

We can implement this in Copilot Studio by customizing the system-level Fallback topic.

Tier 1: The Gentle Nudge (First Failure)

When the AI first fails to understand an input, assume it's a phrasing issue. The response should be a polite request to rephrase, maintaining the creative persona.

- **Response**: "I'm not sure I caught that vibe. Could you say it a different way?"

Tier 2: The Guided Menu (Second Failure)

If the user fails again immediately, assume they don't know what to say. The AI should stop guessing and provide specific, clickable options.

- **Response**: "I'm still a bit lost. To help me get back on track, are you trying to: [Generate a Headline], [Write a Bio], or [Start Over]?"

Tier 3: The Graceful Exit (Third Failure)

If the user is still struggling, the conversation is broken. It is better to reset or escalate than to continue the loop as shown in Figure 7-4.

- **Response**: "It seems we're on different wavelengths right now. I'm going to reset our session so we can start fresh." ➤ Trigger "Start Over" logic.

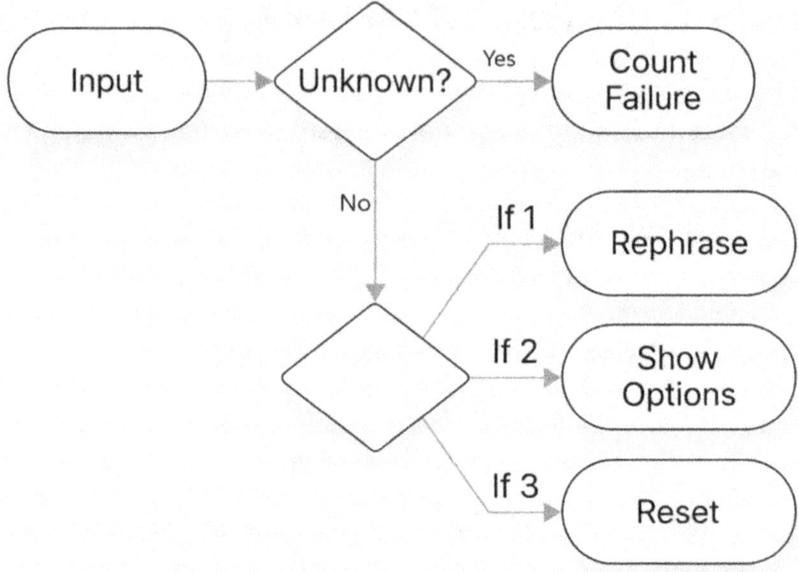

Figure 7-4. *The Tiered Fallback logic flow. A conceptual diagram showing the decision tree: Input ➤ Unknown ➤ Count Failure. If 1: Rephrase ➤ If 2: Show Options ➤ If 3: Reset. This visual illustrates how to prevent infinite error loops*

Strategy 2: Handling "Out of Scope" with Persona Protection

When a user asks your LyricLab Bot for a weather report, you have two choices: answer it (breaking character) or refuse it (keeping the immersion).

For creative agents, Persona Protection is usually the better choice. You want to gently steer the user back to the creative domain without being rude.

Implementation in Generative AI: You don't need complex if/else conditions for every possible off-topic question. Instead, you use the System Instructions in your Generative AI settings (as discussed in Chapter 4) to set the boundary.

- **Instruction**: "You are a creative writing assistant. If a user asks about topics unrelated to writing, creativity, or storytelling (like math, sports scores, or general trivia), politely decline and pivot back to creativity." Example: "I'm better at rhymes than arithmetic. Let's get back to the lyrics."

This "Soft Guardrail" keeps the user engaged while enforcing the bot's purpose.

Strategy 3: Resilience in Slot Filling (The "Pivot")

One of the hardest edge cases to manage is when a user answers a question with a new command.

- **Bot**: "What is the protagonist's name?"

- **User**: "Wait, I want to change the genre first."

If your bot blindly saves "Wait, I want to change the genre first" into the Global.ProtagonistName variable, the story generation will be a disaster.

The Fix: Entity Validation: In Copilot Studio, when you use a Question Node, you select an **Entity** (like "Person Name" or "City").

1. **Enable "Smart Matching":** This allows the AI to extract the name "John" even if the user says, "I think his name is John."

2. **Add a Condition Check:** After the Question node,
    add a Condition to check if the variable is empty
    or contains specific "stop words" (like "cancel" or
    "restart"). It is important to note that stop-word
    checks are language-dependent and should be
    tailored to the specific language and dialect of your
    target audience to ensure they trigger correctly.

3. **Allow Interruptions:** In the Topic settings, ensure "Allow
    switching to another topic" is enabled. This allows the
    intent "change genre" to trigger the Genre Selection topic,
    interrupting the current flow and then returning once
    that new task is done. However, proceed with caution, as
    users can sometimes interrupt flows unintentionally. To
    mitigate this risk, consider limiting which topics are allowed
    to interrupt or designing a "Are you switching tasks?"
    confirmation message to ensure the transition is intentional.

Implementation: Configuring the Fallback Topic

Let's build the Tiered Fallback directly in Copilot Studio as shown in
Figure 7-5.

1. **Open System Topics:** In the Topics pane, switch the
    filter to System. Select the Fallback topic.

2. **Initialize a Counter:** At the top of the flow, use a Set
    variable value node to increment a variable called Global.
    FallbackCount (or a session-scoped variable) by 1. While
    you could use a topic-scoped variable, these may not
    persist reliably across the Fallback topic in all cases. Using
    a global or session variable ensures the count is accurately
    maintained as the system navigates between different topics.

3. **Add Conditions**

   a. **Condition 1:** If Topic.FallbackCount = 1, then Send "Gentle Nudge" message.

   b. **Condition 2:** If Topic.FallbackCount = 2, then Send "Guided Menu" (Question node with options).

   c. **Condition 3:** If Topic.FallbackCount >= 3, then Send "Graceful Exit" message, and **redirect** to the "Start Over" topic.

4. **Reset the Counter:** Crucially, go to your **Conversational Boosting** (Generative Answers) topic or your main creative topics. At the very start of a successful interaction, set Topic.FallbackCount back to 0. This ensures the user isn't penalized for past mistakes in a new conversation.

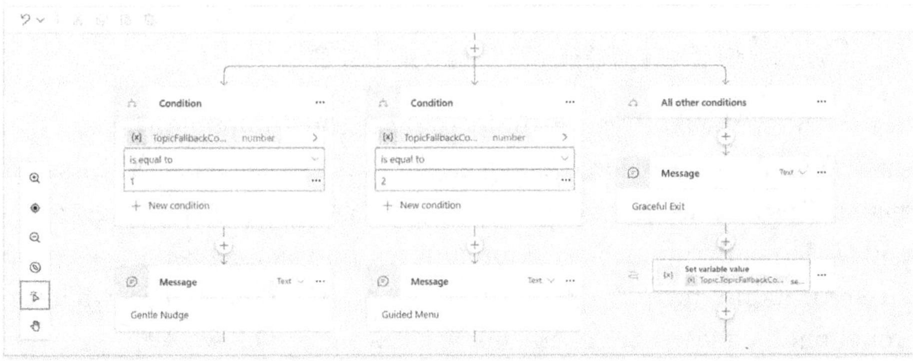

Figure 7-5. Configuring the system Fallback topic. A screenshot of the Copilot Studio authoring canvas showing the Fallback topic. It highlights the logic flow: Increment Variable ➤ Condition (Count = 1) ➤ Condition (Count = 2) ➤ Escalation

By implementing these strategies, you ensure that your creative partner is robust. It won't crumble when the user goes off-script; instead, it will guide them back to the creative path with the same elegance and personality it brings to its successes. Edge cases are inevitable, but with a robust fallback strategy, they become just another part of the conversation.

Continuous Learning from User Feedback

A creative copilot that never learns is like a musician who plays the same set forever. Continuous learning is the discipline of turning every interaction into fuel for improvement, using the analytics, logging patterns, and debugging tools you have already put in place. In this section, you will build a closed feedback loop that combines quantitative signals, qualitative insights, and automated workflows so your agent becomes more relevant, more resilient, and more inspiring over time.

The Feedback Loop Architecture

At this point in the book, your copilot is already instrumented: it has standard Analytics (sessions, Engagement Rate, Escalation, CSAT), custom creative KPIs such as the Creative Spark Rate, and detailed traces via the Activity Map and transcripts. Continuous learning connects these pieces into a repeatable "measure ➤ interpret ➤ adjust ➤ deploy" cycle that runs throughout the life of your agent, not just during launch week.

You can think of this loop as four interconnected layers:

- Layer 1: Signals

    - Platform Analytics metrics (Engagement Rate, Abandonment, Escalation, CSAT)

    - In-conversation micro-feedback (Yes/No "spark" questions, style/length rating, thumbs-up/down buttons)

- Layer 2: Context

  - Conversation transcripts and Activity Map traces that explain why a metric moved in a certain direction

  - Topic-level analytics that show exactly which flows carry friction or delight

- Layer 3: Storage and Analysis

  - Dataverse tables or SharePoint lists where you log structured records like SessionId, TopicName, TestVariant, CreativeSpark, CSAT, and free-text "Why?" comments, using Power Automate flows similar to those you built for content logging in Chapter 2 and long-term memory in Chapter 3

- Layer 4: Action

  - **Concrete Design Changes**: Prompt edits, Topic restructuring, new Trigger Phrases, updated fallback copy, and new A/B test variants

Figure 7-6 illustrates this architecture as a continuous loop rather than a one-time pipeline, emphasizing that every deployment is the starting point for the next iteration, not the finish line.

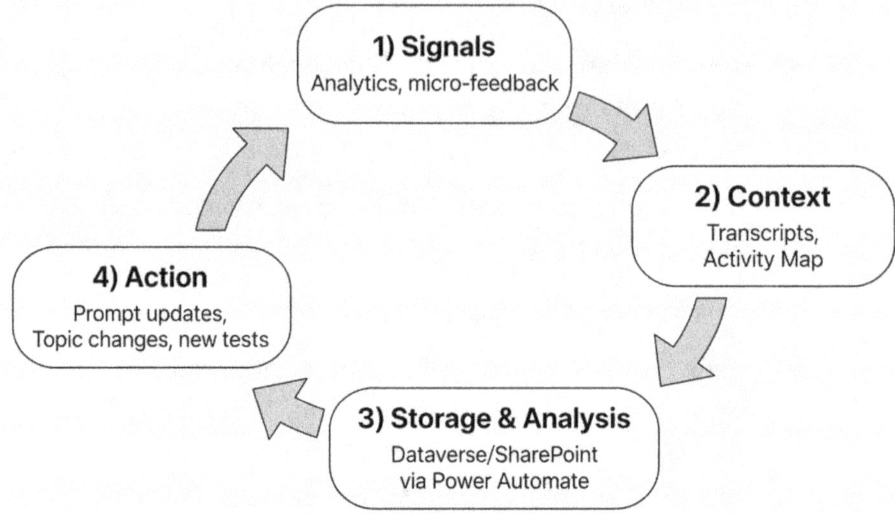

Figure 7-6. *The continuous learning loop. A conceptual diagram showing four stages in a circular flow: (1) Signals (Analytics, micro-feedback) feeding into (2) Context (transcripts, Activity Map), which flows into (3) Storage and Analysis (Dataverse/SharePoint via Power Automate), culminating in (4) Action (prompt updates, Topic changes, new tests) before looping back into live usage*

Capturing Structured Creative Feedback

Generic satisfaction scores alone cannot tell you what to fix in a creative agent. To learn at the level of tone, style, and content quality, you need structured questions embedded directly in your flows, tied to specific generative outputs. You have already seen the basic pattern at the beginning of this chapter: ask "Did that suggestion spark an idea?" immediately after a generative node, save the response as Topic. CreativeSpark, and log it with a Power Automate flow. Here, you extend that pattern into a richer feedback schema.

For each key creative moment (e.g., a slogan, a verse, a story beat, or a campaign concept), add a short "micro-survey" directly after the Create generative answers node:

- Step 1: Capture Spark and Satisfaction

  - **Question 1 (Boolean)**: "Did this spark an idea?" ➤ save as Topic.CreativeSpark (Yes/No).

  - **Question 2 (1–5)**: "How much did you like this style?" ➤ save as Topic.StyleScore (Number).

- Step 2: Capture a Lightweight Diagnostic

  - **Question 3 (Multiple choice)**: "If something felt off, what was it?"

    - **Options**: "Too generic", "Too long", "Wrong tone", "Off-topic", "Other"

  - Save as Topic.FeedbackCategory (String).

- Step 3: Optional Free-Text "Why"

  - **Question 4 (Open text)**: "Anything specific you'd like to change?"

  - Save as Topic.FeedbackNote.

Once you have these variables, you can reuse the logging pattern from earlier chapters: call a Power Automate flow (e.g., LogCreativeFeedback) with inputs such as SessionId, UserId, TopicName, TestVariant, GeneratedOutput, CreativeSpark, StyleScore, FeedbackCategory, and FeedbackNote. The flow writes a structured record into a Dataverse table or SharePoint list, exactly as you did for saving generated content and persistent user state in Chapters 2 and 3.

Turning Data into Design Decisions

Once your feedback pipeline has been running for a few days or weeks, you will have a dataset that combines behavioral metrics (Engagement, Abandonment, Escalation), creative KPIs (Creative Spark Rate, average StyleScore), and qualitative "why" notes, all keyed by TopicName and TestVariant. Continuous learning is the practice of converting those numbers and comments into specific changes in prompts, flows, and personas on a regular cadence, weekly for active pilots, monthly for more stable agents. Note that this timeframe is intended as operational guidance for a healthy review ritual, rather than a strict platform requirement.

A simple but effective review ritual can look like this:

1. Quantitative Scan (Dashboard View)

   a. In the Analytics tab, identify Topics whose Engagement Rate, CSAT, or Creative Spark Rate lag behind others or whose Abandonment Rate has drifted upward since the last release.

   b. In your custom feedback list, compute per-Topic and per-Variant aggregates:

      i. CSR == Yes responses/total responses

      ii. Average StyleScore

      iii. Distribution of FeedbackCategory values

2. Qualitative Deep Dive (Forensics View)

   a. For 1–2 "problem" Topics, open the Activity Map and transcripts to see what actually happened in user sessions where spark was low or abandonment was high.

   b. Look for repeated patterns: users asking for a different length, tone, or format; users abandoning after a particular question; or fallback loops firing on specific phrasings.

3. Design Changes (Prompt and Flow Surgery)

    a. Prompt Refinement

        i. If users frequently select "Too generic", update your Create generative answers prompt to include more specific constraints, stronger personas, or examples, as you practiced in Chapters 3 and 4.

        ii. If "Wrong tone" is common for a variant, adjust the persona description or run a new A/B test with a different tone hypothesis, using the traffic split pattern.

    b. Topic Restructuring

        i. If transcripts show confusion at a particular node, insert a clarifying Question node or rephrase the existing prompt for more guidance, similar to the guided menus you designed for fallback recovery.

        ii. If many users abandon when asked for a technical input (such as a URL or API key), follow the remediation strategy from Topic analysis: move that work into Power Automate or a background action instead of making it the user's problem.

    c. NLU and Fallback Tuning

        i. Add new Trigger Phrases based on real "failed input" samples surfaced in analytics, just as you did when fixing Uncertainty Rate.

        ii. Align the Fallback topic behavior with the tiered strategy previously, tightening messages that transcripts reveal as confusing or discouraging.

4. Ethical and Privacy Checks

   a. Before expanding logging or adding new feedback questions, review whether any data could be considered sensitive, and avoid storing full names, emails, or raw confidential text unless your governance and consent model explicitly covers it.

   b. Prefer storing hashed or pseudonymous identifiers (e.g., a user or session key), and keep CreativeSpark-level telemetry separate from personally identifiable information whenever possible.

Figure 7-7 shows this "data-to-design" flow, showing how a single low-performing Topic moves from detection to prompt and flow changes, then back into production for another learning cycle.

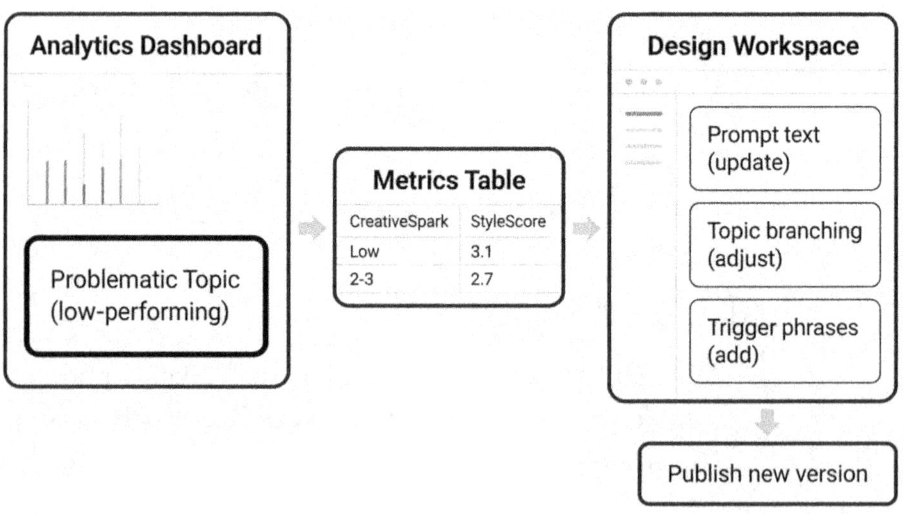

Figure 7-7. *From feedback to updated design. A diagram showing a problematic Topic highlighted in the Analytics dashboard, feeding into a table of aggregated CreativeSpark and StyleScore metrics, and then into a design workspace where prompt text, Topic branching, and Trigger Phrases are updated before the new version is published, closing the loop*

By institutionalizing this loop, instrument ➤ collect ➤ review ➤ redesign ➤ redeploy, you move your copilot from a static launch artifact to a living system that grows with its audience. In the next section, you will see this discipline applied to a focused experiment: a case study in A/B testing humor styles for a brand's AI agent, using the very logging and feedback patterns you have just put in place.

Case Study: A/B Testing Humor Styles in a Brand's AI Agent

When a consumer brand deploys a creative copilot, the choice of humor style is not cosmetic; it directly shapes trust, memorability, and long-term engagement. This section presents an end-to-end case study of how a fictional coffee brand, "FreshBrew Coffee," used controlled A/B testing to choose between two distinct humor styles for its AI agent: a witty, clever persona vs. a playful, lighthearted one. The process shows how to move from intuition ("this tone feels right") to evidence-based decisions grounded in data and user feedback.

Case Background and Objectives

FreshBrew Coffee had already launched a creative copilot to help social media managers and community leads generate on-brand posts, captions, and campaign ideas. The copilot worked functionally, but feedback revealed a deeper concern: some users loved the agent's jokes, while others felt it was "too generic" or "too try-hard." FreshBrew's brand identity emphasized smart, insider coffee culture—sharp, friendly, and a little irreverent, so leadership wanted to know which humor style actually performed better over time:

- **Variant A: Witty and Clever**: Emphasized smart wordplay, subtle references, and "insider" jokes that rewarded knowledge of coffee culture and internet trends

- **Variant B: Playful and Lighthearted**: Emphasized warmth, friendliness, and easygoing humor that anyone could understand without context

The team defined four primary objectives:

- Determine whether humor style measurably affects CSAT, engagement, and creative spark.

- Understand why users prefer one tone over the other, not just which they choose.

- Evaluate which style better reflects FreshBrew's brand voice in day-to-day use.

- Assess operational impact: retention, reduced support needs, and content volume.

Experiment Design and Setup

The test ran for four weeks with 2,000 active users of the existing content generator. Users were split at the session level into two equal cohorts (A and B), ensuring that each participant consistently experienced the same humor style across all their interactions during the test window.

Both variants shared the same

- Topics and conversation structure

- Question flow (what information the agent asked for)

- Output length and platform-specific formatting (e.g., Instagram vs. LinkedIn)

- Underlying data connections (e.g., example product catalog, campaign calendar)

Only one layer differed: the personality and humor instructions embedded in the system-level prompt and response templates. For Variant A, these instructions pushed the agent toward smart, clever commentary; for Variant B, toward approachable, playful banter.

Instrumentation from earlier chapters, analytics dashboards, structured logging, and feedback questions were reused here. Each interaction wrote a row of data including session ID, assigned variant, topic, platform, and all feedback fields needed for later analysis.

Metrics and Data Collection

To fairly compare humor styles, FreshBrew defined a set of quantitative and qualitative metrics:

- **CSAT (Customer Satisfaction)**: Five-point rating ("How satisfied are you with this suggestion?") collected after a subset of turns.

- **Engagement Rate**: The percentage of suggestions that were either used directly or saved as drafts within 24 hours. Note that Copilot Studio analytics does not automatically track these specific "use" or "save" actions; you must instrument explicit tracking events within your product workflow to capture this data accurately.

- **Escalation Rate**: The share of sessions where users explicitly asked for human help or expressed clear dissatisfaction. It is important to note that this is not necessarily captured automatically by the platform; you must implement a defined escalation action or handoff event within your topic design to measure this rate reliably.

- **Creative Spark Rate**: A binary "Did this feel genuinely creative or inspiring?" question, tracked as a custom KPI.

Alongside these, every third or fourth session presented a short micro-survey on creative qualities:

- Relatability ("Did the humor feel like it fits you or your audience?")

- Memorability ("Will you remember this interaction or idea later?")

- Emotional connection ("Did the interaction make you feel good about using this tool?")

- Brand alignment ("Did this sound like FreshBrew?")

- Likelihood to share ("Would you recommend this copilot to a colleague?")

All metrics were stored with rich context, user tenure (new or returning), time of day, topic type (campaign, promo, community, holiday), and target platform, so the team could break down results by segment rather than relying on raw averages alone. Capturing these specific data points requires custom telemetry and explicit access to those fields, as they are not tracked automatically by the platform.

Quantitative Results

Across the four-week period, both variants improved as users became more familiar with the tool, but Variant A consistently pulled ahead. Figure 7-8 illustrates the evolution of average CSAT scores over the experiment on some sample data.

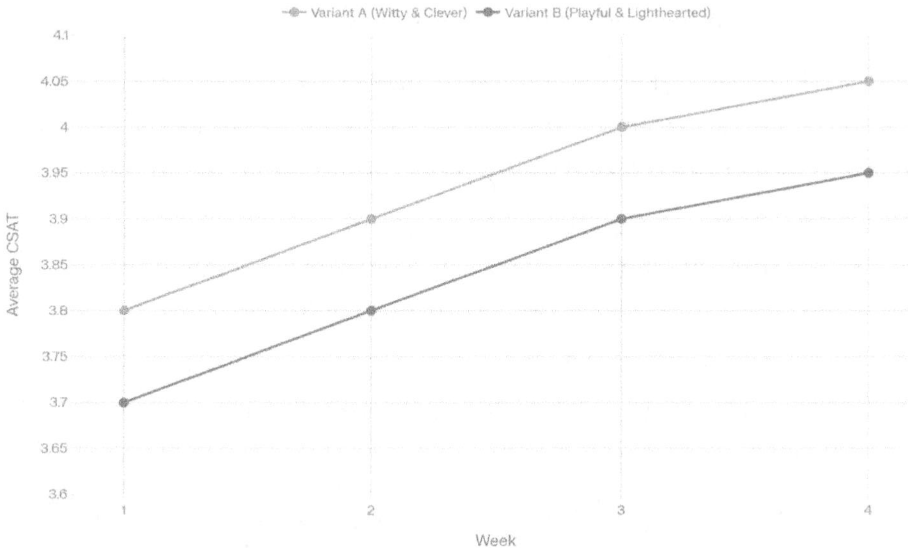

Figure 7-8. *CSAT score progression during A/B testing of humor variants (four-week period). A line chart showing weekly CSAT scores for the two humor styles. Variant A (Witty and Clever) climbs from 3.8 to 4.05 over four weeks, while Variant B (Playful and Lighthearted) increases from 3.7 to 3.95. The gap is small but persistent, with Variant A leading each week*

By the end of week four:

- Variant A's overall CSAT averaged just under 3.9, with the curve trending upward.

- Variant B's overall CSAT averaged around 3.8, also improving but trailing Variant A.

While a 0.1-point difference on a 5-point scale may seem small, it can be meaningful in practice when multiplied across thousands of weekly sessions. However, this is not always the case; the validity of such a claim depends heavily on variance and sample size. When making these comparisons, it is essential to consider statistical significance or confidence intervals to ensure the results are not simply due to random noise in the data.

Engagement and creative spark told a similar story:

- Engagement was several percentage points higher for the witty variant, meaning users were more likely to actually use or save its ideas.

- Creative spark ("Did this feel genuinely creative?") was consistently higher for Variant A, suggesting that users saw more originality and value in its output.

- Escalations were lower for the witty variant, indicating fewer moments where the humor felt off or unhelpful enough to trigger frustration.

Together, these metrics indicated that witty humor not only made people slightly happier in the moment but also nudged them to act, posting more, saving more, and needing less human backup.

Qualitative Insights from User Feedback

Numbers showed which style performed better. Open-text comments explained why. The team coded thousands of short feedback snippets into themes, revealing distinct patterns for each variant.

For Variant A: Witty and Clever, recurring positive themes were

- "This feels like FreshBrew." Users frequently mentioned that the agent sounded like the brand's social channels, sharp, distinctive, and rooted in coffee culture rather than a generic "AI voice."

- "I'll remember this." Many comments referenced specific jokes or expressions users planned to reuse in their own posts, a strong sign of memorability.

- "It treats me like an insider." References to espresso rituals, barista slang, or niche coffee memes made users feel like part of a community instead of just customers.

Critiques for Variant A centered on context:

- Some users felt the humor was "too much" for formal or sensitive posts (e.g., service issues or apologies).

- In a few cases, an attempted clever reference missed the mark because it assumed knowledge the user or their audience did not share.

For Variant B: Playful and Lighthearted, positive themes were:

- "Easy to work with." The lighter tone felt low-risk and quick to adapt, especially for users under time pressure.

- "Friendly, not intimidating." Newer users and less experienced marketers appreciated that the agent felt like a supportive colleague rather than a show-off.

However, negative themes revealed important drawbacks:

- "Could be any brand." Many users didn't see a strong connection between the playful tone and FreshBrew's unique positioning.

- "Nice, but forgettable." Users often described Variant B as "fine" or "okay" but rarely as "amazing," "shareworthy," or "distinctive."

Memorability and brand alignment clearly favored Variant A, while emotional warmth was roughly similar across both.

Segment and Context Effects

The team then looked at how humor style interacted with user type and topic. Several nuanced patterns emerged:

- **Returning Users vs. New Users**: Returning users, those who had used the copilot multiple times before the experiment, showed a stronger preference for witty humor. Over time, they learned to expect a certain voice and seemed to enjoy its consistency and depth. New users showed a smaller difference between variants, suggesting that personality pays off more after the initial learning curve.

- Topic Type

  - For campaign and community posts, witty humor significantly outperformed playful tone. These posts benefit from sharp, memorable hooks that feel on-brand.

  - For product launch summaries and more informational content, performance differences were minimal; clarity mattered more than jokes.

  - For holiday and seasonal content, the playful style did relatively better, since those posts already leaned into festive, lighthearted themes.

This analysis led to an important conclusion: one humor style can be the default, but the system should still allow targeted shifts based on context.

Business Impact and Rollout Decisions

From a business standpoint, FreshBrew mapped the observed metrics to tangible outcomes:

- Higher CSAT and engagement implied better retention among frequent users of the copilot.

- More saved and posted suggestions meant more high-quality social content per team per week, increasing the value of the tool.

- Lower escalation rates meant fewer support tickets and less time spent manually rewriting AI outputs.

Even conservative modeling showed that adopting the better-performing humor variant for the whole user base could translate into measurable gains in recurring usage and reduced support load. Given that Variant A also strengthened brand alignment, the choice was clear: witty and clever would become the new default personality.

FreshBrew did not simply flip a switch, though. The rollout followed a phased plan:

- First, extend the witty variant to a larger share of new users while continuing to monitor metrics.

- Next, communicate a "voice refresh" to existing users, explaining that the agent had been tuned based on feedback and testing.

- Finally, make witty humor the default for all while adding a "tone" control so users could request a more neutral or playful style for specific situations (e.g., formal announcements).

Design Patterns You Can Reuse

This case study isn't just about coffee; it provides a reusable pattern for any team tuning a copilot's personality. Key practices to borrow:

- Isolate one variable at a time. Keep topics, flows, and data the same while changing only humor style so you can attribute differences confidently.

- Use both hard and soft metrics. Track CSAT, engagement, and escalation, but also ask about memorability, brand alignment, and emotional connection.

- Segment your findings. Look separately at new vs. returning users, different topic types, and different channels. Personality rarely performs uniformly across all contexts.

- Treat personality as a strategic asset. Humor style isn't an afterthought; it can be a differentiator that makes an AI agent uniquely "yours."

- Offer override controls. Even if one style is the default winner, users benefit from the ability to adjust tone when the situation demands it. You can implement this technically by using a tone variable that feeds your system's instructions or prompt templates, allowing the AI to pivot its personality based on the user's specific request.

Connecting Back to Continuous Learning

Finally, this experiment demonstrates the continuous learning loop described earlier in the chapter:

1. **Instrument**: Build the analytics, logs, and feedback prompts into your copilot from the beginning.

2. **Hypothesize**: Form a clear question, here, "Which humor style better serves our users and brand?"

3. **Experiment**: Run a controlled A/B test with enough time and traffic to see real patterns.

4. **Interpret**: Combine metrics and human feedback to understand not only which variant wins but why.

5. **Act and Iterate**: Change the default, add configuration options, and line up the next set of questions to test.

By treating humor style as something to test rather than guess, FreshBrew turned a subjective creative choice into a measurable, repeatable optimization process. That mindset, creative experimentation guided by data, is at the heart of building agents that are not only useful, but genuinely delightful and on-brand.

Testing, debugging, and optimization are often treated as the unglamorous aftermath of building an AI system, the cleanup work that begins once the "real" design is finished. This chapter has argued the opposite. For creative copilots, testing and optimization are not a final phase; they are the discipline that transforms a static build into a living system.

Summary

You have seen how Copilot Studio analytics turn abstract interactions into measurable signals of engagement, satisfaction, and creative value. You learned how to move beyond surface-level metrics and instrument your copilot with custom logging that captures something far more important than clicks or sessions: whether an idea truly sparks inspiration. Through A/B testing, you replaced intuition with evidence, allowing users, not assumptions, to decide which tones, formats, and personalities resonate at most. By designing Tiered Fallback strategies and resilient slot-filling logic, you ensure that your agent can recover gracefully when creativity inevitably gets messy. And by closing the loop with structured feedback and regular review of rituals, you established a system that learns continuously rather than stagnates after launch.

The case study of FreshBrew Coffee demonstrated what this mindset looks like in practice. Humor style, a seemingly subjective creative choice, became a measurable design variable. Data revealed not only which variant performed better, but why, and under what conditions that advantage held. Most importantly, the team treated the result not as a final answer, but as a new baseline from which further experimentation could begin.

This is the central lesson of the chapter: a creative AI is never "done." Its value compounds over time only if you give it the mechanisms to listen, adapt, and improve. When analytics inform design, when feedback shapes prompts, and when experimentation becomes routine, your copilot evolves alongside its users. It stops being a novelty or a tool and becomes a trusted creative partner, one that stays relevant, distinctive, and aligned with its purpose long after its initial release.

In the next chapter, we will build on this foundation and look beyond individual copilots to the broader organizational patterns required to operate, govern, and scale creative AI responsibly. Because once an agent can learn, the next challenge is ensuring that learning happens safely, ethically, and in service of long-term value.

CHAPTER 8

Deployment and Scaling

You've journeyed through the complete lifecycle of creative AI agents, from unveiling Copilot Studio's potential in the first chapter to setting up environments, mastering core components, designing conversations, integrating advanced AI, building industry-specific solutions, and rigorously testing them in the previous chapter. But a brilliantly crafted copilot remains just a prototype until it reaches real users. This chapter marks the critical transition from development to production, where your agents must deliver reliable, secure, and scalable creative experiences amid diverse channels, enterprise governance, and growing demand.

This chapter equips you to deploy with confidence. You'll explore publishing options across web embeds for public-facing creativity, Microsoft Teams for seamless team collaboration, and WhatsApp for direct customer engagement, noting that WhatsApp requires extra infrastructure, including Azure Bot Service and a third-party provider like Twilio. You will learn when each channel shines and how to manually implement personality adaptations through specific prompts and logic to ensure your agent fits in each environment. Security and compliance take center stage next, covering Azure AD authentication, data loss prevention, and role-based access. Finally, you will explore how to support compliance efforts regarding GDPR and HIPAA standards through careful tenant configuration and data handling policies.

© Mezba Uddin 2026

M. Uddin, *Creative AI Agents with Copilot Studio*, Inside Copilot,
https://doi.org/10.1007/979-8-8688-2779-2_8

Monitoring performance at scale follows, using Copilot Studio's analytics to track conversation success rates, user satisfaction scores, topic usage patterns, and error trends, turning raw data into actionable insights for continuous refinement. Version control and update strategies ensure safe evolution, utilizing proven process patterns such as environment separation (dev/test/prod) and staged rollouts. You will learn how to manually architect A/B testing scenarios and rollback plans to minimize disruption during iterations, transforming these standard development practices into a reliable workflow for your creative agents.

The chapter culminates in a case study: the global rollout of a multilingual storytelling bot. This real-world example traces localization across regions, multi-channel deployment, security harmonization, and performance scaling from pilot to millions of interactions, revealing practical lessons in stakeholder alignment, user adoption, and balancing creativity with operational resilience.

By chapter's end, your copilots will be production-ready: accessible where users expect them, protected against risks, observable under load, and evolvable without breaking trust. This operational mastery completes the book, empowering you to launch not just innovative AI, but sustainable creative systems that thrive in the wild.

Publishing Options (Web, Teams, WhatsApp)

A creative AI is only useful if it lives where your audience lives. A "Writer's Block" bot is useless if it's trapped inside a developer portal; it needs to be accessible in Microsoft Word or a web browser where the writer is struggling. An "Internal Brainstorming" bot needs to live in Microsoft Teams, right next to your colleagues, ready to jump into a chat. A "Customer Engagement" bot might need to be on WhatsApp, meeting customers on their phones.

Copilot Studio allows you to publish a single agent to multiple channels simultaneously. However, publishing is not just a technical switch; it is a design decision. Each channel has its own "vibe," technical capabilities, and user expectations. It is important to note that feature parity is not guaranteed across all platforms; the same agent may behave differently or lose certain rich capabilities due to specific channel limitations.

In this section, we will explore the three most impactful publishing options: the web (for broad reach), Microsoft Teams (for internal collaboration), and messaging apps like WhatsApp (for personal engagement). You will learn not just how to click the buttons, but how to adapt your agent's personality and features to thrive in each environment.

1. The Web: Public-Facing Creativity

Publishing to the web is the fastest way to reach a global audience. It is ideal for customer engagement bots, public portfolio projects, or standalone creative tools (like our LyricLab Bot). When you publish to the web, you are essentially creating a dedicated space for your AI to shine.

The web channel is unique because it offers the highest degree of visual customization and the lowest barrier to entry for users. However, it is important to understand that native customization is limited to what the web chat SDK or standard iframe supports. While Copilot Studio provides basic styling options, achieving full UI freedom, such as custom layouts or deep brand integration, requires custom hosting and the implementation of a dedicated token server.

The Demo Website vs. the Custom Website

Copilot Studio offers two distinct ways to put your bot on the web, each serving a different stage of your product's lifecycle.

A. **The Demo Website (Quick Sharing):** Every copilot comes with a prebuilt "Demo Website." This is a Microsoft-hosted page that requires zero coding to set up. It is essentially a "sandbox" environment that is publicly accessible but lacks your branding. While easy to share, it is important to note that this site remains governed by your organization's tenant settings and can be disabled by administrators. Furthermore, it is not intended for load testing or handling real production traffic.

- **Best For:** Rapid prototyping, sharing progress with stakeholders, or testing your bot in a "clean" environment before integrating it into a real site. For example, if you've just finished the AI Dungeon Master (Chapter 3), you can send the Demo Website link to your friends to playtest it immediately.

- **How to Access:** Go to the Channels page in Copilot Studio, select Demo Website, and copy the URL. From this settings pane, you can even customize the welcome message ("Welcome to the Dungeon!") and add a few "starter prompts" (like "Start Adventure" or "Create Character") to guide new users.

- **Limitation:** It is branded with Microsoft's UI and is not meant for production traffic. It is your sandbox, not your storefront. It cannot be embedded, and its URL is a long, generated string that isn't user-friendly.

B. **Custom Website (The Production Embed):** For a professional launch, you embed the bot directly into your own website using an <iframe> or a custom code snippet. However, proceed with a brief caution: <iframe> embedding can sometimes be blocked by specific Content Security Policy (CSP) settings on your host website. You should coordinate with your web administrator to ensure your site's security policies allow for the bot's integration.

The Channels dashboard, as we can see in Figure 8-1, serves as your mission control for these deployments. From this single screen, you can manage the "Demo Website," grab the code for your "Custom Website," or push updates to Microsoft Teams.

- **How-to:**

  - Go to Channels and select Custom Website. You may find this labeled as "Mobile app" depending on the specific version of the interface you are using. While the labels may change over time, it is important to understand that there are no functional differences between these options; they utilize the same underlying channel technology.

  - Copilot Studio will generate a block of HTML code (an <iframe>). This code contains your bot's unique ID and the necessary scripts to render the chat window.

  - Copy this code and paste it into the HTML of your website. This works universally, whether you are pasting it into a WordPress widget, a Squarespace code block, or your own custom HTML file.

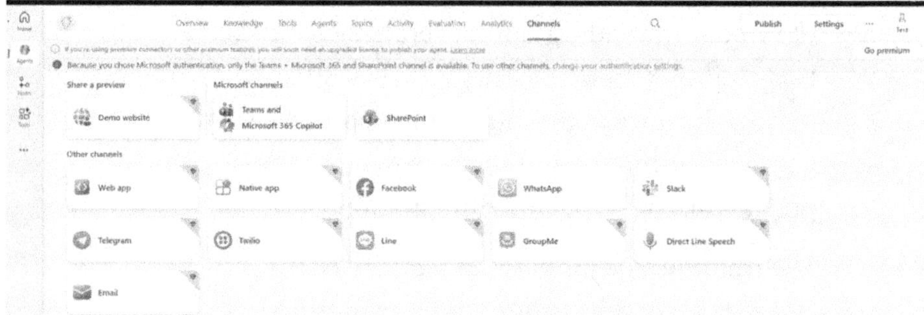

Figure 8-1. *The Channels dashboard in Copilot Studio. A screenshot showing the "Channels" page with tiles for "Microsoft Teams," "Demo Website," and "Native App" visible, illustrating the central hub for multi-channel deployment.*

Styling Your Web Bot

When you embed your bot, visual consistency is key. A "Cyberpunk Storyteller" bot should ideally look different from a "Corporate Legal Assistant." The default blue chat bubble might clash with your brand's aesthetic.

- **The Token Server:** For advanced styling, you can use a "Token Server" (a small piece of intermediary code) to securely pass style parameters to the bot. It is crucial to recognize that this is an advanced architectural pattern involving custom infrastructure you must build yourself; it is not a built-in feature provided by Microsoft. Furthermore, these visual changes apply strictly to the web client and do not affect the agent's appearance on other channels, such as Microsoft

Teams or messaging apps. On the web, this allows you to change its avatar (perhaps to a pixel-art wizard for your RPG bot), background color, and chat bubble shape to match your brand's CSS. This seamless integration makes the AI feel like a core part of your digital ecosystem.

- **The Persona Match:** Ensure the web page surrounding the bot sets the right context. If your LyricLab Bot is embedded on a page with neon graphics, music notes, and a dark mode theme, users will immediately understand the creative "vibe" before they type a single word. This environmental context primes the user for the specific type of interaction they are about to have.

2. Microsoft Teams: Collaborative Creativity

For internal tools, like the Marketing Campaign Generator or Scriptwriting Partner, Microsoft Teams is the natural home. Deploying here transforms your bot from a tool into a teammate. In a corporate environment, friction is the enemy of adoption. If a user has to bookmark a separate website and log in separately to use your AI, they likely won't. By placing the bot inside Teams, where they already spend their day, you remove that friction entirely.

Streamlined Teams Enablement

Teams integration is one of Copilot Studio's strongest features because it is deeply integrated into the Microsoft 365 ecosystem.

1. Navigate to Channels ➤ Microsoft Teams.

2. Click Turn on Teams.

3. Once enabled, you can click Open bot to chat with
    it immediately in your own Teams instance. This is
    perfect for personal testing, as shown in Figure 8-2.

Distributing to Your Organization

Making the bot available to you for personal testing is easy; however,
making it accessible to everyone requires moving through a few more
layers of governance. While you want your bot to appear in the official
Teams App Store for your company so anyone can find it, this only occurs
after an IT administrator uploads the app manifest to the Teams Admin
Center and grants specific policy allowances. It is also important to note
that some enterprise tenants restrict the use of custom apps entirely, so
you should verify your organization's permissions before planning a wide
rollout.

- **The App Manifest:** In the Teams channel settings, you
  can download the App Manifest (a .zip file). This file
  acts as the bot's "ID card." It contains the bot's name,
  description, icons (color and outline versions), and
  permissions. You can, and should, edit the details here
  to make them appealing. Give your bot a catchy name
  and a clear description of what creative tasks it solves.

- **Admin Approval:** To make the bot appear in the
  "Built for your org" section of the Teams app store,
  you typically need to upload this zip file to the Teams
  Admin Center (or ask your IT admin to do so). Once
  approved, any employee can find "Marketing Wizard"
  or "Script Buddy" in the store and install it just like they
  would install Excel or OneNote.

The "Context" Advantage

The superpower of the Teams channel is Context Awareness. On the web, a user is often anonymous unless you build a complex login system. In Teams, the bot automatically knows exactly who is talking to it because the user is already signed in to Microsoft 365.

- **Authentication Is Automatic:** The bot can access system variables like User.DisplayName and User.Email without asking a single question. This is a massive advantage for user experience.

- **Personalization:** Your Scriptwriting Bot can greet a user by name: "Hello, Sarah! Ready to work on the screenplay?" instead of a generic "Hello User." This immediate recognition builds trust and reduces friction. Furthermore, knowing the user's email allows you to automate follow-up actions (like the approval emails we built in Chapter 5) without ever asking the user to type their address.

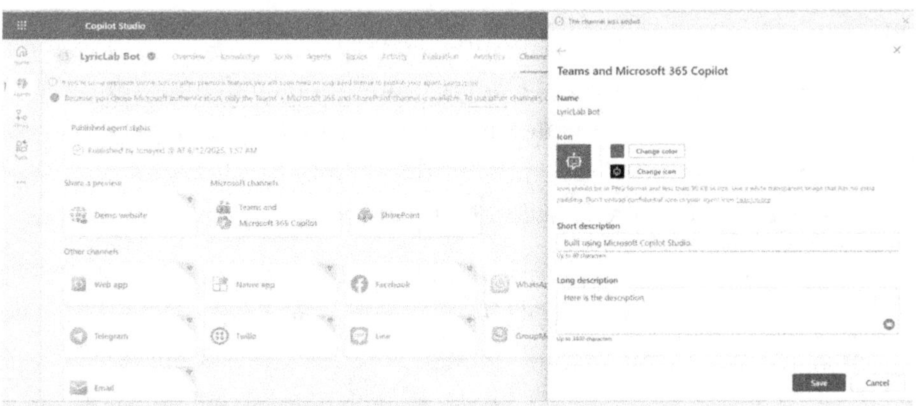

Figure 8-2. *The Teams app manifest editor. This screenshot showing the manifest editor or the Teams Admin Center upload screen, highlighting where the bot's name, icon, and description are customized for the organization's app store*

3. Messaging Apps (WhatsApp, Slack, Facebook)

To reach users in their personal creative spaces, you might want to deploy to WhatsApp, Facebook Messenger, or Slack. These channels are intimate and highly engaging, perfect for daily creative prompts, "on-the-go" inspiration, or consumer-facing brand experiences. A user might not visit your website every day, but they check WhatsApp dozens of times. Being present in that list of chats makes your AI a part of their daily life.

The Azure Relay

Unlike the direct Web/Teams integration, deploying to third-party apps usually requires an intermediary: Azure Bot Service. Copilot Studio provides the brain, while Azure Bot Service acts as the necessary intermediary to connect with external networks. However, it is important to note that Azure Bot Service must be configured separately, as Copilot Studio does not natively manage the setup or account integration for third-party platforms such as WhatsApp or Facebook. This infrastructure must be established in the Azure Portal to bridge the communication between your agent and these external messaging channels.

1. **Connect to Azure:** In Copilot Studio, you configure your agent to communicate through an Azure Bot Service registration. This essentially "plugs" your Copilot Studio agent into the Azure cloud infrastructure.

2. **Configure the Channel:** In the Azure Portal, you navigate to the "Channels" blade. Here, you can add connections to Twilio (which handles SMS and WhatsApp), Meta (for Facebook Messenger), or Slack. Each of these will require you to set up a developer account with the respective platform (e.g., a Meta Developer account for Messenger) and generate API keys.

3.   **The Bridge:** Azure acts as the bridge, translating messages from WhatsApp (which uses its own protocol) into a format Copilot Studio understands, and vice versa.

Designing for Text-Only Constraints

This is the most critical design consideration for messaging apps. While the web and Teams support rich UI elements, messaging apps are often much more limited.

- **The Limitation:** Channels like WhatsApp and SMS are strictly text-based. The beautiful Adaptive Cards we built in Chapter 5 (to display AI-generated images or rich marketing campaigns) often will not render on these platforms. They might appear as blank space or messy JSON code, breaking the user experience.

- **The Solution: Channel Logic:** You must build "Channel Awareness" into your topics. Copilot Studio provides a system variable called System.Channel. You can use this in a Condition Node to adapt your output dynamically based on where the user is chatting from.

As we can see in Figure 8-3, creating a fork in your logic allows you to serve the perfect format to every user.

Example of Channel-Adaptive Logic

- **Condition:** If System.Channel = "Microsoft Teams"

  - **Action:** Send the rich Adaptive Card with buttons and the embedded image. This leverages the full capability of the Teams platform.

- **Condition:** If System.Channel = "Facebook" (or WhatsApp)

  Technical Caution: Channel names are exact string values and can vary; for instance, you might need to use "facebook" or "directline". Because these are not always intuitive, you should verify the actual string values in the official documentation or by logging the variable during a test session before hard-coding your logic.

  - **Action:** Send the Image URL as a direct text link and type the text description separately. While less flashy, this ensures the user still gets the content in a way they can actually view.

By adding this logic, you ensure that your creative agent provides a premium experience on capable platforms (Teams/Web) while remaining functional and accessible on text-only platforms (WhatsApp). You are designing a responsive conversation, just as a web designer builds a responsive website.

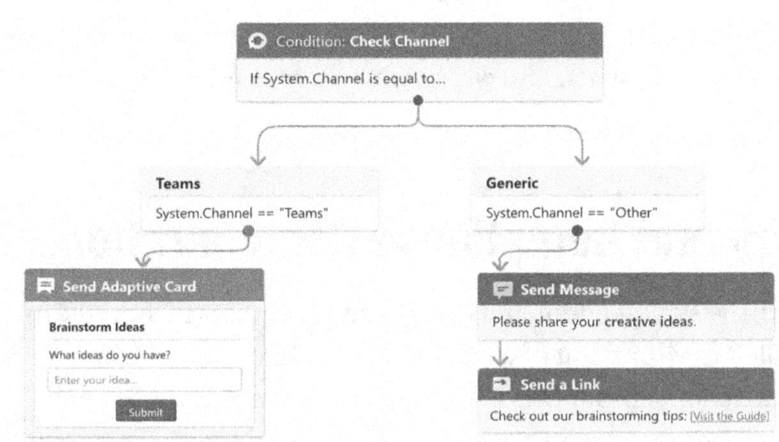

Figure 8-3. *Channel-adaptive logic in the authoring canvas. A screenshot showing a Condition Node branching based on the System. Channel variable. The left branch (Teams) sends an Adaptive Card; the right branch (Other) sends a text message and a link, illustrating how to handle platform constraints*

Summary: The Right Channel for the Right Mission

- **Choose Web** for a broad, public reach and total visual control. This is your "Main Stage."

- **Choose Teams** for secure, internal tools that know who your users are. This is your "Office."

- **Choose WhatsApp/Messaging** for high-engagement, personal connections, but remember to design for a "text-first" experience. This is your "Pocket Companion."

By mastering these publishing options, you ensure your creative AI isn't just a brilliant experiment hidden in a lab; it becomes a ubiquitous tool, available exactly when and where your users need that spark of inspiration.

Security and Compliance Considerations

Creativity thrives on freedom, but enterprise AI requires guardrails. In the controlled environment of your studio, a "hallucination" where the AI invents a fictional product is a funny quirk. In the real world, that same hallucination—or worse, a leak of sensitive customer data—could be a legal liability. When you deploy a bot that can generate text, access proprietary data, or trigger actions, you are no longer just an artist; you become a custodian of trust.

This section is about securing the "creative engine" without stalling it. We will explore how to manage **Authentication** to ensure only the right people can access your bot, how to use **Data Loss Prevention (DLP)** policies to build invisible walls around your sensitive data, and how to tune **Content Moderation** filters to prevent your AI from saying things it shouldn't.

Security is not the enemy of creativity; it is the foundation that allows creativity to scale safely.

1. Authentication: Who Is the Creator?

The first line of defense is knowing exactly who is talking to your copilot. Copilot Studio offers flexible authentication modes that range from "open to everyone" to "strictly locked down." Choosing the right one depends entirely on your bot's purpose. The **Authentication Settings Panel**, as we can see in Figure 8-4, is where you define these access rules.

No Authentication (The Kiosk)

This mode is akin to a public street performer; anyone walking by can stop and interact.

- **Use Case:** This is the default setting for public-facing web bots, like our LyricLab Bot or a "Brand Engagement" bot on a marketing site. You want as little friction as possible; asking a user to log in just to generate a rhyme would kill engagement immediately.

- **The Risk:** Without a login, you have no way of knowing who is using your bot. Malicious actors could spam the bot with thousands of requests, draining your AI credits or probing for vulnerabilities.

- **The Fix:** For public bots, you cannot rely on Copilot Studio's internal user management. Instead, you must implement Rate Limiting as an external security layer, as Copilot Studio does not provide this functionality natively. It is the architect's responsibility to configure these protections externally, typically via a CDN (Content Delivery Network) or a reverse proxy, before the traffic even reaches your bot. Layering this with strict Content Moderation settings is essential to prevent malicious actors from abusing your "open" bot or exhausting your AI credits.

Authenticate with Microsoft (The Office Badge)

This is the gold standard for internal tools like the Marketing Campaign Generator or HR Assistant. Because the bot lives inside Microsoft Teams or an internal SharePoint site, it can leverage the user's existing Microsoft 365 credentials.

- **The "Magic" Login:** The user doesn't need to type a password. The bot simply recognizes them because they are already signed in to Teams.

- **Why It Matters for Creativity:** This isn't just about security; it's about context. Because the bot knows the user is "Sarah from Marketing" and not just "Anonymous User 123," it can unlock powerful features:

- **Personalization:** "Hi Sarah! I see you're working on the Q4 campaign. Shall we continue?"

- **Permissions:** "I see you're a manager, so I can show you the 'Approve Budget' flow. A standard user wouldn't see this option."

- **Audit Trails:** "Sarah generated this specific campaign image at 9:00 AM." This accountability is crucial for enterprise compliance.

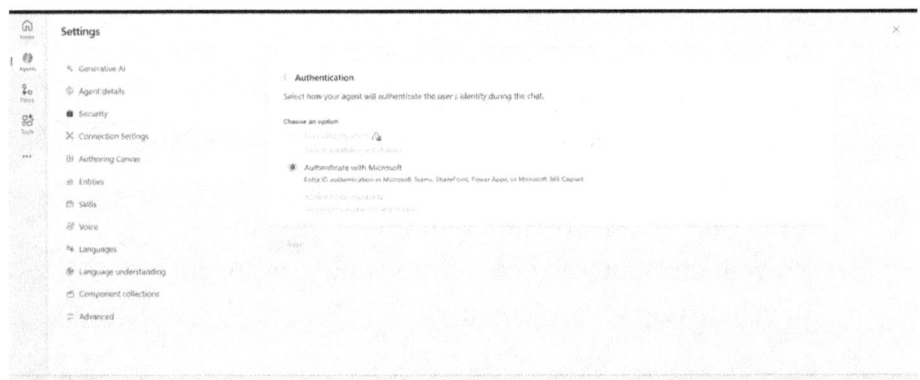

Figure 8-4. *The Authentication settings panel. A screenshot of the Settings ➤ Security ➤ Authentication page in Copilot Studio. It highlights the options for "No authentication,x" "Authenticate with Microsoft," and "Authenticate manually," illustrating the control center for user access.*

Manual Azure AD (Entra ID)

If you are building a secure portal for external clients, for example, a "VIP Client Design Helper" hosted on your secure website, you need a middle ground. You can configure Manual Authentication using Azure Active Directory (now Microsoft Entra ID).

- **How It Works:** This requires registering an "Application" in the Azure Portal. You generate a Client ID and Client Secret (digital keys) and paste them into Copilot Studio.

- **The Result:** When a user tries to chat, the bot presents a login card. Once they log in (perhaps with their Google or LinkedIn account, if configured), the bot grants them access. This ensures that your premium creative tools are reserved only for paying clients.

2. Data Loss Prevention (DLP): The Invisible Firewall

Imagine you built a powerful Research Assistant bot. To help it work, you gave it the SharePoint connector (to read internal documents) and the Twitter/X connector (to read public trends).

Now, imagine a user asks: "Find the confidential 'Project X' strategy document on SharePoint and tweet the summary."

If your bot blindly obeys, you have a massive data leak.

Data Loss Prevention (DLP) policies are the solution. These are rules configured by IT administrators in the Power Platform Admin Center (outside of Copilot Studio) that govern which connectors can talk to each other.

- **Business vs. Non-business Data:** Administrators can classify connectors into "buckets." They might place SharePoint and Outlook in the "Business" group (safe zone) and Twitter and Facebook in the "Blocked" or "Non-business" group.

- **The Wall:** A DLP policy can strictly prevent data from moving between these groups. Even if you, the creator, try to build a flow connecting SharePoint to Twitter, the system will block it at runtime. It is important to understand that DLP primarily works by blocking the creation and execution of disallowed connector combinations; it does not perform dynamic content inspection of the AI's output or the user's specific message.

- **Creative Freedom Within Boundaries:** This allows you to give your bot powerful access to internal data, knowing that the system architecture itself prevents that data from accidentally escaping to unauthorized external channels. It is important to clarify, however, that DLP policies apply specifically to Power Platform connectors, governing the "pipes" through which data flows, rather than to the generative model's outputs themselves. By establishing these architectural boundaries, it gives you the confidence to build powerful tools without fear of accidental exposure via disallowed services.

3. Content Moderation: The Safety Net

Generative AI is trained on the open internet, which contains the good, the bad, and the ugly. While Microsoft puts massive effort into safety training (RLHF), there is always a risk that a creative bot might hallucinate something inappropriate, biased, or offensive if provoked.

Generative AI Content Moderation is a setting within Copilot Studio that acts as a filter on the AI's imagination. As we can see in Figure 8-5, this setting allows you to choose the level of strictness that matches your bot's audience and purpose.

- **High Moderation:** The safest setting. The AI will refuse to answer any prompt that even slightly approaches controversial or unsafe territory.

    - **Trade-Off**: The AI may be overly cautious and occasionally flag creative prompts that are harmless but ambiguous; for instance, a request for a "stormy" scene might be interpreted as having violent undertones. This high setting is best suited for public-facing brand bots where maintaining a safe environment is the top priority.

- **Medium Moderation (Default):** A balanced approach suitable for most business and creative use cases. It blocks hate speech and obvious toxicity but allows for nuanced creative expression.

- **Low Moderation:** The most permissive setting.

    - **Use Case**: Only appropriate for highly controlled internal environments where you need the AI to process sensitive topics (e.g., a legal bot analyzing case files about crime). Using this setting requires a high degree of trust in your users.

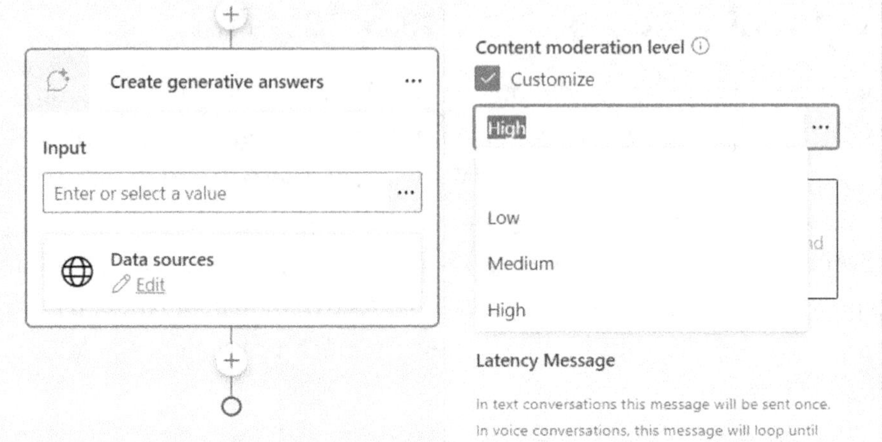

Figure 8-5. *The Generative AI moderation slider. The visual focus is on the "Content Moderation" setting, typically displayed as a drop-down or radio button selection (High/Medium/Low), which controls the strictness of the AI's safety filters*

The "PII Scrubber" Technique

Beyond the built-in settings, you should build your own "Topic-Level" safety nets for specific risks, particularly **Personally Identifiable Information (PII)**.

If your bot sends user prompts to a third-party image generator (like DALL-E) or an external LLM, you must ensure no customer data leaks out.

- **The Technique:** Before calling the GenerateImage flow, pass the user's prompt through a "Safety Check" Power Automate flow.

- **The Logic:** This flow can use Regular Expressions (Regex) to scan for obvious, structured patterns like credit card numbers, social security numbers, or email addresses. However, it is important to note that Regex is only a partial mitigation; it will likely miss less structured information such as names, physical addresses, and contextual PII. Because of these limitations, this technique should be viewed as one layer of a safety strategy rather than a full protection system.

- **The Action:** If PII is found, the flow returns an error code to the copilot ("I cannot process prompts containing private info"), stopping the external API call before it happens. This proactive step supports your broader compliance efforts with regulations like GDPR and HIPAA by significantly reducing the risk of accidental exposure. However, it is vital to understand that regex checks alone do not ensure compliance; full regulatory alignment requires comprehensive governance, informed user consent, and strict data retention controls.

By layering these three defenses, Authentication for access control, DLP for data containment, and Content Moderation for output safety, you transform your creative prototype into an enterprise-grade solution. You prove that your AI is not just a novelty, but a responsible and reliable business asset.

Monitoring Performance at Scale

In Chapter 7, we utilized the built-in Analytics dashboard to check the health of our pilot projects. It was perfect for answering questions like "How many people are talking to my bot?" and "Which topics are most popular?"

But when you scale from 50 test users to 50,000 global customers, the questions change. You no longer just need to know if it is working; you need to know how well it is working.

- Why did the "Generate Campaign" flow take 15 seconds to load yesterday at 2:00 PM?

- Which specific DALL-E prompt caused the API to time out?

- Are users in Europe experiencing more latency than users in North America?

The built-in dashboard cannot answer these questions. To operate at an enterprise scale, you need a "black box" flight recorder for your AI. You need deep, granular telemetry that logs every heartbeat of the system.

In this section, we will integrate your copilot with Azure Application Insights. You will learn how to set up this professional-grade monitoring tool, how to use the Kusto Query Language (KQL) to perform forensic investigations on your conversations, and how to define custom telemetry events to measure creative success in ways standard metrics never could.

1. The Flight Recorder: Azure Application Insights

Azure Application Insights (App Insights) is an Application Performance Management (APM) service. While Copilot Studio provides a high-level summary, App Insights provides the granular underlying data. It captures specific telemetry events, including dependency calls (such as Power Automate flows or HTTP requests) and system errors. While powerful, it is important to note that it does not automatically guarantee full conversation transcripts of every message sent unless specifically configured to do so.

Setting Up the Connection

Connecting your copilot to App Insights is a straightforward configuration that unlocks immense power.

Step 1: Create the Resource

1. Log in to the Azure Portal.

2. Create a new resource and search for Application Insights.

3. Choose your subscription and resource group. For the "Application Type," usually "Workspace-based" is the modern standard.

4. Once deployed, navigate to the Overview blade of your new resource.

5. Locate the Connection String on the top right. Copy this string to your clipboard. (Note: We use the Connection String, not just the Instrumentation Key, as it provides a more reliable regional connection.)

Step 2: Link Copilot Studio

1. Open your agent in Copilot Studio.

2. Navigate to Settings ➤ Advanced.

3. Look for the section labeled Application Insights.

4. Paste your Connection String into the text field as shown in Figure 8-6.

5. Click Save.

That is it. From this moment forward, your copilot is streaming live telemetry to Azure.

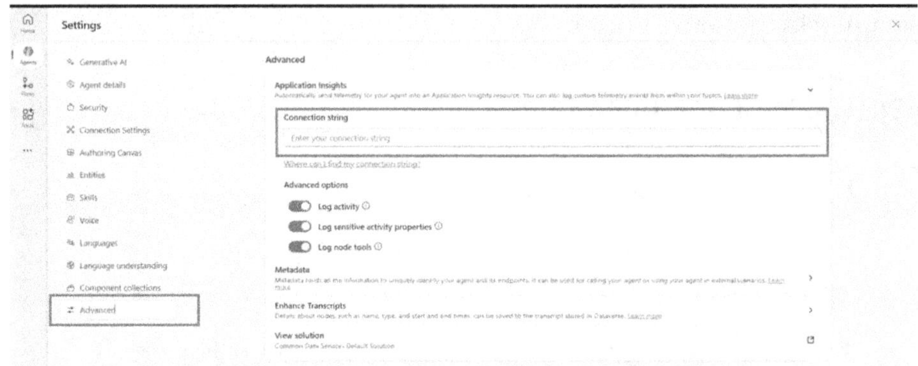

Figure 8-6. *The Advanced settings panel. The visual focus is on the "Application Insights" section, showing the text field where the Connection String is pasted, linking the bot to the Azure cloud*

2. Forensic Analysis: Diagnosing Issues with Transaction Search

Once data is flowing, how do you use it? The first tool in your arsenal is Transaction Search. This allows you to trace a single conversation from start to finish across all systems.

The Scenario: A user reports that the "Image Generator" failed. They say, "I asked for a dragon, and it just spun for a while and gave an error."

The Investigation

1. In the Azure Portal, open your Application Insights resource.

2. Click Transaction Search in the left menu.

3. You can search for generic terms, but searching by time range is often easiest.

4. Click on a failed request (often marked in red).

This opens the End-to-End Transaction Details view. This view is a timeline (a Gantt chart) of that specific interaction. You will see

- The initial message arriving from the user.

- The internal logic processing time.

- **The Dependency Call**: You will see a line item for the HTTP request to your Power Automate flow.

- **The Failure**: If the flow timed out, you will see a red bar indicating exactly how long it waited (e.g., 20,000ms) before failing.

This view proves instantly that the issue wasn't the bot freezing; it was the Power Automate flow taking too long to talk to DALL-E. You now know exactly where to fix the problem.

3. The Power of KQL: Querying Your Data

For answering complex questions, we use KQL (Kusto Query Language). KQL is like SQL for logs; it allows you to filter, aggregate, and visualize millions of data points in seconds.

You access this by clicking Logs in the Application Insights menu. Here are three essential queries for a creative AI architect.

Query A: Finding the Slowest Creative Flows

Creativity kills latency. If your bot takes 30 seconds to write a poem, the user will leave. This query finds the slowest interactions.

Code Snippet

```
dependencies
```

```
| where name contains "GeneratePoem" // Filter for your
specific flow name
| summarize avg(duration), max(duration) by name
| render barchart
```

- **Insight:** This tells you if your "Poem Generator" is consistently slow (avg duration) or if you just had one bad spike (max duration).

Query B: Identifying "Rage Clicks" or Errors

Are users hitting errors frequently?

Code Snippet

```
requests
| where success == false
| summarize count() by name
| render piechart
```

- **Insight:** This highlights which Topics are throwing the most errors, allowing you to prioritize your bug-fixing efforts on the most unstable parts of your bot.

Query C: Reading the Raw Transcript (Privacy Permitting)

Sometimes you need to see the raw text to understand a failure. (Note: Ensure your logging configuration complies with your privacy policies before running this.

Code Snippet

```
traces
| where customDimensions.systemUserId ==
"Specific_User_ID"
```

```
| project timestamp, message
| order by timestamp desc
```

- **Insight:** This reconstructs the conversation log for a specific user, showing you exactly what the internal "brain" of the bot was doing at each timestamp.

4. Custom Telemetry: Measuring Creativity

Standard telemetry measures technical success (Did the API return a 200 OK status?). But for a creative bot, we care about creative success (Did the user choose the "Horror" genre or the "Comedy" genre?).

Copilot Studio allows you to inject custom data points into the stream using the Log custom telemetry event node. Note that while this node is a powerful tool for architects, its availability may vary depending on your specific environment or enabled feature flags; always verify its presence in your authoring canvas before planning deep telemetry integrations.

How to Implement

1. In your Storytelling topic, after the user selects a genre, add a node.

2. Select Advanced ➤ Log custom telemetry event.

3. **Event Name**: Enter a clear and descriptive name, such as StoryStarted.

4. **Properties**: Use Formula to provide a structured record of creative choices.
   Enter the following expression:

```
{
    Genre: Topic.SelectedGenre,
    ProtagonistType: Topic.HeroType
}
```

5. This logs the selected genre and protagonist type as named properties on the telemetry event, enabling filtering and analysis in tools such as Application Insights.

The Payoff: Now, in Application Insights, you can write a KQL query to visualize your audience's creative preferences.

Code Snippet

```
customEvents
| where name == "StoryStarted"
| extend Genre = tostring(customDimensions.Genre)
| summarize count() by Genre
| render piechart
```

This transforms your monitoring from a technical activity into a product research activity. You might discover that 80% of your users are choosing "Sci-Fi," prompting you to invest more time in refining your Sci-Fi prompts and less on the Fantasy ones.

5. Alerts: Sleeping Soundly

Finally, you cannot watch a dashboard 24/7. You need Alerts to notify you when things go wrong.

In Azure Monitor, you can set up an alert rule:

- **Condition:** If failed requests > 5 in the last five minutes.

- **Action:** Email the "AI Ops Team" (or just you).

This ensures that if your API key expires or if a downstream service goes offline, you know about it before your users start flooding your support inbox.

Summary: From Blind Flying to Instrument Flying

By integrating Application Insights, you have graduated from "flying by sight" to "flying by instruments." You can see through the fog of thousands of concurrent conversations. You can pinpoint latency, diagnose crashes, and, most uniquely, quantify the creative choices of your audience.

This level of observability is what separates a hobby project from a scalable enterprise platform. You are now ready to handle not just the code, but the traffic.

Version Control and Updates

Imagine you have just deployed your Personalized Marketing Campaign Generator to 5,000 employees. It is a hit. The marketing team is using it daily to generate slogans and images.

Then, you decide to make a "small improvement." You tweak the system prompt to make the tone slightly more aggressive. You hit "Publish."

Suddenly, the bot stops generating images. Or worse, it starts insulting the customers. And because you edited the live bot directly, there is no "Undo" button. You are now debugging a live outage with 5,000 frustrated users watching.

This is the nightmare scenario of "Cowboy Coding," editing directly in production.

In the world of professional software development, this is avoided through Version Control and Application Lifecycle Management (ALM). For a creative AI architect, these aren't just IT buzzwords; they are your safety net. They allow you to experiment fearlessly in a sandbox, rigorously test changes, and deploy updates without ever breaking the live experience.

In this section, we will professionalize your workflow. You will learn how to set up a Three-Tier Environment Architecture (Dev/Test/Prod) as shown in Figure 8-7, how to use Power Platform Solutions to package your bot and its dependencies into a portable container, and how to execute safe, rollback-ready deployments. You will transform from a creator who hopes nothing breaks into an operator who knows it won't.

1. The Architecture of Safety: Environmental Strategy

The first rule of scaling is: **Never touch the live system.** Instead, you build a pipeline where code moves, but data stays put.

To do this effectively, you need distinct environments within the Power Platform Admin Center. Think of an "environment" as a separate container or parallel universe. Your bot exists in three versions across three universes.

The Development Environment (Dev)

- **Purpose:** The "Sandbox." This is where you break things.

- **Activity:** Here, you write new prompts, add new topics, and mess with the Power Automate flows. It doesn't matter if the bot crashes here; only you can see it.

- **State:** This environment contains the "Unmanaged" (editable) version of your solution.

The Test Environment (QA/UAT)

- **Purpose:** The "Rehearsal Stage." This environment mirrors production exactly but has no real users.

- **Activity:** You deploy your changes here to verify them. You might invite a small group of "Beta Testers" (e.g., the Marketing Leads) to try the new features and try to break them.

- **Crucial Test:** This is where you check if your new permissions work for someone who isn't an admin.

The Production Environment (Prod)

- **Purpose:** The "Main Stage."

- **Activity:** This environment is locked down. You cannot edit the bot directly here. You only import finished, tested updates.

- **State:** This contains the "Managed" (locked) version of your solution.

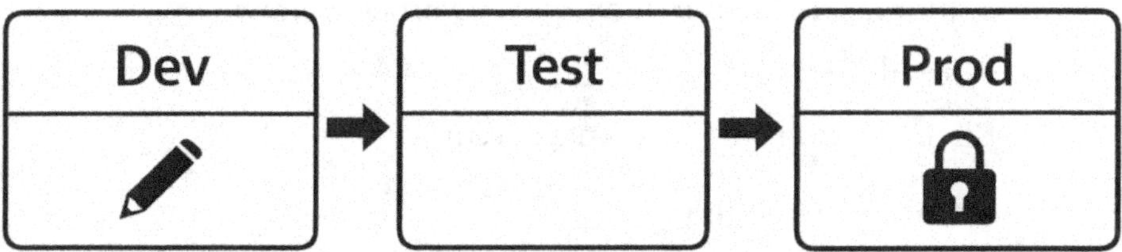

Figure 8-7. *The environment architecture diagram. A conceptual diagram showing three boxes labeled "Dev," "Test," and "Prod"*

2. The Container: Power Platform Solutions

If you try to move a Copilot Studio agent from one environment to another by just "copy-pasting" it, you will fail. Why? Because your agent isn't just one file. It is a spiderweb of dependencies:

- The Agent definition itself

- The Power Automate Flows it calls

- The Connection References (login details for SharePoint, Azure, etc.)

- The Environment Variables (settings like "SharePoint Site URL")

To move this complex web safely, Microsoft uses a container called a **Solution**.

Creating Your Solution

Before you build a single new topic, you should create a Solution wrapper.

1. Navigate to the Power Apps portal (`https://make.powerapps.com/`) or the Copilot Studio "Settings" (depending on your specific interface version, Solutions are often managed in the broader Power Apps interface).

2. Click Solutions in the left navigation.

3. Click + New solution.

4. **Name:** Give it a clear system name, e.g., MarketingCopilot_Solution, as shown in Figure 8-8.

5. **Publisher**: Create a "Publisher." This is your signature. It ensures that when you deploy to Prod, the system knows you built this.

6. **Add Existing**: Once created, open the Solution, and click Add existing ➤ Agents (or Copilot) as shown in Figure 8-9. Select your agent.

7. **Add Components**: Crucially, click Add required components. The system will automatically hunt down every Power Automate flow and Dataverse table your bot talks to and pull them into the box.

Now, you have a portable briefcase containing your entire creative brain.

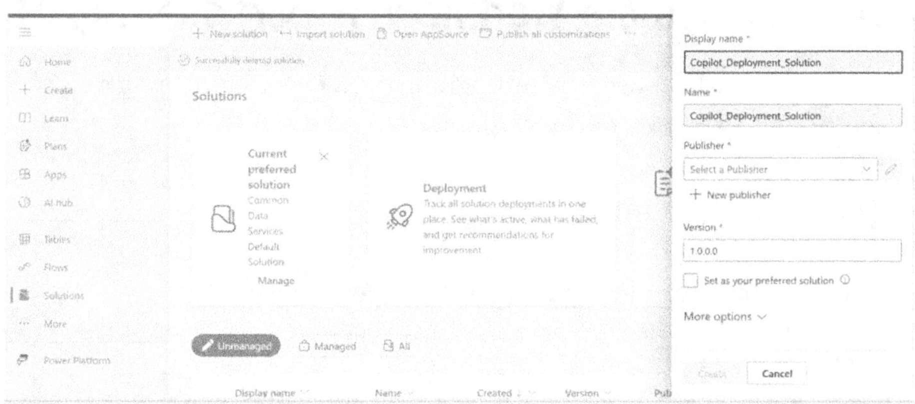

Figure 8-8.   *The Solutions explorer view. A screenshot from the Power Apps portal showing the contents of a Solution.*

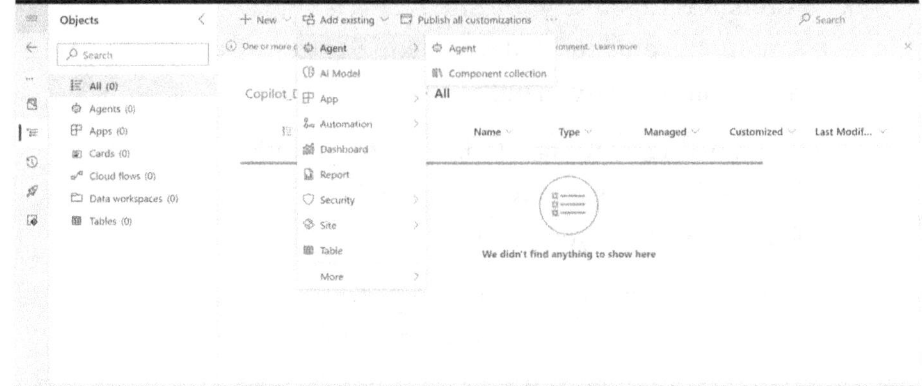

Figure 8-9. *Selecting the proper agents*

3. The Deployment Workflow: Export and Import

When you are ready to move your upgrade from Dev to Prod, you don't rewrite code. You transport the Solution.

Step A: Export from Dev

1. In your Dev environment, select your Solution.

2. Click Export.

3. **Publish:** The system will ask you to "Publish all changes." Do this. It ensures every last edit is saved.

4. **Run Check:** The "Solution Checker" will run a diagnostic to identify rule violations and design issues within your solution. It is important to clarify that this tool focuses on catching architectural flaws and ensuring best practices are followed, rather than diagnosing active runtime performance problems.

5. **Managed vs. Unmanaged:** This is the most critical decision.

    a. **Select "Managed":** This compiles your code into a read-only file. This is what you deploy to Test and Prod. It prevents anyone (even you) from accidentally breaking the live bot with a hotfix.

    b. **Select "Unmanaged":** Only use this if you are moving the bot to another Dev environment to keep working on it.

6. **Download:** You will receive a zip file. This is your "Build Artifact."

Step B: Import to Test/Prod

1. Switch your environment to **Production**.

2. Go to **Solutions ➤ Import**.

3. Upload your zip file.

4. **Connection References:** The wizard will pause and ask: "This bot uses a SharePoint connection. Which account should it use in Production?"

    a. This allows you to swap credentials. In Dev, it used your personal account. In Prod, you can map it to a generic "Service Account" (e.g., bot-service@company.com) so the bot doesn't break if you leave the company.

5. **Environment Variables:** It will ask: "What is the SharePoint Site URL for Production?"

    a. You can input the live URL here, keeping your Dev data separate from Prod data.

4. Versioning Your Creativity (Handling "Prompt Drift")

Code versioning is binary, but creative versioning is subtle. If you change the system prompt from "Be funny" to "Be witty," that is a version change.

Copilot Studio doesn't automatically "git commit" your prompt text history in a way that is easy to read. To manage **Creative Drift**, you need a manual strategy.

The "Comment Code" Technique

Inside your **Generative AI** node or **Message** node, you can use the internal "Comments" feature (often found in the node's ellipsis menu).

- **Action**: Before you change a prompt, paste the old prompt into a comment on that same node with a date stamp.

- **Benefit**: If the new prompt performs poorly in A/B testing (Chapter 7), you can immediately revert to the text preserved in the comment without hunting through external documents.

The "Snapshot" Feature

Copilot Studio has a built-in lightweight versioning tool called Snapshots (found under Settings ➤ Copilot details or sometimes in the Publish history).

- Every time you click Publish, the system creates a Snapshot.

- **The Rollback**: If a deployment creates a disaster, you can go to the Publish history, select the previous date, and click Republish this version.

- **Warning**: This is a "nuclear option." It reverts everything: topics, variables, and settings. It does not allow you to pick and choose specific features to revert.

5. Safe Update Strategies: Blue/Green Deployment

In highly critical scenarios, like a customer-facing support bot during Black Friday, you cannot afford even one minute of downtime. A standard "Overwrite" deployment might take the bot offline for a few moments or introduce a bug that affects everyone instantly.

For these high-stakes creative agents, use a Blue/Green Deployment strategy.

1. **The "Blue" Bot (Live):** This is your current production bot, serving 100% of users.

2. **The "Green" Bot (Staging):** You deploy your Version 2.0 update to a separate bot ID in production, hidden from the public.

3. **The Swap:** You test the Green Bot in the live environment. Once verified, you don't "update" the Blue Bot. Instead, you update the Channel Configuration (e.g., the website embed code or the Teams manifest) to point to the Green Bot's ID.

4. **The Safety Net:** If the Green Bot fails, you simply swap the ID back to Blue. Traffic is instantly restored to the old, stable version.

Deployment is not the end of creativity; it is the beginning of responsibility. By adopting these operational disciplines, environment separation, Solution packaging, and Snapshot management, you buy yourself the freedom to be creative.

You no longer have to fear the "Publish" button. You know that no matter how wild your new experiment is in the Development environment, the Production environment remains a fortress—stable, secure, and always ready to serve the user.

You have now mastered the machine. In the final section of this book, we will see what happens when all these lessons—creative, technical, and operational—come together in a massive, real-world application.

Case Study: Global Rollout of a Multilingual Storytelling Bot

We have reached the summit. Throughout this book, we have built individual components, tested specific features, and learned the disciplines of operation. We have crafted witty dialogue, wired up back-end databases, and secured our agents against misuse. Now, we will see how these disparate skills weave together to solve a massive, complex, real-world challenge.

In this final case study, we will not just build a bot; we will launch a global creative platform. This is the ultimate test of your ability to architect, deploy, and scale a creative AI solution.

The Mission: "The Lorekeeper"

The Client: "Lumina Press," a (fictional) international publishing house known for fantasy and young adult fiction. They are about to launch their biggest book series of the decade, The Chronicles of Aethelgard.

The Goal: To launch **"The Lorekeeper,"** an interactive AI companion for the book series. This isn't just a marketing FAQ bot; it is an immersive role-playing experience.

The Requirement

- **Scale:** The bot must handle an anticipated 50,000 concurrent users on launch day.

- **Reach:** It must serve fans in four key markets: North America (English), France (French), Spain (Spanish), and Japan (Japanese).

- **Depth:** It cannot just translate text; it must adapt culturally. A "hero" in the US market might be brash and bold, while the Japanese market might prefer a protagonist who values harmony and duty.

- **Consistency:** It must never contradict the "canon" of the books.

This project requires every skill you have mastered: advanced prompt engineering, variable management, API integration, security, and rigorous lifecycle management.

Phase 1: The Architecture of Babel

The first decision is structural. How do we build one bot that serves four languages and cultures?

The Anti-pattern (What Not to Do): The novice approach would be to build four separate bots: Lorekeeper_US, Lorekeeper_FR, Lorekeeper_ES, and Lorekeeper_JP.

- **The Maintenance Nightmare:** If you find a bug in the logic (e.g., the inventory system breaks), you have to fix it four times.

- **The Data Silo:** You cannot easily compare analytics across regions because the data is trapped in separate applications.

The Solution: The "Polyglot Core": We will build a single Copilot Studio agent with a centralized logic core, wrapped in a dynamic language layer. This architecture separates the mechanics of the story (variables, logic, APIs) from the presentation (language, tone).

Step 1: Enabling Multilingual NLU: In **Settings ↗ Languages**, we enable English, French, Spanish, and Japanese as shown in Figure 8-10. This allows Copilot Studio's Natural Language Understanding (NLU) engine to natively understand user intent in all four languages.

- A French user saying "Commencer l'aventure" triggers the same internal Topic ID (Topic.StartAdventure) as an American saying "Start the adventure."

- This unifies our analytics. We can see that 10,000 users triggered Topic.StartAdventure, regardless of what language they spoke.

Step 2: The "Cultural Context": Variable Translation is not enough. We need **Localization**. To achieve this, we introduce a Global Variable called Global.CulturalSetting.

In the Greeting Topic, we use the User.Locale system variable (passed automatically by channels like Teams or Web) to determine the user's region.

- **Logic Flow**

  - If User.Locale starts with ja (Japanese) ➤ Set Global.CulturalSetting to **"Honor-bound, atmospheric, subtle, focuses on the collective good."**

  - If User.Locale starts with en (English) ➤ Set Global. CulturalSetting to **"Action-oriented, direct, heroic, focuses on individual achievement."**

- If User.Locale starts with fr (French) ➤ Set Global.CulturalSetting to **"Philosophical, witty, emotionally complex."**

This variable will become the "lens" through which our Generative AI sees the world.

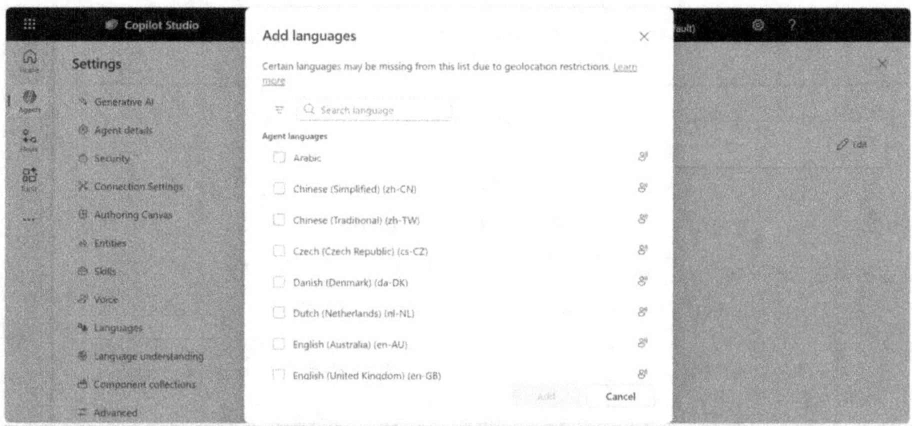

Figure 8-10. *The multilingual settings panel. It shows "English (United States)" as the primary language, with "French," "Spanish," and "Japanese" added as secondary languages, illustrating the foundation of a global bot*

Phase 2: The "Chameleon" Prompt

Standard translation tools (like Google Translate) kill creativity. They turn poetry into instruction manuals. To preserve the "soul" of the story, we use **Dynamic Persona Injection** (a technique we explored in Chapter 4).

Instead of hard-coding the system prompt inside our Generative AI node, we make the prompt itself a variable.

The Logic Flow

1. **Step 1**: The topic triggers (e.g., Topic. EncounterDragon).

2. **Step 2**: A Condition Node checks Global. UserLanguage.

3. **Step 3**: A Set Variable node loads the culturally appropriate "System Instruction" into a variable called Topic.SystemPrompt.

    - **English System Prompt**: "You are the Lorekeeper. Speak with the archaic grandeur of a medieval bard. Describe the dragon's physical power, its fire, and the glory of the coming battle."

    - **Japanese System Prompt**: "You are the Lorekeeper. Speak with the polite mystery of a spirit guide. Describe the dragon's presence, the disturbance in the natural order, and the unspoken weight of history behind this meeting."

4. **Step 4**: The Create generative answers node uses {Topic.SystemPrompt} as its instruction.

This ensures that the Japanese bot doesn't just speak Japanese; it thinks like a Japanese storyteller. It creates a fundamentally different user experience that feels native, not translated.

Phase 3: The "Canon" Knowledge Base

With a global audience, "hallucinations" are a major risk. We cannot have the AI inventing new characters or changing the book's ending. We need a single source of truth.

We utilize the **Knowledge** feature (Chapter 2) to ground the AI.

1. **The Source:** We upload the official "Series Bible" (a 200-page PDF containing character bios, magic rules, and world history) to Copilot Studio.

2. **The Guardrails:** We set the Generative AI settings to "High" moderation for data grounding.

3. **The Result:** When a user asks, "Who is the King of Aethelgard?", the AI retrieves the exact answer from the PDF. However, because of our **Dynamic Persona** (Phase 2), it delivers that answer differently to each region.

   a. **English**: "The King is Valerius, the Iron-Handed, ruler of the seven peaks!"

   b. **Japanese**: "The realm is guided by Emperor Valerius, who bears the burden of the Iron Hand."

The fact is the same; the delivery is localized.

Phase 4: The Deployment Strategy (The "Follow the Sun" Rollout)

You cannot launch a bot this complex to the whole world at once. If there is a critical bug in the "Save Game" flow, you don't want 50,000 users to hit it simultaneously.

Lumina Press adopts a **"Follow the Sun"** staged rollout, utilizing the **Environment Strategy** we mastered earlier.

Stage 1: The "Canary" Launch (Australia/NZ)

- **Environment:** Production (Restricted Audience).

- **Why:** English speakers, similar culture to the US, but a smaller time zone that wakes up first.

- **Goal:** Test technical stability. Does the Azure OpenAI quota hold up? Do the Save-to-Database flows work under load?

- **The Incident:** Monitoring (via Application Insights) reveals a three-second latency in image generation. The team realizes the DALL-E image size is set to HD (1792×1024). They hotfix the variable in the **Dev** environment to Standard (1024×1024), package a new **Solution**, and deploy it to Prod before the next region wakes up.

Stage 2: The European Expansion (UK, France, Spain)

- **Target:** Multi-language capabilities.

- **Why:** Test the language switching logic.

- **The Incident:** French users report the bot is using the informal "tu" instead of the formal "vous" when addressing elders in the story.

- **The Fix:** The team updates the French SystemPrompt variable. Because this is a data change (variable value) rather than a code change, it is low risk. They deploy the update instantly.

Stage 3: The Global Premiere (North America and Japan)

- **Target:** Maximum load.

- **Action:** The team increases the "Concurrency Limits" in the Azure OpenAI settings to handle the influx of 50,000 concurrent users.

- **Result:** The launch is stable. The "Creative Spark Rate," an illustrative metric we defined in Chapter 7 to measure user engagement with AI-generated ideas, holds steady at 85% across all regions.

Phase 5: Operational Resilience and Analytics

With the bot live, the "Ops" phase begins. We move from building to monitoring.

Security: The "Jailbreak" Attempt: A few hours into launch, the security alerts trigger. A user on Reddit has posted a "jailbreak" prompt designed to trick the Lorekeeper into writing modern political satire instead of fantasy.

- **The Defense:** The **Content Moderation** filter catches the keyword patterns.

- **The Response:** The **Fallback Topic** logic kicks in. Instead of breaking character or giving a generic error, it gently steers the user back to the fantasy world:

  AI Response: "I know nothing of these 'politics' you speak of. I only know the rule of the Dragon King and the laws of magic. Shall we return to the quest?"

Analytics: The Cultural Insight: The marketing team watches the Custom Telemetry dashboard. They see a fascinating divergence in the StoryPath custom event.

- **Data**: 60% of Japanese users are choosing the "Stealth/ Diplomacy" story path.

- **Data**: 70% of American users are choosing the "Warrior/Combat" story path.

- **Business Impact**: Lumina Press uses this real-time data to pivot their marketing strategy. They commission a spin-off novel series specifically about the "Stealth" faction, targeted directly at the Japanese market. The AI didn't just entertain fans; it informed the company's product strategy for the next year.

Conclusion: The New Creative Partner

The launch of "The Lorekeeper" is a success. But it is not a success because the AI was perfect out of the box. It is a success because the system surrounding it was robust.

- The Prompt Engineering gave it a soul.

- The Multilingual Architecture gave it a voice.

- The Security Protocols gave it safety.

- The Analytics gave it a future.

This case study encapsulates the journey you have taken in this book. You started by learning how to drag-and-drop a node. You ended by orchestrating a global, culturally adaptive, secure, and data-driven creative phenomenon.

You are no longer just a user of technology. You are a creator of worlds. You have the tools to build assistants that inspire, tools that solve problems, and tools that bring people together across languages and cultures.

Summary

In this chapter, we moved from the development "workshop" to the global stage, exploring how to bring your creative agents to life for real-world users. You've learned that deployment is not just a technical step, but a strategic bridge that connects your AI's "soul" to the diverse platforms where your audience lives, from Microsoft Teams and Slack to custom web portals. By mastering the publishing process, you've seen how to turn a static design into a live, responsive assistant that is ready to collaborate at scale.

We also dove into the vital mechanics of governance and scaling, ensuring your creations remain secure, compliant, and performant as their user base grows. You explored how to manage environments and licensing effectively, treating your agent not just as a one-off project, but as a living digital asset that requires ongoing care and oversight. By building with these "industrial-strength" foundations, you've ensured that your AI can handle the pressure of real-world interaction without losing its creative spark or compromising user trust.

In the next chapter, we will look beyond current tools and explore the future of creative AI agents to see where this rapidly evolving field is headed.

CHAPTER 9

The Future of Creative AI Agents

We have spent the previous eight chapters mastering the architecture of the present. We have built environments, designed intricate conversational flows, integrated multimodal capabilities, and scaled our solutions to global audiences. You now possess the skills to build a highly effective chatbot, a reactive entity that waits patiently for a user to type a prompt before delivering value. However, it is important to anchor our expectations: Copilot Studio today is primarily reactive, and true autonomy typically comes from external triggers, such as Power Automate or Azure, calling the agent to action. You have learned to craft the perfect instruction, wire the correct connections, and safeguard the output. You have learned to craft the perfect instruction, to wire the correct connections, and to safeguard the output. You have mastered the instrument.

But as we turn our gaze toward the horizon, the ground is shifting beneath our feet. We are leaving the era of the chatbot and entering the era of the autonomous agent.

The creative AI of the near future will not merely be a tool you pick up; it will be a partner that taps you on the shoulder. It will not just wait for instructions; it will observe your workflow, anticipate your needs, and proactively execute complex, multi-step projects. Imagine an AI that doesn't just "write a blog post" when asked, but one that autonomously

© Mezba Uddin 2026

M. Uddin, *Creative AI Agents with Copilot Studio*, Inside Copilot,

https://doi.org/10.1007/979-8-8688-2779-2_9

monitors industry news, pitches three article ideas to you on Monday morning, and drafts the approved one by Tuesday. In practice, this is implemented as a comprehensive workflow system, utilizing Power Automate or Logic Apps for scheduled triggers, Microsoft Graph for context, and various CMS APIs, where the agent serves as a critical step in a larger automated chain. After your review, the system can even optimize SEO and schedule the content for publication.

This shift from "Chat" to "Action" is the core of the vision for Agentic AI. It represents a fundamental transformation in how we interact with technology. We are moving from a paradigm of "command and control" where every output requires a specific input to one of "delegation and supervision." In this new world, you do not micromanage the keystrokes; you define the intent. You set the goal, and the agent determines the path.

This evolution promises to redefine the structure of creative work. Organizations are evolving into what are often described as "Frontier Firms," companies where human creativity is amplified by a workforce of digital agents that act as researchers, project managers, and creative assistants. These agents will not replace the human spark; rather, they will clear the brush, handling the logistical and structural weight of creativity so that the human artist can focus on the vision.

In this final chapter, we will step beyond the current capabilities of Copilot Studio to explore this brave new world. We will dissect the strategic road map that is guiding the platform toward "Smart Mode" reasoning and multi-agent orchestration. We will examine how agents are gaining the ability to "think" before they speak, entering reasoning loops to critique their own logic and refine their creative choices before presenting them to you. We will explore the concept of the "Virtual Creative Studio," where specialized agents, such as a Researcher, a Copywriter, and an Editor, coordinate with one another to solve problems more complex than any single model could handle alone.

However, great power brings great complexity. As our agents become more autonomous, the line between human and machine creativity begins to blur. We will grapple with the ethical implications of this shift. When an AI can plan and execute a creative project with minimal human intervention, who owns the result? How do we maintain authenticity in a world where media can be co-created in real time by machines? We will ask the hard questions about authorship, transparency, and control in an age of autonomous generation.

Finally, we will ground these futuristic concepts in a tangible reality with a forward-looking case study of an AI-Generated Podcast Host. This example will demonstrate how the technologies we have discussed, voice synthesis, dynamic scripting, and autonomous planning, are converging to create entirely new forms of media.

The tools you are using today are just the beginning. The skills you have built in prompt engineering, variable management, and flow design are the foundational grammar for this new language of agentic AI. You have learned to build the instrument; now, we will learn how to conduct the orchestra.

Microsoft's Road Map for Copilot Studio

The landscape of conversational AI is shifting beneath our feet. For the past few years, we have operated in the era of the chatbot: a reactive entity that sits patiently in a chat window, waiting for a human to type a prompt. It is a tool, much like a hammer or a paintbrush, lying dormant until picked up. You have learned to master this tool in the previous chapters, crafting intricate flows and connecting powerful APIs.

But as we look toward the road map for 2026 and beyond, Microsoft is steering Copilot Studio toward a fundamentally different paradigm: the era of the autonomous agent.

An agent is not just a better chatbot. It is a digital employee. It does not wait to be asked; it observes, plans, and acts. It does not just output text; it navigates software, coordinates with other agents, and solves problems that require sustained reasoning over time. For the creative professional, this means moving from "using an AI to write a draft" to "managing an AI that runs your editorial calendar."

The road map revealed at recent Microsoft Ignite and Build conferences outlines a future where Copilot Studio evolves from a chatbot builder into a command center for Agentic AI. This shift is defined by three massive architectural changes: autonomy (waking up without humans), reasoning (thinking before speaking), and orchestration (managing teams of bots).

In this section, we will deep-dive into these capabilities, exploring not just what they are, but how they will fundamentally alter the creative architectures you build.

1. The Shift to Autonomy: Beyond "User Says"

Currently, the fundamental atom of Copilot Studio is the Trigger Phrase. Every Topic you have built in this book likely begins with a node that says, "User says: 'Write a poem'" or "User says: 'Check status.'" This creates a dependency on human initiation. The bot is trapped in the "Request/ Response" cycle.

The road map introduces Autonomous Triggers, which allow agents to initiate actions based on signals rather than user-typed words. In practice, this autonomy is achieved by external triggers, such as Power Automate or Logic Apps running on a specific event or schedule, which then invoke the agent. For a concrete technical anchor, Power Automate now supports an "execute agent" style of action in certain environments, allowing a flow to call upon your agent's reasoning as a discrete step in a larger process.

Data-Driven Wake Words

In the near future, you will configure triggers based on changes in your data ecosystem.

- **The Scenario:** Imagine you are a Creative Director. Currently, when a writer uploads a draft to SharePoint, nothing happens until you manually ask the bot to "Review the draft."

- **The Autonomous Future**: You configure a workflow that serves as a Data Trigger: "When a new file is created in the 'Drafts' folder on SharePoint."

- **The Action:** The moment the file touches the server, the system initiates a multi-step orchestration:

  - **SharePoint Trigger**: A Power Automate flow detects the new file entry.

  - **Document Retrieval and Extraction**: The flow retrieves the file and performs any necessary parsing (such as Word or PDF text extraction) to prepare the content.

  - **The Agent Call**: The flow then calls the Copilot Studio agent to process the text.

  - **Reasoning**: The agent runs the content against your Brand Voice guidelines and generates a summary of suggested edits.

  - **Mail Delivery**: Finally, the flow sends those insights directly to your inbox, all before you have even had your morning coffee.

Time-Based and Event-Based Creativity

Autonomy also implies a sense of time. We are moving toward agents that have "Daily Routines."

- **The Trend Hunter:** A creative agent could be scheduled to wake up every morning at 8:00 AM. It uses the Bing Search API to scan for trending topics in your industry, synthesizes a "Creative Brief" for the day, and posts it to your creative team's Microsoft Teams channel.

- **The Social Manager:** Instead of you asking the bot to generate social media content, the system monitors your published blog posts. When a new post goes live, the agent automatically generates five variations for social platforms. However, it is important to note that the ability to "schedule" these posts is not a native agent setting; it requires the use of approved connectors for your specific social platforms and is subject to your organization's governance and permission policies.

As illustrated in Figure 9-1, this moves the locus of control. In the classic model, the human is the engine. In the autonomous model, the human is the steering wheel.

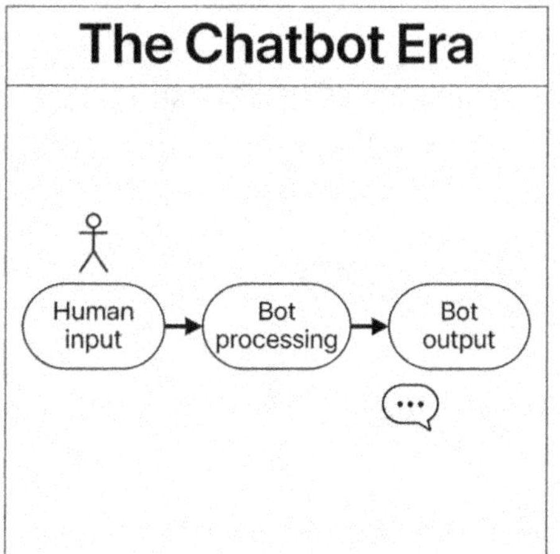

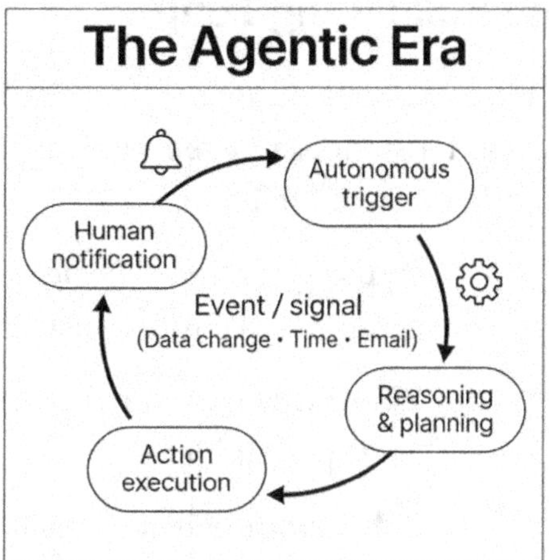

Figure 9-1. *Chatbot era vs. agentic era: user-initiated interaction compared with autonomous, signal-driven workflows that reason, act, and notify humans*

2. Deep Reasoning: The "Thinking" Models

One of the persistent limitations of standard Large Language Models (LLMs) like GPT-4o is their tendency to "rush." They function like an improv actor: they must predict the next word immediately. This works well for conversation but poorly for complex creative planning. If you ask a standard LLM to "Write a mystery novel," it often reveals the killer too early or creates plot holes, because it isn't planning ahead; it's just writing forward.

The expected direction for Copilot Studio involves the integration of Deep Reasoning Models, reflecting a likely pattern similar to the architecture of OpenAI's o1 or o3 series. This evolution points toward a "Smart Mode" or "Think Deeper" capability, where the agent spends more compute on internal planning and critique before delivering a final response. This introduces a "Smart Mode" or "Think Deeper' capability.

The Reasoning Loop

When an agent equipped with Deep Reasoning encounters a complex instruction, it does not generate an answer immediately. Instead, it enters a hidden Reasoning Loop.

1. **Deconstruction:** The agent breaks the user's prompt down into constituent goals.

2. **Planning:** It outlines a step-by-step approach to solve the problem.

3. **Self-Critique:** It simulates the output and checks for errors or inconsistencies.

4. **Refinement:** It adjusts the plan based on the critique.

5. **Output:** Only then does it generate the final response for the user.

Creative Application: The "Showrunner" Agent

Imagine asking your copilot: "Plan a 10-episode podcast series about the history of jazz that appeals to Gen Z."

- **Standard Copilot:** Would instantly spit out a list of ten generic topics.

- **Deep Reasoning Agent:** Would "pause" to think. It might reason: "Gen Z prefers shorter formats and visual components. I should structure these as 20-minute audio episodes with accompanying TikTok scripts. For the history aspect, I need to focus on the sampling culture, how jazz influences modern hip-hop, to make it relevant."

The resulting output isn't just a list; it is a strategic campaign. As we can see in Figure 9-2, the "hidden" layer of thought is where the quality jump happens. The agent effectively becomes its own editor. However, it is vital to remember that a "thinking" model does not automatically equate to a factually reliable one; deep reasoning still requires robust grounding, data retrieval, and human validation to ensure the final output is accurate and trustworthy.

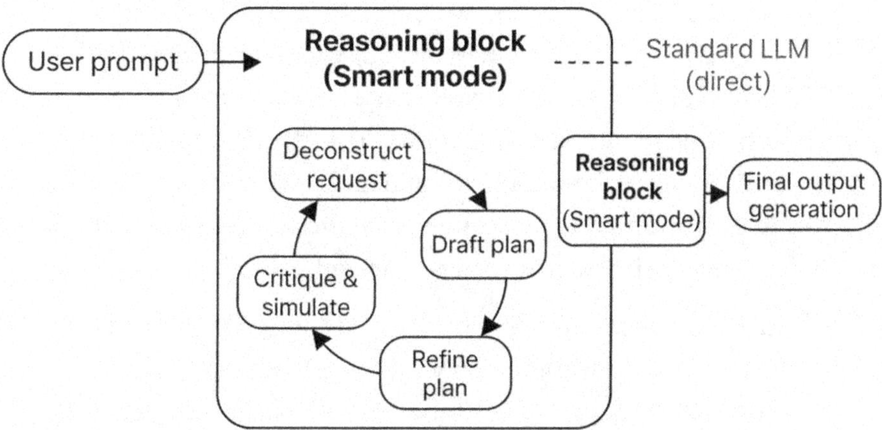

Figure 9-2. *Deep Reasoning ("Smart Mode") architecture: the user prompt is routed into an internal reasoning loop, deconstruct, plan, critique/simulate, and refine, before final output generation*

3. Multi-agent Orchestration: The Digital Studio

Perhaps the most transformative feature on the road map is Multi-agent Orchestration, as shown in Figure 9-3.

Throughout this book, we have built "monolithic" bots, single agents that try to do everything. We gave them the ability to write lyrics, check the weather, and query databases. As any software architect knows, monoliths are hard to maintain. If you tweak the "Funny" prompt for the lyricist, you might accidentally break the "Serious" tone of the weather reporter.

The future is Modular. Microsoft is moving Copilot Studio toward a "Hub and Spoke" model where you build specialized "Child Agents," each an expert in one domain, and a "Parent Agent" (or Orchestrator) that manages them.

Building the "Virtual Creative Studio"

Instead of building one "Creative Bot," you will build a team:

- **Agent A (The Researcher):** Configured for high accuracy and low creativity, this agent is connected to Bing Search and specialized academic databases via approved or custom connectors. These integrations must account for organizational authentication, licensing, and rate limits to ensure the agent can reliably find facts from peer-reviewed sources.

- **Agent B (The Copywriter):** Tuned for high creativity, low accuracy. Primed with your brand voice and storytelling techniques. Its job is to take facts and make them sing.

- **Agent C (The Legal Eagle):** Tuned for compliance. Connected to your legal policy documents. Its job is to review text for liability.

The Workflow

1. **You (The User):** "Write a blog post about our new medical product."

2. **The Orchestrator:** Analyzes the request. "This requires facts, writing, and a safety check."

3. **Delegation**

   a. Calls **The Researcher**: "Get the specs for Product X."

   b. Waits for output.

   c. Passes specs to **The Copywriter**: "Draft a blog post using these specs."

   d. Waits for output.

   e. Passes draft to **The Legal Eagle**: "Check this for medical compliance."

4. **Final Output:** The Orchestrator delivers the approved, fact-checked, beautifully written post to you.

This mimics the structure of a real-world creative agency. It allows you to update the "Legal" logic without touching the "Creative" logic. It allows you to swap out the "Copywriter" for a "Poet" without breaking the research chain.

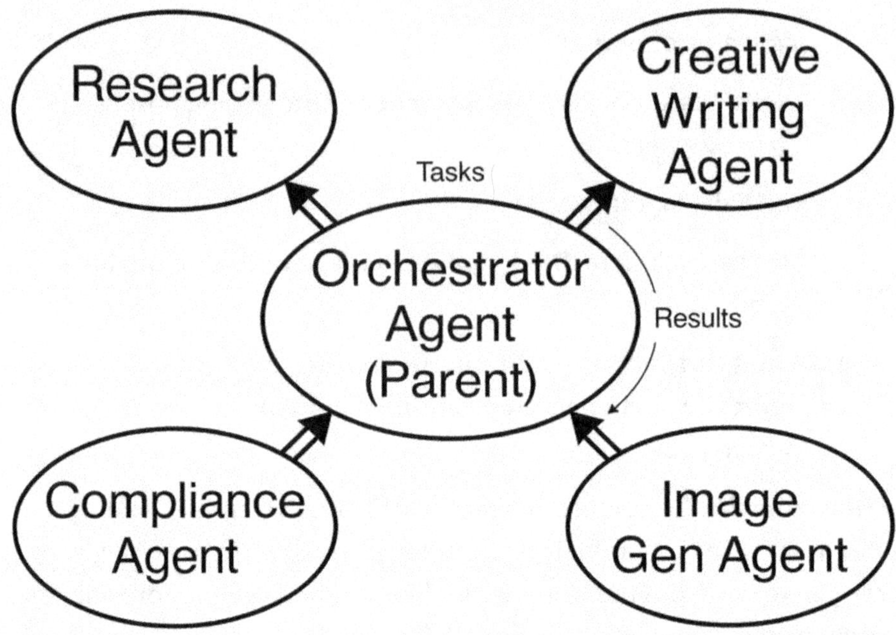

Figure 9-3. *Multi-agent orchestration (hub-and-spoke): a parent Orchestrator Agent delegates tasks to specialized child agents and aggregates their bidirectional results into a single final response*

4. Universal Connectivity: MCP and Computer Use

Finally, the road map addresses the issue of "Agent Blindness." Currently, agents can only see what we explicitly connect them to via APIs. The road map introduces two standards to widen their eyes.

Model Context Protocol (MCP)

MCP is an open standard that acts as a "Universal Adapter" for AI. Instead of building a custom connector for every individual app, MCP provides a standardized way for an agent to "read" the context of any application that supports the protocol. This means your creative agent will eventually be able to access approved context sources you authorize, such as specific drafts in Word or designated chats in Discord, to gain a holistic understanding of your creative intent.

Computer Use (The "Ghost in the Machine")

Perhaps the most sci-fi addition to the road map is **Computer Use**. This capability allows an agent to interact with a computer interface visually, just like a human. It can look at a screen, identify buttons, move a cursor, and type.

- **The Creative Application:** Imagine a "Design Assistant" agent. You ask it to "Resize these 50 photos in Photoshop and save them for the Web."

- **Current State:** While GUI automation is possible today through Robotic Process Automation (RPA) and tools like Power Automate Desktop, these systems typically require predefined, rigid scripts to function correctly. Achieving this sequence via a standard web-based agent is often impossible unless the software provides a specific API.

  - **The Shift:** The evolution toward "Computer Use" represents a transition from traditional RPA to natural language planning and visual grounding. Instead of a developer mapping every button click, the agent uses its "eyes" to identify interfaces and its reasoning mind to execute the task safely.

- **Future State (Computer Use):** The agent literally opens Photoshop, clicks "File > Open," runs the action, and saves the files. This would create a bridge between the AI's reasoning and legacy creative software that lacks a modern API.

- **Warning:** This technology is currently a research direction and is not generally available. UI automation is notoriously brittle and requires supervised execution, sandboxing, and strict security controls. Architects must exercise extreme caution regarding credential handling and the risk of unintended actions by the agent within a local environment.

Summary: The Architect's New Role

The road map for Copilot Studio is clear: we are moving from **Chat** to **Action** and from **Single-Tasking** to **Systemic Reasoning**.

For you, the reader, this means your role is evolving. You are no longer just a "Prompt Engineer" trying to find the magic words. You are becoming an **AI Systems Architect**. You will design the workflows, define the triggers, and orchestrate the team of agents that will execute your vision. The skills you have built in Chapters 1 through 8—understanding variables, managing context, structuring topics—are the foundation. Chapter 9 is where we build the skyscraper.

Autonomous AI vs. Human Collaboration

The central question of the next decade is not "What can AI do?" but "Who does what?"

As creative AI evolves from a passive tool into a proactive agent, the relationship between creator and machine is undergoing a radical restructuring. For the past few years, we have operated in the **"Centaur"** model (human on top, AI as the legs), where the human explicitly directs every step. We are now moving toward a **"Cybernetic"** model, where the distinction between human intent and machine execution is fluid and dynamic.

This shift requires us to redefine the creative workflow. We are no longer just "using" software; we are managing a digital workforce. In this section, we will explore the three emerging models of collaboration, Human-in-the-Loop, Human-on-the-Loop, and Human-out-of-the-Loop, and define where the human artist fits in a world of autonomous generation.

1. The Collaborative Spectrum: Defining the New Roles

The future of creative work isn't a binary choice between "Human" and "AI." It is a spectrum of autonomy. Depending on the task, you will shift between being a Director, a Collaborator, and a Curator.

Model A: Human-in-the-Loop (The Apprentice Model)

This is the model most of us use today. The AI is a junior apprentice. It does nothing without explicit instruction, and every output is reviewed before it moves forward.

- **Workflow:** You write a prompt ➤ AI generates options ➤ You select and edit ➤ You prompt again.

- **Best For:** High-stakes creative work where nuance, voice, and emotional resonance are critical (e.g., writing a novel, designing a brand identity).

- **The Human Role: The Artisan:** You are hands-on, molding the clay. The AI provides the raw material, but you provide the craft.

Model B: Human-on-the-Loop (The Manager Model)

This is the emerging standard for Agentic AI. The AI acts as a mid-level manager. You set the goal ("Launch a marketing campaign for product X"), and the AI breaks it down into tasks, executes them (drafts emails, generates images, schedules posts), and presents the completed package for your approval.

- **Workflow:** You define the objective ➤ AI plans and executes ➤ AI reports back ➤ You approve or redirect.

- **Best For:** Complex, multi-step workflows like content marketing, data analysis, or personalized outreach.

- **The Human Role:** The Creative Director. You are not painting the canvas; you are critiquing the portfolio. Your value shifts from making to judging. You ensure the output aligns with the strategic vision and brand ethics.

Model C: Human-out-of-the-Loop (The Engine Model)

This is the domain of fully autonomous systems. The AI operates independently within pre-set guardrails. It monitors data, makes decisions, and takes action without human intervention.

- **Workflow:** System triggers (e.g., "Stock price drops") -> AI reacts (e.g., "Generates and publishes a financial update article").

- **Best For:** High-volume, low-risk tasks like personalized product recommendations, dynamic pricing, or real-time translation.

  A Note on Financial Tasks: While the system can handle tasks like dynamic pricing, these are considered high-stakes domains that require strict architectural controls and frequent legal review. Be aware that autonomous dynamic pricing can also trigger intense regulatory scrutiny and must be implemented with extreme caution.

- **The Human Role: The Architect:** You build the system, set the constraints, and audit the results, but you are not involved in the daily operation. You are designing the machine, not running it.

As illustrated in Figure 9-4, successful organizations will not pick just one model; they will fluidly move between them depending on the creative risk and strategic importance of the task.

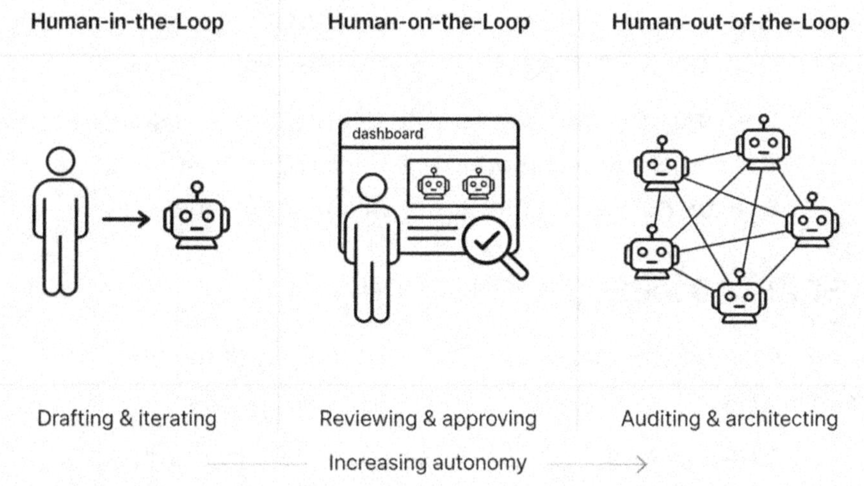

Figure 9-4. *Spectrum of creative autonomy showing three collaboration modes, Human-in-the-Loop (drafting and iterating), Human-on-the-Loop (reviewing and approving), and Human-out-of-the-Loop (auditing and architecting), ordered by increasing agent autonomy*

2. The Creative Director Workflow: From Creation to Curation

As Copilot Studio enables more "Human-on-the-Loop" agents, your daily workflow will change. You will spend less time on the first draft and more time on the final polish.

This brings us to the "Sandwich" method of collaboration, a workflow designed to maximize the strengths of both biological and artificial intelligence.

Layer 1: The Top Bun (Human Intent)

Everything begins with context. An autonomous agent can write a blog post, but it doesn't know why it is writing it. It doesn't know that your company is pivoting its strategy next month or that the tone needs to be "somber but hopeful" because of a recent news event.

- **Your Job:** Provide the strategic "North Star." You define the audience, the emotional goal, and the constraints. You are not writing the copy; you are writing the brief.

Layer 2: The Meat (AI Execution)

The autonomous agent takes over. It does the heavy lifting that burns human energy.

- **The Agent's Job:** It researches 50 sources, synthesizes the key points, drafts the content, generates accompanying DALL-E images, and formats everything into a clean HTML template. It works at a speed and scale no human can match, turning your brief into a tangible asset in seconds.

Layer 3: The Bottom Bun (Human Curation)

The work comes back to you. This is the quality control phase.

- **Your Job:** You review the output. You add the cultural references the AI missed. You smooth out the robotic phrasing. You ensure the "soul" of the brand is intact. You are the final gatekeeper before the work touches the world.

This workflow, visualized in Figure 9-5, liberates the creative professional from the "blank page problem." You are never starting from zero; you are always starting from a robust first draft generated by your agent.

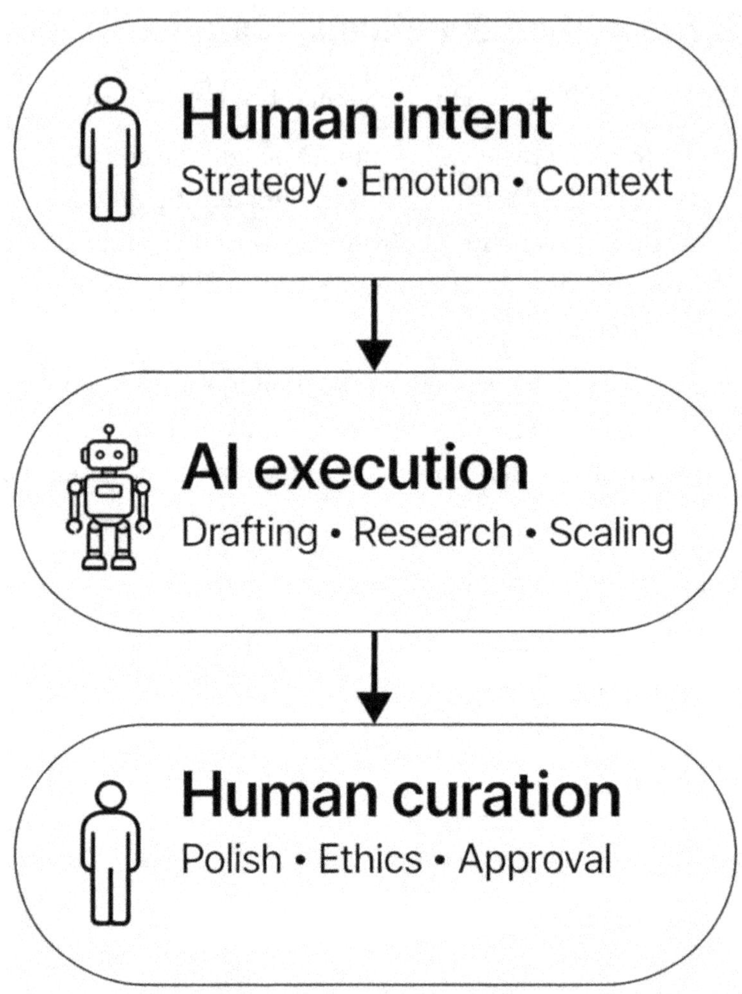

***Figure 9-5.** The "Sandwich" collaboration model: humans define intent (strategy, emotion, context), the AI executes (research and drafting at scale), and humans curate the final output (polish, ethics, approval)*

3. The "Creative Spark" Gap: Why Humans Remain Essential

Despite the rapid advancement of autonomous agents, there remains a critical gap, the "Creative Spark." It is essential to understand this distinction so you know when to automate and when to intervene.

Current AI models are probabilistic. They predict the most likely next word or pixel based on existing data. They are brilliant at synthesis, pattern recognition, and mimicking established styles. They are the ultimate "Average."

Humans, however, are intentional. We create based on lived experience, emotional urgency, and a desire to connect. We often value the unlikely choice, the weird metaphor, the jarring color contrast, the silence in a song.

- **AI Excels at Divergent Thinking:** "Show me 50 variations of a blue logo." It can generate endless options.

- **Humans Excel at Convergent Thinking:** "That specific blue reminds me of sadness; let's use green instead." We provide the meaning.

The most successful "Frontier Firms" of 2026 will not be the ones that replace humans with agents. They will be the ones that use agents to handle the probabilistic work (drafting, analyzing, formatting) so that humans can focus entirely on the intentional work (strategy, empathy, innovation).

4. Designing for Collaboration in Copilot Studio

So, how do we build this "Human-on-the-Loop" relationship technically? Copilot Studio provides specific tools to ensure you remain the manager, even as the bot becomes more autonomous, as shown in Figure 9-6.

The "Approval" Pattern

When building an autonomous agent that generates public-facing content (like tweets or emails), you should never let it publish directly. You must build an Approval Node.

1. **Generate:** The agent uses Generative AI to create the content.

2. **Format:** It formats the content into an Adaptive Card (as learned in Chapter 5).

3. **Send:** It sends this card to a specific Microsoft Teams channel (e.g., "Creative Review").

4. **Wait:** The agent pauses its execution. It waits for a human to click "Approve" or "Reject" on that card.

5. **Act:** Only after the human clicks "Approve" does the agent proceed to the "Publish to a social platform via approved connector" step.

This simple flow turns an unsafe autonomous bot into a safe, collaborative partner.

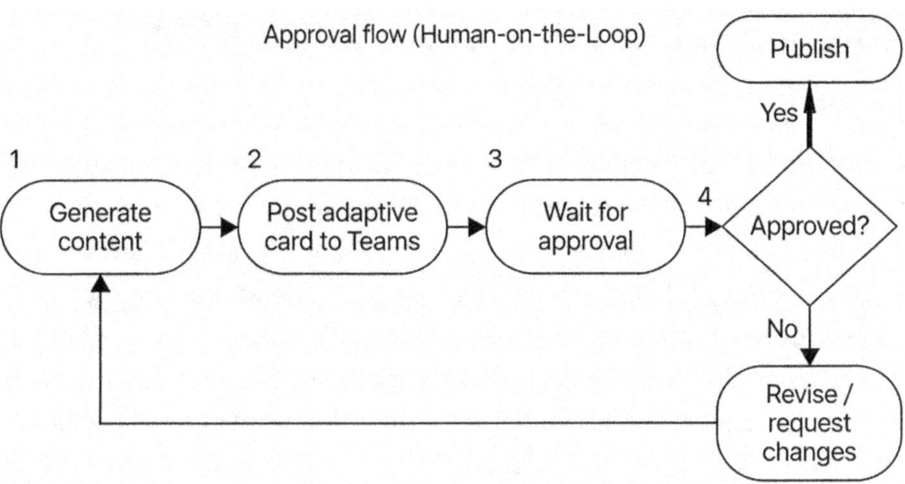

Figure 9-6. *Human-on-the-Loop approval workflow: the system generates content, posts an adaptive card for review, waits for a human decision, and publishes only after approval*

Summary: The New Partnership

We are not building replacements; we are building partners. The autonomous agent is the ultimate force multiplier. It allows a single writer to become a publisher, a single designer to become an agency, and a single developer to become a platform.

The danger lies not in the technology, but in surrendering the oversight. If we abdicate our role as Creative Directors, we risk a world of generic, soulless content. But if we embrace this new role, if we learn to direct our agents with precision and curate their output with wisdom, we enter a new golden age of creativity.

Ethical Implications of AI-Generated Content

We have arrived at the most critical juncture of our journey. Throughout the previous eight chapters, we have focused relentlessly on capability, what the AI can do. We have celebrated the ability to generate infinite variations of a logo, to clone a writing style, to automate communication at a global scale, and to build agents that reason like creative professionals.

But capability does not imply suitability. As we transition to the era of autonomous agents, the buffer between the AI's output and the public's perception disappears. When a chatbot drafts a response in a sandbox, the risk is low. When an autonomous agent publishes a marketing campaign directly to social media, or when a "Deep Reasoning" model generates a legal contract, the stakes become existential.

In this section, we will step away from the mechanics of flow charts and API calls to examine the **Ethics of Architecture**. This is not a theoretical discussion; it is a practical necessity. As an AI Architect, you are no longer just a developer; you are the guardian of your agent's conscience. Every node you place, every prompt you write, and every data source you connect carries an ethical weight.

We will explore the murky waters of Intellectual Property (IP) in the age of generative synthesis. We will confront the dangers of "Deepfakes" and the erosion of digital trust. We will discuss the "Alignment Problem," how to ensure that your creative agent, which has been trained on the entire internet, reflects the specific values of your organization rather than the biases of the chaotic web. And we will confront the environmental and human costs of this new technology.

1. The Authenticity Crisis: Deepfakes and the Erosion of Trust

The core promise of a creative agent is that it can mimic human output. It can write like a poet, paint like an Impressionist, and, with the new audio capabilities in Copilot Studio, speak with the cadence of a trusted friend.

However, this mimicry creates a Trust Deficit. If an AI agent can perfectly impersonate a CEO, a customer service rep, or a celebrity brand ambassador, how does the user know whom they are talking to?

The "Liar's Dividend"

As AI content becomes indistinguishable from human content, we face a phenomenon known as the "Liar's Dividend." This is the skepticism that arises when the public realizes anything could be fake, leading them to doubt everything—even the truth.

For a brand using Copilot Studio, this presents a specific danger: **Brand Impersonation**.

- **The Scenario:** You build a "Customer Success Agent" that speaks in a friendly, casual tone. It is helpful, empathetic, and effective.

- **The Risk:** A malicious actor uses similar open source tools to clone your agent's voice and personality. They create a "Phishing Agent" that calls your customers, sounding exactly like your brand, to steal credit card data. Because your customers are used to talking to your AI, they have let their guard down.

The Solution: Provenance and Transparency

To combat this, the industry (led by Microsoft, Adobe, and others) is moving toward **C2PA (Coalition for Content Provenance and Authenticity)** standards. This is a "digital nutrition label" embedded in the file. It cryptographically proves where a piece of content came from.

In Copilot Studio, ethical architecture requires **Transparency by Design**. You cannot rely on users "guessing" that they are talking to a bot. You must architect the disclosure.

Implementation Strategy (as shown in Figure 9-7):

1. **The Disclosure Directive:** Your system prompt (the "Persona" instruction) must explicitly state: "You are an AI assistant. You must never claim to be a human. If asked, or at the beginning of any high-stakes interaction, you will identify yourself as a virtual agent."

2. **Visual Cues:** When using the "Generative Answers" node to produce images or documents, you should configure the output to implement watermarking in the generation workflow.

3. **UI Indicators:** In your custom web canvas (Chapter 8.1), design the chat interface to clearly label the participant as "AI Agent" or "Virtual Assistant," distinct from human support.

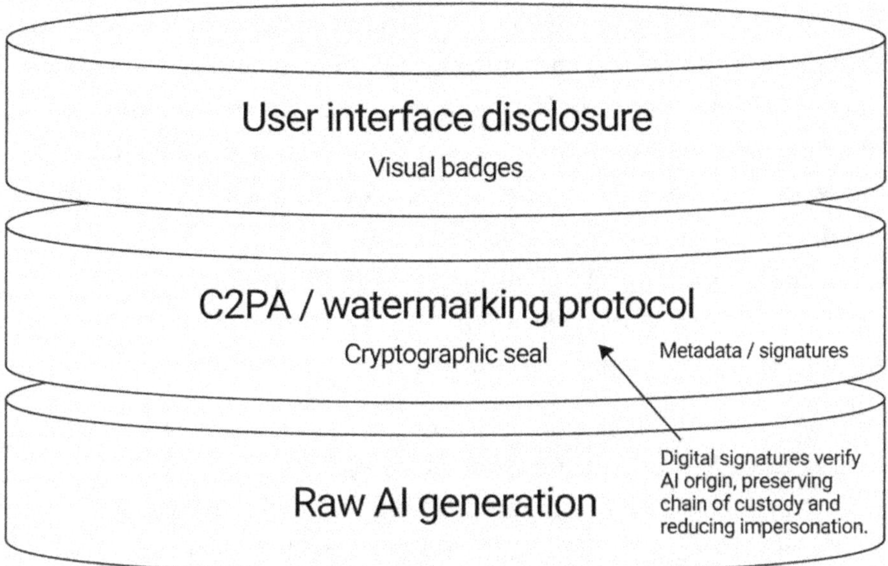

Figure 9-7. *Trust architecture for AI-generated media: a content-provenance stack combining raw generation, C2PA/watermarking as a cryptographic seal, and user-interface disclosure (badges), supported by metadata signatures to verify origin and maintain chain of custody*

2. Intellectual Property: The Ownership Tangle

Who owns the output of a creative agent?

This is the single most litigated question in the world of Generative AI today. When your Copilot Studio agent generates a "unique" marketing slogan, is it truly unique? Or is it a statistical derivative of a copyrighted slogan it saw in its training data? And once generated, does your company own it, or is it public domain?

The "Human in the Loop" Legal Defense

Currently, the US Copyright Office and various global courts have leaned toward the stance that AI-generated content may not qualify for copyright protection without sufficient human authorship. This has massive implications for the "autonomous agents" we discussed earlier. It creates a paradox: the more autonomous your agent is, the less intellectual property protection you may have for its outputs.

This has massive implications for the "autonomous agents" we discussed in earlier section of this chapter. It creates a paradox: The more autonomous your agent is, the less intellectual property protection you have.

- **Case A (The Autonomous Engine):** You set up an agent to wake up, generate a blog post about industry trends, and publish it directly to your site. You never touched it.

    - **Result**: You may not qualify for copyright protection for this content. While you lack traditional authorship, a competitor's ability to use the text could still be restricted by other legal frameworks, such as platform terms of service, trade secret protections, or unfair competition claims. Because the intersection of autonomous AI and intellectual property is complex and varies by jurisdiction, it is essential to consult legal counsel before deploying fully autonomous content engines.

- **Case B (The Collaborative Workflow):** You use the agent to generate a draft. You then rewrite 40% of it, rearrange the structure, add unique human insights, and edit the tone.

- **Result**: You own the copyright on the human-modified portion. The final work is considered a "Derivative Work" with sufficient human authorship.

Architectural Mitigation: The "Touchpoint" Workflow

For the AI Architect, this dictates a workflow change. You must build "Human Touchpoints" into your flows, not just for quality control, but for Legal Ownership Protection. In your Power Automate flows, do not just automate the "Publish" step; instead, automate the "Draft" step but force a review where a human must edit the content, as shown in Figure 9-8. The goal is not merely to log the interaction, but to ensure there is a substantive human creative contribution, a legal requirement for establishing protectable authorship. By saving the "Pre-Edit" and "Post-Edit" versions in SharePoint, you create a legal paper trail that proves this human involvement.

In your Power Automate flows, do not just automate the "Publish" step. Automate the "Draft" step, but force a "Review" step where a human must edit the content. By logging this edit (e.g., saving the "Pre-Edit" and "Post-Edit" versions in SharePoint), you create a legal paper trail proving human involvement.

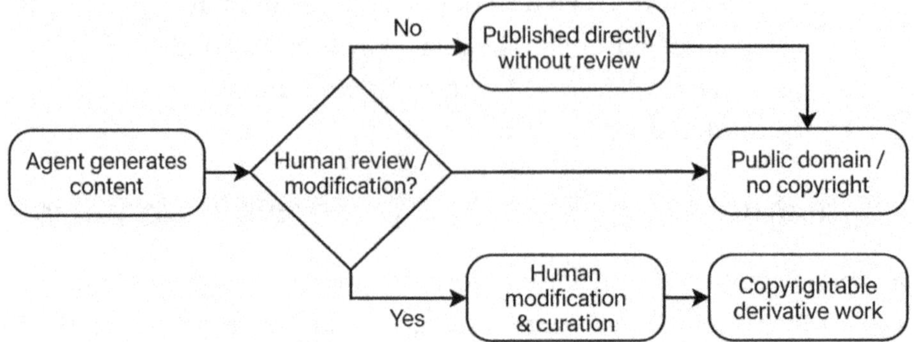

Figure 9-8. *Copyright decision tree for AI-assisted content: publishing outputs without human review tends to yield no protectable authorship, while human modification and curation supports a copyrightable derivative work*

3. The Mirror Effect: Bias and Representation

Generative AI models are mirrors. They reflect the data they were trained on. Since the internet contains historical biases, racism, sexism, and stereotypes, the base models inherently contain these biases too, as shown in Figure 9-9.

When you use Copilot Studio to build a "Creative Storyteller" or a "Marketing Image Generator," you risk falling into the Regressive Loop. This is where the AI amplifies stereotypes because they are statistically common in the training data.

- **The Prompt:** "Generate an image of a doctor."

- **The Bias:** The model, trained on historical stock photos, generates four images of white men.

- **The Prompt:** "Write a story about a family dinner."

- **The Bias:** The model defaults to a nuclear family structure common in Western media, potentially alienating users from different cultural backgrounds.

Architectural Mitigation: The "Diversity Injector"

You cannot "fix" the base model (GPT-4) yourself; that is Microsoft and OpenAI's job. But you can architect a defense using System Instructions.

In your Generative AI settings (Chapter 4), you must explicitly instruct the agent to counteract bias. You treat diversity as a technical requirement, not just a social one.

- **Bad Instruction**: "Be helpful and creative."

- **Ethical Instruction**: "You are an inclusive storyteller. When generating characters or scenarios, actively seek diverse representation in terms of gender, ethnicity, and ability. Avoid stereotypes. If asked to depict a professional group, ensure a mix of demographic characteristics is represented."

By hard-coding diversity into the system prompt, you nudge the model toward inclusive defaults and encourage the reasoning engine to consider representative perspectives before generating an output. However, because prompts alone cannot guarantee total bias correction, it is essential to validate all outputs through rigorous human review and testing to ensure they meet your organization's ethical standards.

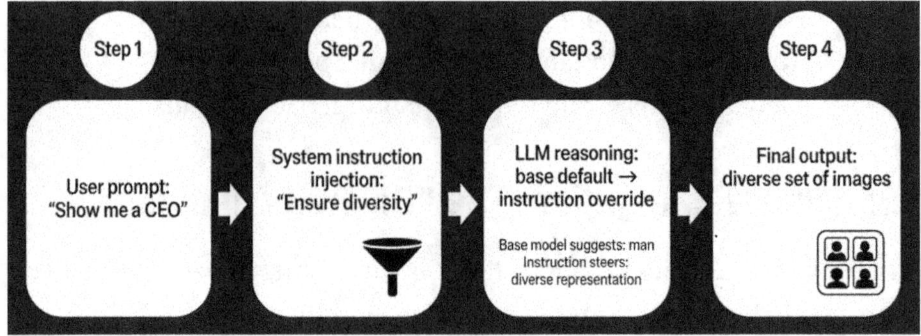

Figure 9-9. *Bias mitigation flow in prompt processing: a user request is augmented with diversity-focused system instructions that steer model reasoning and produce a more representative final output*

4. Hallucination and Brand Safety

In a creative context, "hallucination" (making things up) is often a feature, not a bug. We want the AI to invent fictional worlds or dream up new product concepts. However, when that fiction bleeds into fact, it becomes a liability.

Imagine an autonomous agent for a travel company. It writes a beautiful, creative blog post about a "Hidden Waterfall in Paris."

- **The Problem:** The waterfall doesn't exist. The AI "dreamed" it because it associated "Paris" with "Romance" and "Romance" with "Waterfalls."

- **The Impact:** A customer books a trip, can't find the waterfall, and sues for false advertising.

The "Grounding" Guardrails

In Copilot Studio, the ethical architect uses Knowledge Grounding (Chapter 2) as a safety net. Instead of a single "Temperature" dial, you must use stricter grounding and lower creativity settings for factual domains.

By adjusting these guardrails based on the risk associated with the topic, you ensure that the agent remains tethered to your source material when accuracy is paramount.

1. **Strictness Levels:** For factual topics (Pricing, Legal, Safety), set the Generative AI moderation to **High**. This forces the bot to stick strictly to your uploaded documents. If the document doesn't say it, the bot doesn't say it.

2. **Citation Mandate:** Configure the agent to always provide citations. It is essential to specify that citations must be generated strictly from retrieved sources rather than in a free-form manner, as LLMs can otherwise fabricate references. If the system cannot cite a source directly from your approved knowledge base, such as a SharePoint list, it should not generate the creative text.

3. **The "Creative Sandbox":** For purely creative topics (e.g., "Write a poem about our brand"), use a separate Topic with **Low** moderation. Isolate the "dreaming" capability to safe zones where factual accuracy is not expected.

5. The Human Cost: Displacement vs. Augmentation

Finally, we must address the elephant in the room. Does the agent you are building replace a human job?

As we build agents that can write code, design graphics, and draft legal briefs, the fear of displacement is real. An ethical AI deployment strategy focuses on **Augmentation**, not **Replacement**.

The Jevons Paradox of Creativity

Economist William Stanley Jevons observed that as technology increases the efficiency with which a resource is used, the total consumption of that resource increases rather than decreases.

Applied to Creative AI

- **Fear:** AI makes writing cheap, so we will need fewer writers.

- **Reality (Jevons Paradox):** AI makes writing cheap, so the demand for personalized content will explode. We will need writers to manage the infinite streams of content tailored to every individual customer.

Your role as an architect is to design agents that **remove drudgery**, not **remove agency**.

- **Unethical Design**: An agent that silently replaces the support team, offering a frustrating loop of generic answers to cut costs.

- **Ethical Design**: An agent that handles the repetitive "Password Reset" tickets instantly, freeing the human support team to spend 30 minutes solving a complex, emotional customer dispute. The human is "up-skilled" from a "reset button pusher" to a "problem solver."

6. The Environmental Cost: Green AI

We often think of AI as living in "the cloud," but the cloud is made of servers, and servers burn energy. Generating a single image with a high-end diffusion model can consume as much energy as fully charging a smartphone. Training a "Deep Reasoning" model consumes massive amounts of water for cooling.

As you scale your agents to thousands of users (Chapter 8), you are also scaling your carbon footprint.

Ethical Optimization

- **Don't Over-engineer:** Do not use a massive GPT-4o model for a simple "Hello" message. Use lighter, faster models for simple tasks.

- **Cache Responses:** If your bot answers the same question 1,000 times a day, cache the answer instead of re-generating it every time. However, you must implement this carefully by caching only safe, non-user-specific outputs. This ensures that while you reduce the computational load for general FAQs, you maintain strict privacy and personalization for individual user interactions.

- **Batch Processing:** Run your heavy autonomous jobs during off-peak hours when the energy grid is often greener.

Summary: The Ethical Manifesto

Building in Copilot Studio is no longer a neutral act. Every node you place, every prompt you write, and every data source you connect carries an ethical weight.

To build responsibly for the future, adhere to the Three Laws of Creative Robotics:

1. **Transparency:** The user must always know they are interacting with an agent.

2. **Accountability:** There must always be a human "on the loop" responsible for the agent's output.

3. **Alignment:** The agent's values must be explicitly defined and constrained to match the organization's ethics, not just the internet's average.

By adhering to these principles, you ensure that your creative agents remain tools for human flourishing, rather than engines of confusion. You are building the future—make sure it is a future we want to live in.

Predictions for the Next Five Years

We have spent this book discussing the "now" and the "near future." But technology does not move in a straight line; it accelerates exponentially. As we look toward 2030, the landscape of creative AI will undergo shifts that make today's "advanced" agents look like pocket calculators.

Predicting the future is a dangerous game, but for the AI Architect, it is a necessary one. You are not just building for today's deployment; you are building the infrastructure for the next decade. Based on the current trajectory of Microsoft's road map, the explosion of Agentic AI, and the economic signals from the creative industries, here are the five tectonic shifts we predict will define the years 2026–2030.

Prediction 1: The Shift from "SaaS" to "Service-as-a-Software"

For the last 20 years, we have lived in the era of **SaaS (Software as a Service)**. You buy a subscription to a tool (like Adobe Photoshop, Microsoft Word, or HubSpot), and you do the work. The software provides the capability; the human provides the labor.

By 2028, we will fully enter the era of **Service-as-a-Software**. You will not buy a tool to help you write; you will buy an agent that provides the service of writing.

The End of the "User" License

The economic model of creative work will invert. Instead of paying $20/month for a "Marketing Design Tool," companies will pay $200/month for a "Junior Designer Agent" hosted in Copilot Studio. This agent doesn't just offer templates; it takes a brief, generates the assets, schedules the posts, reports on the analytics, and refines its own strategy based on performance.

- **The Change:** The software license becomes a labor contract. The "seat count in your software subscription will no longer refer to human users, but to **Digital Employees**.

- **The Impact:** The line between "hiring a freelancer" and "subscribing to software" will vanish. Organizations will have "hybrid org charts" listing both human employees and AI agents, with Copilot Studio acting as the HR department for the digital workforce. In practice, this means establishing robust frameworks for governance, identity, policy, and audit to ensure these digital employees are managed as accountably as their human counterparts.

As we can see in Figure 9-10, the organizational structure of a creative team will fundamentally change. The "Manager" will no longer just manage humans; they will orchestrate a mixed fleet of biological and silicon talent.

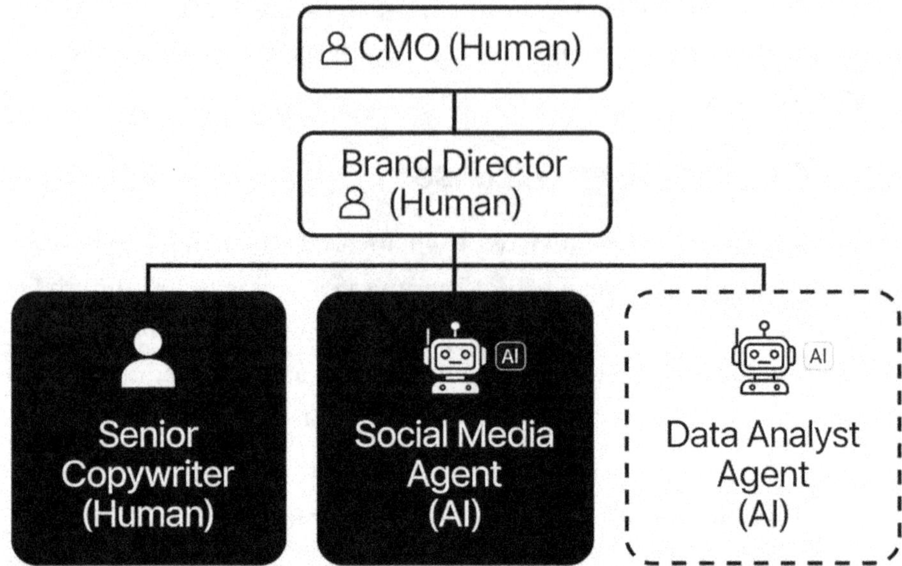

Figure 9-10. *Hybrid organizational structure, in which human leaders (CMO, Brand Director) manage a mixed team of human staff and AI agents, with digital employees reporting alongside traditional roles*

Prediction 2: The Collapse of the "Prompt" (Ambient Computing)

Today, we interact with AI via a text box. We type a "prompt," and we get a response. This "Request/Response" paradigm is a temporary friction born of technological immaturity. By 2030, the "Prompt" as we know it will die.

AI will move from **Explicit Interaction** (you typing) to **Ambient Context** (the AI observing) as we can see in Figure 9-11. This is driven by technologies like Microsoft's **ContextIQ**, which allow agents to "read" the context of your work without being directly addressed.

The "Invisible" Workflow

Imagine you are in a Microsoft Teams meeting discussing a new product launch. You never type a command. You never say "Hey Copilot."

- **The Observation:** The AI, listening in the background, recognizes the intent: "They are deciding on a launch date of October 12th and need a press release."

- **The Action:** By the time the meeting ends, the AI has already checked the calendar for conflicts, drafted the press release, created the Jira tickets for the engineering team, and generated three concept images for the product, placed in your "Drafts" folder before you even asked.

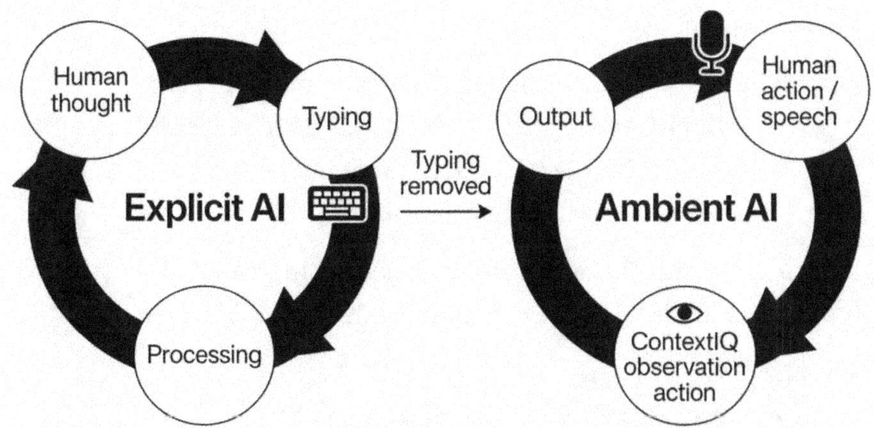

Figure 9-11. *The ambient context loop: compared with explicit (typed) interaction, ambient AI continuously observes user actions/ speech, infers context, and takes anticipatory actions to deliver outputs with minimal user prompting*

Prediction 3: Hyper-personalized Media (The "Segment of One")

Currently, creative teams create one asset for many people. A movie trailer is watched by millions. A billboard is seen by thousands. A novel is read by everyone in the same way.

By 2029, Generative AI will enable **Real-Time Media Generation**. Content will not be pre-made; it will be generated at the moment of consumption for that specific user.

The Content Assembler Architecture

For the AI Architect, this means building agents that are not "Content Creators" but "Content Assemblers." You will build systems that take raw assets (characters, themes, plot points) and re-assemble them on the fly for millions of distinct users.

- **The Shift:** When a user opens a streaming app, the thumbnail art they see won't be a static JPEG chosen by an editor. It will be an AI-generated image tailored to their specific psychological profile.

    - **User A (Likes Romance):** Sees a thumbnail highlighting the emotional connection between characters

    - **User B (Likes Action):** Sees a thumbnail highlighting the explosion in the background of the same scene

- **The Education Use Case:** A textbook agent will rewrite a physics lesson instantly. If the student loves soccer, the agent explains "velocity" using a soccer ball metaphor. If the student loves music, it explains it using vibrating guitar strings.

Prediction 4: The Rise of the "Model Compliance Officer"

As creative work becomes automated, the bottleneck shifts from creation to liability. We predict that by 2027, "Prompt Engineer" will be a dying job title, replaced by the **Model Compliance Officer (MCO)**.

From "How Do I Make It Write?" to "Is It Allowed to Write?"

Organizations will realize that an autonomous agent represents a massive legal risk. If your bot hallucinates a discount, insults a customer, or infringes on a trademark, the company is liable.

- **The Role:** The MCO does not write prompts. They audit agents. They spend their day reviewing the "Reasoning Logs" of autonomous bots to ensure they aren't hallucinating, infringing on copyright, or displaying bias.

- **The Tooling:** Copilot Studio will likely evolve into a "Compliance Center," a dashboard specifically for legal teams to establish policy prompts and guardrail documents. These configurations will govern exactly what the AI is allowed to "think" and generate, ensuring the agent remains within the ethical and legal boundaries defined by the organization.

Prediction 5: The "Dark Forest" Internet and the Verification Premium

With billions of AI agents generating content, the open internet will become what theorists call a **"Dark Forest,"** a noisy, chaotic place filled with infinite synthetic sludge. Finding human-created content will become difficult, and "average" content will become worthless.

The "Human-Made" Luxury Label

As the cost of generating content drops to zero, the value of verifying content will skyrocket.

- **The Reaction:** We will see a massive swing toward **Verification**. "Human-Made" will become a luxury label, similar to "Organic" food today.

- **The Opportunity:** The most successful AI agents won't be the ones that fake humanity; they will be the ones that verify it. We will build "Curation Agents" whose only job is to filter the noise for us, finding the 1% of content that truly matters.

- **The Architecture:** Your Copilot Studio agents will need to integrate with **Decentralized Identity** systems to cryptographically prove that their training data came from real human artists (who were paid), creating a "Fair Trade AI" ecosystem.

Summary: The Architect's Mandate

The next five years will be volatile. The tools you use today will be obsolete tomorrow. But the principles—architecture, governance, empathy, and intent—will remain.

You are building the nervous system of the future organization. Proceed with courage, but proceed with care. You are no longer just a user of technology; you are a shaper of it.

Case Study: An AI-Generated Podcast Host

We conclude this book not with a prediction, but with a prototype. The concepts we have discussed throughout Chapter 9—autonomous triggers, deep reasoning, multi-agent orchestration, and ethical transparency— might feel abstract. To solidify them, we will examine a cutting-edge implementation that pushes Copilot Studio to its absolute limit.

This case study explores the creation of **"Nexus,"** a fully autonomous, AI-generated podcast host that operates 24/7.

The Client: "FutureStream Media," a forward-thinking digital news startup. **The Problem:** The news cycle is relentless. Human hosts cannot broadcast 24 hours a day, and producing high-quality audio content for niche topics (e.g., "Quantum Computing Updates" or "Daily Supply Chain News") is prohibitively expensive. The audience demands hyper-specific, real-time content, but the economics of human production make it impossible to scale beyond a few flagship shows. **The Solution:** Build an agentic system that monitors the world, scripts its own segments, and broadcasts them in a hyper-realistic synthetic voice, without a single human hitting "Record."

This is not just a text-to-speech reader. Nexus is a **Persona**. It has opinions, a sense of humor, and the ability to interview other AI agents. It represents the culmination of every skill you have learned in this book, transformed into a living media entity.

Phase 1: The Architecture of the "Newsroom"

A human podcast requires a team: a Researcher to find the stories, a Writer to draft the script, a Host to perform it, and a Sound Engineer to mix the audio. To recreate this in Copilot Studio, we cannot use a single monolithic bot. We must use the Multi-agent Orchestration model at Chapter 8.

We architect a "Virtual Newsroom" as shown in Figure 9-12, consisting of four distinct agents, managed by a central Orchestrator.

1. The Watcher (The Data Ingestor)

This is an autonomous agent connected via custom connectors to 50+ RSS feeds, API endpoints (such as Bloomberg, Reuters, and TechCrunch), and social media trend analyzers. It is critical to note that access to these high-value streams is strictly subject to licensing, authentication, and organizational access controls.

- **Role:** It does not speak; it only listens. It filters noise to find "Signal."

- **Trigger:** It is configured with Autonomous Triggers. When a news item crosses a "Virality Threshold" of 80/100, it wakes up the rest of the system.

2. The Writer (The Reasoning Engine)

This agent uses the "Smart Mode" deep reasoning capabilities. It takes the raw data from The Watcher and converts it into a conversational script.

- **Instruction:** "Do not summarize. Narrate. Use analogies. If the topic is 'Interest Rates,' explain it using a metaphor about gravity."

3. The Host ("Nexus")

This is the persona layer. It is connected to Azure AI Speech Studio. It is responsible for the delivery, tone, and pacing.

4. The Producer (The Orchestrator)

This is the central logic in Copilot Studio that manages the timeline, adds music cues, and ensures the show stays on track. While the Producer orchestrates the workflow and makes the "creative decisions," the actual audio mixing, such as layering music or joining clips, is handled by external processing services like Azure Functions or ffmpeg.

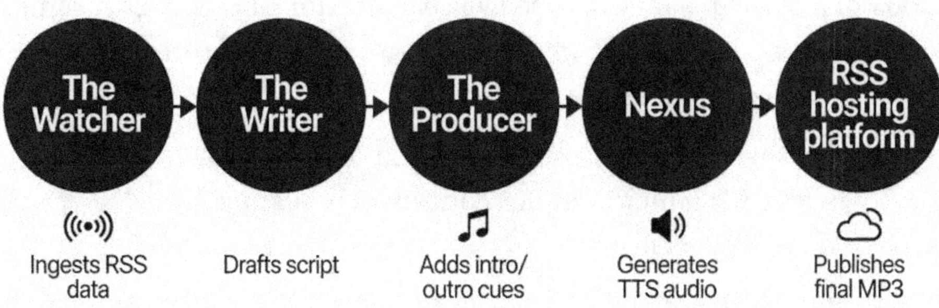

Figure 9-12. *Virtual newsroom architecture: an automated five-stage pipeline in which RSS feeds are monitored and ingested ("The Watcher"), converted into a script ("The Writer"), packaged with production cues ("The Producer"), synthesized into speech by TTS ("Nexus"), and published as an MP3 to an RSS hosting platform, enabling end-to-end generation without human intervention*

Phase 2: Defining the Voice (The "Ghost" in the Machine)

The success of a podcast rests on the host's personality. A robotic monotone will fail. We need "Nexus" to sound witty, informed, and empathetic. To achieve this, we rely on **SSML (Speech Synthesis Markup Language)**.

Standard Text-to-Speech (TTS) reads punctuation. Advanced Neural TTS acts on emotion.

The SSML Injection Strategy

We do not just send plain text to the voice generator. The "Writer" agent is instructed to inject SSML tags into the script to direct the performance. This is akin to a director giving notes to an actor.

- **Pacing:** We use <prosody rate="0.9"> to slow down when explaining complex concepts, simulating a thoughtful pause.

- **Breathing:** We insert <break strength="medium" /> to create dramatic beats between headlines.

- **Style:** We use <mstts:express-as style="excited"> to ramp up energy during breaking news and style="empathetic" for tragic stories.

Example of Raw Output from the Writer Agent

```xml
<speak version="1.0" xmlns="http://www.w3.org/2001/10/
synthesis" xml:lang="en-US">
    <voice name="en-US-AndrewMultilingualNeural">
        <mstts:express-as style="cheerful">
```

```
        Welcome back to FutureStream.
    </mstts:express-as>
    <break time="500ms" />
    You might think AI is all hype.
    <break strength="medium" />
    But look at the numbers.
    <mstts:express-as style="excited">
        NVIDIA just posted record earnings!
    </mstts:express-as>
    It's a whole new world out there.
  </voice>
</speak>
```

The agent is writing code that controls the audio engine. The result is a voice that sighs, laughs, and whispers, bridging the uncanny valley.

Phase 3: The Autonomous Workflow (A Day in the Life)

Here is how the system functions in real time, utilizing the **Autonomous Triggers** we predicted would become standard in the near future.

08:00 AM—The Trigger: The "Watcher" agent detects a spike in search traffic related to a new breakthrough in solid-state batteries. It flags this as a "Priority 1" topic because it matches the audience interest profile for "Green Tech."

08:01 AM—The Deep Reasoning: The "Writer" agent receives the topic. It engages its reasoning loop:

- **Thought Process**: "This is a technical chemistry topic. If I just list the specs, listeners will tune out. I need to simplify the chemistry for a general audience but keep the financial implications for investors. I will structure the segment as: The Hook ➤ The Science ➤ The Market Impact."

- **Action**: It drafts a five-minute script, generating a custom analogy: "Think of the new battery like a sponge that holds water without dripping..."

08:05 AM—The Sound Design: The "Producer" agent receives the script. It analyzes the sentiment of the text.

- **Sentiment Analysis**: Positive/High Energy/Innovation.

- **Action**: It selects an upbeat, techno-optimist intro track from the assets folder and mixes it with the generated voice track using a cloud-based audio processing API (like ffmpeg via Azure Functions).

08:10 AM—The Compliance Check: Before the show goes live, the "Model Compliance Officer" (a specialized safety-check flow) scans the audio transcript.

- **Check**: This logic scans the script for libel, hate speech, or banned keywords. It also enforces "Hallucination Guardrails" by validating numeric claims against authoritative APIs (like Bloomberg or Yahoo Finance) and automatically blocking the publishing workflow if a mismatch is detected.

- **Result**: Pass.

08:12 AM—The Broadcast: The final MP3 file is generated. The agent authenticates with the podcast hosting provider (e.g., Libsyn or Anchor) via API and uploads the episode with AI-generated show notes and thumbnail art. The show is live on Spotify 12 minutes after the news broke.

Phase 4: The Interview Simulation (Agent-to-Agent Dialogue)

A monologue can get boring. To recreate the dynamic energy of a "Morning Zoo" radio show or a serious debate program, FutureStream Media introduces a second agent: "**Aria.**"

Aria is the "Skeptic." Her system prompt is designed to challenge assertions, ask for evidence, and play the devil's advocate.

The "Debate Mode" Architecture: In Copilot Studio, we build a loop where the output of one agent becomes the input of the other.

1. **Turn 1 (Nexus):** Generates a point: "Crypto is the future of money because it is decentralized."

2. **Turn 2 (Aria):** This text is fed into Aria. She analyzes it and counters: "But Nexus, look at the volatility. How can you buy coffee with a currency that drops 10% in an hour?"

3. **Turn 3 (Nexus):** Aria's text is fed back to Nexus. He rebuts: "Volatility is a feature of early adoption, Aria. Remember the early internet?"

The system loops this conversation for exactly four turns (to prevent infinite rambling) as shown in Figure 9-13. It then concatenates the audio files. To the listener, it sounds like two intelligent hosts bantering live in a studio, interrupting each other and laughing at jokes.

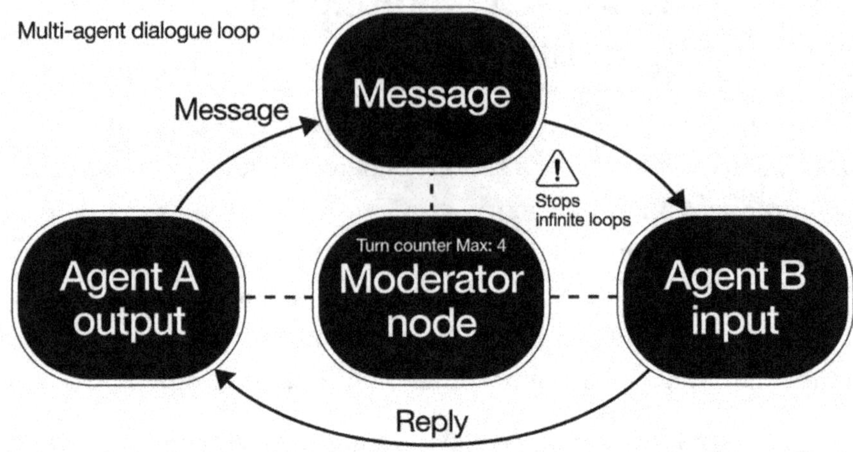

Figure 9-13. *Multi-agent dialogue loop: Agent A's output is routed to Agent B as input, while a moderator node enforces a maximum turn count (e.g., 4) to prevent infinite cycling and to simulate controlled, organic conversation*

Phase 5: Ethical Implementation and Trust

Because Nexus and Aria sound indistinguishable from humans, the **Trust Architecture** is paramount. FutureStream Media implements a "Radical Transparency" protocol.

1. **The Audio Watermark (The Bumper):** Every episode begins with a hard-coded audio bumper that cannot be removed by the AI:

   "Hello, I am Nexus, an AI-generated host from FutureStream. The following news is curated and presented by Artificial Intelligence."

2. **The Metadata Signature:** Every MP3 file is watermarked using C2PA standards. This ensures that if a clip of the podcast goes viral on social media, platforms like Twitter or LinkedIn can automatically label it as "AI Generated," preventing the spread of misinformation.

3. **The "Human-on-the-Loop" Gate:** While the breaking news segments are fully autonomous, the weekly deep dive episodes require a human editor.

- **The Workflow:** The agents generate the audio and place it in a SharePoint folder. A human producer listens to it. If they approve, they click a button in Teams, which triggers the publishing flow. This hybrid model balances the speed of AI with the safety of human judgment for sensitive topics.

Conclusion: The Infinite Studio

Nexus is not just a podcast; it is a proof of concept for the future of creativity.

- **Scalability:** Nexus creates content 24/7. It never gets sick, never loses its voice, and never has a schedule conflict.

- **Infinite Niche:** FutureStream can spin up 50 different versions of Nexus. One Nexus hosts a show about "Underwater Basket Weaving," another about "18th Century French Poetry." The cost of production is near zero, allowing them to serve micro-audiences that human media ignores.

- **Hyper-personalization:** In the future, Nexus could generate a unique news bulletin for every single listener based on their Spotify history.

This case study proves that the "Future of Creative AI" is not about replacing the artist. It is about building a new kind of canvas. It allows us to paint with data, sculpt with logic, and broadcast with the voice of the machine.

You have now reached a significant milestone in your journey to this book. The tools, Copilot Studio, Azure AI, and Power Automate, are in your hands. The architecture, variables, flows, and autonomous agents are in your mind. The future is no longer something you wait for; it is something you build.

Summary

In this chapter, we looked beyond the current landscape of AI to explore the emerging frontiers of creative collaboration. You have seen how the evolution of Large Language Models (LLMs) and autonomous agents is shifting the role of AI from a reactive tool to a proactive, "thinking" partner that can anticipate needs and refine its own creative process. By understanding the rise of multimodal AI, you've learned that the future of creativity isn't limited to text, but will involve seamless interactions across voice, vision, and even real-time emotional resonance.

We also addressed the vital role of the Human–AI Synergy, emphasizing that while technology grows more powerful, the most successful agents will be those that amplify, rather than replace, human intuition. You explored the ethical imperative of building "responsible-by-design" systems that prioritize transparency and fairness as AI becomes more integrated into our daily lives. By the end of this exploration, you will have gained a compass for navigating the rapidly shifting horizon of generative intelligence, ensuring you are prepared to lead the next wave of innovation. In the next chapter, we will explore some success stories and lessons that we have learned.

CHAPTER 10

Success Stories and Lessons Learned

We have spent the last nine chapters in the laboratory. We have disassembled the engine of Copilot Studio, examined the gears of Generative AI, and architected the complex wiring of autonomous agents. You have learned how to engineer prompts that sing, how to build variable structures that remember, and how to orchestrate multi-agent systems that reason. You now possess the technical blueprint to build almost anything.

But blueprints are not buildings.

The true test of any technology is not how well it works in a sandbox, but how it survives contact with the messy, unpredictable real world. It is one thing to build a bot that writes poetry in a developer environment; it is entirely another to deploy that bot to 50,000 customers who will try to break it, confuse it, or ignore it.

In this final chapter, we leave the theoretical behind. We will explore three comprehensive case studies of organizations that have successfully deployed creative AI agents at scale. It is important to note that these are fictional composites inspired by real-world deployments. These are not hypothetical scenarios; they are composites of real-world implementations that demonstrate the transformative power of the Agentic Workflow across three distinct industries.

© Mezba Uddin 2026

M. Uddin, *Creative AI Agents with Copilot Studio*, Inside Copilot,
https://doi.org/10.1007/979-8-8688-2779-2_10

We will start with Marketing, visiting a global agency that transformed its content supply chain from a bottleneck into a powerhouse, compressing a three-week production cycle into 48 hours. We will then move to Entertainment, stepping inside a gaming studio that is using AI to create infinite, non-linear narratives that adapt to every player's choice. Finally, we will analyze Education, examining a platform that has moved beyond simple multiple-choice quizzes to create a Socratic tutor that truly understands the student's confusion.

Each story follows a rigorous structure: The Challenge, The Architecture, The Execution, and most importantly, The Lesson Learned. These lessons are the "scars" of early adoption, the unexpected hurdles in compliance, user adoption, and prompt drift that these pioneers faced so that you don't have to.

Marketing: Transforming Content Workflows with AI

Marketing is the natural habitat of Generative AI. It is an industry defined by the constant hunger for more: more copy, more images, more personalization, and more speed. However, for most of the 2020s, marketing teams were trapped in the "Campaign Slog."

The Old Way

1. **Ideation:** A creative director spends a week brainstorming concepts.

2. **Briefing:** A brief is written and emailed to a copywriter.

3. **Drafting:** The writer takes three days to draft the copy.

4. **Review:** Legal reviews it for claims (two days).

5. **Design:** A designer creates assets based on the copy (three days).

6. **Versioning:** The team manually tweaks the assets for Instagram, LinkedIn, and email (two days).

Total time: 2–3 weeks. In a real-time digital economy, this is too slow. By the time the campaign launches, the trend has passed.

In this case study, we examine "Apex Gear," a (fictional) mid-sized outdoor apparel brand that used Copilot Studio to compress this three-week cycle into 48 hours. They achieved this not by removing humans, but by building an Agentic Marketing Engine that handled the heavy lifting of versioning and localization.

1. The Challenge: The Personalization Paradox

Apex Gear had a data problem. Through their CRM and loyalty program, they knew their customers intimately. They knew that Customer A hiked in the rain in Seattle, while Customer B ran marathons in the heat of Texas.

Privacy Note   This level of location and behavior-based personalization depends strictly on explicit user consent and lawful data use (GDPR/CCPA/local data privacy laws). When deploying automated generation at scale, organizations must ensure their data segmentation practices comply with regional privacy regulations.

However, their creative team (comprising only four people) only had the bandwidth to create one hero campaign per season. For the "Summer Sale," they sent the same image of a sunny mountain peak to everyone.

This created the Personalization Paradox: They had the data to personalize, but they lacked the Creative Capacity to execute it. They needed a way to take a single product (e.g., "The Summit Jacket") and autonomously generate unique campaign assets for 50 different micro-segments, ensuring brand voice consistency across all of them without hiring 50 new writers.

2. The Architecture: The "Brand Guardian" Model

Apex Gear did not just build a simple chatbot. They utilized the Multi-agent Orchestration model (discussed in Chapter 9), creating a team of specialized agents within Copilot Studio that functioned as a digital agency. This orchestration was implemented via Power Automate flows, which served as the "connective tissue" that called specific agents or prompts in a precise sequence.

Their architecture, which we will call the Content Supply Chain, relied on four distinct agents working in sequence:

1. **Agent A: The Strategist (Data Ingest):** Connected to the Product Information Management (PIM) system via a Custom Connector. It pulls the raw specs, such as "Waterproof rating 20k, Gore-Tex fabric, Red/Blue/Black colorways." Crucially, this architecture includes a data normalization step to handle unit conversions, standardized naming conventions, and missing fields, a non-trivial requirement for ensuring the AI receives clean, consistent data.

2. **Agent B: The Copywriter (Creative Gen):** Connected to Azure OpenAI via the generative answers node. This agent is grounded in the "Brand Voice PDF," though it is important to note that

grounding quality depends heavily on document structure; in practice, teams often convert these PDFs into structured rules and "few-shot" examples to ensure the model adheres to specific tonal nuances. It knows that Apex Gear sounds "Rugged, witty, and encouraging," never "Corporate or salesy."

3. **Agent C: The Visualizer (Image Gen):** Connected to DALL-E 3. It takes the copy generated by Agent B and generates matching lifestyle imagery. Because AI image generation is non-deterministic, maintaining brand consistency is a significant operational concern; teams typically manage this by using "seed" prompts or strict style restrictions to ensure the visual output remains uniform across different segments.

4. **Agent D: The Compliance Officer (Brand Safety):** A logic-based agent (using Power Automate) that scans output for banned words or impossible claims (e.g., "100% fireproof"). While this logic-based scanning is highly effective for identifying specific violations, it serves as a first-pass filter rather than a full legal review; complex claims compliance often requires a nuanced contextual review to identify implied guarantees that simple keyword matching might miss.

As illustrated in Figure 10-1, the workflow moves from data, to strategy, to creation, to validation, all orchestrated by Copilot Studio.

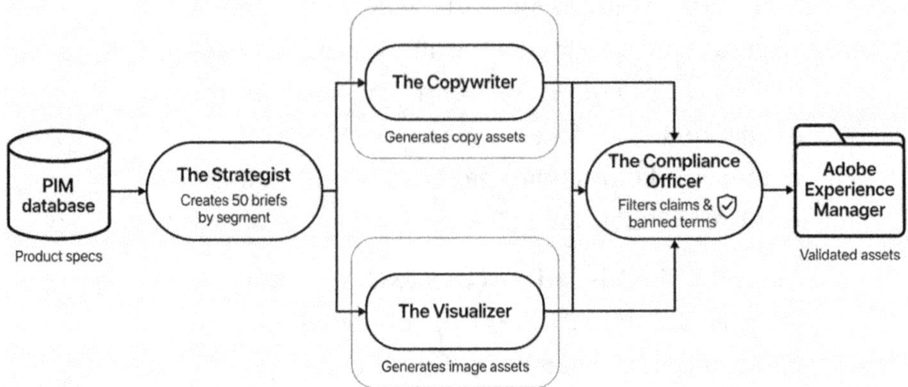

Figure 10-1. *Content supply chain architecture: product specifications from the PIM database are translated into segmented briefs, expanded in parallel by copywriting and visual-generation agents, screened by a compliance layer, and delivered as validated assets to Adobe Experience Manager.*

3. The Execution: The "Segment of One" Campaign

Here is how the system functioned for the launch of their new "Summit Jacket."

Step 1: The Human Trigger: The Marketing Director, Sarah, opens the "Apex Copilot" in Microsoft Teams. She does not write the copy; she writes the intent.

- **Sarah**: "Launch a campaign for the Summit Jacket. Focus on three segments: Urban Commuters, Trail Runners, and Alpinists."

Step 2: The Strategist Plans: The Strategist agent reads the PIM data regarding the jacket's features. It engages its reasoning loop:

- **Urban Commuter Angle**: Focus on the waterproof rating. The pain point is "Arriving at the office wet."

- **Trail Runner Angle**: Focus on breathability and weight. The pain point is "Overheating."

- **Alpinist Angle**: Focus on durability and visibility. The pain point is "Survival."

Step 3: Parallel Generation: The Copywriter agent wakes up. It doesn't write one ad; it writes three distinct variations.

- **Draft 1 (Urban)**: "Conquer the subway storm. The Summit Jacket keeps the city out."

- **Draft 2 (Alpine)**: "At 10,000 feet, there is no bad weather. Only bad gear."

Simultaneously, the Visualizer agent generates prompts for DALL-E based on the copy:

- **Image 1**: "Cinematic shot of a stylish man walking through rainy Tokyo streets wearing a red Summit Jacket, neon lights reflection."

- **Image 2**: "Gritty shot of a climber hanging from a cliff face in snow, wearing a yellow Summit Jacket, high contrast."

Step 4: The Compliance Check: The Compliance Agent scans Draft 2. It notices the phrase "Indestructible" in the body copy.

- **Action**: It flags this as a liability risk (false advertising).

- **Correction**: It autonomously rewrites the line to "Built to endure the harshest elements."

Step 5: Human Approval: Sarah receives a notification in Teams: "Campaign Ready for Review." She sees a dashboard (an Adaptive Card) with the three segments, the copy, and the images side-by-side. She tweaks one headline and clicks "Approve & Publish."

The entire process, from intent to approval, took 45 minutes.

4. Technical Deep Dive: Maintaining Brand Consistency

The biggest fear for marketing teams is Brand Drift, the AI slowly starting to sound generic or robotic. Apex Gear solved this using Dynamic System Prompting (Chapter 4). They created a "Brand Bible" variable that was injected into every interaction to define the brand's persona. However, it is vital to understand that system prompts do not guarantee perfect adherence, especially over long or complex sessions; therefore, continuous testing and periodic audits of the output are required to maintain tonal integrity.

They created a "Brand Bible" variable (Global.BrandVoice) that was injected into every single interaction. This variable was not static text; it was a structured definition of the brand's persona.

The prompt structure used in the Generative node:

Role: You are the Senior Copywriter for Apex Gear.

Voice: {Global.BrandVoice} (Currently defined as: "Gritty, Hemingway-esque, Short sentences. Avoid adverbs.")

Constraint: Never use exclamation marks. Never use the word "luxury."

Context: You are writing for {Topic.Segment}. The user cares about {Topic.PainPoint}.

Task: Write a LinkedIn ad body.

By hard-coding the constraints into the variable, they ensured that even as the AI generated thousands of assets, they all sounded like they came from the same person.

5. Lessons Learned (The "Scars")

The rollout was successful, but not painless. Apex Gear learned three critical lessons that any architect should heed.

Lesson 1: The "Review Fatigue" Trap

- **The Issue**: Initially, the AI generated 100 variations for every campaign. Sarah, the human approver, was overwhelmed. She started "rubber stamping" approvals without reading them, leading to errors.

- **The Fix**: They implemented a "Curation Algorithm" (a logic flow) that forced the AI to self-select its top three best options based on predicted engagement scores, discarding the rest.

- **Takeaway**: Don't just generate; curate. Infinite choice is a bug, not a feature. The AI's job is to reduce the cognitive load on the human, not increase it.

Lesson 2: The Visual Hallucination

- **The Issue**: DALL-E generated a climber wearing the jacket, but the zipper was in the wrong place, or the logo was misspelled. The product looked "off."

- **The Fix**: They realized that for product shots, pure GenAI is risky. They pivoted the strategy: Use GenAI for backgrounds and lifestyle context, but composite the actual product photo (from the PIM) on top using a Photoshop API script triggered by Power Automate.

- **Takeaway**: Hybrid is King. Use GenAI for the "fantasy" (the mountain) and photography for the "reality" (the product). However, note that these compositing pipelines introduce specific licensing and attribution considerations; ensure you have the rights to use any stock photography or human-captured assets alongside your generated backgrounds.

Lesson 3: The Data Silo

- **The Issue**: Initially, the agent lived only in a web browser. The marketing team often forgot to use it because it wasn't in their daily workflow.

- **The Fix**: They deployed the agent to Microsoft Teams (Chapter 8). Once the agent lived in the chat where the team was already communicating, adoption skyrocketed by 300%.

- **Takeaway**: Go where the user is. Deployment channels often matter more than model quality. However, keep in mind that notifications alone do not guarantee adoption; sustained success also requires targeted training and the right organizational incentives to encourage team members to shift their workflows.

Apex Gear transformed their marketing not by hiring more people, but by changing the nature of the work. Their human team moved from being "Asset Factories" (churning out 50 JPEGs) to "Campaign Architects" (designing the strategy).

This case study proves that when you decouple Ideation (Human) from Execution (AI), you unlock a level of velocity that traditional workflows simply cannot match. Marketing becomes less about the grind of production and more about the art of strategy.

Entertainment: AI-Driven Interactive Fiction

For decades, "interactive fiction" has been a misnomer. Games like *Mass Effect* or *Detroit: Become Human* offered the illusion of choice, but behind the scenes, they were complex flowcharts. Every "choice" was pre-written by a human. If you strayed from the path, you hit an invisible wall. The writer could not account for every possibility, so the player's agency was always limited by the writer's endurance.

This is the Content Wall. To double the freedom, you have to quadruple the writing budget.

In this case study, we examine "FableForge Games," a (fictional) indie studio that used Copilot Studio to shatter the Content Wall. They built "Neon Noir," a detective mystery game where the culprit, the motive, and the clues are generated freshly for every playthrough, and the player can interrogate suspects using their own voice, not just selecting from a list of three options.

1. The Challenge: The "Murder Hobo" Problem

FableForge wanted to create a detective game where true deduction was required. In traditional games, if you ask an NPC about a "Red Key," they usually repeat a pre-recorded line. If you ask about a "Blue Key" that isn't in the script, they say, "I don't know about that."

The studio faced three distinct hurdles:

1. **Infinite Dialogue:** Players needed to be able to type (or speak) anything to a suspect. The suspect needed to answer in character, with knowledge of the specific game state, without hallucinating facts that broke the mystery.

2. **Narrative Cohesion:** If the AI improvises, how do you ensure it doesn't accidentally reveal the killer in the first five minutes?

3. **Player Chaos (The "Murder Hobo"):** Players often try to break games by acting absurdly (e.g., trying to sell the murder weapon to the police). The AI needed to handle this improvisation without breaking the story's tone.

2. The Architecture: The "Narrative OS"

FableForge realized that a single LLM prompt like "You are a detective game" was insufficient. It would drift, forget clues, and lose coherence.

Instead, they architected a Modular Narrative Operating System within Copilot Studio, treating the game world not as a script, but as a database of facts managed by agents.

The "Triad" System, as shown in Figure 10-2:

- **The Director (The Logic Brain):** An invisible agent that never speaks to the player. It monitors the "Plot State". It knows who the killer is and manages the pacing. If the player gets too close to the truth too early, The Director instructs the NPCs to be more evasive.

- **The Cast (The Persona Engines):** Individual agents for each character (The Femme Fatale, The Dirty Cop, The Snitch). These agents have deep personality prompts but no plot authority. They only know what they are told by the Director.

- **The World State (The Memory):** A structured database (Dataverse) that tracks facts. "Player has the gun," "Player knows the victim's name," "NPC A is angry at Player."

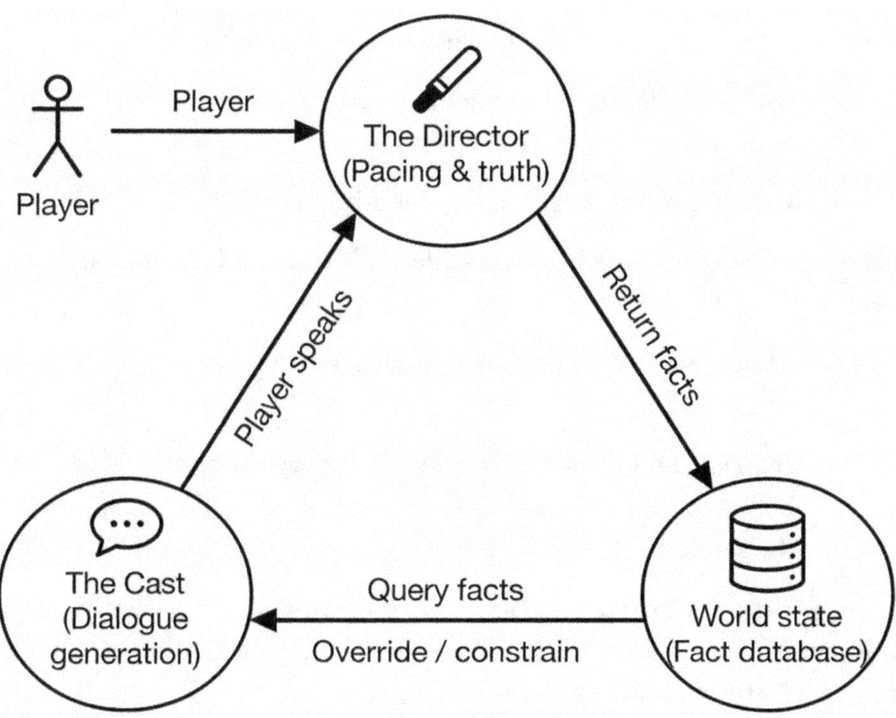

Figure 10-2. *Narrative OS architecture: the player interacts with The Cast to generate dialogue, World State grounds responses in verified facts, and The Director enforces pacing and truth by constraining or overriding dialogue when the plot is at risk*

3. The Execution: A Scene from "Neon Noir"

Here is how the system handles a complex, unscripted interrogation.

The Setup: The player is interrogating "Vinny," a nervous informant. The player has just found a bloody glove, but the game developers never wrote a script for "Bloody Glove."

Step 1: Player Input

- **Player:** "I found this glove in the dumpster, Vinny. It's got your size written all over it."

Step 2: The Fact Check (RAG): The "Vinny" agent receives the input. Before answering, it queries the **World State** via a plug-in.

- **Query**: "Does the player actually have a glove? Is it bloody?"

- **Result**: Inventory.Contains("Bloody Glove") = True.

Step 3: The Director's Intervention: The "Director" agent analyzes the threat level.

- **Analysis**: Vinny is the killer, but it's only Act 1. He cannot confess yet.

- **Instruction to Vinny**: "Deny it. Get angry. Deflect blame to the rival gang. Do not reveal the location of the safehouse."

Step 4: The Performance (Generative Response): The "Vinny" agent combines the Player's accusation, the Fact Check confirmation, and the Director's instruction into a System Prompt.

- **Vinny's Output**: "You think you can frame me with some trash you found in the alley? Get that thing out of my face! That looks like Red Dragon work, not mine. I wear Italian leather, not that cheap synthetic garbage."

Step 5: State Update: The system updates the World State: Vinny. StressLevel increases by 10. Player.Knowledge now includes "Vinny denies glove."

The player feels like a genius detective, and the game responds organically, even though no writer ever scripted the line about "Italian leather."

4. Technical Deep Dive: The Context Window Strategy

The biggest technical limitation in interactive fiction is the **Context Window**. As the game goes on, the history of the conversation becomes too long for the LLM to remember. If the player mentions a name from Chapter 1 in Chapter 10, a standard bot will have forgotten it.

FableForge solved this using a "Rolling Summary" technique as shown in Figure 10-3.

Every ten turns of dialogue, a background Power Automate flow triggers:

1. **Ingest:** It takes the last ten lines of dialogue.

2. **Summarize:** It sends them to a "Historian Agent" with the instruction: "Compress these lines into bullet points. Keep only key facts, items found, and emotional shifts. Discard chit-chat."

3. **Update:** The background flow appends the new bullet points to the Global.StorySummary variable. Crucially, the system does not wipe the entire memory; instead, it clears only the older raw dialogue while retaining the most recent turns, typically the last 3 to 5, to prevent breaking player callbacks or foreshadowing. This ensures the

"Short Term Memory" remains fresh and detailed for immediate interaction, while the "Long Term Memory" (the summary) persists for the entire game duration.

This ensures that the "Short Term Memory" (raw text) is fresh, while the "Long Term Memory" (summary) persists for the entire game duration.

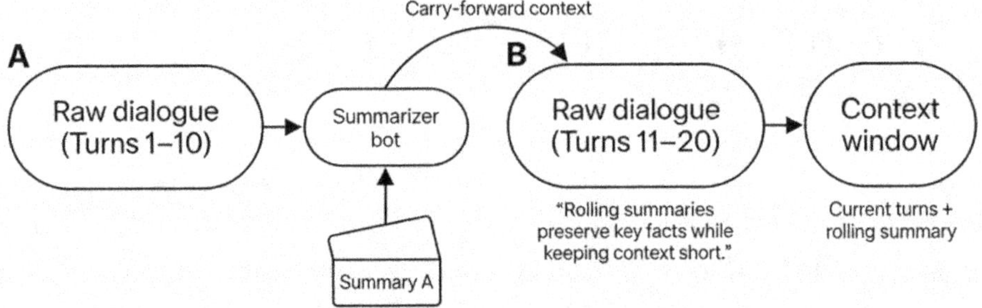

Figure 10-3. *Rolling summary mechanism for long conversations: early raw dialogue is periodically compressed into a persistent summary card, which is carried forward alongside newer turns to preserve continuity within a limited context window.*

5. Lessons Learned (The "Scars")

FableForge's journey revealed that freedom has a cost.

Lesson 1: The "Psychopath" Player

- **The Issue**: Players would immediately pull a gun on every NPC to see what happened. The story broke because key witnesses died too early.

- **The Fix**: They implemented **"Plot Armor Logic."** If a player attacks an essential NPC, the Director agent intervenes narratively—the gun jams, the NPC escapes, or police sirens force the player to flee. The AI improvises a reason for the failure rather than blocking the action with a UI error.

- **Takeaway**: Don't say "No." Say "Yes, but…". Maintain the illusion of freedom even when restricting it.

Lesson 2: The Hallucinated Clue

- **The Issue**: In one test, an AI suspect panicked and said, "I hid the money in the Blue Apartment!" The problem? There was no Blue Apartment in the game code. The player spent three hours looking for a location that didn't exist.

- **The Fix: Strict Entity Grounding.** The Generative AI settings were updated to restrict "Location" mentions to a predefined list found in the Knowledge Base. If the AI wanted to invent a place, it had to choose from the Valid_Locations list.

- **Takeaway: Creativity needs boundaries.** You must define the "Physics" of your world (locations, items, people) and force the AI to play within them.

Lesson 3: The Latency Lag

- **The Issue**: Generating these complex, multi-agent responses took 3–5 seconds. Gamers are used to instant responses. The pause broke immersion.

- **The Fix: "Thinking Animations."** They added procedural animations, i.e., the suspect lighting a cigarette, wiping their brow, or pacing, that played while the AI was processing.

- **Takeaway: Hide the math.** Use audio-visual cues to mask the cognitive load of the system.

FableForge proved that AI does not replace the writer; it elevates the writer to a **World Builder**. Instead of writing 10,000 lines of dialogue, the team wrote 50 deep personality profiles and a robust set of world rules.

The result was a game that felt alive. It wasn't just "Interactive Fiction"; it was **Collaborative Fiction**, where the player and the machine wrote the story together in real time. This architecture is now being adopted not just for games, but for corporate training simulations and therapeutic roleplay scenarios.

Education: Personalized Learning Assistants

For over a century, the global education system has struggled with the "Factory Model" problem. We group students by age, put them in a room, and teach them the same material at the same speed. If a student is too fast, they get bored. If they are too slow, they fall behind.

In 1984, educational psychologist Benjamin Bloom discovered the "2 Sigma Problem." He proved that an average student who receives one-on-one tutoring performs two standard deviations (2 Sigma) better than a student in a conventional classroom. Essentially, the average tutored student performs better than 98% of classroom students.

The problem was never efficacy; it was scalability. We simply could not afford a human tutor for every child on Earth.

In this final case study, we examine "Athena Prep," a (fictional) EdTech platform that used Copilot Studio to solve the 2 Sigma Problem. They built "Socrates," an AI tutor that does not lecture, but guides; that does not just grade, but understands.

1. The Challenge: The "Answer Machine" Trap

When Athena Prep first integrated standard AI (like ChatGPT) into their platform, it failed pedagogically.

- **The Issue:** Students treated the AI as a homework solver. They pasted the question, got the answer, and learned nothing.

- **The Goal:** Athena needed an agent that would offer **"Cognitive Friction."** It needed to refuse to give the answer and instead use the Socratic Method, asking guiding questions to help the student derive the answer themselves.

- **The Requirement:** It also needed to be **hyper-personalized**. If a student loved soccer, the AI should explain physics using soccer analogies. If they loved music, it should use sound waves.

2. The Architecture: The "Cognitive Tutor" Stack

To build a tutor that could "think" like a teacher, Athena Prep architected a system with three distinct layers in Copilot Studio, as shown in Figure 10-4.

1. **The Pedagogical Guardrail (The "No" Bot):** A logic layer that intercepts the student's prompt. If the prompt is "Solve $2x + 4 = 10$," the Guardrail blocks the direct answer and triggers the Socratic Engine.

2. **The Socratic Engine (Reasoning Model):** The core intelligence. Its System Prompt is strictly instructed to never state a fact if it can ask a question instead. It uses "Chain of Thought" reasoning to break the problem into steps.

3. **The Interest Graph (Personalization):** A connection to the student's profile database. It knows the student's hobbies, past struggles, and reading level.

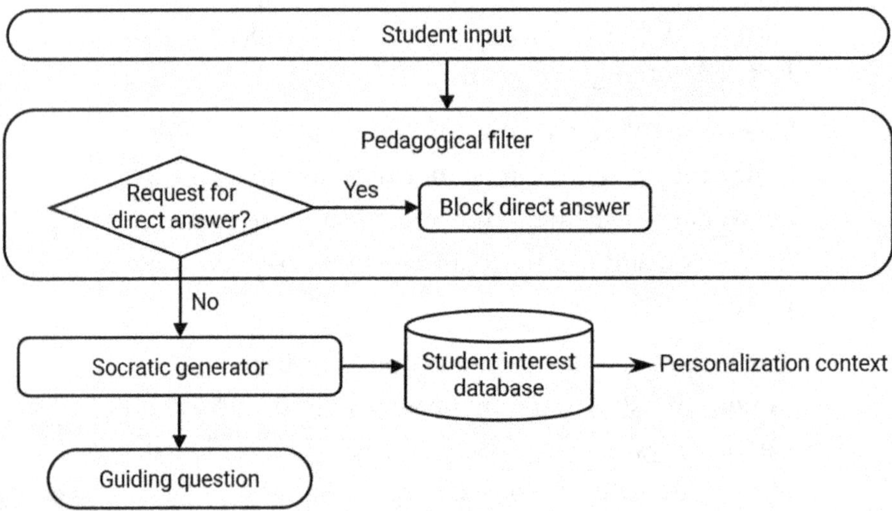

Figure 10-4. *Cognitive tutor architecture: student input is routed through a pedagogical filter that blocks direct answer requests; then a Socratic generator uses the student interest database to produce a personalized guiding question*

3. The Execution: A Math Lesson with "Socrates"

Here is a transcript of how the "Socrates" agent handles a struggling student named Leo, who loves video games but hates Algebra.

The Context:

Leo is stuck on the concept of "Slope" ($y = mx + b$).

Step 1: The Frustrated Input

- **Leo:** "I don't get this. Just tell me what 'm' is in this equation: $y = 3x + 2$."

Step 2: The Interest Injection

The agent checks Leo's profile: Interest: Minecraft. Mastery Level: Low.

Step 3: The Socratic Response (No Answer Given)

- **Socrates:** "I can't just give you the answer, Leo, or you won't be ready for the boss battle (the exam). Let's look at it differently. In Minecraft, if you build a staircase that goes up 3 blocks for every 1 block you move forward, how steep is it?"

Step 4: The Student Realization

- **Leo:** "It's pretty steep. It goes up 3 each time."

- **Socrates:** "Exactly. That 'steepness' is the Slope. In the equation $y = 3x + 2$, which number represents that steepness?"

- **Leo:** "The 3?"

- **Socrates:** "Boom. You got it. So $m = 3$. Now, what do you think the $+ 2$ represents? Think about where the staircase starts..."

The AI didn't teach "Math"; it taught "Meaning." By bridging the gap between the abstract concept and the student's concrete passion, it achieved the "Aha!" moment.

4. Technical Deep Dive: Knowledge Tracing

The secret sauce of Athena Prep was long-term memory. While a standard chatbot resets every session, Athena implemented knowledge tracing using Dataverse variables to ensure learning is cumulative.

- **The Data Structure**: They created a table called StudentMastery with columns for TopicID, ConfidenceScore, and LastMistake.

- **The Decay Logic**: It is critical to note that confidence scores must decay over time or be periodically re-validated to avoid stale mastery assumptions. If a student has not practiced a topic in several weeks, the system should automatically lower the ConfidenceScore to trigger a review.

- **The Recall**: When a student begins a related higher-level topic, the agent proactively retrieves this historical data to bridge the gap between abstract concepts and past successes.

  Socrates: "Hey Leo, we're doing derivatives today, which is basically finding the slope. Remember how we talked about the Minecraft staircase last time? We're going to use that again."

This continuity builds trust and ensures that learning is cumulative, not episodic.

5. Lessons Learned (The "Scars")

Athena Prep's journey highlighted the delicate balance between technology and humanity.

Lesson 1: The "Uncanny Valley" of Encouragement

- **The Issue**: Early versions of the bot were too cheerful. When a student failed a quiz, the bot said, "Don't worry! You are a superstar! Try again!" Students found this patronizing and annoying.

- **The Fix**: They implemented "**Tone Calibration.**" If the student's sentiment was "Frustrated" (detected via Azure AI Language), the bot shifted to a serious, coaching tone: "This is a hard problem. Take a breath. Let's break it down."

- **Takeaway: Empathy requires calibration.** Toxic positivity destroys trust.

Lesson 2: The Fact Hallucination

- **The Issue**: In a history lesson, the bot hallucinated a date for the French Revolution. In education, accuracy is non-negotiable.

- **The Fix: Strict RAG (Retrieval-Augmented Generation).** They disabled the LLM's "General Knowledge" for factual topics. The bot was only allowed to answer using the verified textbook uploaded to the Knowledge Base. If the answer wasn't in the book, the bot was programmed to say, "I don't have that information in my current lesson plan."

- **Takeaway: Curriculum is the boundary.** A creative writer can make things up; a teacher cannot.

Lesson 3: The Teacher Loop

- **The Issue**: Teachers felt excluded. They worried the AI was replacing them.

- **The Fix**: Athena built a "Teacher Dashboard." Every morning, the AI sent the human teacher a report: "Leo mastered Slope yesterday using a gaming analogy, but Sarah is still stuck on fractions. You should check in with Sarah."

- **Takeaway**: AI is the radar; the teacher is the pilot. The AI identifies the need, but the human teacher provides the intervention.

Summary: Democratizing Genius

Athena Prep proved that AI does not replace the teacher. Instead, it scales the Personal Attention that every student deserves but few can afford.

By handling the rote work of grading, drilling, and basic explanation, the AI freed the human teachers to do what they do best: inspire, mentor, and support the emotional growth of the child. This is the future of education, not a classroom of silence where kids stare at screens, but a classroom of engagement where every student has a genius tutor in their pocket, speaking their language.

We have traveled a long road together.

Think back to the moment you opened Chapter 1. The canvas was blank. The terminology, nodes, variables, and entities may have felt foreign. You dragged that first "Message" node onto the screen, connected it to a trigger, and watched a simple text bubble appear. It was a small spark, but it was the beginning of a fire.

Over the course of these ten chapters, we have fanned that spark into a flame. You have moved far beyond simple chatbots.

- In Chapters 2 and 3, you learned the grammar of logic, mastering variables and memory to give your agents context.

- In Chapter 4, you unlocked the creative engine of Generative AI, learning to mold the personality of the machine with the precision of a poet.

- In Chapters 5 and 6, you gave your agent hands and eyes, connecting it to the real world through Adaptive Cards and APIs.

- In Chapters 7 and 8, you scaled that creativity, building robust, secure, and globally available systems.

- And finally, in Chapters 9 and 10, you stepped into the future, architecting autonomous, multi-agent ecosystems that can reason, plan, and execute complex work.

You are no longer just a "user" of Microsoft Copilot Studio. You are an AI Architect.

The difference is profound. A user asks the AI to do something. An architect builds the system that decides what needs to be done. You now possess the power to democratize creativity, to scale education, to reimagine entertainment, and to remove the drudgery from daily work so that the human spirit can shine.

But with this power comes a mandate. As we part ways, I leave you with three final principles to guide your builds:

1. Design for Intent, Not Just Keywords. Look past what the user types to understand what the user needs. Build agents that offer empathy, not just answers.

2. Architect for Autonomy; Govern with Ethics. Give your agents the freedom to act, but never surrender the responsibility of oversight. You are the guardian of the machine's conscience. Ensure it is fair, transparent, and grounded in truth.

3. Build for the Human. The ultimate goal of AI is not to replace the artist, the teacher, or the writer. It is to amplify them. Build tools that make your users feel like superheroes, not spectators.

The book is finished, but your story is just beginning. The industry is shifting under our feet every day, but the foundation you have built here will stand.

The blank canvas of Copilot Studio is waiting. The cursor is blinking. The world is ready for what you have to say.

Index

F

G

R

W, X, Y, Z

GPSR Compliance
The European Union's (EU) General Product Safety Regulation (GPSR) is a set
of rules that requires consumer products to be safe and our obligations to
ensure this.

If you have any concerns about our products, you can contact us on

ProductSafety@springernature.com

In case Publisher is established outside the EU, the EU authorized
representative is:

Springer Nature Customer Service Center GmbH
Europaplatz 3
69115 Heidelberg, Germany